# MeruPuri™

Märchen ✦ Prince

# Volume 4

**Story & Art by Matsuri Hino**

# Contents

**MeruPuri: Märchen Prince**

**Chapter 17** °°°°°°°°°°°°°°°°°°°°°°°°°°°° 3

**Chapter 18** °°°°°°°°°°°°°°°°°°°°°°°°°°°° 35

**Chapter 19** °°°°°°°°°°°°°°°°°°°°°°°°°°°° 67

**Chapter 20** °°°°°°°°°°°°°°°°°°°°°°°°°°°° 97

**Chapter 21** °°°°°°°°°°°°°°°°°°°°°°°°°°°°° 127

**MeruPuri Secret Story I** °°°° 163

**MeruPuri: Märchen Prince**
**Final Chapter** °°°°°°°°°°°°°°°°°°°°°°°° 170

**MeruPuri Secret Story II** °°°° 202

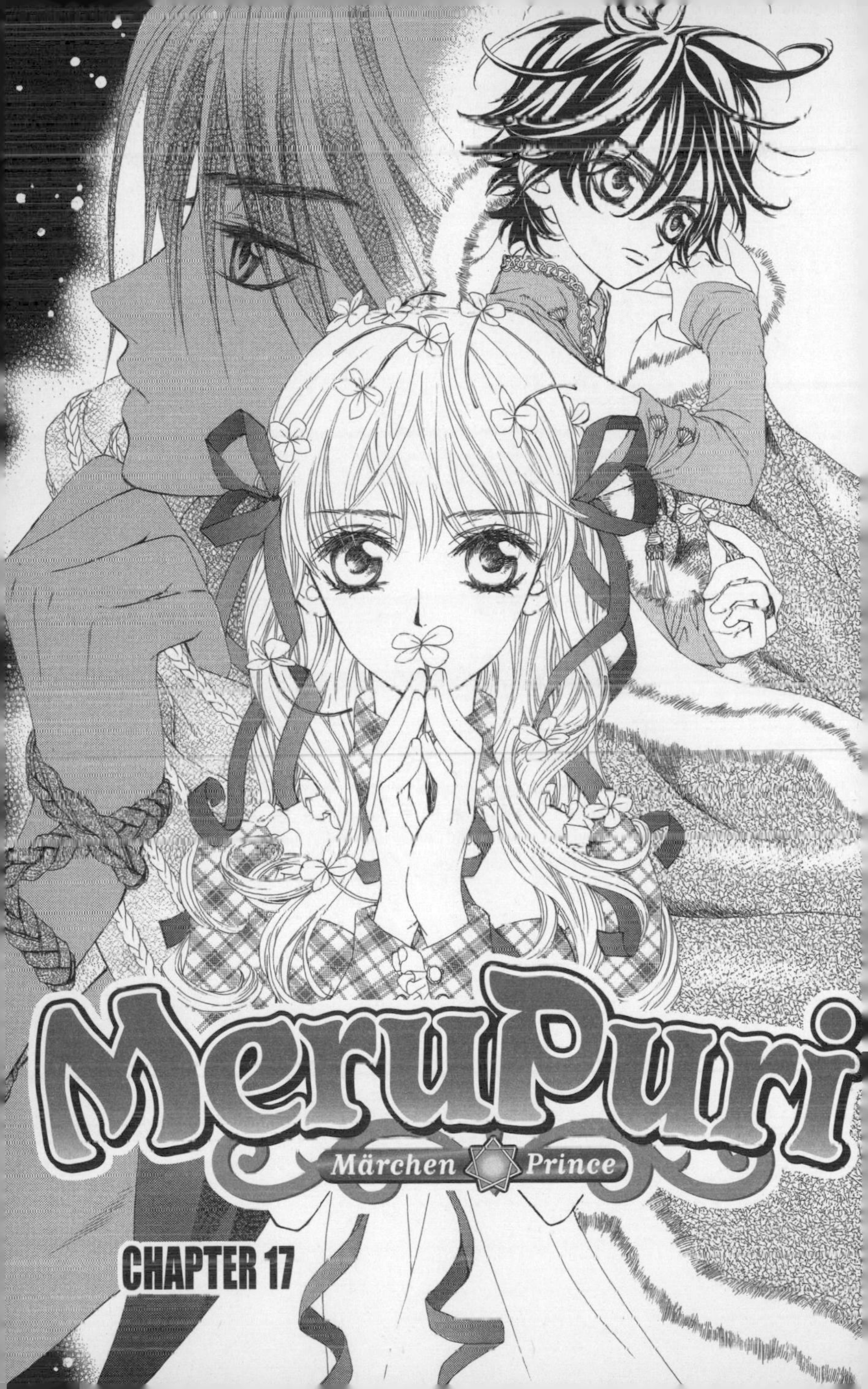
MeruPuri
Märchen Prince
CHAPTER 17

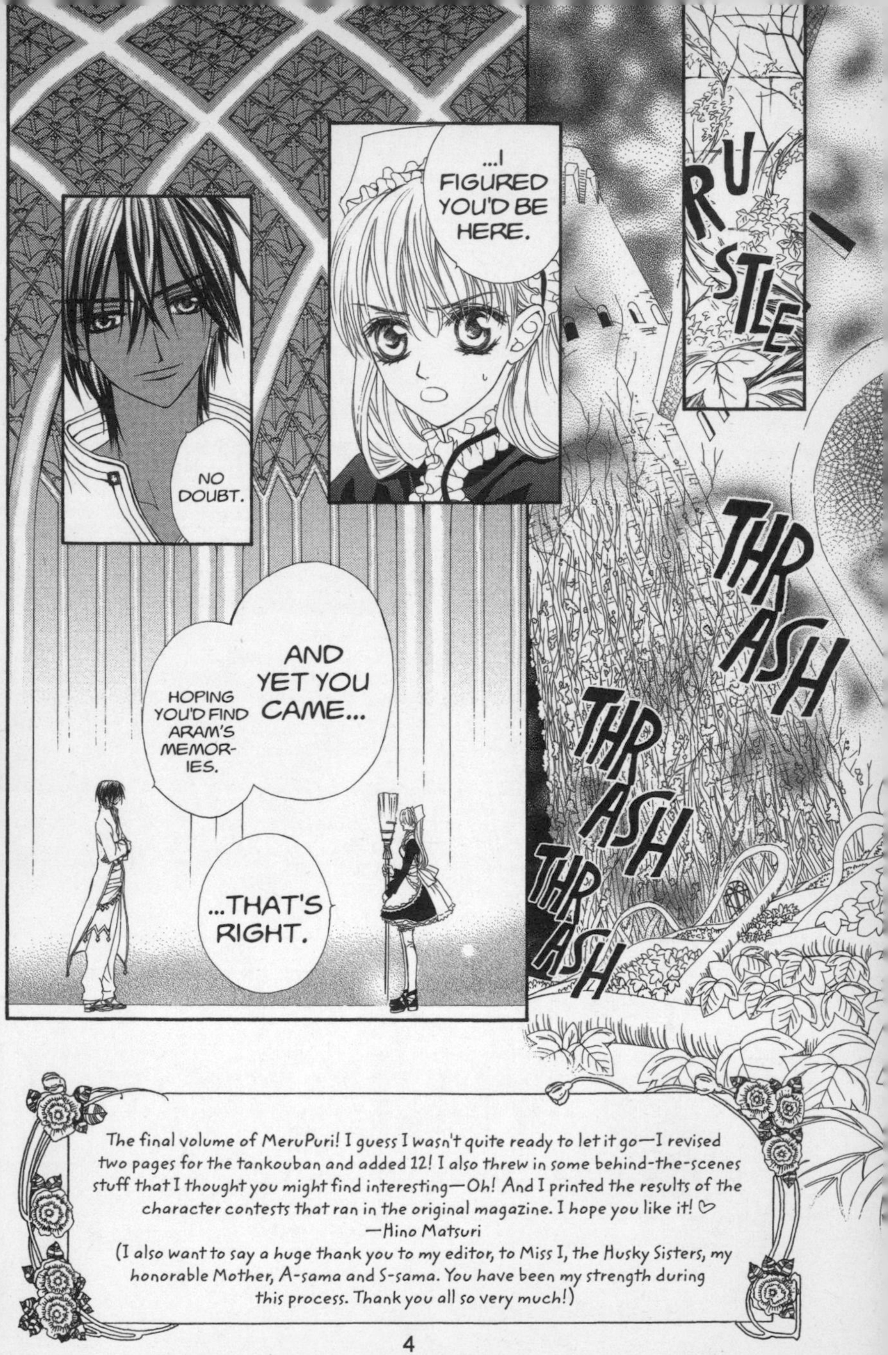
RUSTLE
THRASH
THRASH
THRASH
...I FIGURED YOU'D BE HERE.
NO DOUBT.
AND YET YOU CAME...
HOPING YOU'D FIND ARAM'S MEMOR-IES.
...THAT'S RIGHT.

The final volume of MeruPuri! I guess I wasn't quite ready to let it go—I revised two pages for the tankouban and added 12! I also threw in some behind-the-scenes stuff that I thought you might find interesting—Oh! And I printed the results of the character contests that ran in the original magazine. I hope you like it! ♡

—Hino Matsuri

(I also want to say a huge thank you to my editor, to Miss I, the Husky Sisters, my honorable Mother, A-sama and S-sama. You have been my strength during this process. Thank you all so very much!)

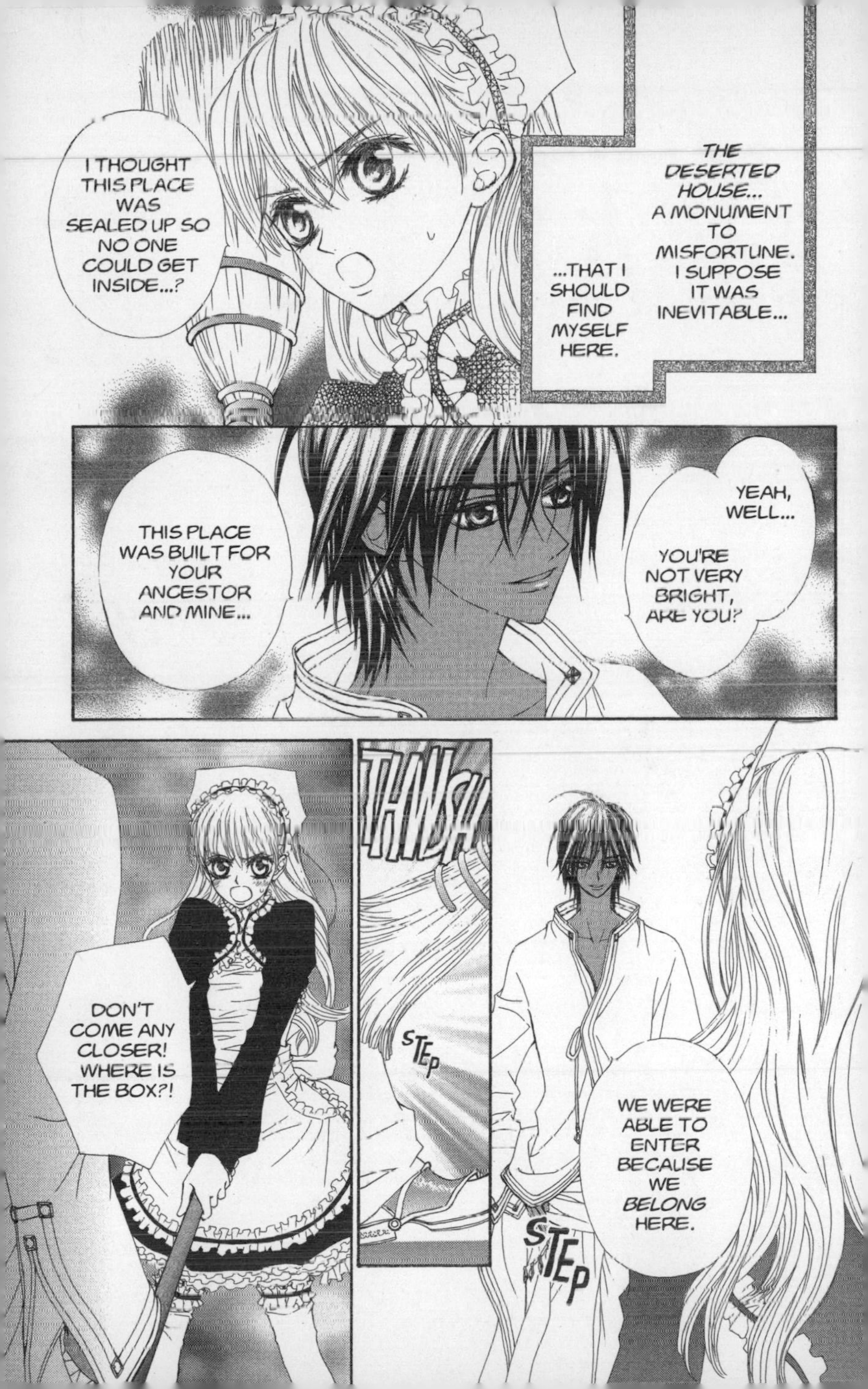
THE DESERTED HOUSE... A MONUMENT TO MISFORTUNE. I SUPPOSE IT WAS INEVITABLE...
...THAT I SHOULD FIND MYSELF HERE.
I THOUGHT THIS PLACE WAS SEALED UP SO NO ONE COULD GET INSIDE...?
YEAH, WELL...
YOU'RE NOT VERY BRIGHT, ARE YOU?
THIS PLACE WAS BUILT FOR YOUR ANCESTOR AND MINE...
WE WERE ABLE TO ENTER BECAUSE WE BELONG HERE.
STEP
THWSH
STEP
DON'T COME ANY CLOSER! WHERE IS THE BOX?!

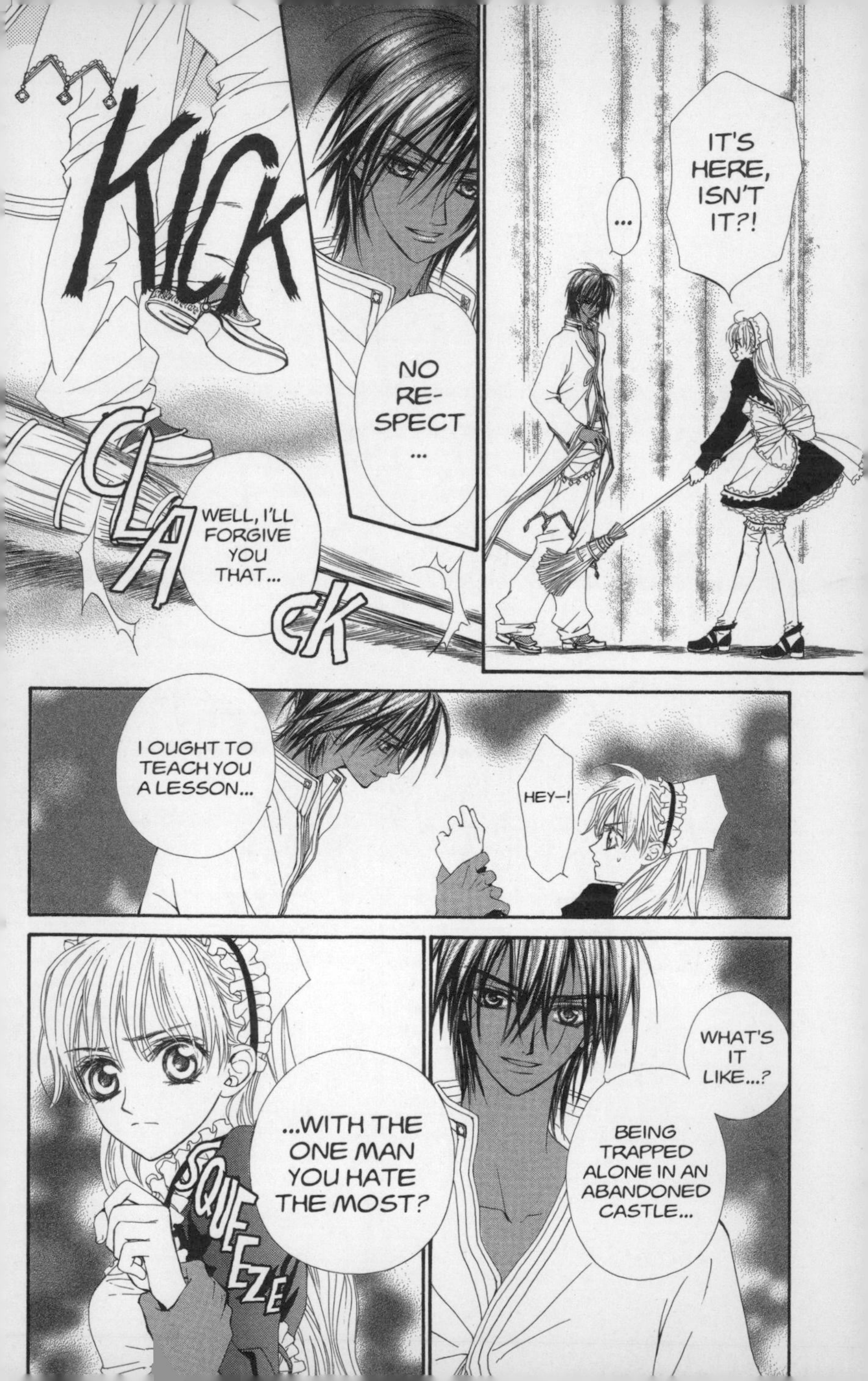
IT'S HERE, ISN'T IT?!
...
NO RE-SPECT ...
KICK
WELL, I'LL FORGIVE YOU THAT...
CLACK
HEY—!
I OUGHT TO TEACH YOU A LESSON...
WHAT'S IT LIKE...?
BEING TRAPPED ALONE IN AN ABANDONED CASTLE...
...WITH THE ONE MAN YOU HATE THE MOST?
SQUEEZE

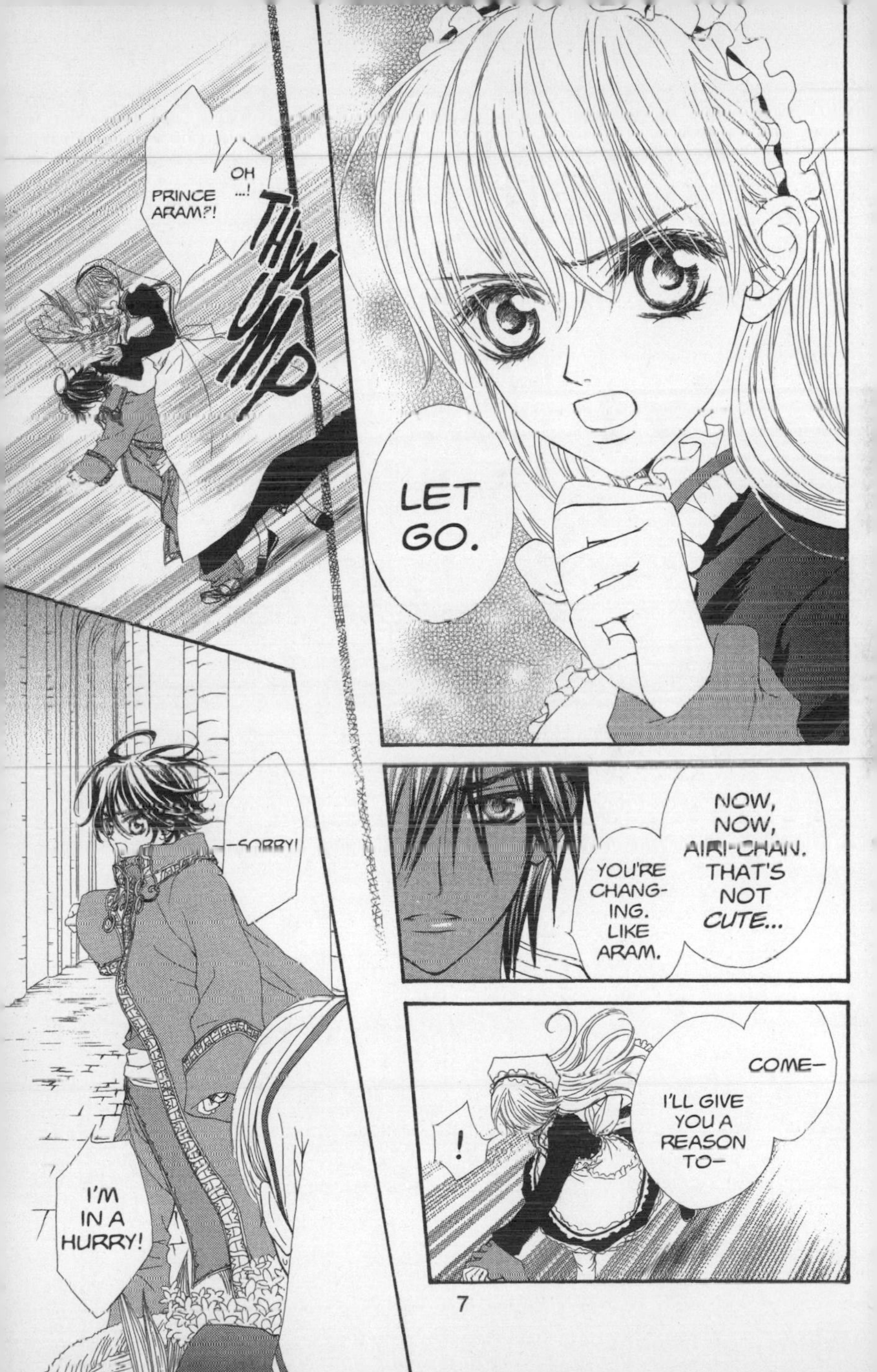
LET GO.
NOW, NOW, AIRI-CHAN. THAT'S NOT CUTE...
YOU'RE CHANGING. LIKE ARAM.
COME—
I'LL GIVE YOU A REASON TO—
!
OH ...!
PRINCE ARAM?!
THWUMP
—SORRY!
I'M IN A HURRY!

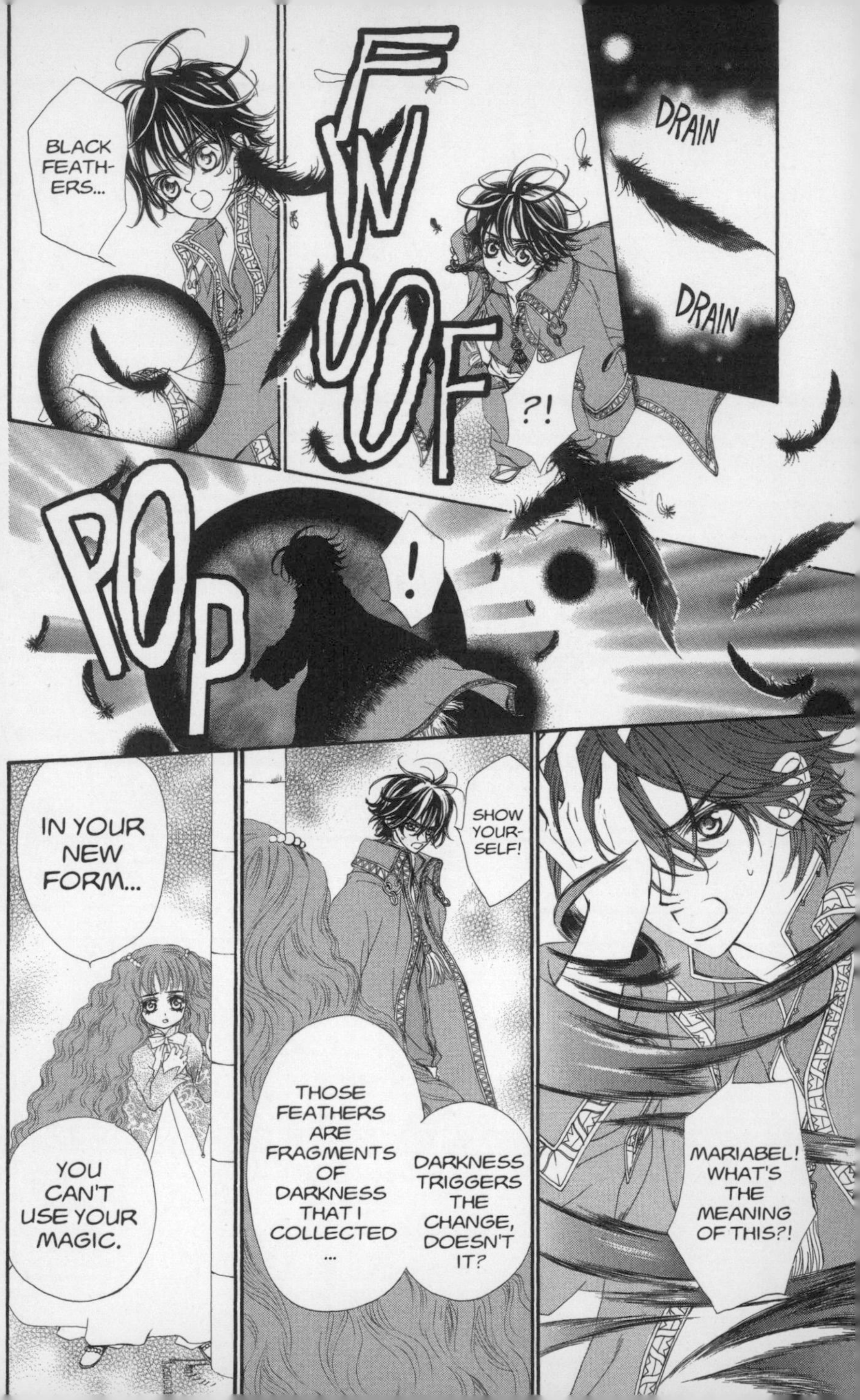
DRAIN
DRAIN
FWOOF
?!
BLACK FEATHERS...
POP
!
MARIABEL! WHAT'S THE MEANING OF THIS?!
SHOW YOURSELF!
DARKNESS TRIGGERS THE CHANGE, DOESN'T IT?
THOSE FEATHERS ARE FRAGMENTS OF DARKNESS THAT I COLLECTED...
IN YOUR NEW FORM...
YOU CAN'T USE YOUR MAGIC.

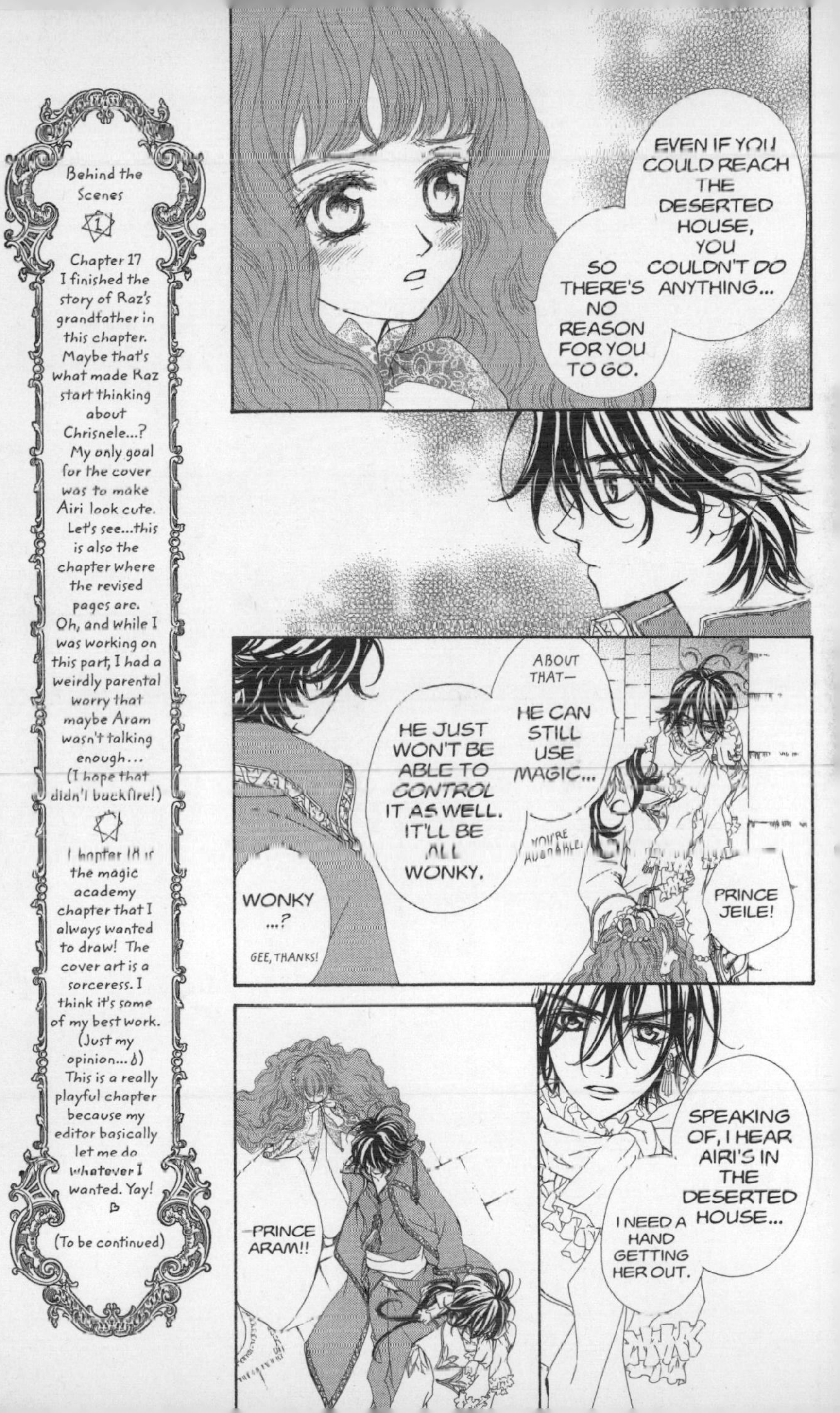
EVEN IF YOU COULD REACH THE DESERTED HOUSE, YOU COULDN'T DO ANYTHING...
SO THERE'S NO REASON FOR YOU TO GO.
ABOUT THAT—
HE CAN STILL USE MAGIC...
HE JUST WON'T BE ABLE TO CONTROL IT AS WELL. IT'LL BE ALL WONKY.
PRINCE JEILE!
WONKY ...?
GEE, THANKS!
SPEAKING OF, I HEAR AIRI'S IN THE DESERTED HOUSE...
I NEED A HAND GETTING HER OUT.
—PRINCE ARAM!!

Behind the Scenes

1

Chapter 17 I finished the story of Raz's grandfather in this chapter. Maybe that's what made Raz start thinking about Chrisnele...? My only goal for the cover was to make Airi look cute. Let's see...this is also the chapter where the revised pages are. Oh, and while I was working on this part, I had a weirdly parental worry that maybe Aram wasn't talking enough... (I hope that didn't backfire!)

Chapter 18 is the magic academy chapter that I always wanted to draw! The cover art is a sorceress. I think it's some of my best work. (Just my opinion...) This is a really playful chapter because my editor basically let me do whatever I wanted. Yay!

(To be continued)

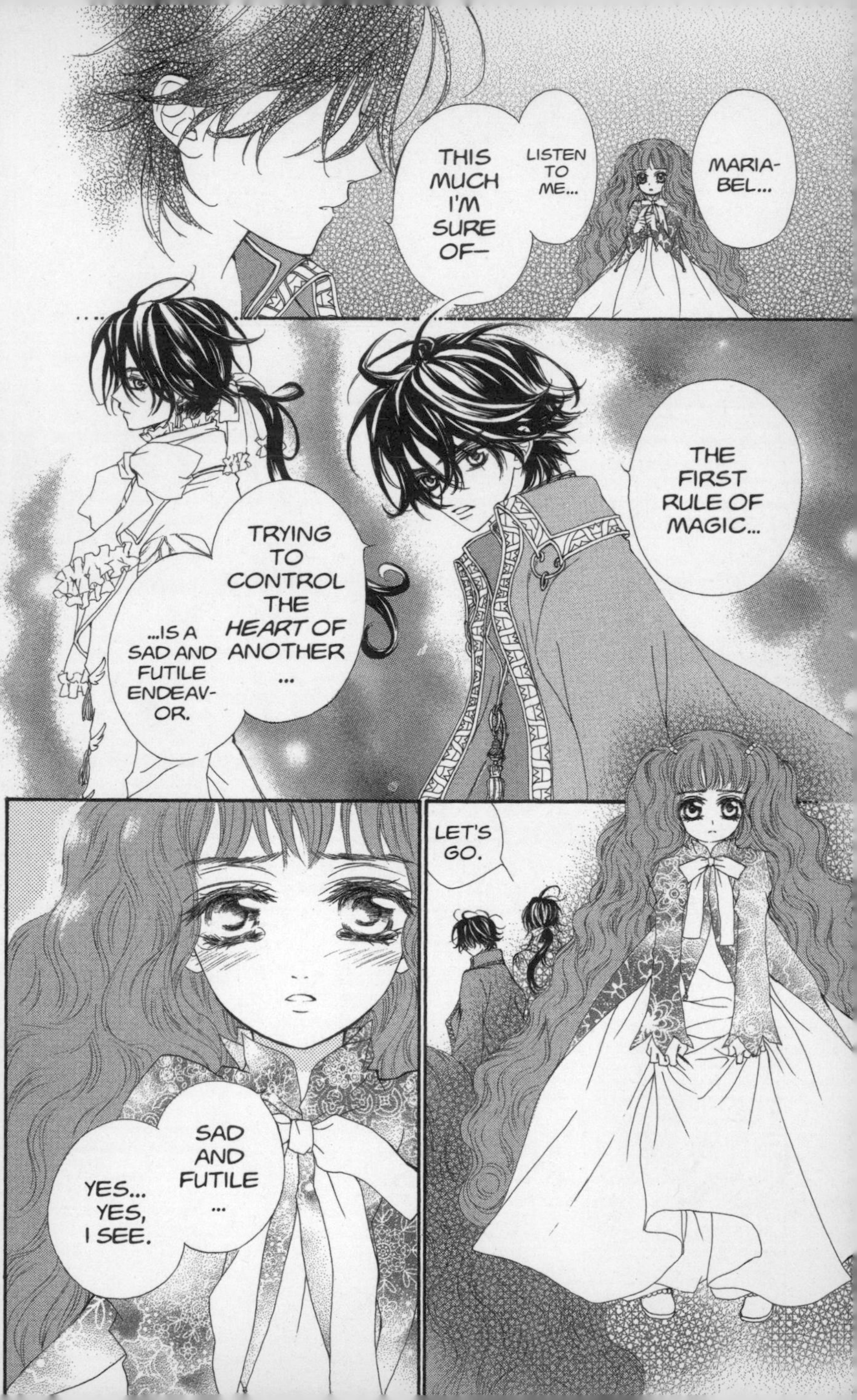
MARIA-BEL...
LISTEN TO ME...
THIS MUCH I'M SURE OF—
THE FIRST RULE OF MAGIC...
TRYING TO CONTROL THE *HEART* OF ANOTHER...
...IS A SAD AND FUTILE ENDEAV-OR.
LET'S GO.
SAD AND FUTILE...
YES... YES, I SEE.

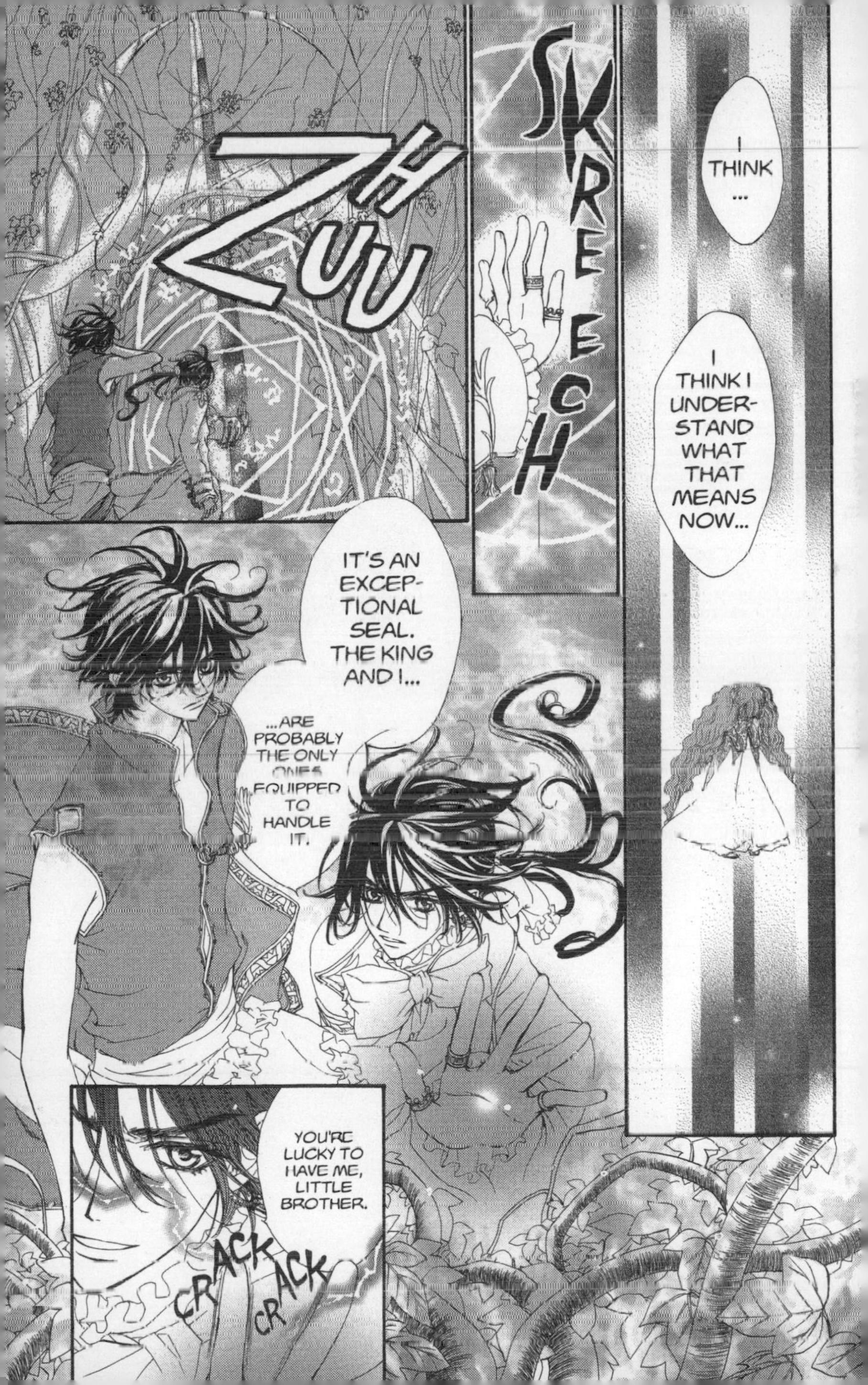
I THINK...
I THINK I UNDERSTAND WHAT THAT MEANS NOW...
SKREECH
ZHUU
IT'S AN EXCEPTIONAL SEAL. THE KING AND I...
...ARE PROBABLY THE ONLY ONES EQUIPPED TO HANDLE IT.
YOU'RE LUCKY TO HAVE ME, LITTLE BROTHER.
CRACK
CRACK

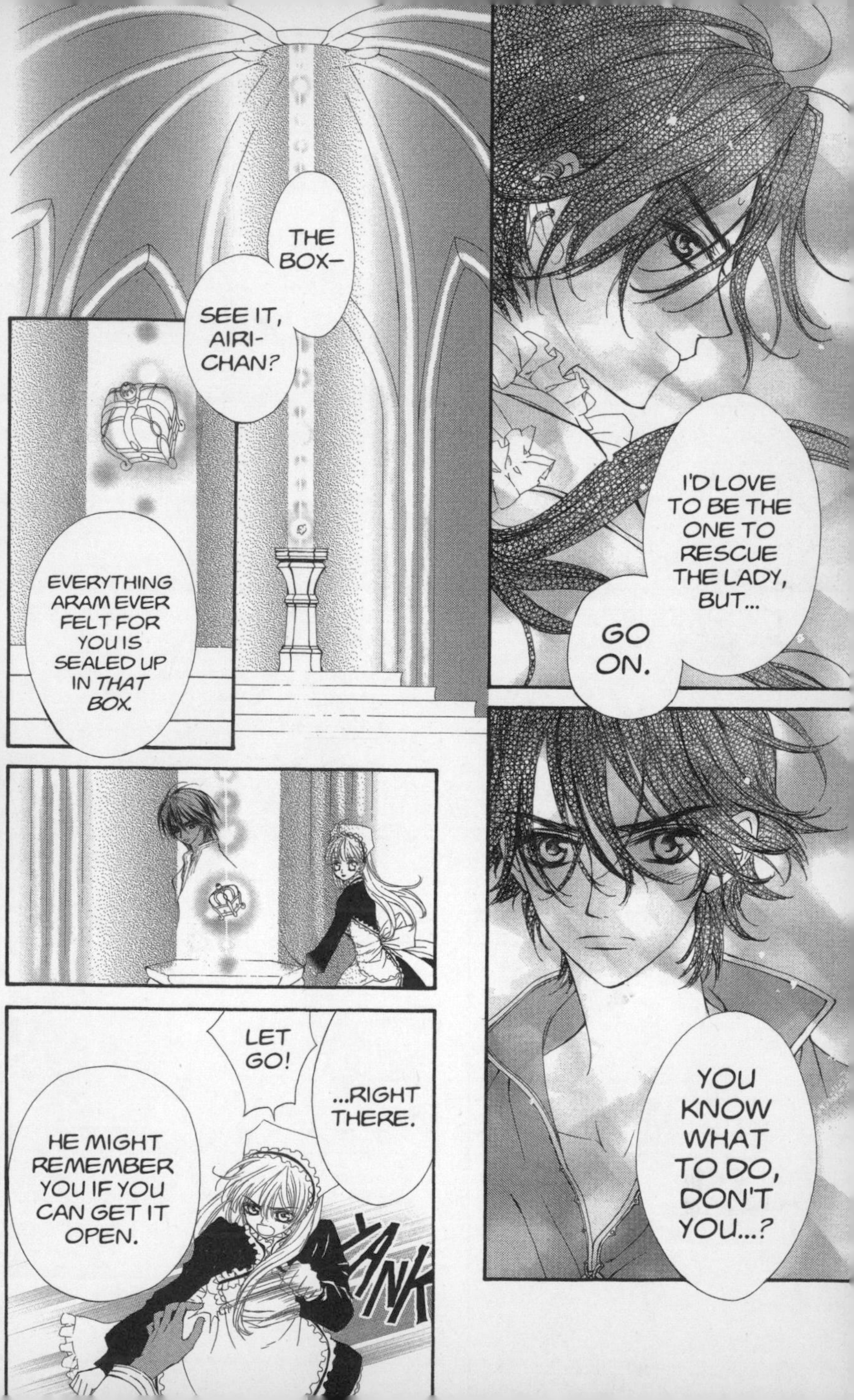
I'D LOVE TO BE THE ONE TO RESCUE THE LADY, BUT...
GO ON.
YOU KNOW WHAT TO DO, DON'T YOU...?
THE BOX—
SEE IT, AIRI-CHAN?
EVERYTHING ARAM EVER FELT FOR YOU IS SEALED UP IN *THAT* BOX.
...RIGHT THERE.
LET GO!
HE MIGHT REMEMBER YOU IF YOU CAN GET IT OPEN.
YANK

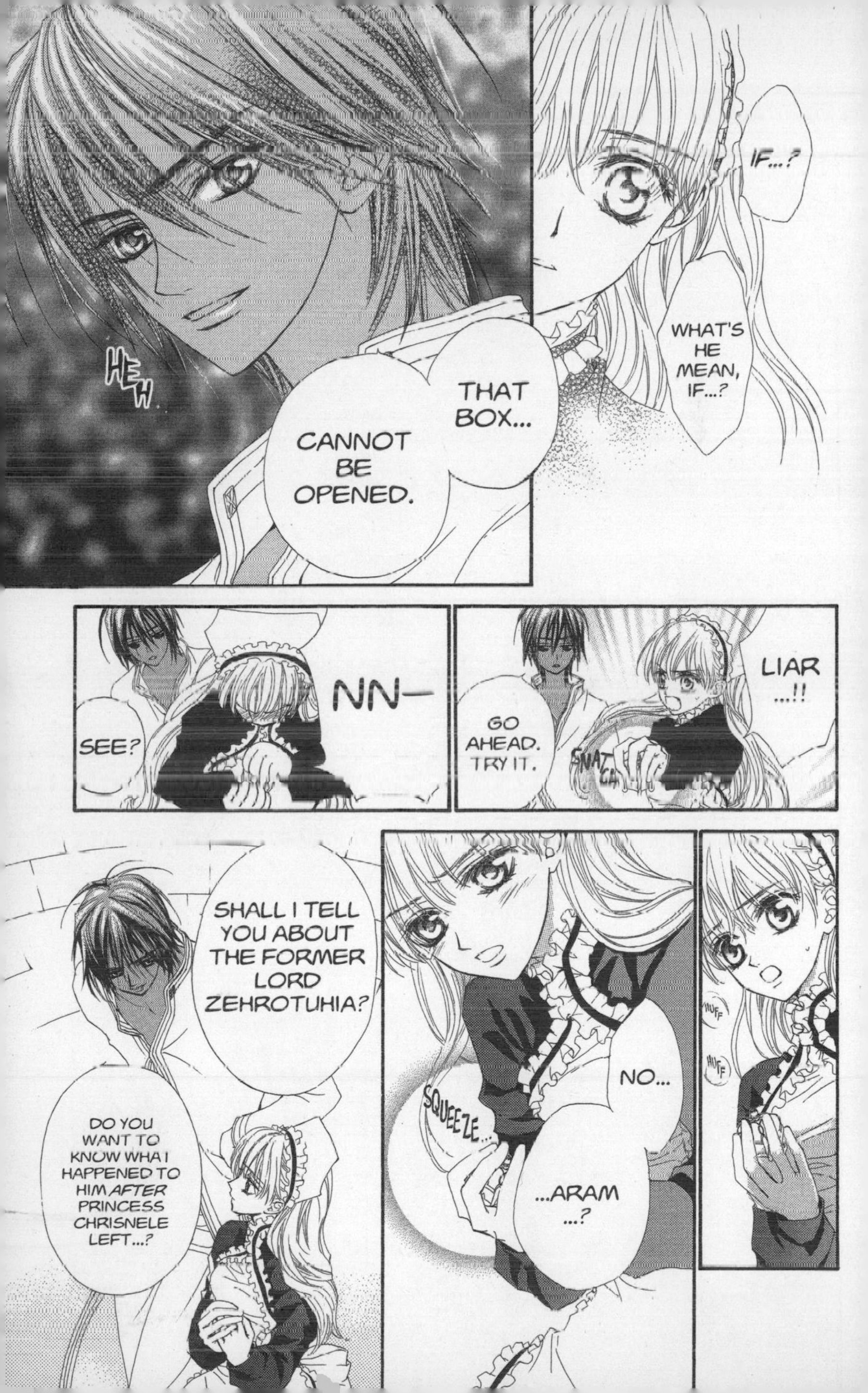
IF...?
WHAT'S HE MEAN, IF...?
HEH
THAT BOX...
CANNOT BE OPENED.
LIAR ...!!
SNATCH
GO AHEAD. TRY IT.
NN—
SEE?
HUFF
HUFF
NO...
SQUEEZE...
...ARAM ...?
SHALL I TELL YOU ABOUT THE FORMER LORD ZEHROTUHIA?
DO YOU WANT TO KNOW WHAT HAPPENED TO HIM *AFTER* PRINCESS CHRISNELE LEFT...?

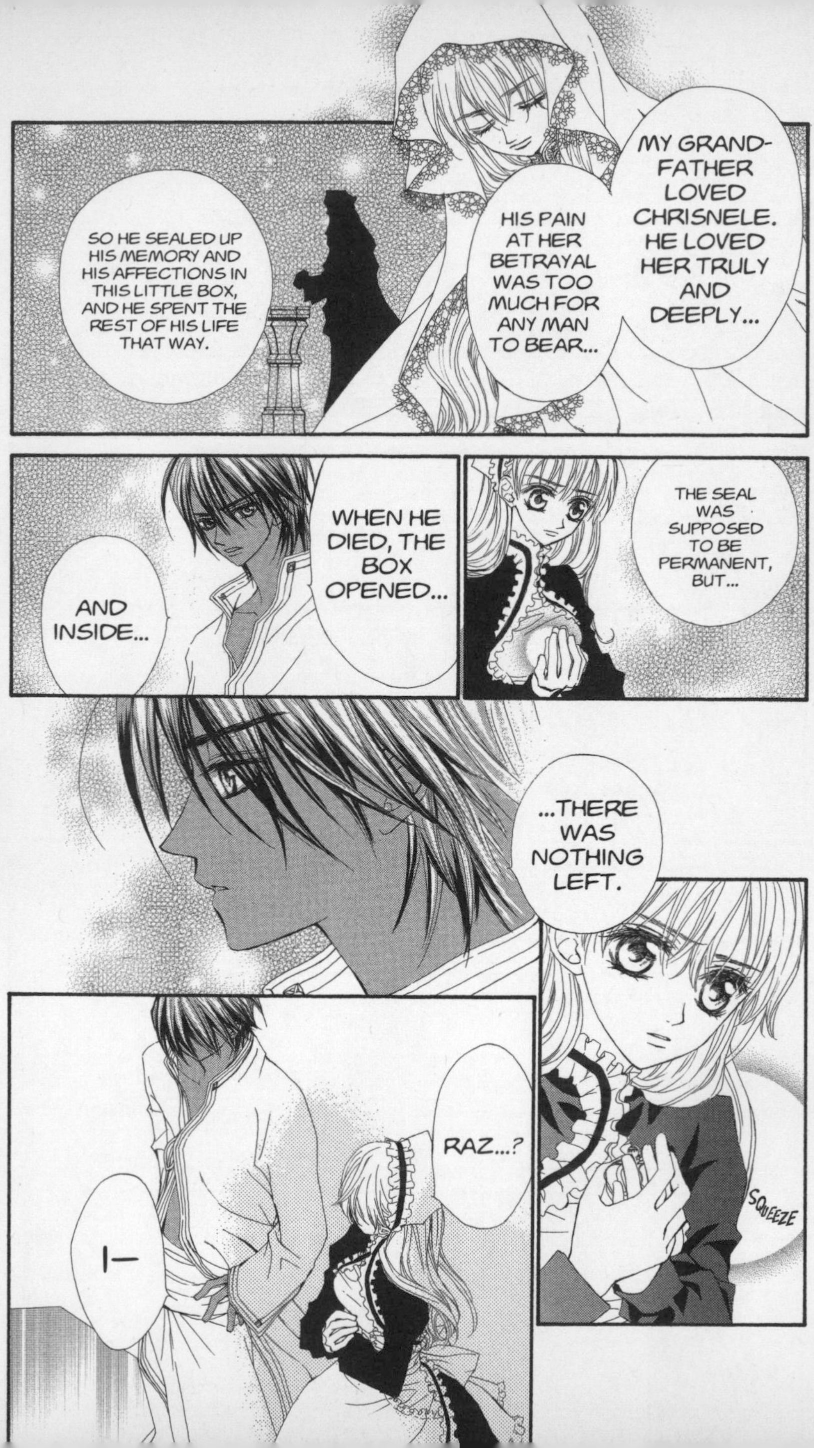
MY GRAND-FATHER LOVED CHRISNELE. HE LOVED HER TRULY AND DEEPLY...
HIS PAIN AT HER BETRAYAL WAS TOO MUCH FOR ANY MAN TO BEAR...
SO HE SEALED UP HIS MEMORY AND HIS AFFECTIONS IN THIS LITTLE BOX, AND HE SPENT THE REST OF HIS LIFE THAT WAY.
THE SEAL WAS SUPPOSED TO BE PERMANENT, BUT...
WHEN HE DIED, THE BOX OPENED...
AND INSIDE...
...THERE WAS NOTHING LEFT.
SQUEEZE
RAZ...?
I—

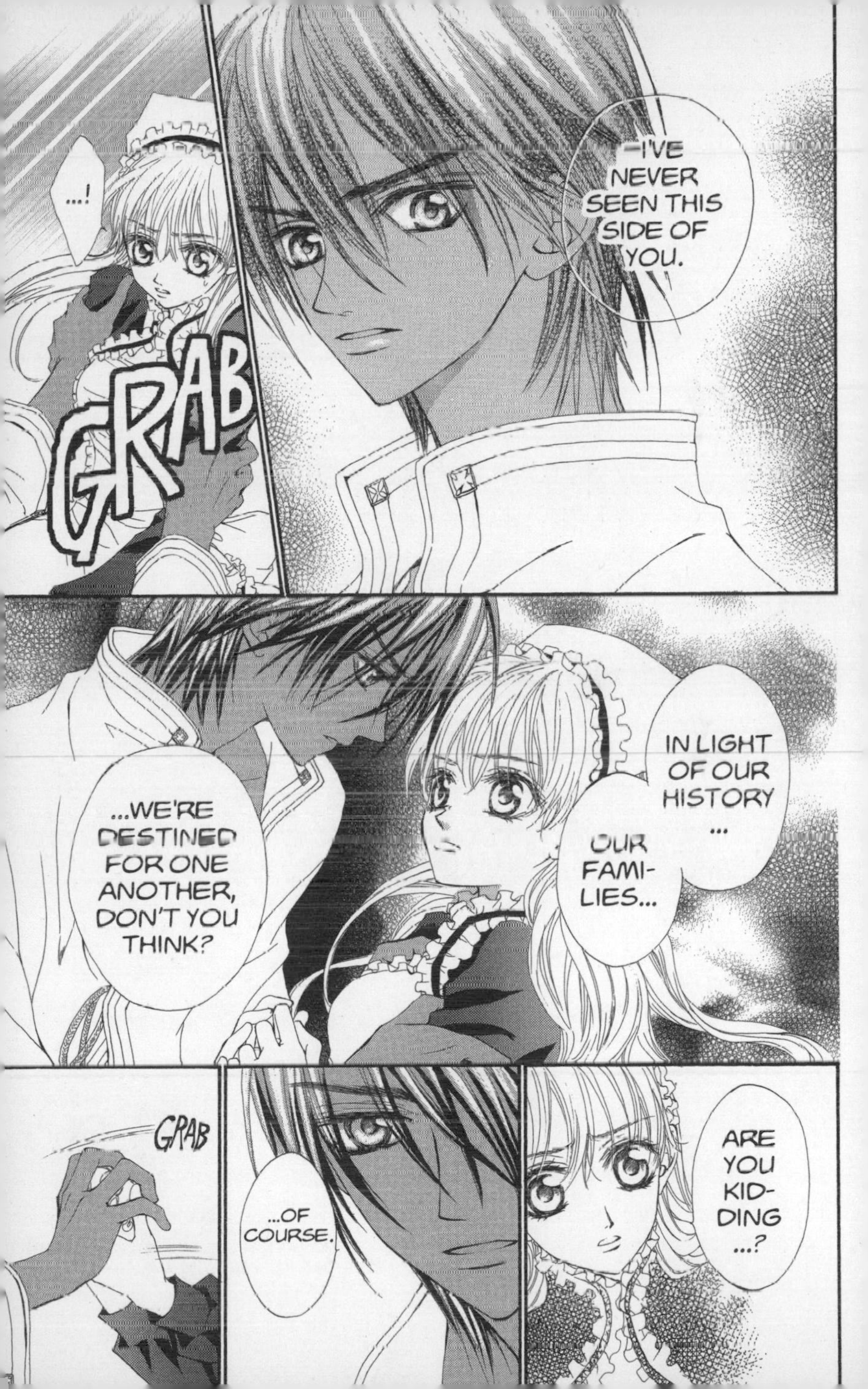
—I'VE NEVER SEEN THIS SIDE OF YOU.
...!
GRAB
IN LIGHT OF OUR HISTORY ...
OUR FAMI-LIES...
...WE'RE DESTINED FOR ONE ANOTHER, DON'T YOU THINK?
ARE YOU KID-DING ...?
...OF COURSE.
GRAB

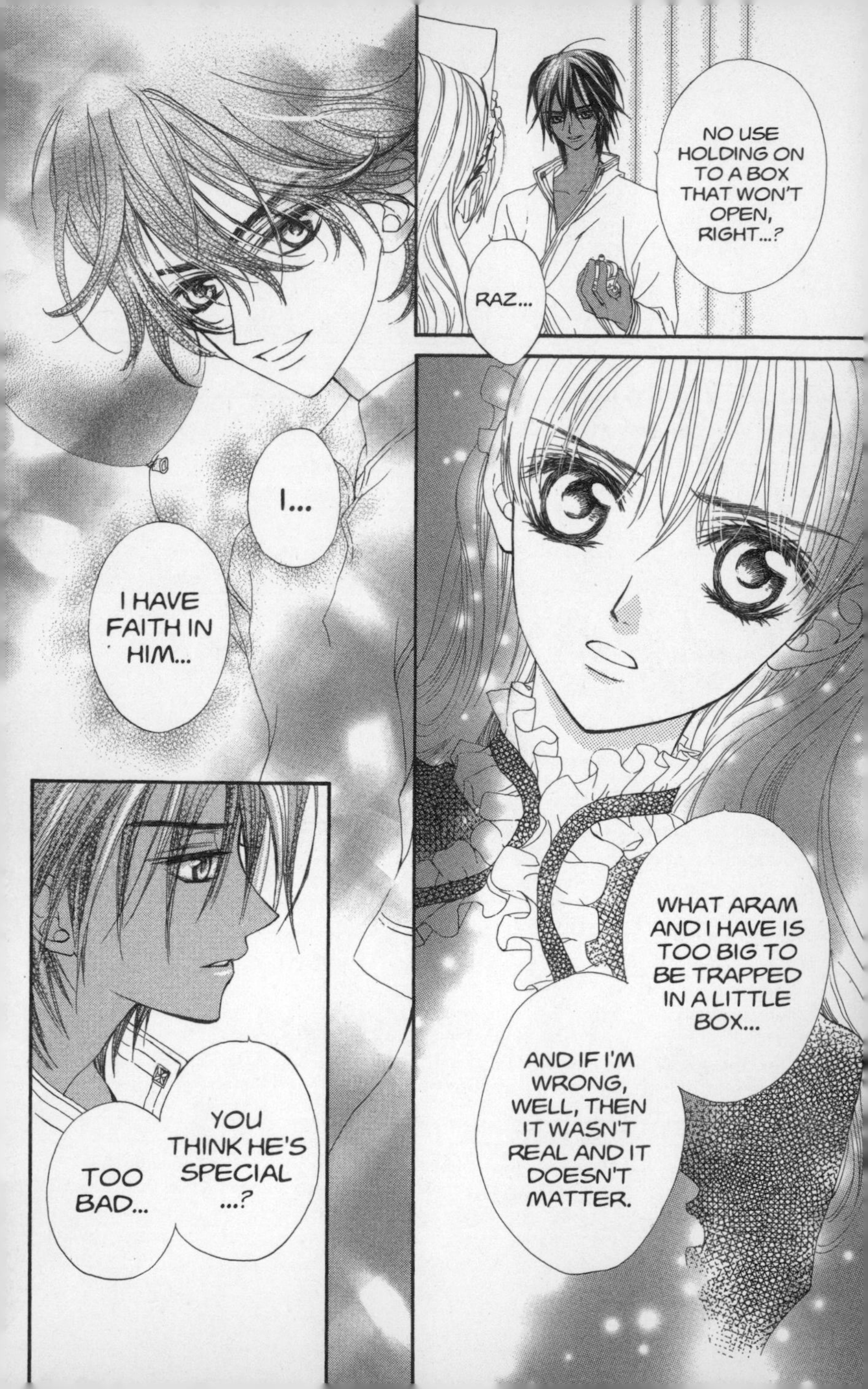
NO USE HOLDING ON TO A BOX THAT WON'T OPEN, RIGHT...?
RAZ...
WHAT ARAM AND I HAVE IS TOO BIG TO BE TRAPPED IN A LITTLE BOX...
AND IF I'M WRONG, WELL, THEN IT WASN'T REAL AND IT DOESN'T MATTER.
I...
I HAVE FAITH IN HIM...
YOU THINK HE'S SPECIAL ...?
TOO BAD...

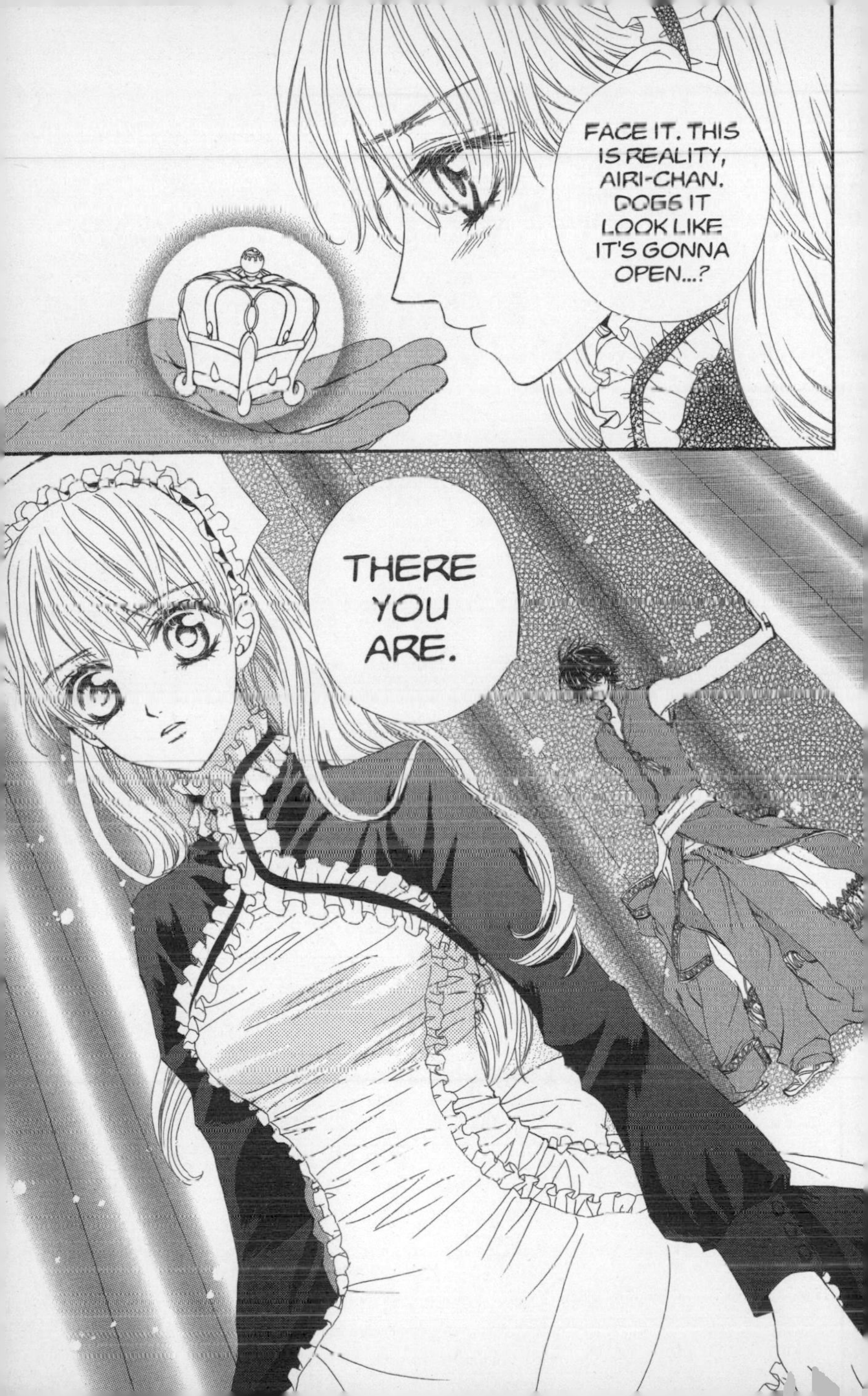
FACE IT. THIS IS REALITY, AIRI-CHAN. DOES IT LOOK LIKE IT'S GONNA OPEN...?
THERE YOU ARE.

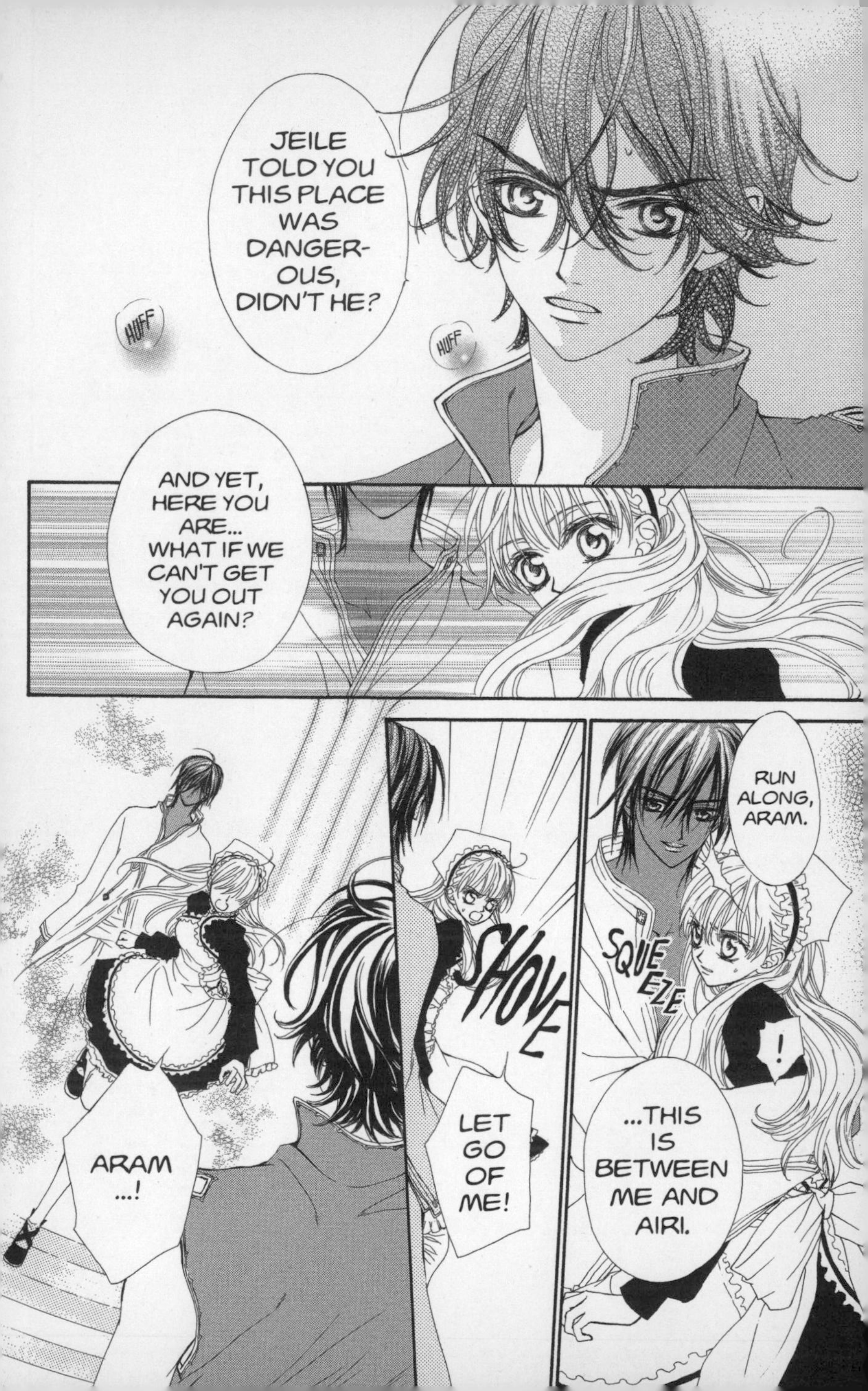
JEILE TOLD YOU THIS PLACE WAS DANGER-OUS, DIDN'T HE?
HUFF
HUFF
AND YET, HERE YOU ARE... WHAT IF WE CAN'T GET YOU OUT AGAIN?
RUN ALONG, ARAM.
SQUEEZE
!
...THIS IS BETWEEN ME AND AIRI.
SHOVE
LET GO OF ME!
ARAM ...!

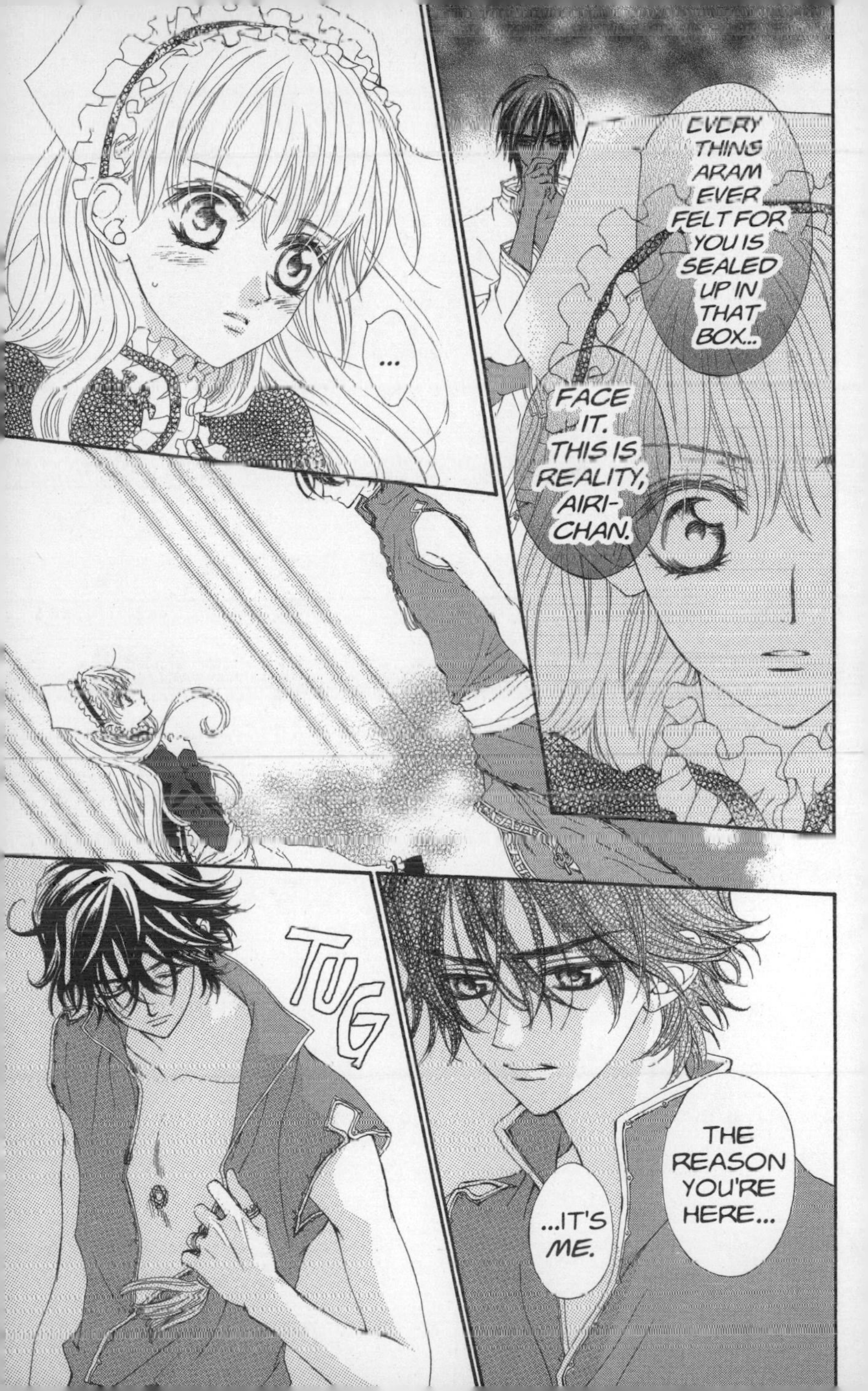
EVERY THING ARAM EVER FELT FOR YOU IS SEALED UP IN THAT BOX...
FACE IT. THIS IS REALITY, AIRI-CHAN.
...
THE REASON YOU'RE HERE...
...IT'S ME.
TUG

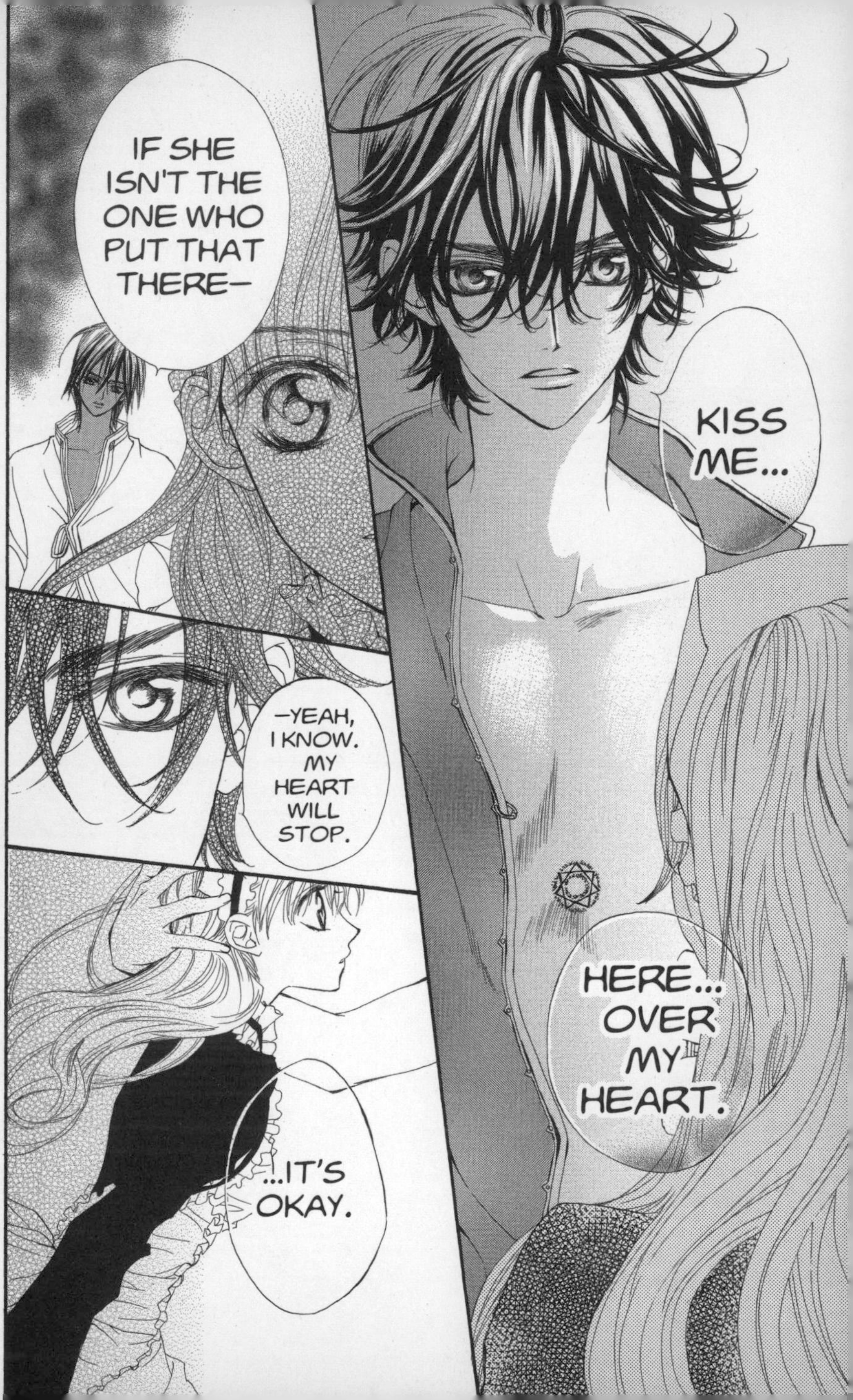
KISS ME...
HERE... OVER MY HEART.
IF SHE ISN'T THE ONE WHO PUT THAT THERE—
—YEAH, I KNOW. MY HEART WILL STOP.
...IT'S OKAY.

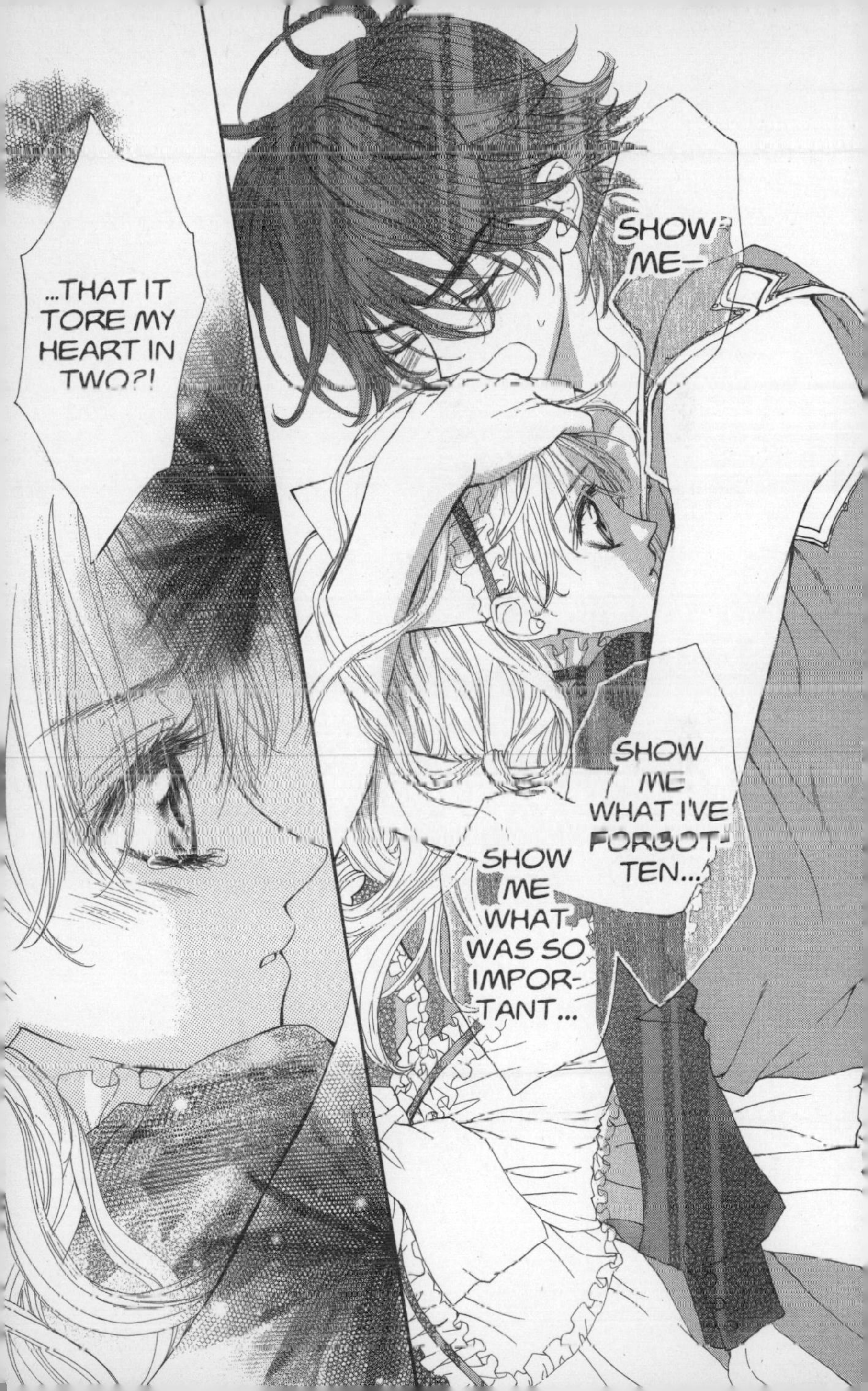
SHOW ME—
SHOW ME WHAT I'VE FORGOT-TEN...
SHOW ME WHAT WAS SO IMPOR-TANT...
...THAT IT TORE MY HEART IN TWO?!

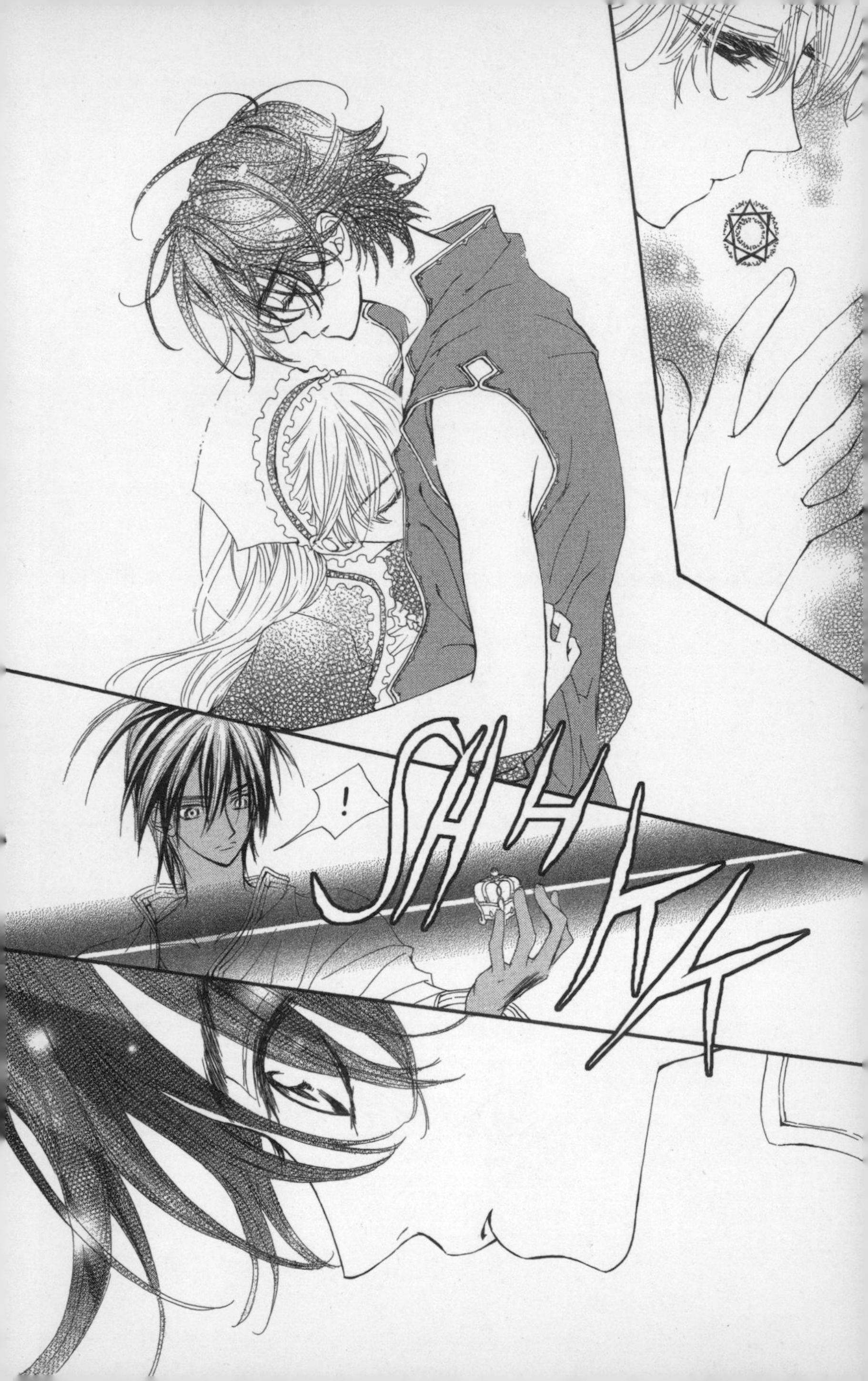
!
SHHKK

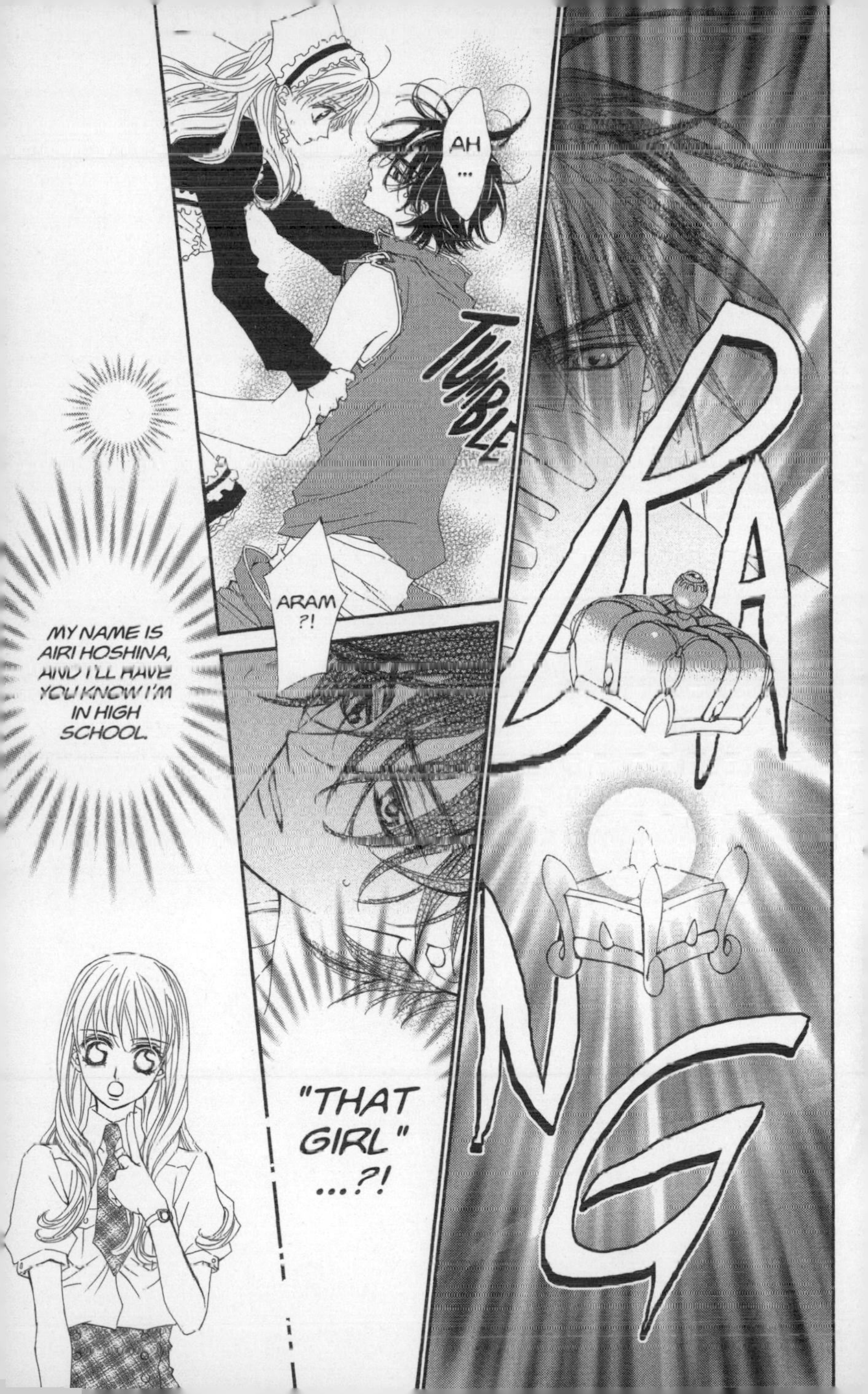
RANG
AH ...
TUMBLE
ARAM ?!
"THAT GIRL" ...?!
MY NAME IS AIRI HOSHINA, AND I'LL HAVE YOU KNOW I'M IN HIGH SCHOOL.

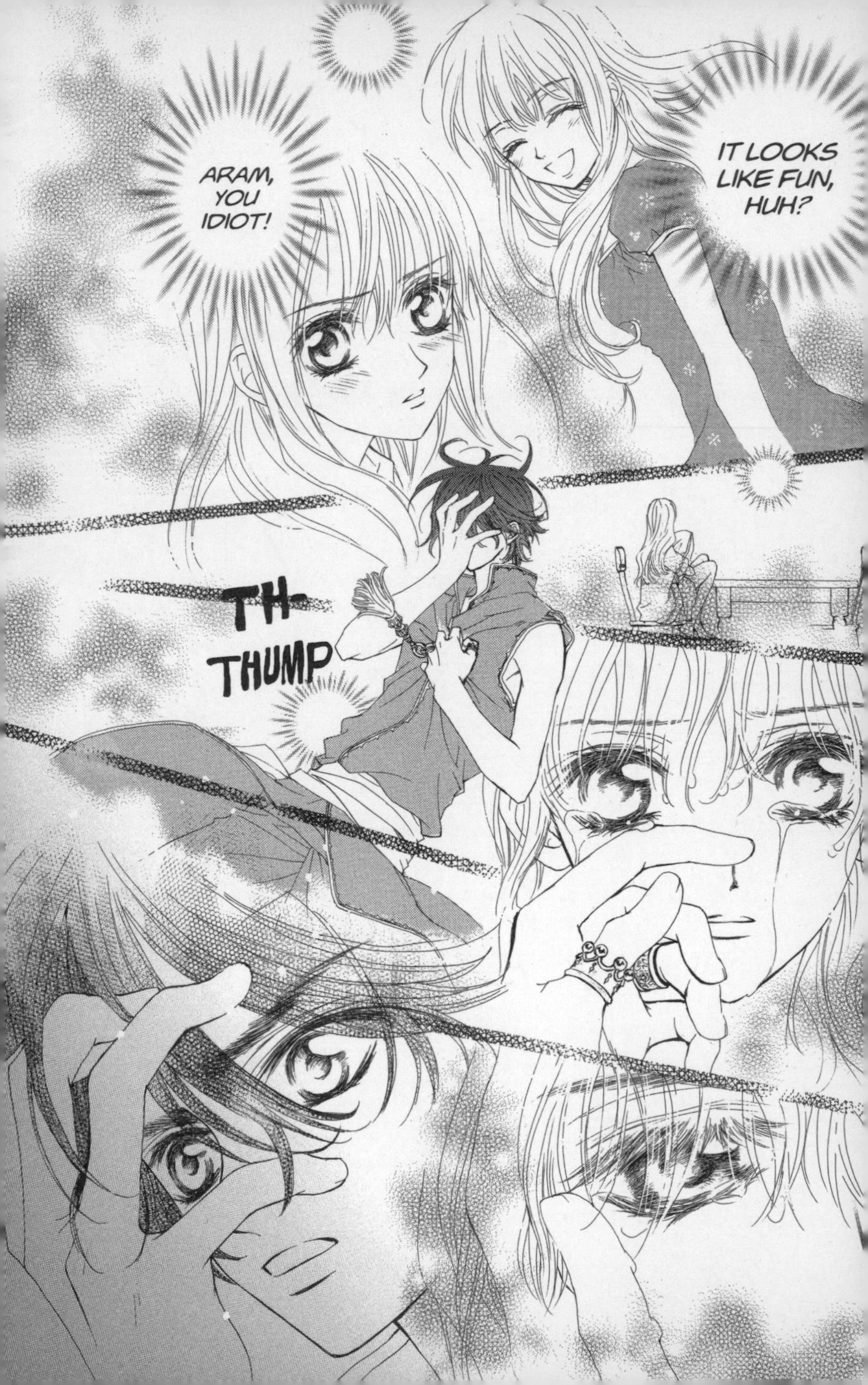
IT LOOKS LIKE FUN, HUH?
ARAM, YOU IDIOT!
TH- THUMP

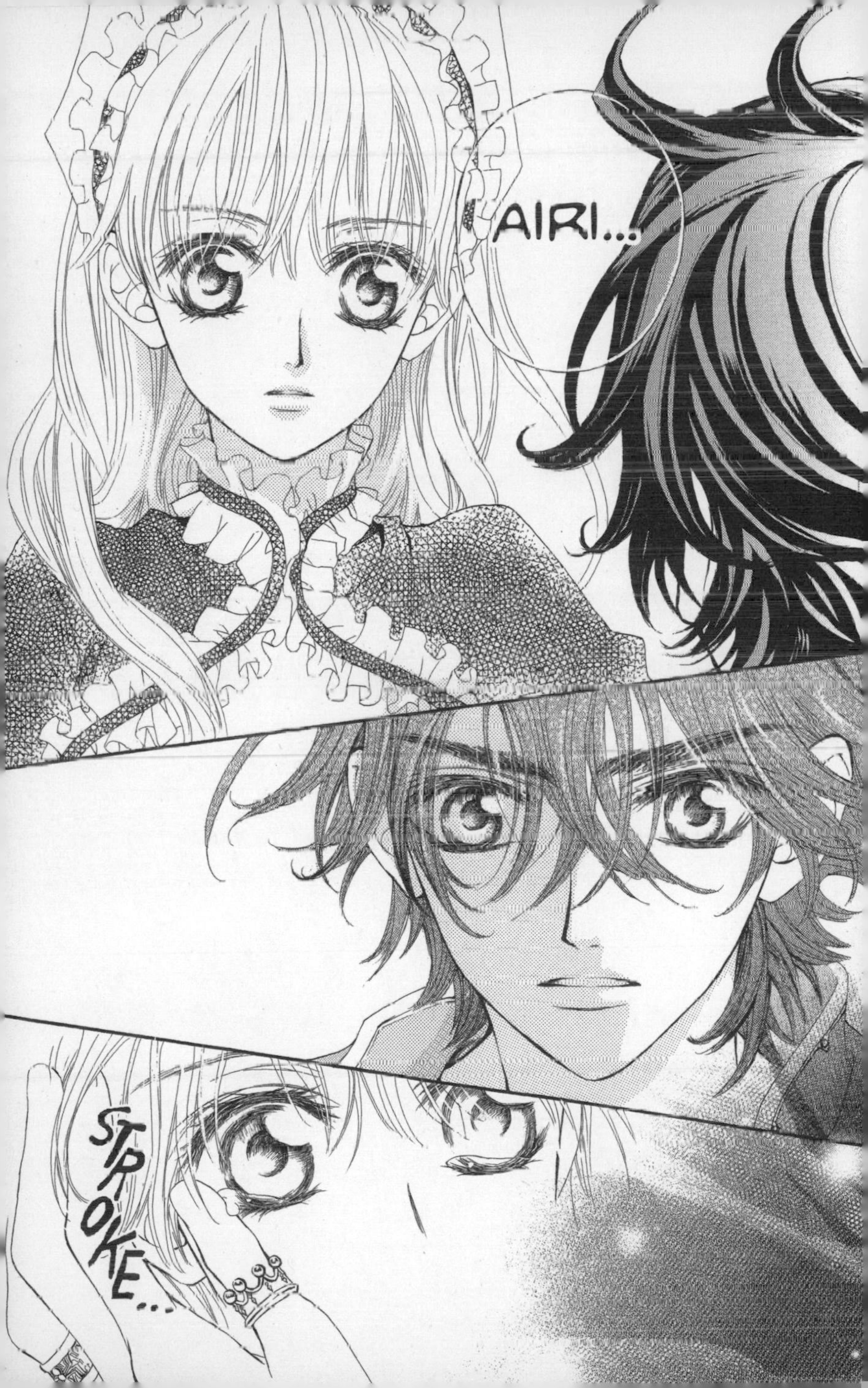
AIRI...
STROKE...

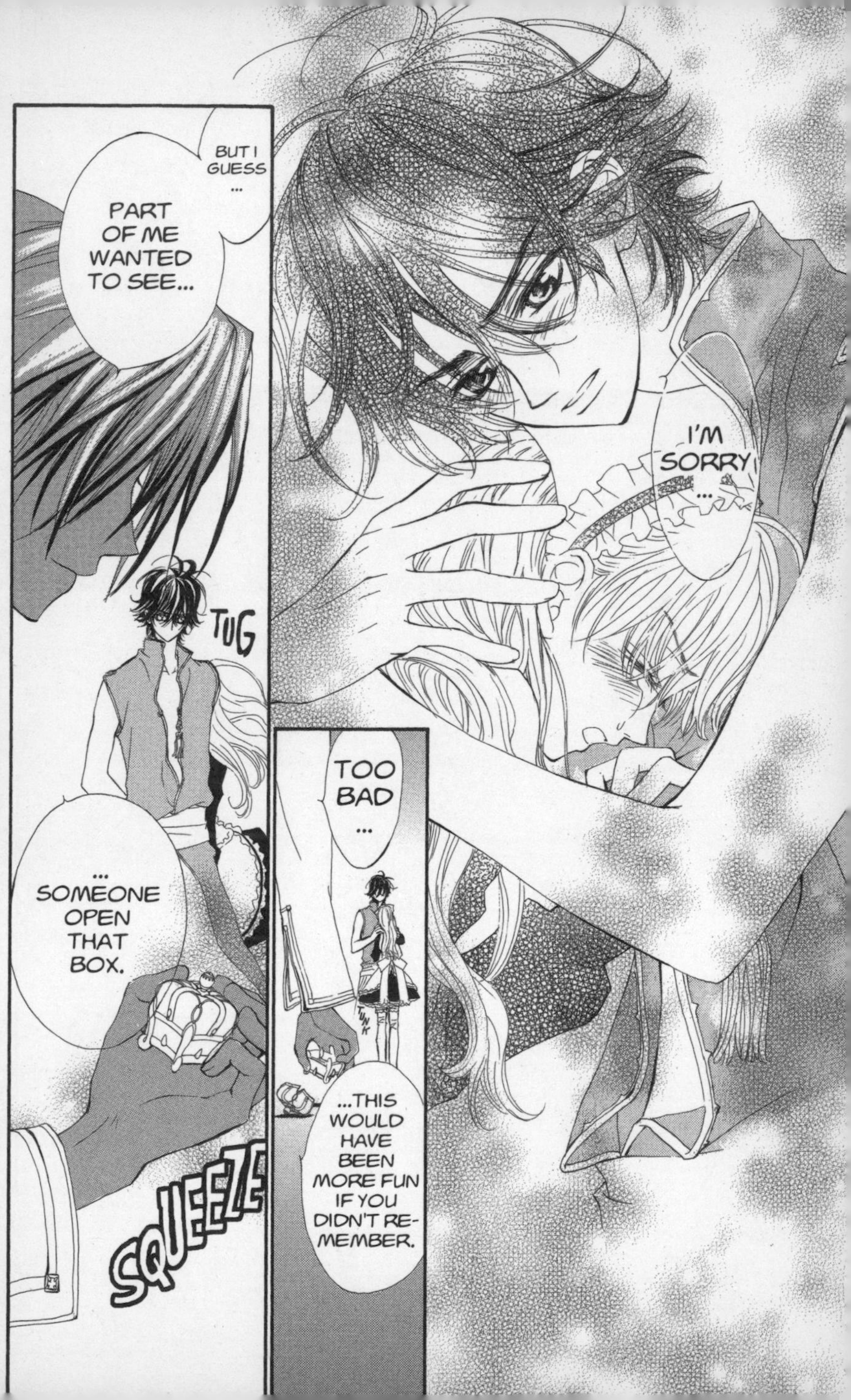
I'M SORRY ...
TOO BAD ...
...THIS WOULD HAVE BEEN MORE FUN IF YOU DIDN'T RE-MEMBER.
BUT I GUESS ...
PART OF ME WANTED TO SEE...
TUG
... SOMEONE OPEN THAT BOX.
SQUEEZE

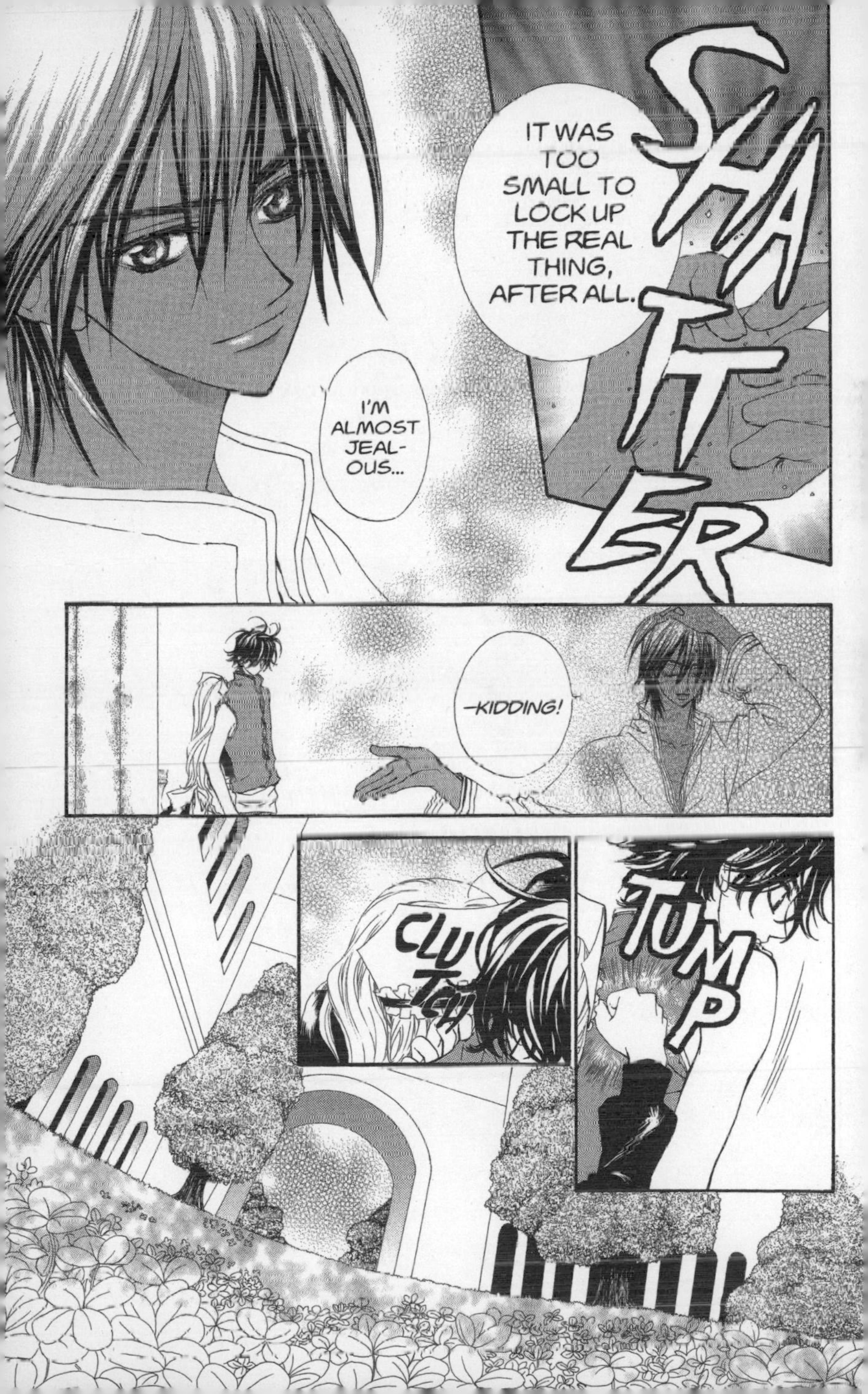
IT WAS TOO SMALL TO LOCK UP THE REAL THING, AFTER ALL.
SHATTER
I'M ALMOST JEAL-OUS...
-KIDDING!
TUMP
CLUTCH

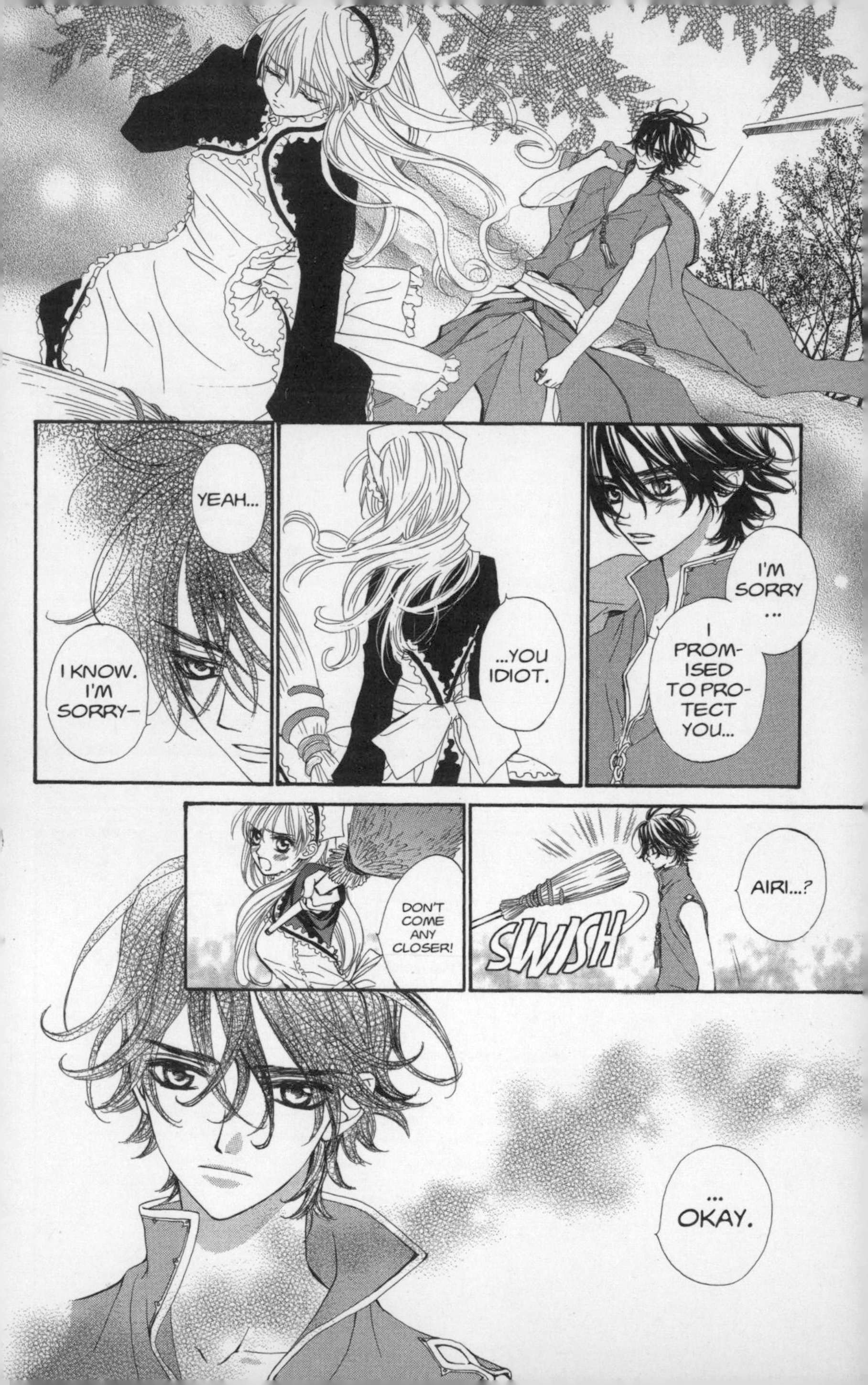
I'M SORRY ...
I PROMISED TO PROTECT YOU...
...YOU IDIOT.
YEAH...
I KNOW. I'M SORRY—
AIRI...?
SWISH
DON'T COME ANY CLOSER!
... OKAY.

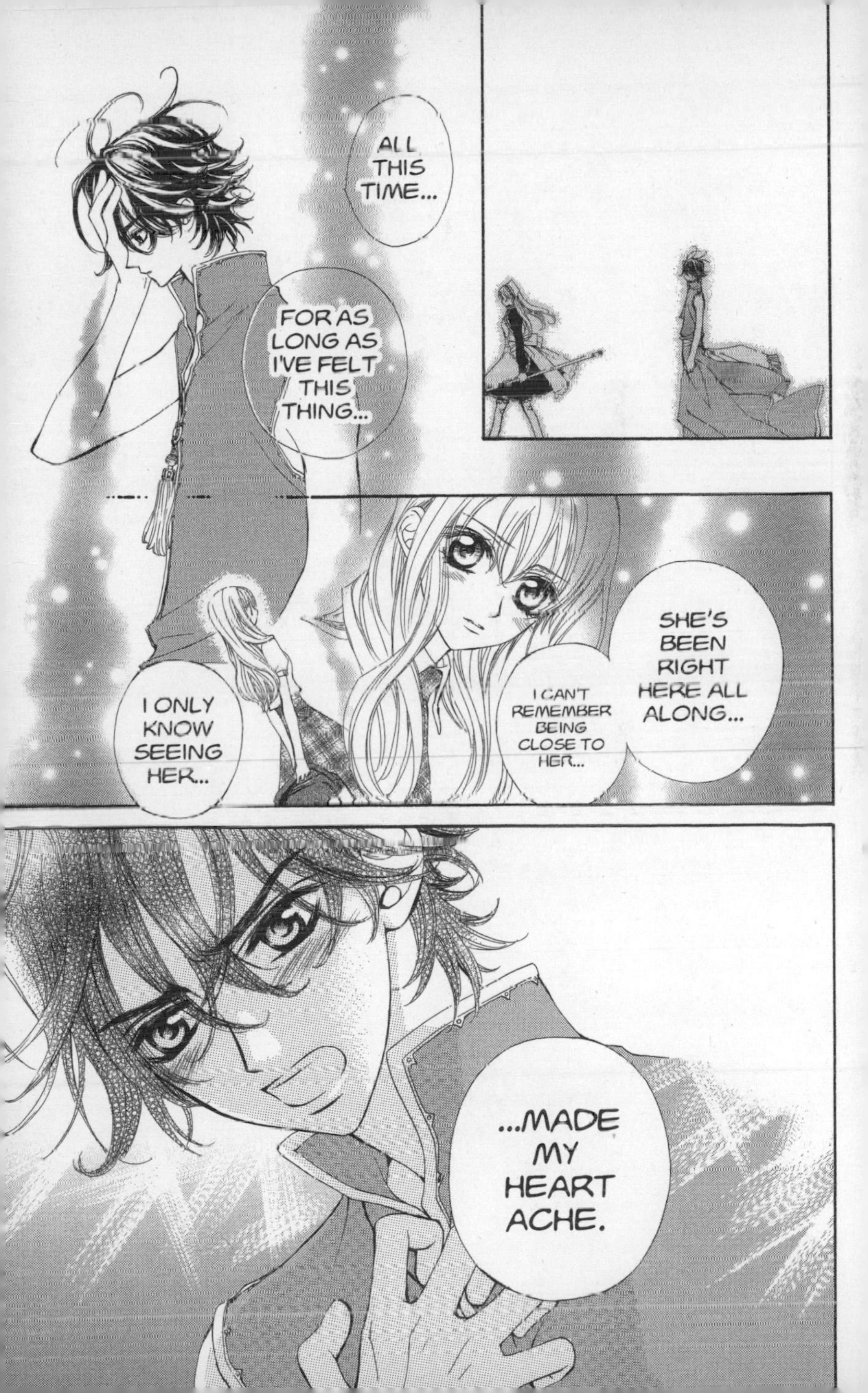
ALL THIS TIME...
FOR AS LONG AS I'VE FELT THIS THING...
SHE'S BEEN RIGHT HERE ALL ALONG...
I CAN'T REMEMBER BEING CLOSE TO HER...
I ONLY KNOW SEEING HER...
...MADE MY HEART ACHE.

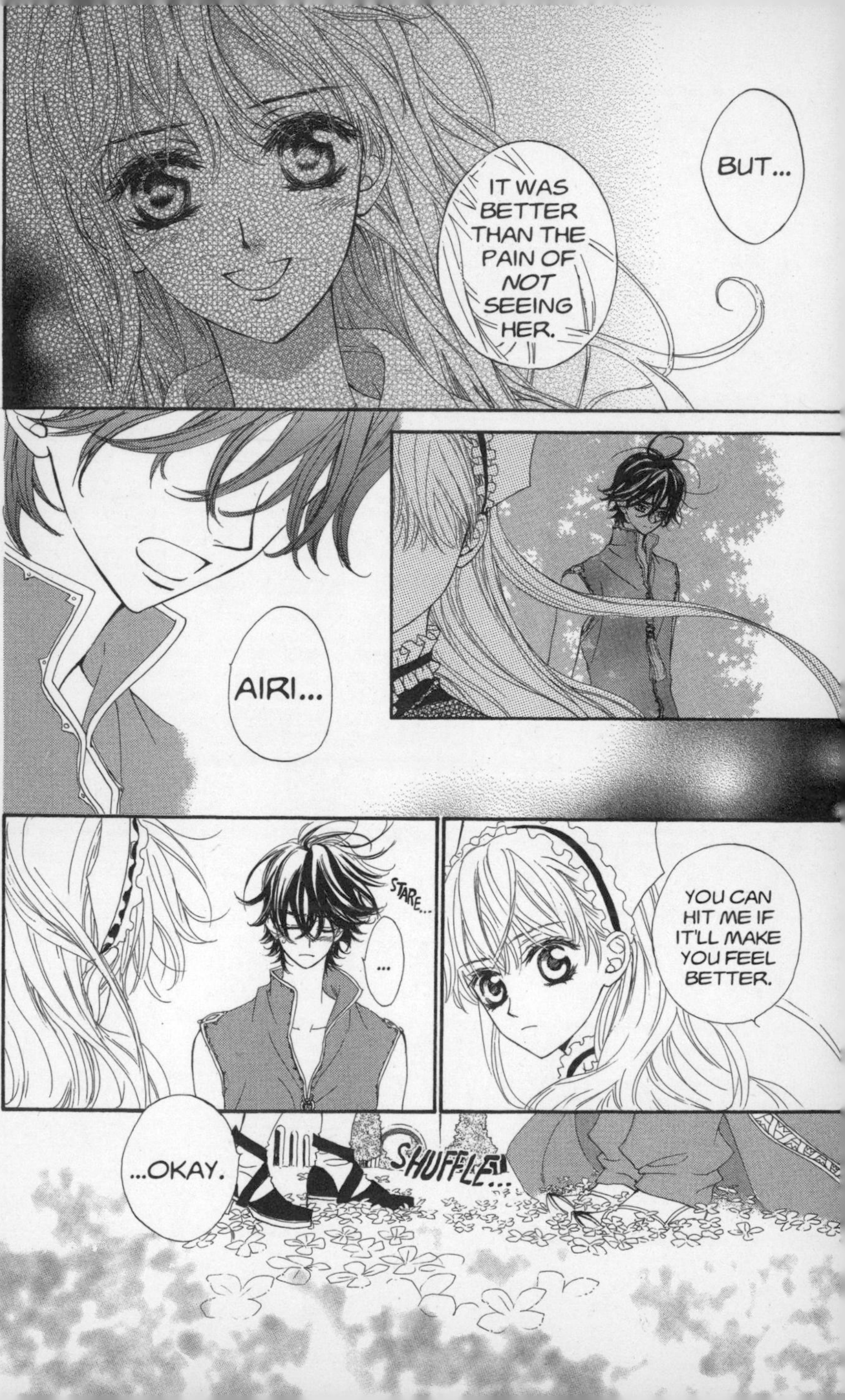
BUT...
IT WAS BETTER THAN THE PAIN OF NOT SEEING HER.
AIRI...
YOU CAN HIT ME IF IT'LL MAKE YOU FEEL BETTER.
STARE...
...
SHUFFLE...
...OKAY.

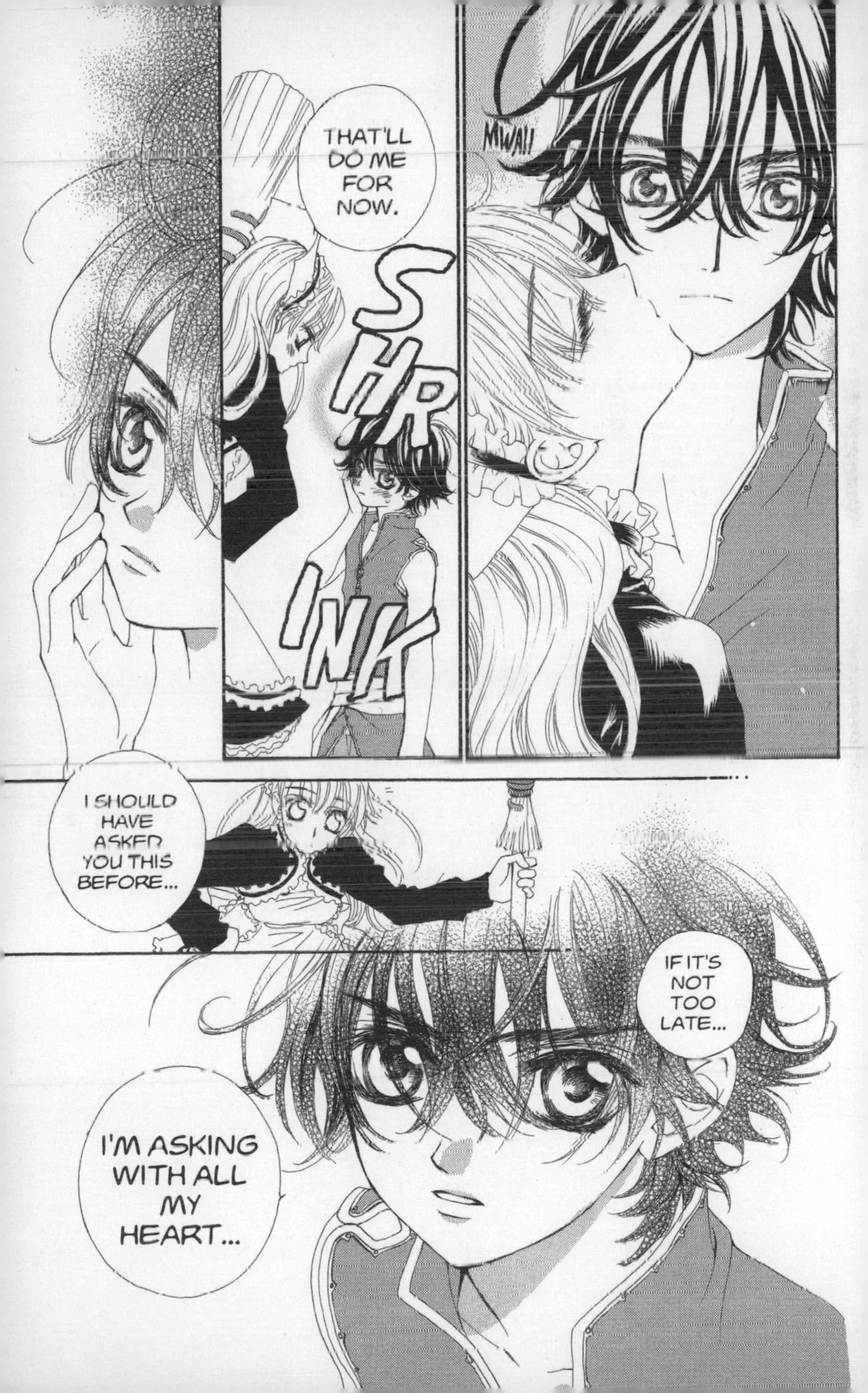
MWAH
THAT'LL DO ME FOR NOW.
SHRINK
I SHOULD HAVE ASKED YOU THIS BEFORE...
IF IT'S NOT TOO LATE...
I'M ASKING WITH ALL MY HEART...

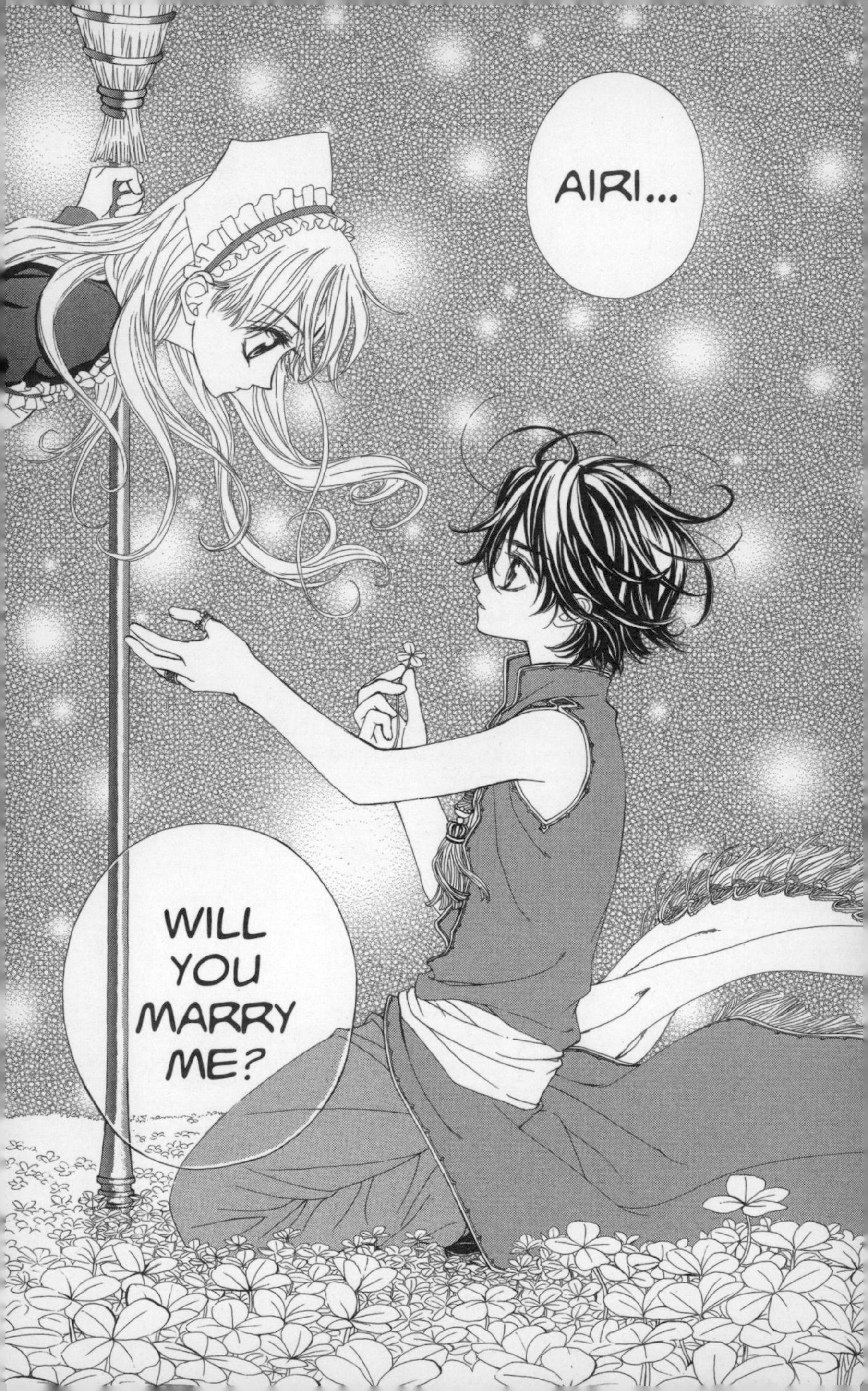
AIRI...
WILL YOU MARRY ME?

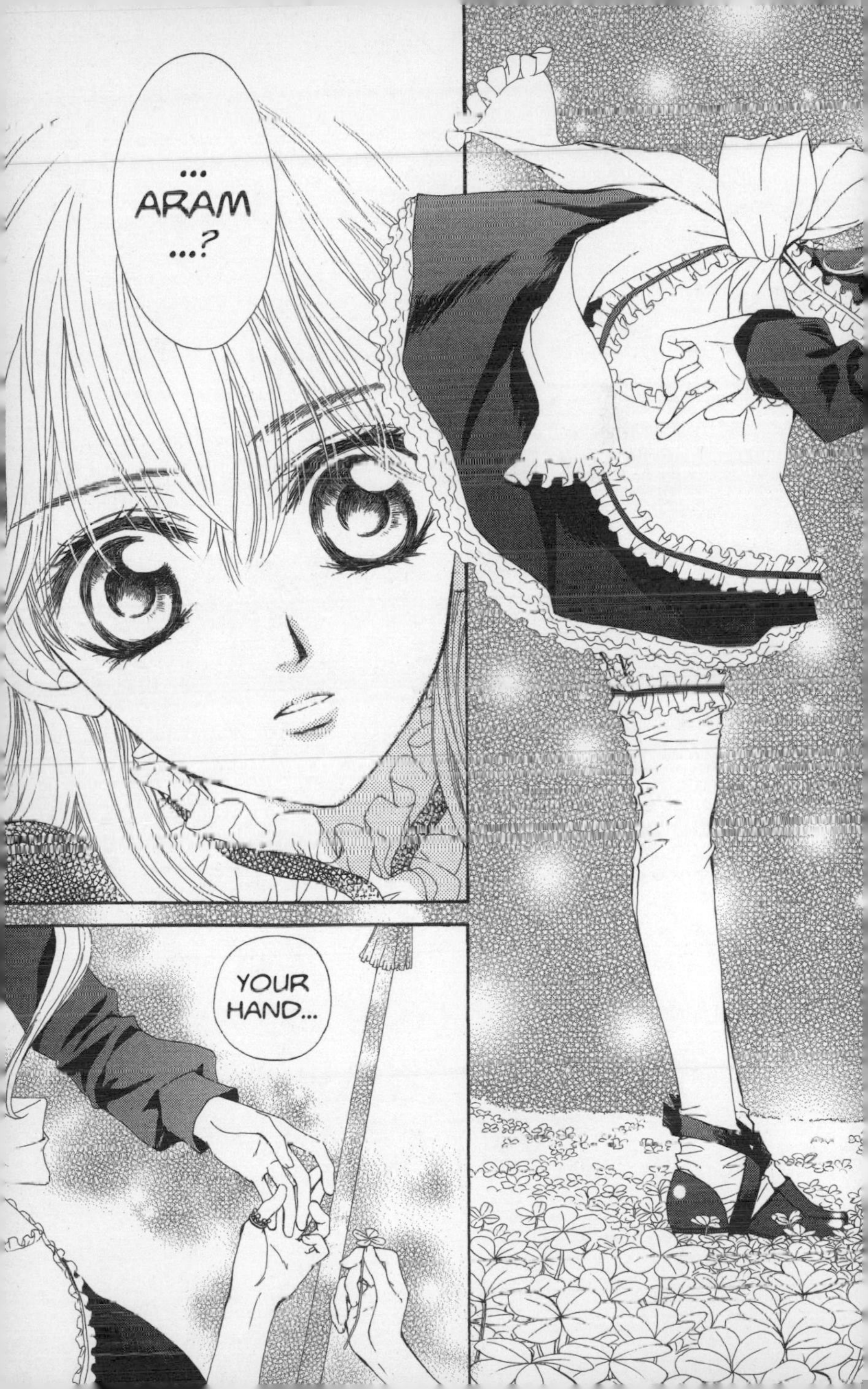

... ARAM ...?
YOUR HAND...

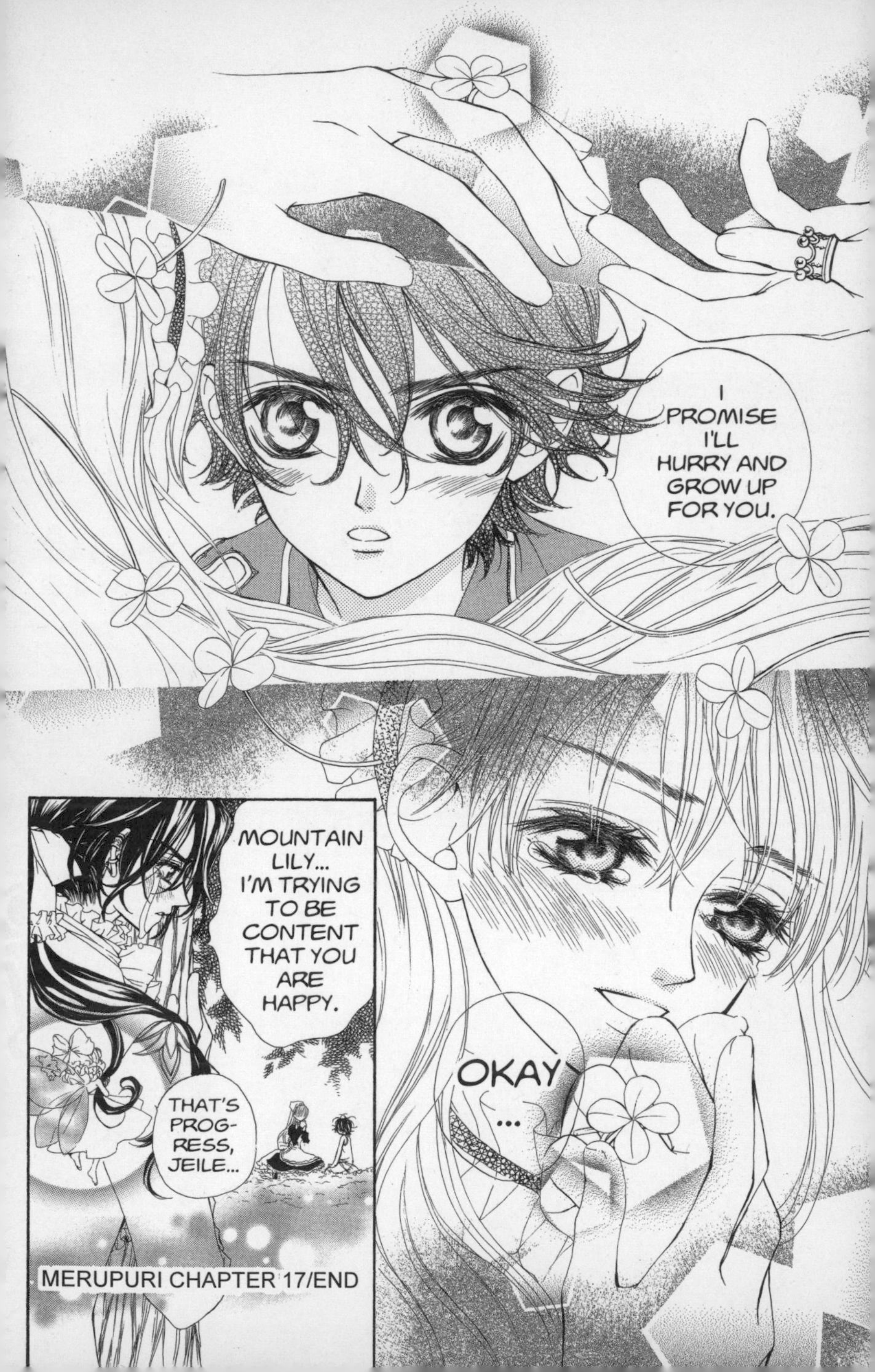
I PROMISE I'LL HURRY AND GROW UP FOR YOU.
OKAY ...
MOUNTAIN LILY... I'M TRYING TO BE CONTENT THAT YOU ARE HAPPY.
THAT'S PROG-RESS, JEILE...
MERUPURI CHAPTER 17/END

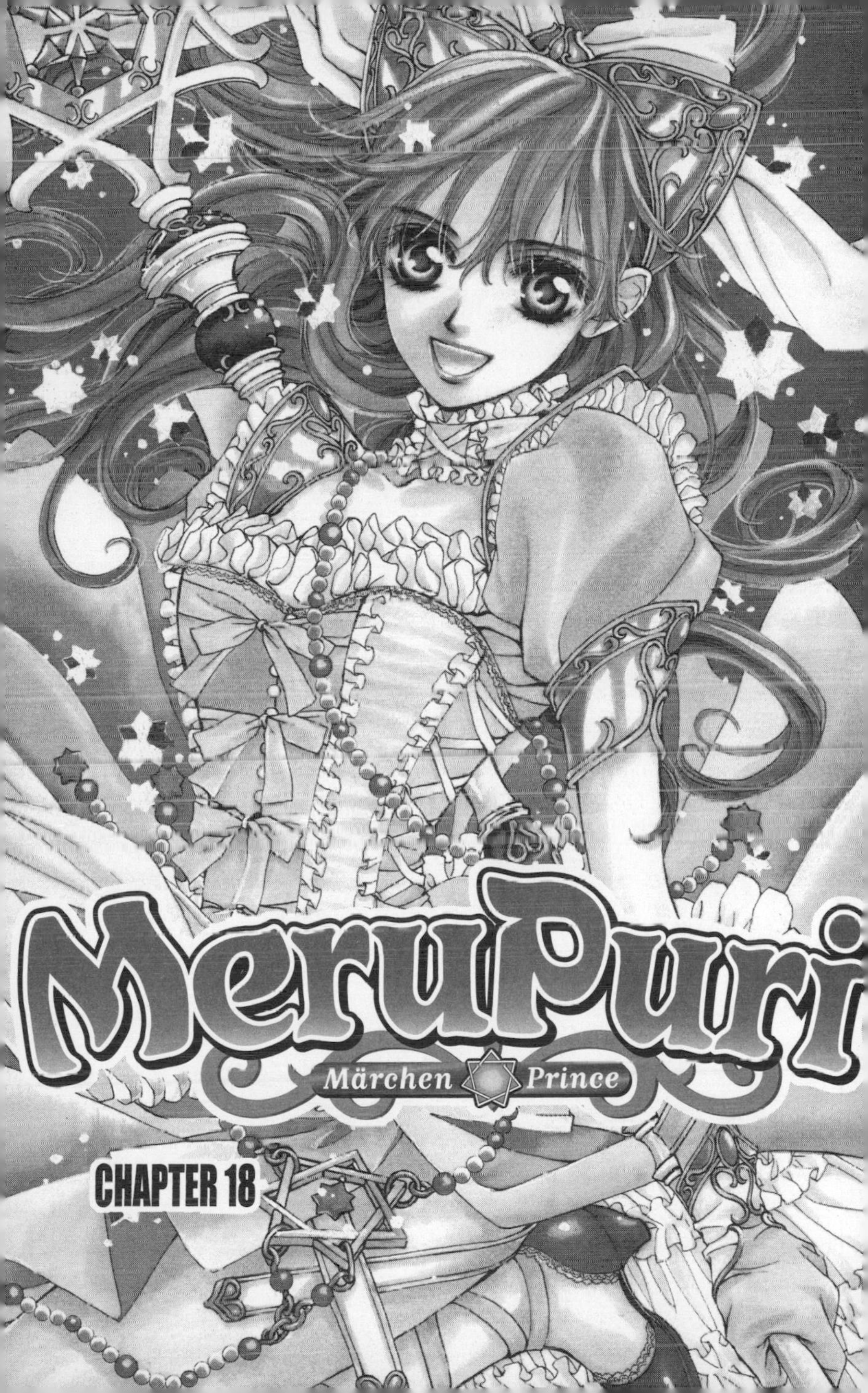
MeruPuri
Märchen Prince
CHAPTER 18

ARAM LEARNED ABOUT ENGAGEMENT RINGS FROM AIRI'S VIDEOS.

TALES OF MARRIAGE ON THE PLAINS...

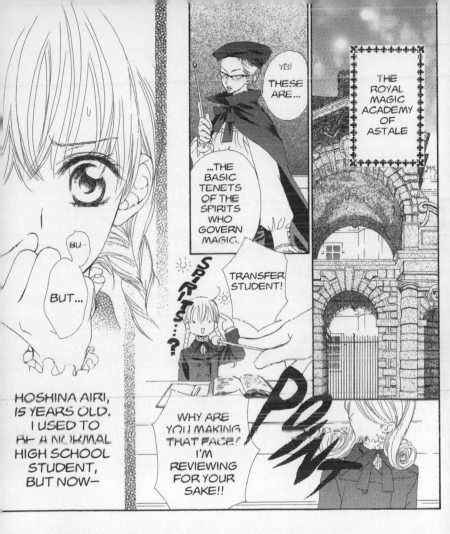

THE ROYAL MAGIC ACADEMY OF ASTALE
YES!
THESE ARE...
...THE BASIC TENETS OF THE SPIRITS WHO GOVERN MAGIC.
TRANSFER STUDENT!
SPIRITS...?
POINT
WHY ARE YOU MAKING THAT FACE? I'M REVIEWING FOR YOUR SAKE!!
BU—
BUT...
HOSHINA AIRI, 15 YEARS OLD. I USED TO BE A NORMAL HIGH SCHOOL STUDENT, BUT NOW—

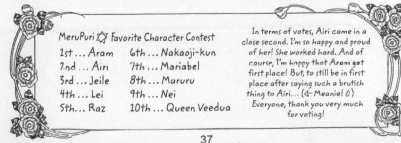

MeruPuri ✡ Favorite Character Contest

1st ... Aram
2nd ... Airi
3rd ... Jeile
4th ... Lei
5th... Raz
6th ... Nakaoji-kun
7th ... Mariabel
8th ... Maruru
9th ... Nei
10th ... Queen Veedua

In terms of votes, Airi came in a close second. I'm so happy and proud of her! She worked hard. And of course, I'm happy that Aram got first place! But, to still be in first place after saying such a brutish thing to Airi... (← Meanie! ()) Everyone, thank you very much for voting!

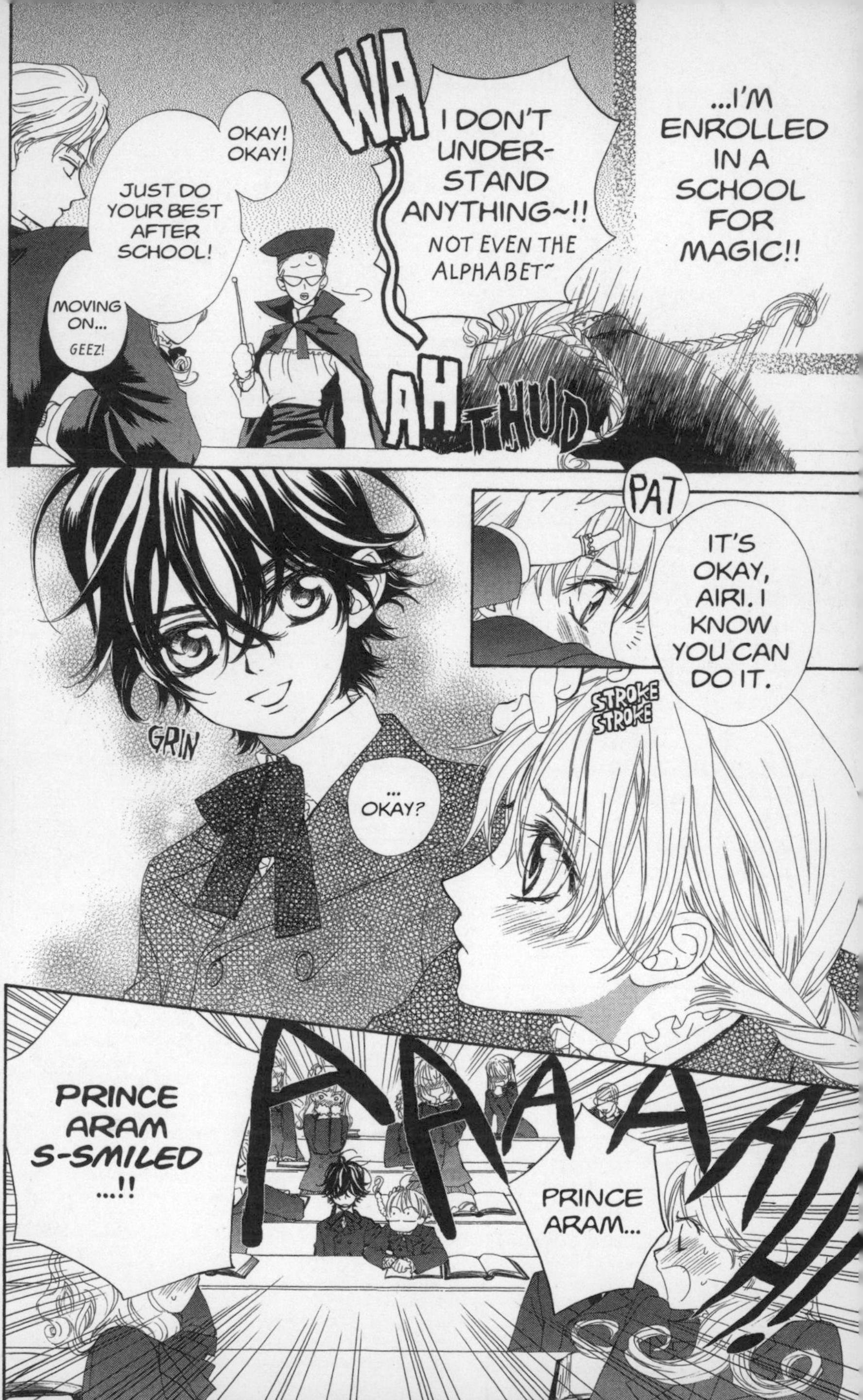

...I'M ENROLLED IN A SCHOOL FOR MAGIC!!
WA
I DON'T UNDERSTAND ANYTHING~!!
NOT EVEN THE ALPHABET~
AH
THUD
OKAY! OKAY!
JUST DO YOUR BEST AFTER SCHOOL!
MOVING ON...
GEEZ!
PAT
IT'S OKAY, AIRI. I KNOW YOU CAN DO IT.
STROKE STROKE
GRIN
...OKAY?
AAAAAH!!
PRINCE ARAM...
PRINCE ARAM S-SMILED ...!!

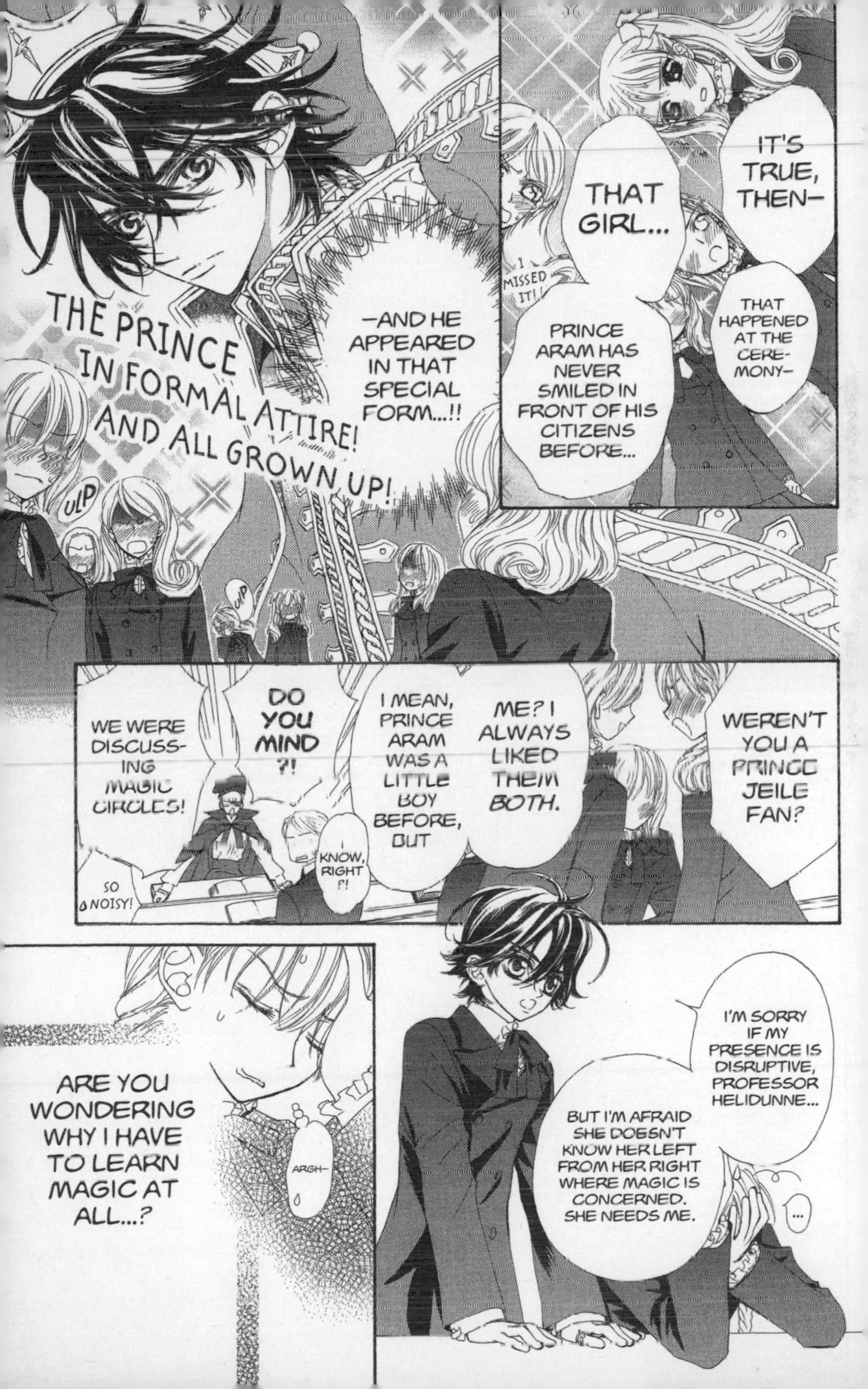
IT'S TRUE, THEN—
THAT GIRL...
I MISSED IT!!
THAT HAPPENED AT THE CERE-MONY—
PRINCE ARAM HAS NEVER SMILED IN FRONT OF HIS CITIZENS BEFORE...
—AND HE APPEARED IN THAT SPECIAL FORM...!!
THE PRINCE IN FORMAL ATTIRE! AND ALL GROWN UP!
ULP
ULP
WEREN'T YOU A PRINCE JEILE FAN?
ME? I ALWAYS LIKED THEM BOTH.
I MEAN, PRINCE ARAM WAS A LITTLE BOY BEFORE, BUT
I KNOW, RIGHT?!
DO YOU MIND?!
WE WERE DISCUSS-ING MAGIC CIRCLES!
SO NOISY!
I'M SORRY IF MY PRESENCE IS DISRUPTIVE, PROFESSOR HELIDUNNE...
BUT I'M AFRAID SHE DOESN'T KNOW HER LEFT FROM HER RIGHT WHERE MAGIC IS CONCERNED. SHE NEEDS ME.
...
ARGH—
ARE YOU WONDERING WHY I HAVE TO LEARN MAGIC AT ALL...?

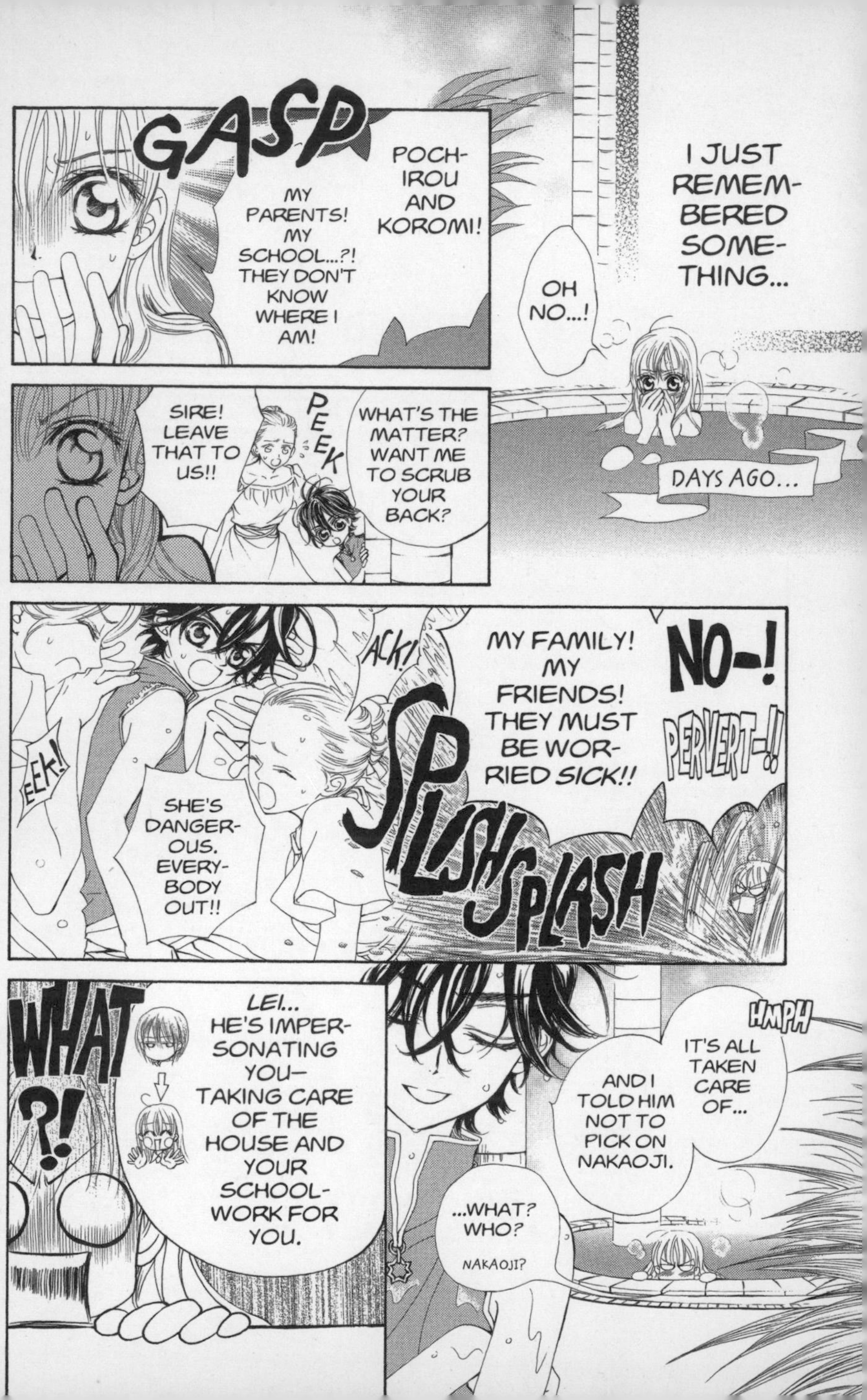
I JUST REMEMBERED SOMETHING...
OH NO...!
DAYS AGO...
GASP
POCH-IROU AND KOROMI!
MY PARENTS! MY SCHOOL...?! THEY DON'T KNOW WHERE I AM!
WHAT'S THE MATTER? WANT ME TO SCRUB YOUR BACK?
PEEK
SIRE! LEAVE THAT TO US!!
NO-!
PERVERT-!!
MY FAMILY! MY FRIENDS! THEY MUST BE WORRIED SICK!!
SPLISH SPLASH
ACK!
SHE'S DANGEROUS. EVERYBODY OUT!!
EEK!
HMPH
IT'S ALL TAKEN CARE OF...
AND I TOLD HIM NOT TO PICK ON NAKAOJI.
...WHAT? WHO?
NAKAOJI?
WHAT?!
LEI... HE'S IMPERSONATING YOU— TAKING CARE OF THE HOUSE AND YOUR SCHOOLWORK FOR YOU.

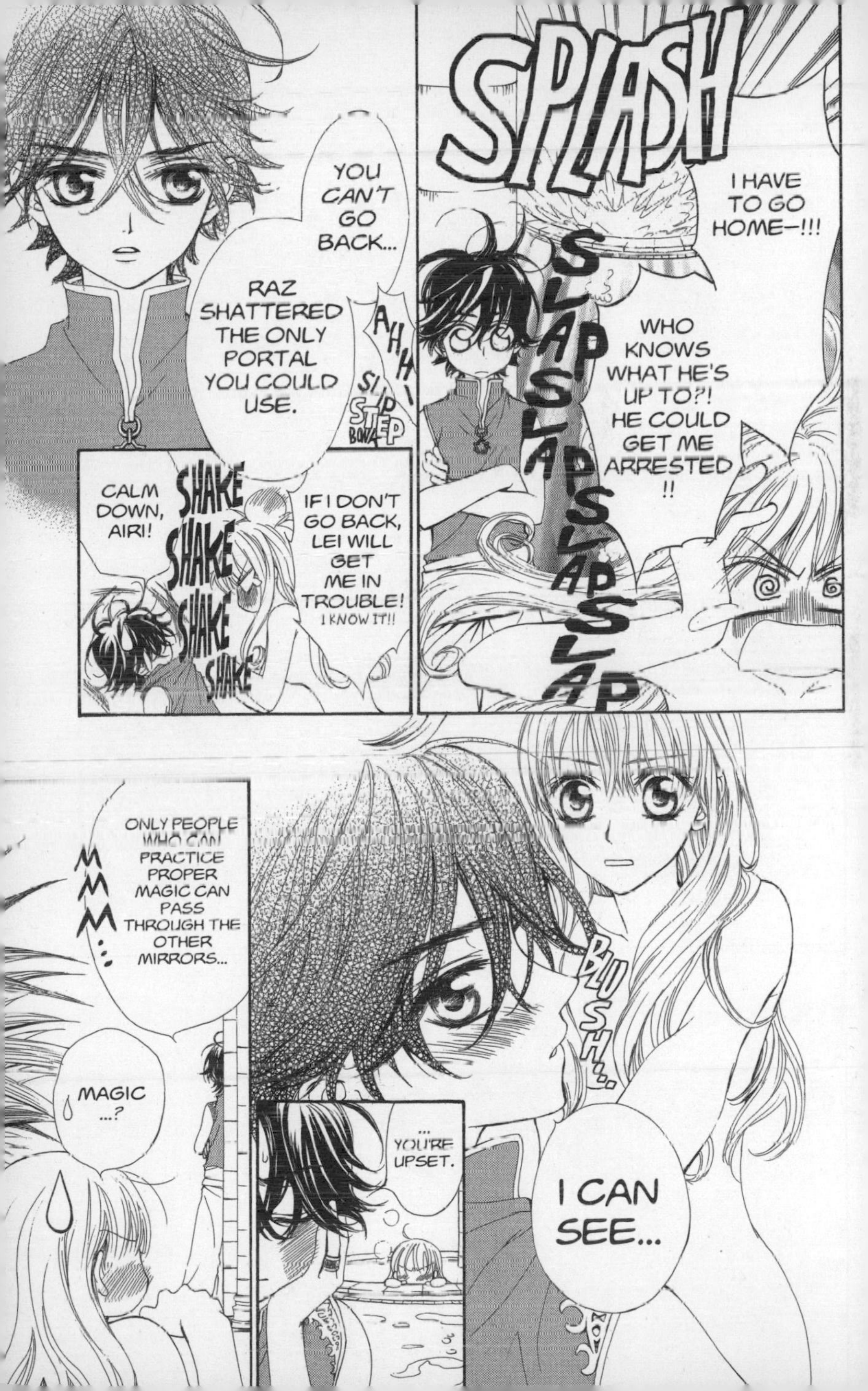
SPLASH
I HAVE TO GO HOME-!!!
WHO KNOWS WHAT HE'S UP TO?! HE COULD GET ME ARRESTED!!
SLAP SLAP SLAP SLAP SLAP
YOU CAN'T GO BACK...
RAZ SHATTERED THE ONLY PORTAL YOU COULD USE.
AHH!
SLIP STEP
BONK
IF I DON'T GO BACK, LEI WILL GET ME IN TROUBLE! I KNOW IT!!
SHAKE SHAKE SHAKE SHAKE
CALM DOWN, AIRI!
BLUSH...
I CAN SEE...
...YOU'RE UPSET.
ONLY PEOPLE WHO CAN PRACTICE PROPER MAGIC CAN PASS THROUGH THE OTHER MIRRORS...
MMM...
MAGIC...?

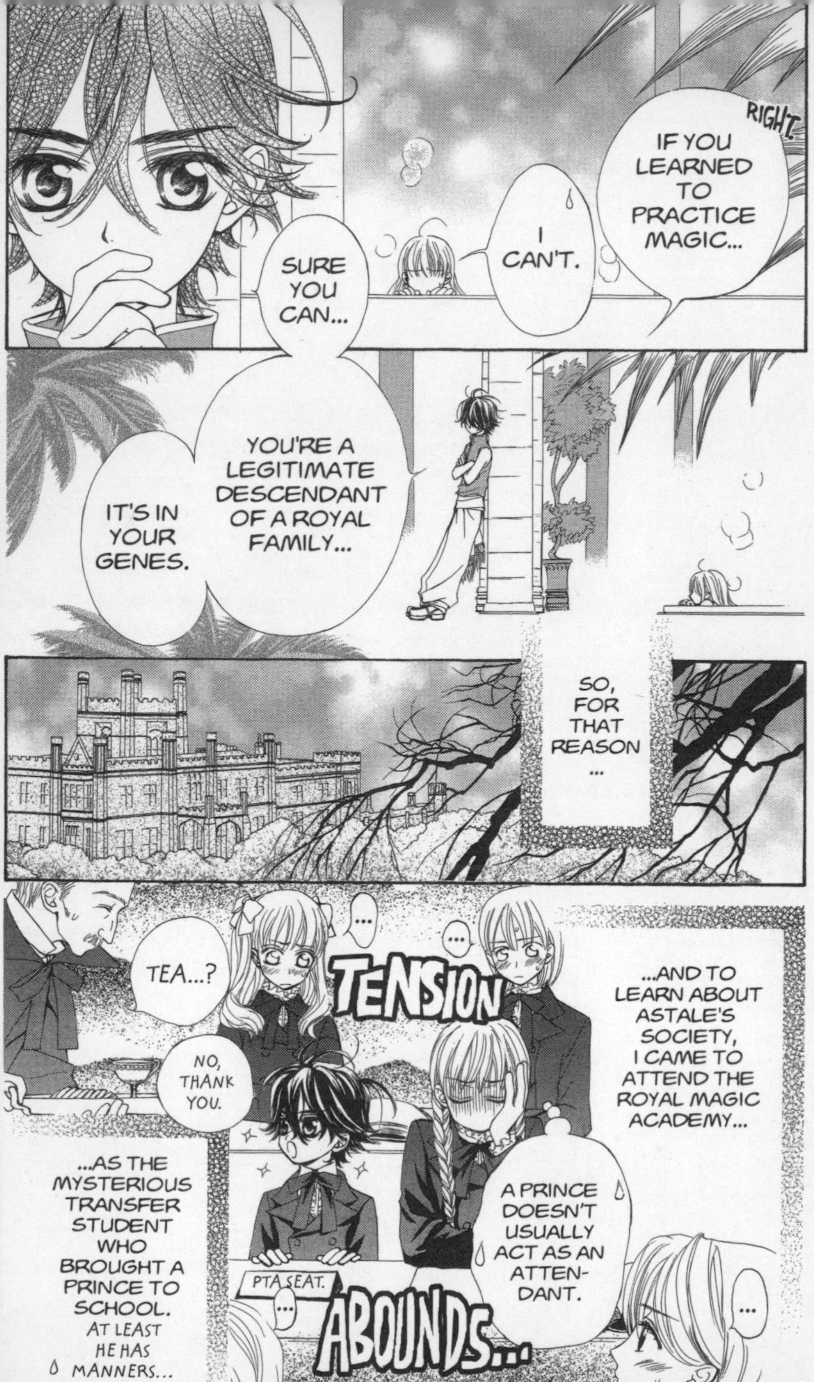
RIGHT!
IF YOU LEARNED TO PRACTICE MAGIC...
I CAN'T.
SURE YOU CAN...
YOU'RE A LEGITIMATE DESCENDANT OF A ROYAL FAMILY...
IT'S IN YOUR GENES.
SO, FOR THAT REASON ...
...AND TO LEARN ABOUT ASTALE'S SOCIETY, I CAME TO ATTEND THE ROYAL MAGIC ACADEMY...
...
...
TENSION
TEA...?
NO, THANK YOU.
A PRINCE DOESN'T USUALLY ACT AS AN ATTEN-DANT.
...
PTA SEAT.
ABOUNDS...
...
...AS THE MYSTERIOUS TRANSFER STUDENT WHO BROUGHT A PRINCE TO SCHOOL.
AT LEAST HE HAS MANNERS...

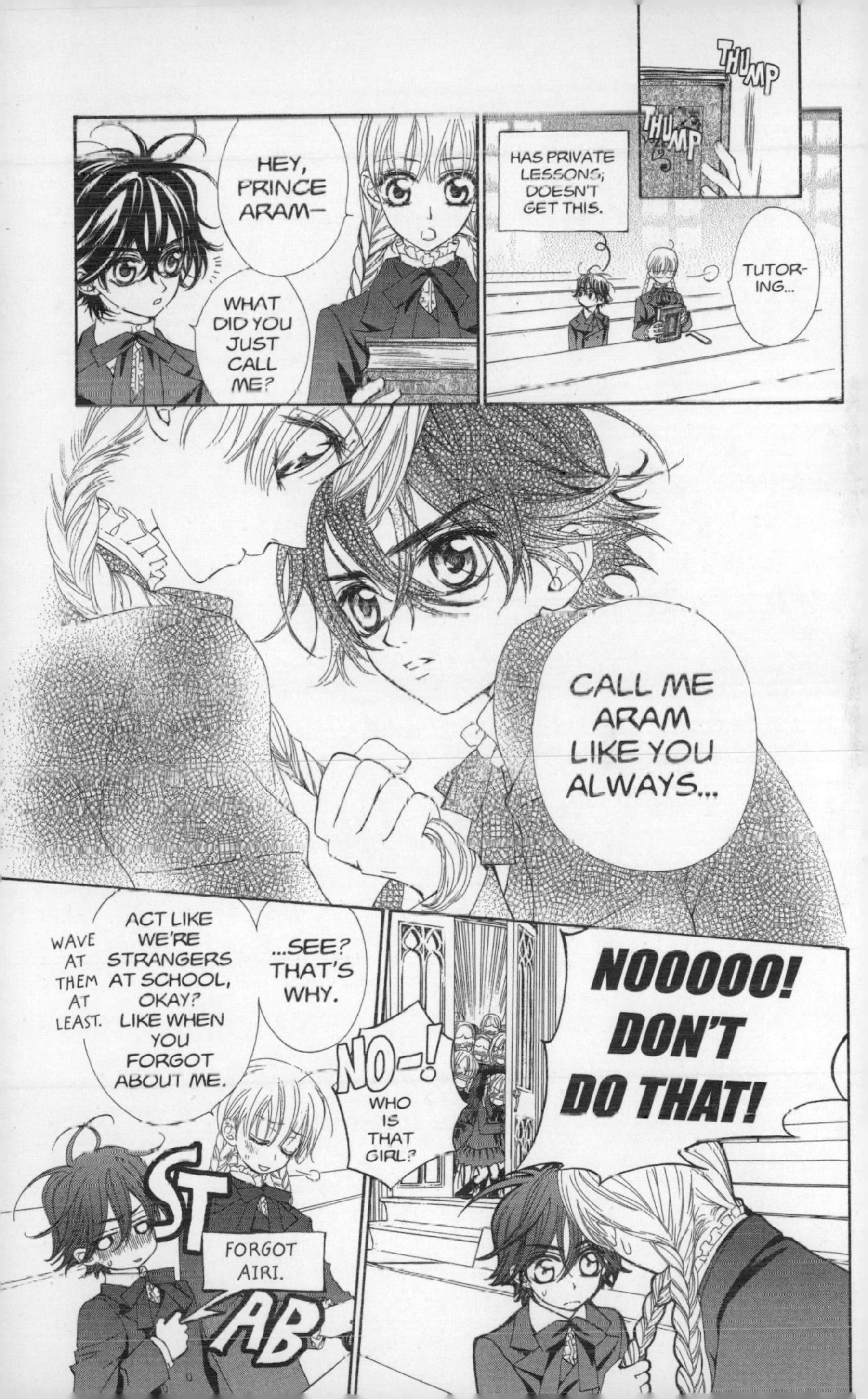

THUMP
THUMP
HAS PRIVATE LESSONS; DOESN'T GET THIS.
TUTORING...
HEY, PRINCE ARAM—
WHAT DID YOU JUST CALL ME?
CALL ME ARAM LIKE YOU ALWAYS...
NOOOOOO! DON'T DO THAT!
NO—!
WHO IS THAT GIRL?
...SEE? THAT'S WHY.
ACT LIKE WE'RE STRANGERS AT SCHOOL, OKAY? LIKE WHEN YOU FORGOT ABOUT ME.
WAVE AT THEM AT LEAST.
STAB
FORGOT AIRI.

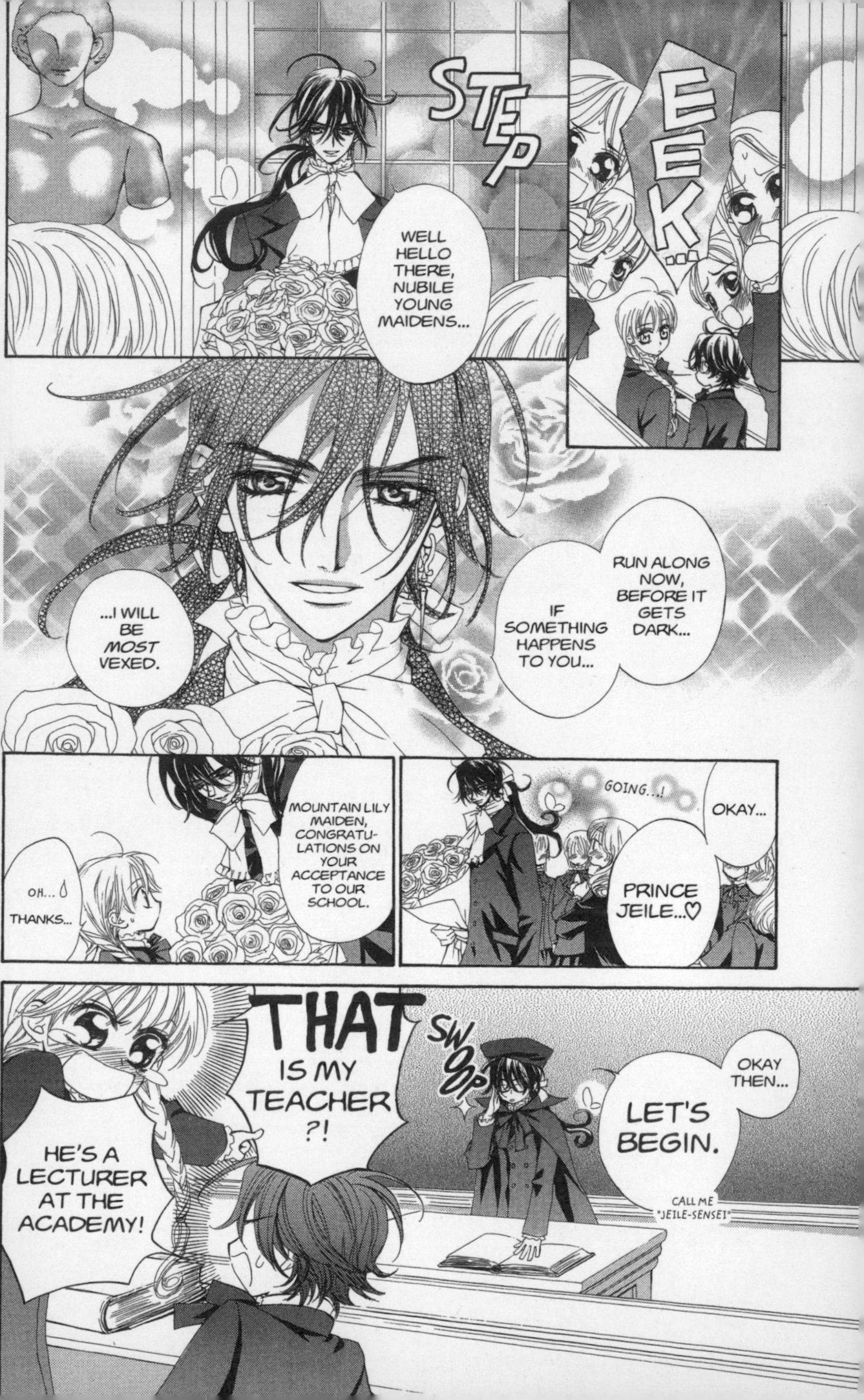
EEK...
STEP
WELL HELLO THERE, NUBILE YOUNG MAIDENS...
RUN ALONG NOW, BEFORE IT GETS DARK...
IF SOMETHING HAPPENS TO YOU...
...I WILL BE MOST VEXED.
OKAY...
GOING...!
PRINCE JEILE...♡
MOUNTAIN LILY MAIDEN, CONGRATU-LATIONS ON YOUR ACCEPTANCE TO OUR SCHOOL.
OH...
THANKS...
OKAY THEN...
LET'S BEGIN.
CALL ME "JEILE-SENSEI"
SWOOP
THAT IS MY TEACHER?!
HE'S A LECTURER AT THE ACADEMY!

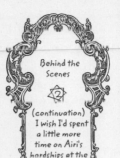

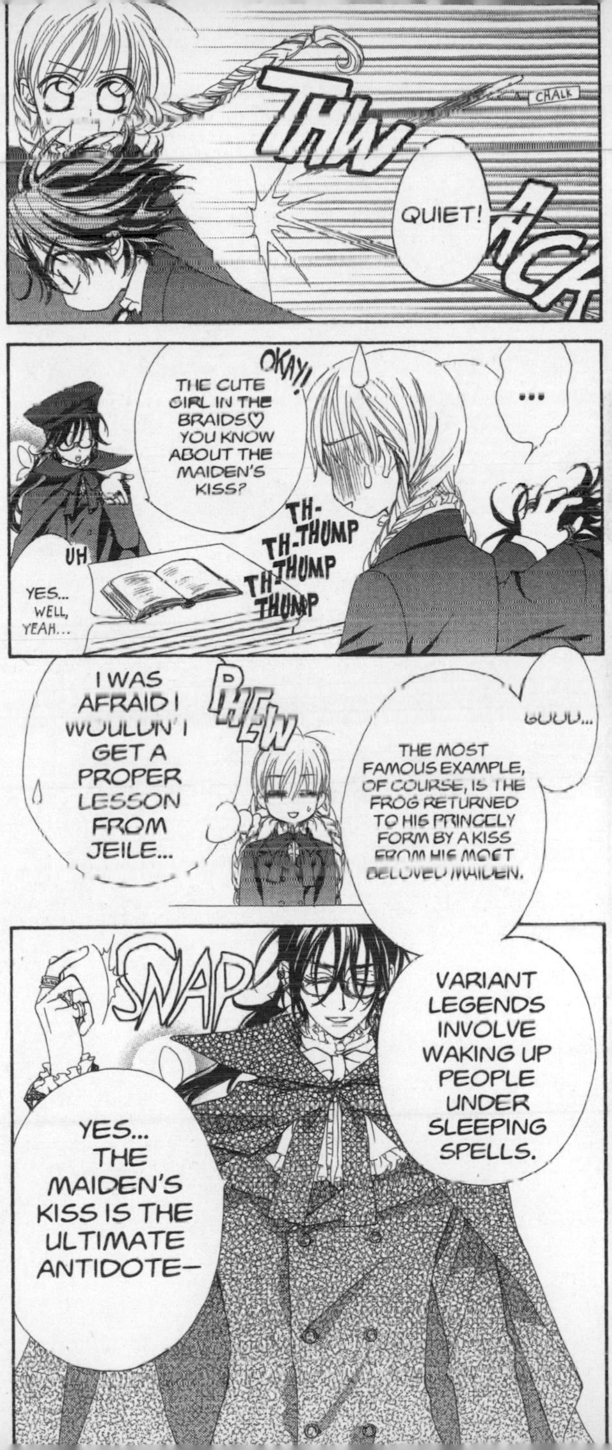
THWACK
CHALK
QUIET!
...
OKAY!
THE CUTE GIRL IN THE BRAIDS♡ YOU KNOW ABOUT THE MAIDEN'S KISS?
TH-TH-THUMP THUMP TH-THUMP
UH
YES... WELL, YEAH...
GOOD...
THE MOST FAMOUS EXAMPLE, OF COURSE, IS THE FROG RETURNED TO HIS PRINCELY FORM BY A KISS FROM HIS MOST BELOVED MAIDEN.
PHEW
I WAS AFRAID I WOULDN'T GET A PROPER LESSON FROM JEILE...
SNAP
VARIANT LEGENDS INVOLVE WAKING UP PEOPLE UNDER SLEEPING SPELLS.
YES... THE MAIDEN'S KISS IS THE ULTIMATE ANTIDOTE—

Behind the Scenes

2

(continuation) I wish I'd spent a little more time on Airi's hardships at the Academy.

Chapter 19 is a celebration! For the first time, MeruPuri was on the opening page and the front cover. I really liked the cover image (June issue). I used the same composition for the cover of this volume.

♡

(I had the opening spread put on the cover flap for the tankobon.) The subject matter was a bit more on the adult side (ha ha!), but I wanted a chance to draw them in a calm place, so I thought it was nice. Small Jeile... I guess I hadn't learned my lesson—I brought him back again (Ha!).

(To be continued)

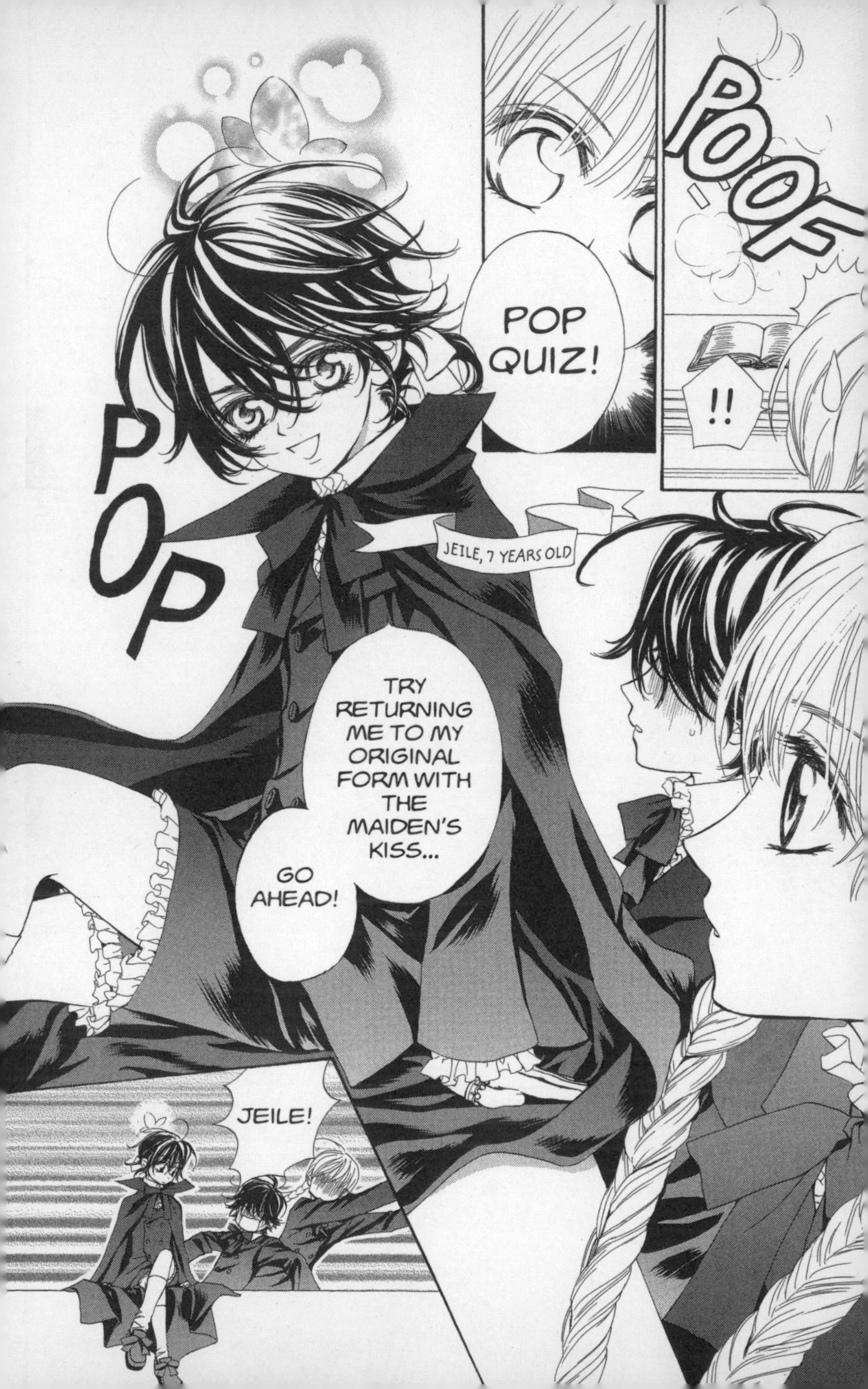
POOF
!!
POP QUIZ!
POP
JEILE, 7 YEARS OLD
TRY RETURNING ME TO MY ORIGINAL FORM WITH THE MAIDEN'S KISS...
GO AHEAD!
JEILE!

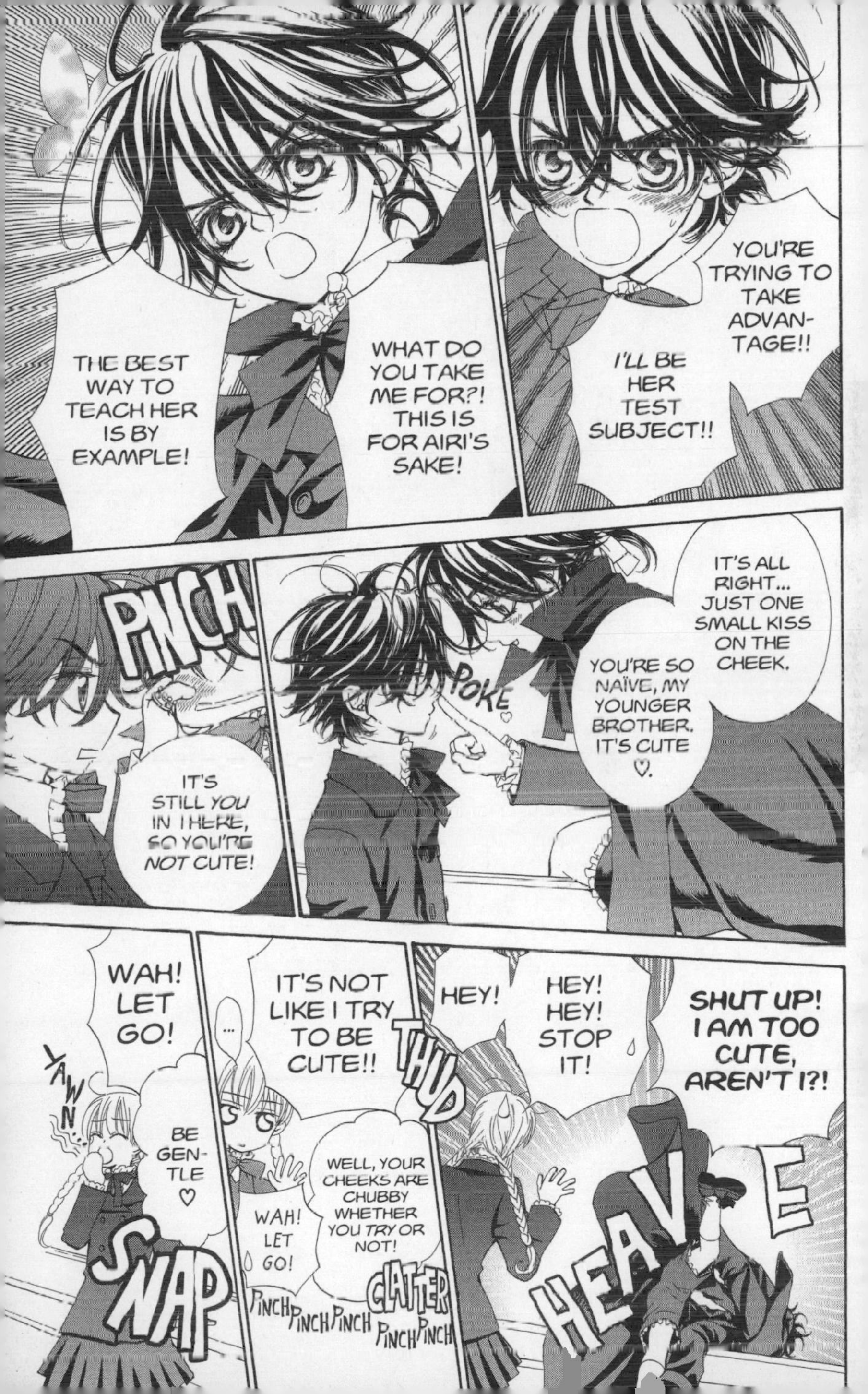
YOU'RE TRYING TO TAKE ADVANTAGE!!
I'LL BE HER TEST SUBJECT!!
WHAT DO YOU TAKE ME FOR?! THIS IS FOR AIRI'S SAKE!
THE BEST WAY TO TEACH HER IS BY EXAMPLE!
IT'S ALL RIGHT... JUST ONE SMALL KISS ON THE CHEEK.
YOU'RE SO NAÏVE, MY YOUNGER BROTHER. IT'S CUTE ♡.
POKE
PINCH
IT'S STILL YOU IN THERE, SO YOU'RE NOT CUTE!
SHUT UP! I AM TOO CUTE, AREN'T I?!
HEY! HEY! STOP IT!
HEY!
HEAVE
THUD
IT'S NOT LIKE I TRY TO BE CUTE!!
...
WELL, YOUR CHEEKS ARE CHUBBY WHETHER YOU TRY OR NOT!
WAH! LET GO!
PINCH PINCH PINCH
CLATTER
PINCH PINCH
WAH! LET GO!
BE GENTLE ♡
YAWN
SNAP

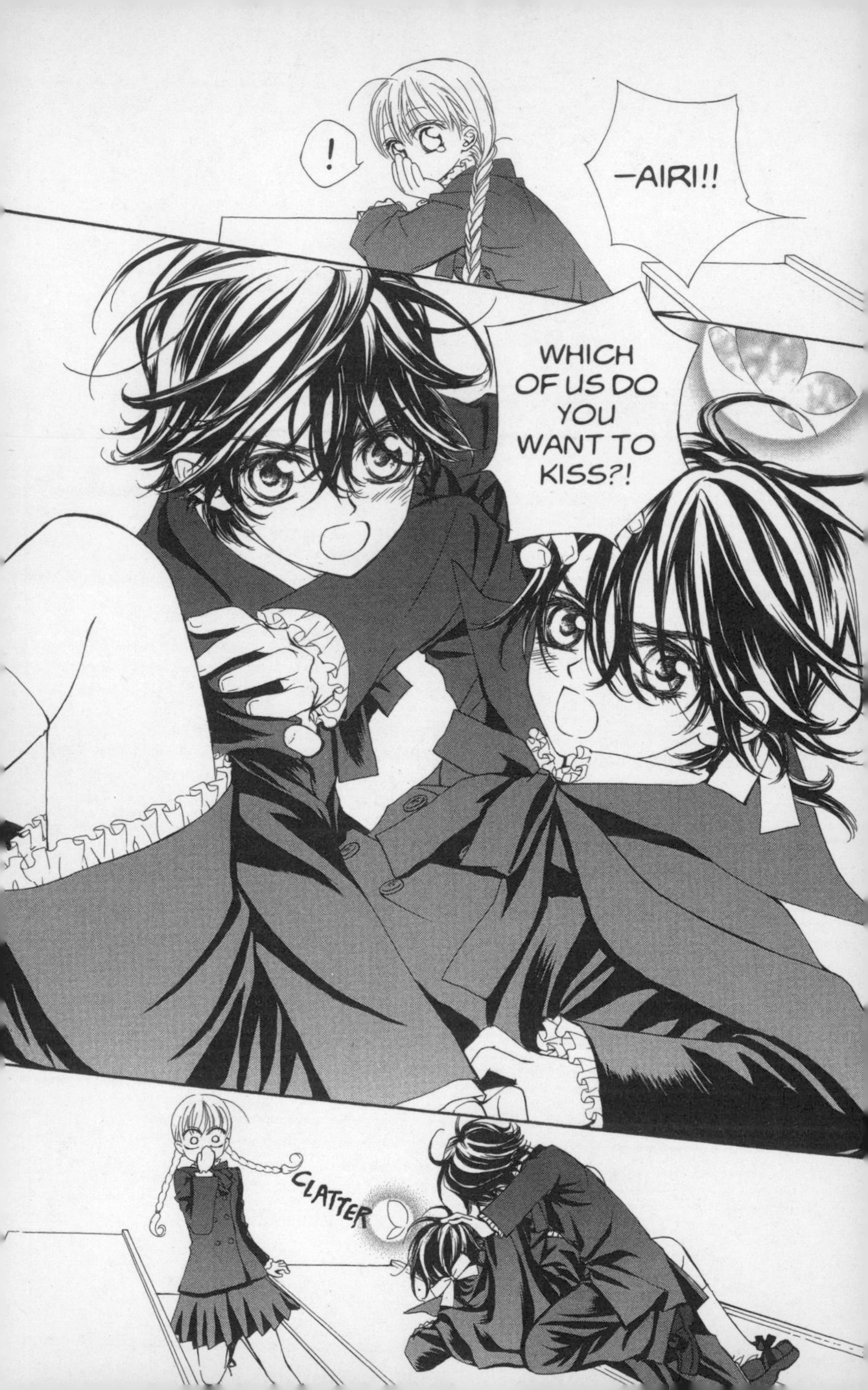
—AIRI!!
!
WHICH OF US DO YOU WANT TO KISS?!
CLATTER

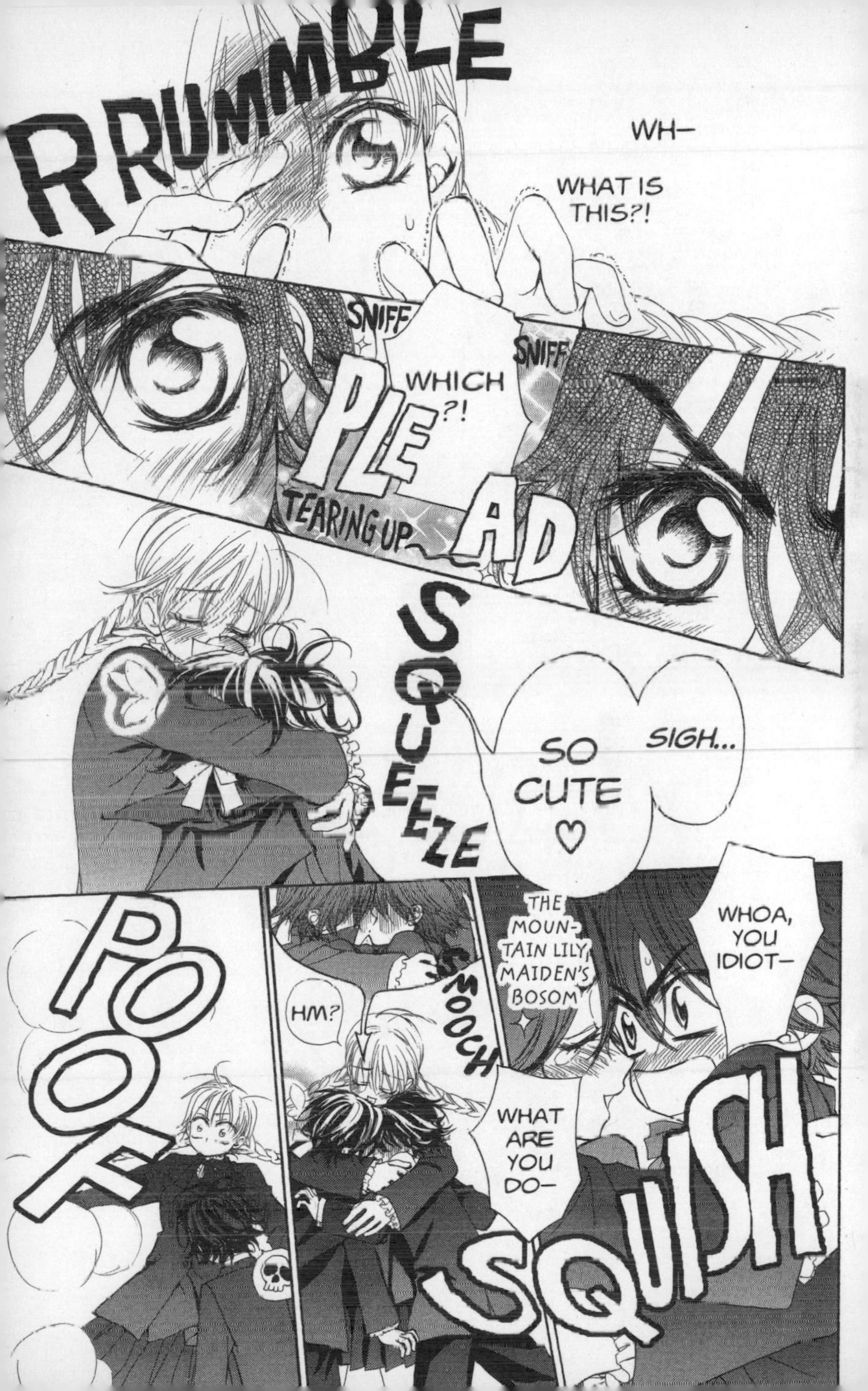
WH—
WHAT IS THIS?!
RRUMMBLE
SNIFF
SNIFF
WHICH?!
PLEAD
TEARING UP
SQUEEZE
SIGH...
SO CUTE ♡
WHOA, YOU IDIOT—
THE MOUNTAIN LILY MAIDEN'S BOSOM
SQUISH
WHAT ARE YOU DO—
SMOOCH
HM?
POOF

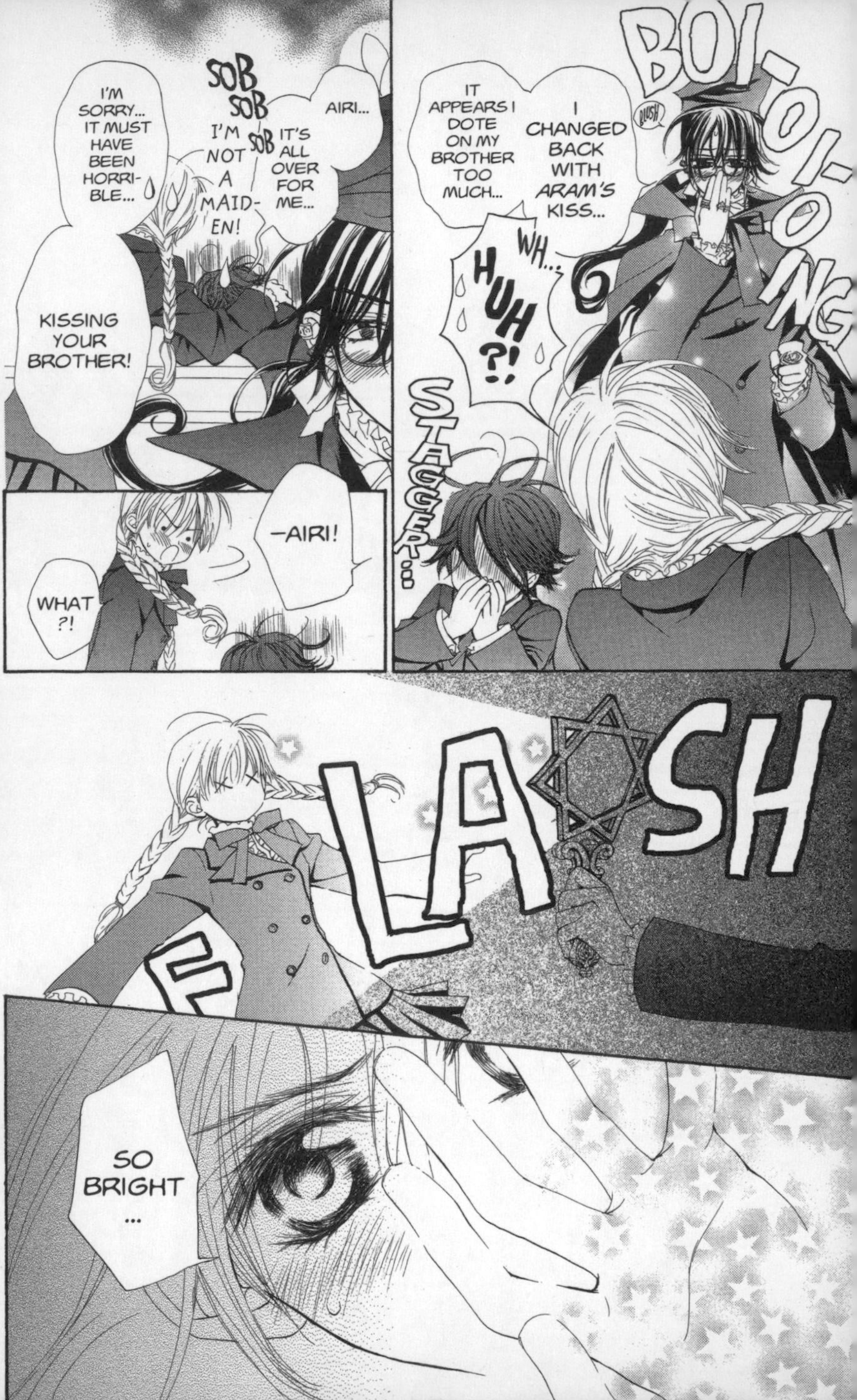
BOI-OI-OING
BLUSH
I CHANGED BACK WITH ARAM'S KISS...
IT APPEARS I DOTE ON MY BROTHER TOO MUCH...
WH... HUH?!
STAGGER...
AIRI...
IT'S ALL OVER FOR ME...
SOB SOB SOB
I'M NOT A MAIDEN!
I'M SORRY... IT MUST HAVE BEEN HORRIBLE...
KISSING YOUR BROTHER!
—AIRI!
WHAT?!
FLASH
SO BRIGHT...

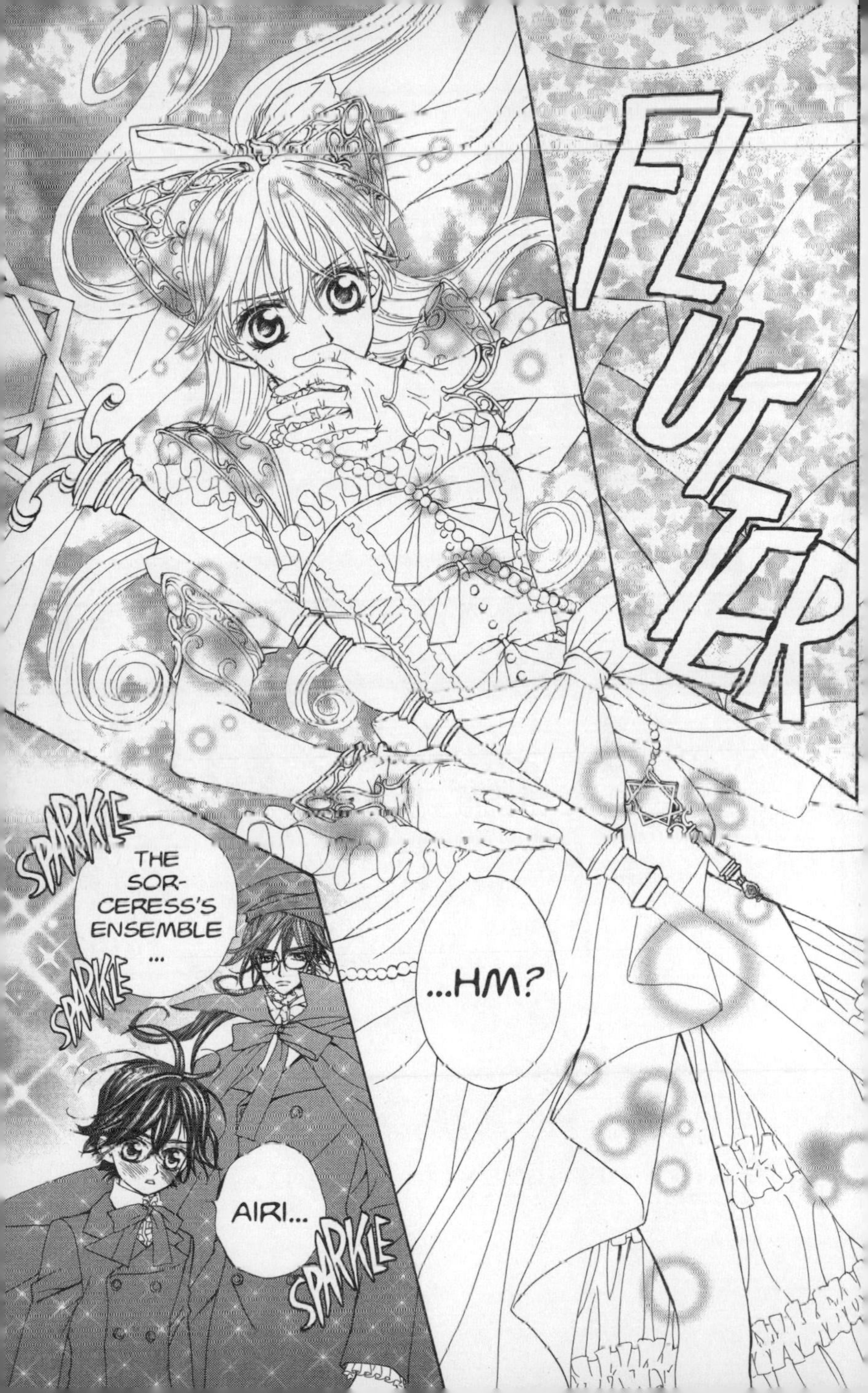
FLUTTER
...HM?
SPARKLE
THE SOR-CERESS'S ENSEMBLE ...
SPARKLE
AIRI...
SPARKLE

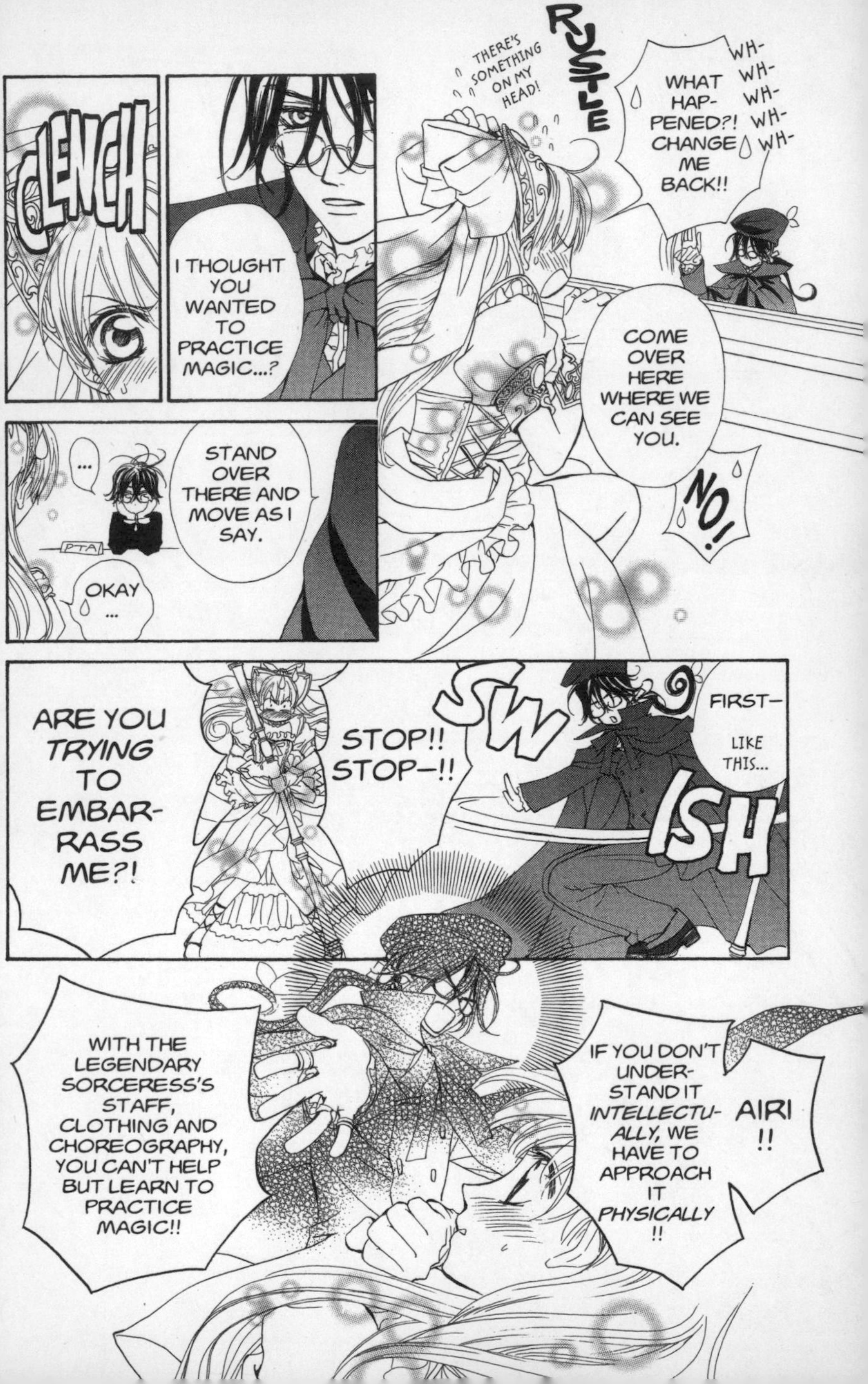
WH- WH- WH- WH- WH-
WHAT HAPPENED?! CHANGE ME BACK!!
RUSTLE
THERE'S SOMETHING ON MY HEAD!
COME OVER HERE WHERE WE CAN SEE YOU.
NO!!
I THOUGHT YOU WANTED TO PRACTICE MAGIC...?
CLENCH
STAND OVER THERE AND MOVE AS I SAY.
...
PTA
OKAY ...
FIRST—
LIKE THIS...
SWISH
STOP!! STOP—!!
ARE YOU *TRYING* TO EMBARRASS ME?!
AIRI !!
IF YOU DON'T UNDERSTAND IT *INTELLECTUALLY*, WE HAVE TO APPROACH IT *PHYSICALLY* !!
WITH THE LEGENDARY SORCERESS'S STAFF, CLOTHING AND CHOREOGRAPHY, YOU CAN'T HELP BUT LEARN TO PRACTICE MAGIC!!

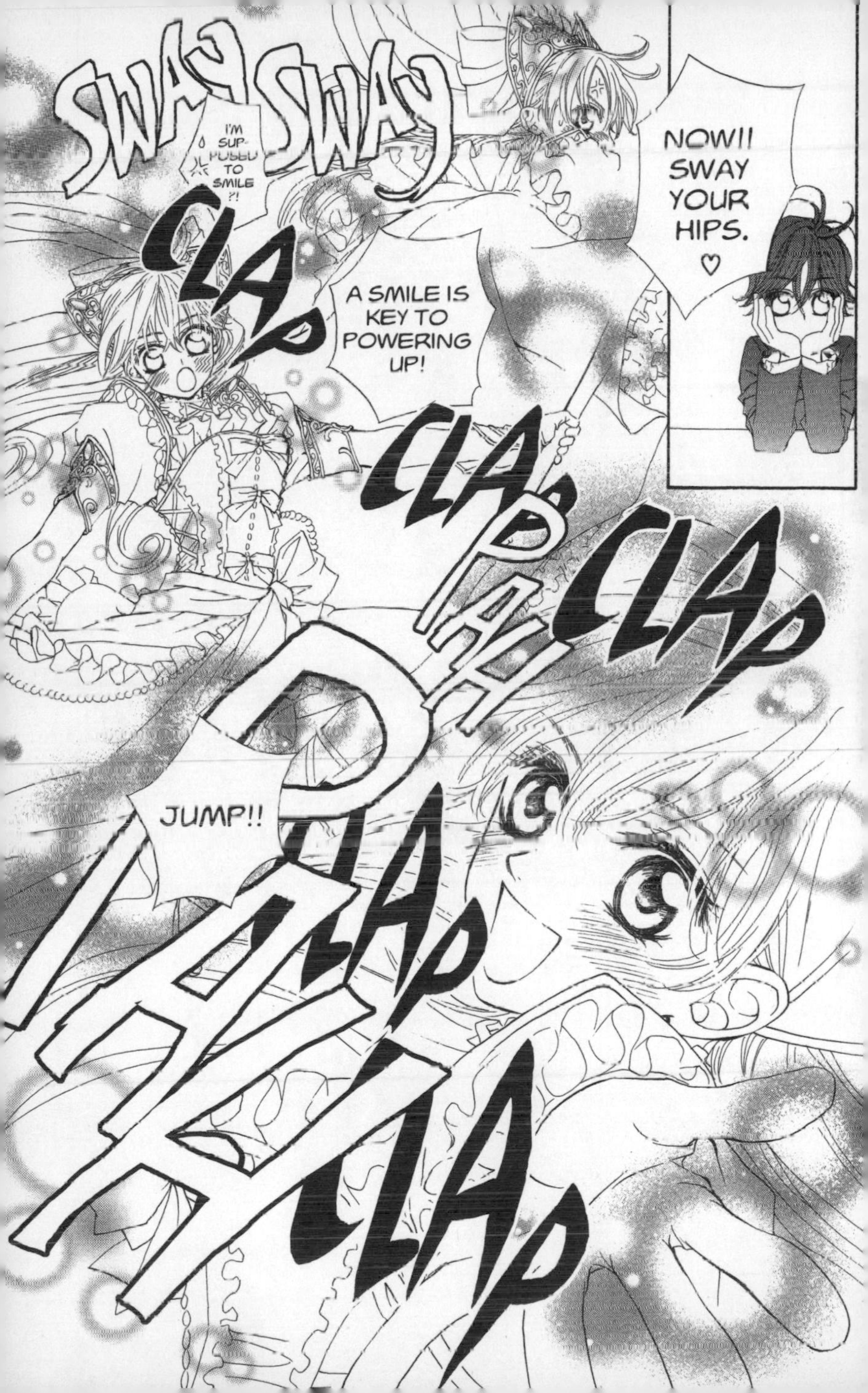
NOW!! SWAY YOUR HIPS. ♡
SWAY SWAY
I'M SUPPOSED TO SMILE?!
CLAP
A SMILE IS KEY TO POWERING UP!
CLAP
CLAP
CLAP
JUMP!!
CLAP
CLAP

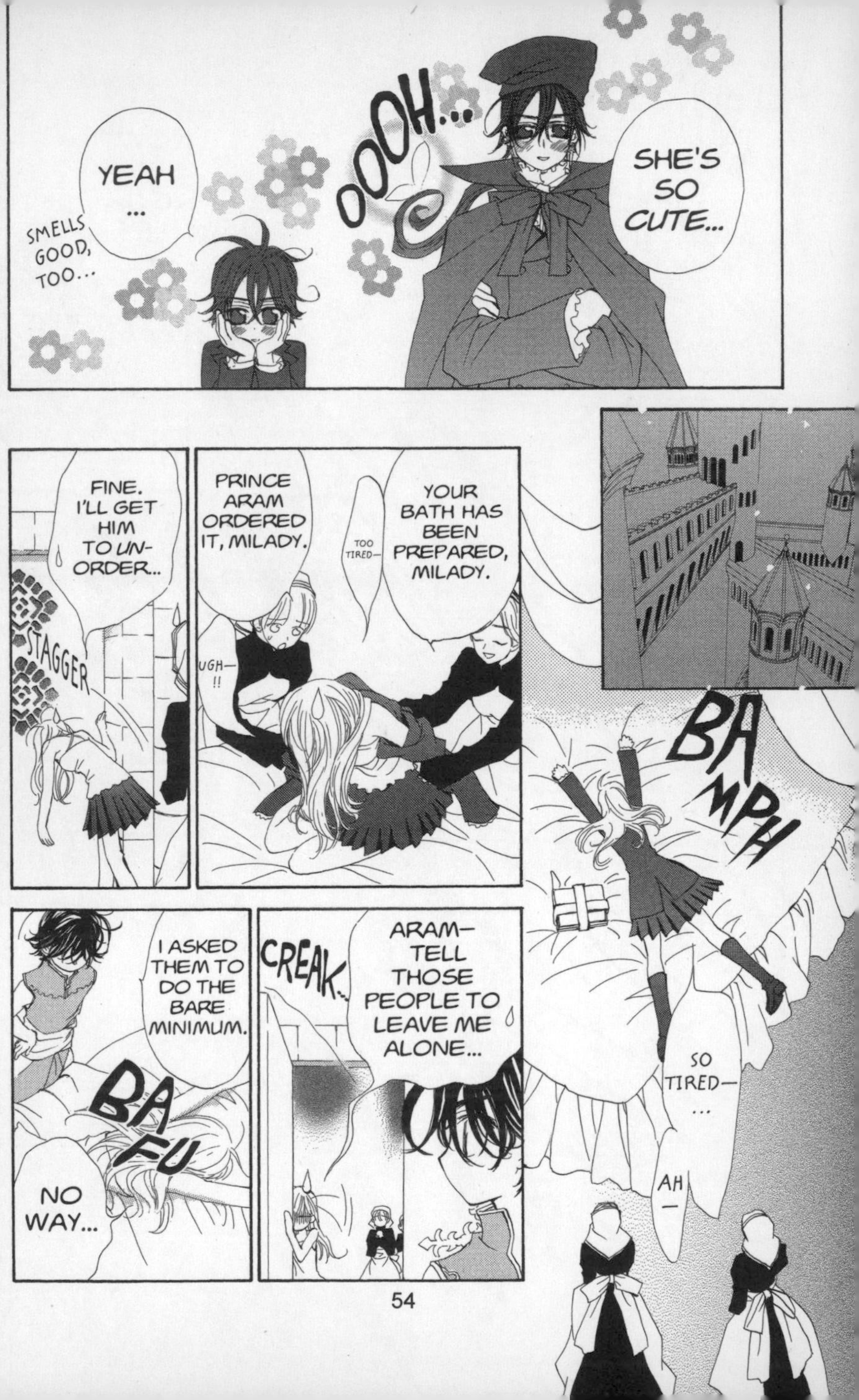
SHE'S SO CUTE...
OOOH...
YEAH ...
SMELLS GOOD, TOO...
BAMPH
SO TIRED— ...
AH —
YOUR BATH HAS BEEN PREPARED, MILADY.
TOO TIRED—
PRINCE ARAM ORDERED IT, MILADY.
UGH— !!
FINE. I'LL GET HIM TO UN-ORDER...
STAGGER
CREAK...
ARAM— TELL THOSE PEOPLE TO LEAVE ME ALONE...
I ASKED THEM TO DO THE BARE MINIMUM.
BAFU
NO WAY...

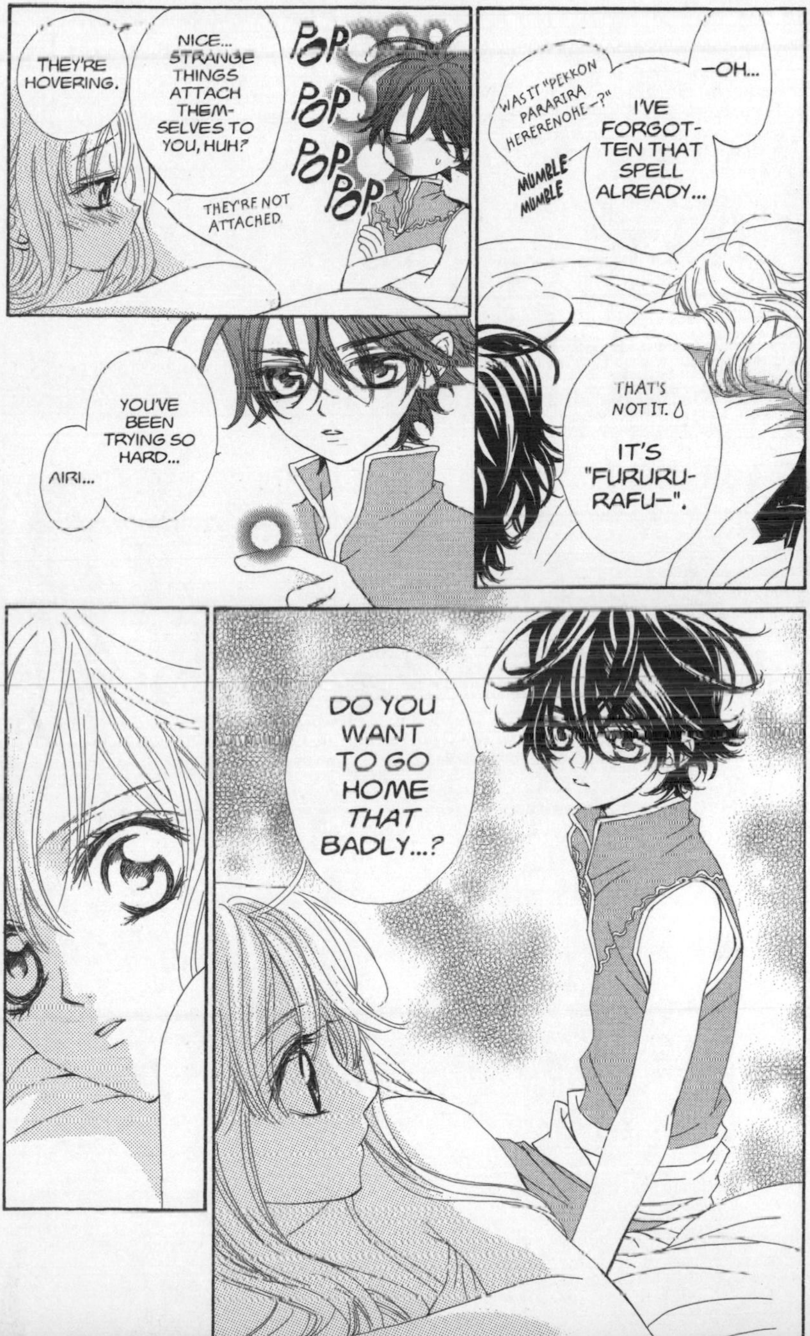

—OH...
I'VE FORGOTTEN THAT SPELL ALREADY...
WAS IT "PEKKON PARARIRA HERERENOHE—?"
MUMBLE MUMBLE
THAT'S NOT IT.
IT'S "FURURU-RAFU—".
POP POP POP POP POP
NICE... STRANGE THINGS ATTACH THEMSELVES TO YOU, HUH?
THEY'RE HOVERING.
THEY'RE NOT ATTACHED
YOU'VE BEEN TRYING SO HARD...
AIRI...
DO YOU WANT TO GO HOME THAT BADLY...?

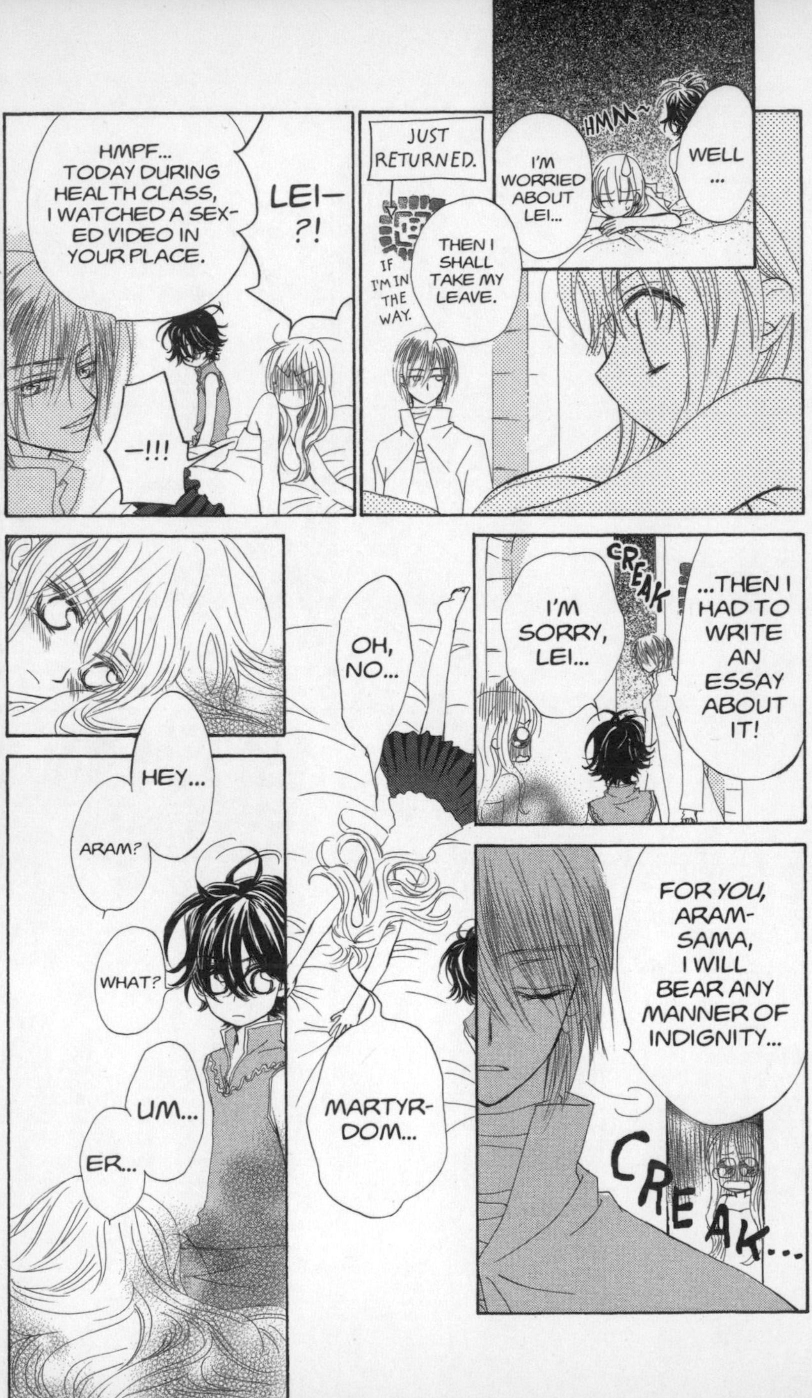
HMM~
WELL...
I'M WORRIED ABOUT LEI...
JUST RETURNED.
THEN I SHALL TAKE MY LEAVE.
IF I'M IN THE WAY.
HMPF... TODAY DURING HEALTH CLASS, I WATCHED A SEX-ED VIDEO IN YOUR PLACE.
LEI—?!
—!!!
CREAK
...THEN I HAD TO WRITE AN ESSAY ABOUT IT!
I'M SORRY, LEI...
OH, NO...
FOR YOU, ARAM-SAMA, I WILL BEAR ANY MANNER OF INDIGNITY...
CREAK...
MARTYR-DOM...
HEY...
ARAM?
WHAT?
UM...
ER...

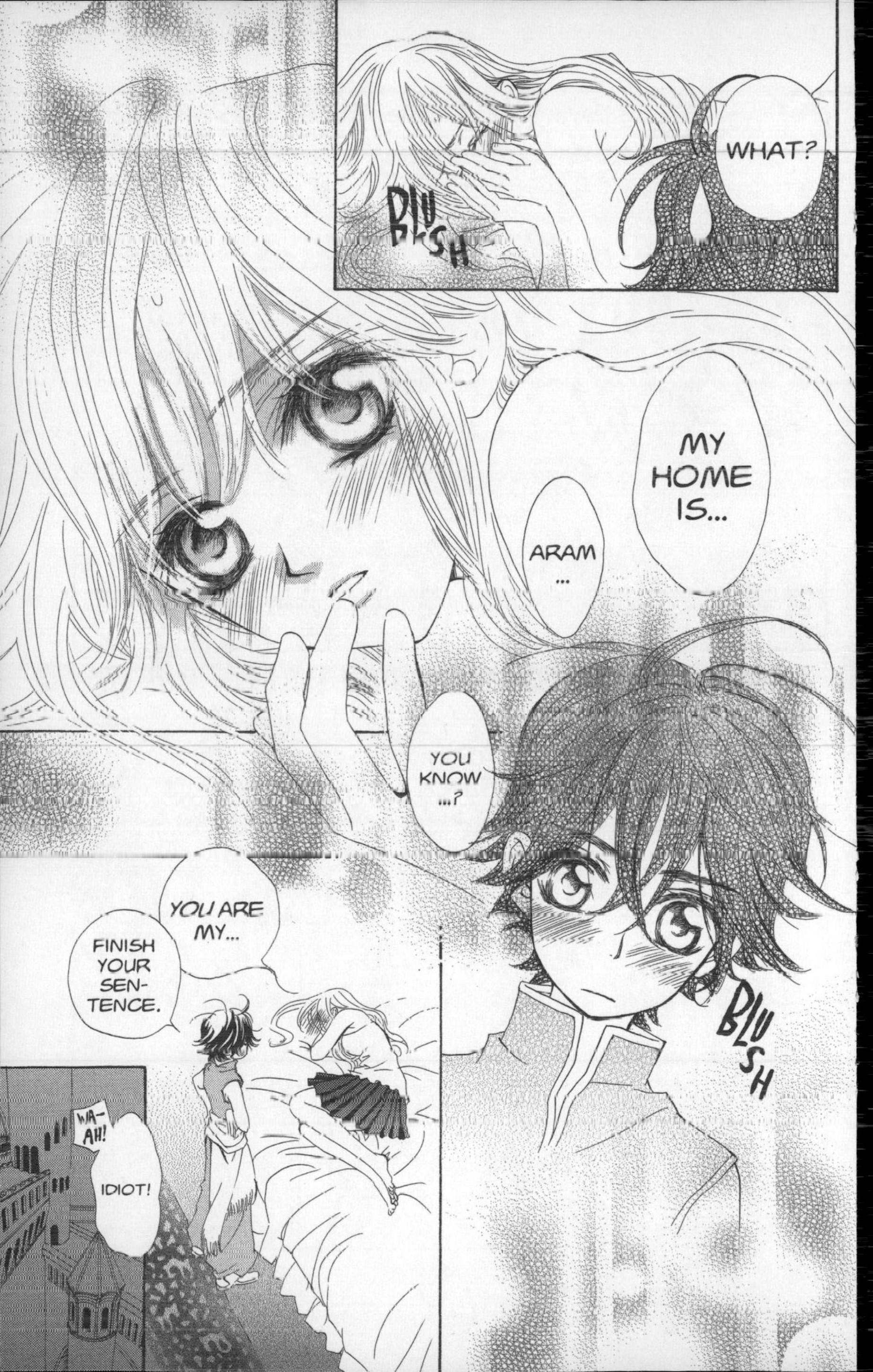
WHAT?
BLUSH
MY HOME IS...
ARAM ...
YOU KNOW ...?
BLUSH
YOU ARE MY...
FINISH YOUR SEN-TENCE.
WA-AH!
IDIOT!

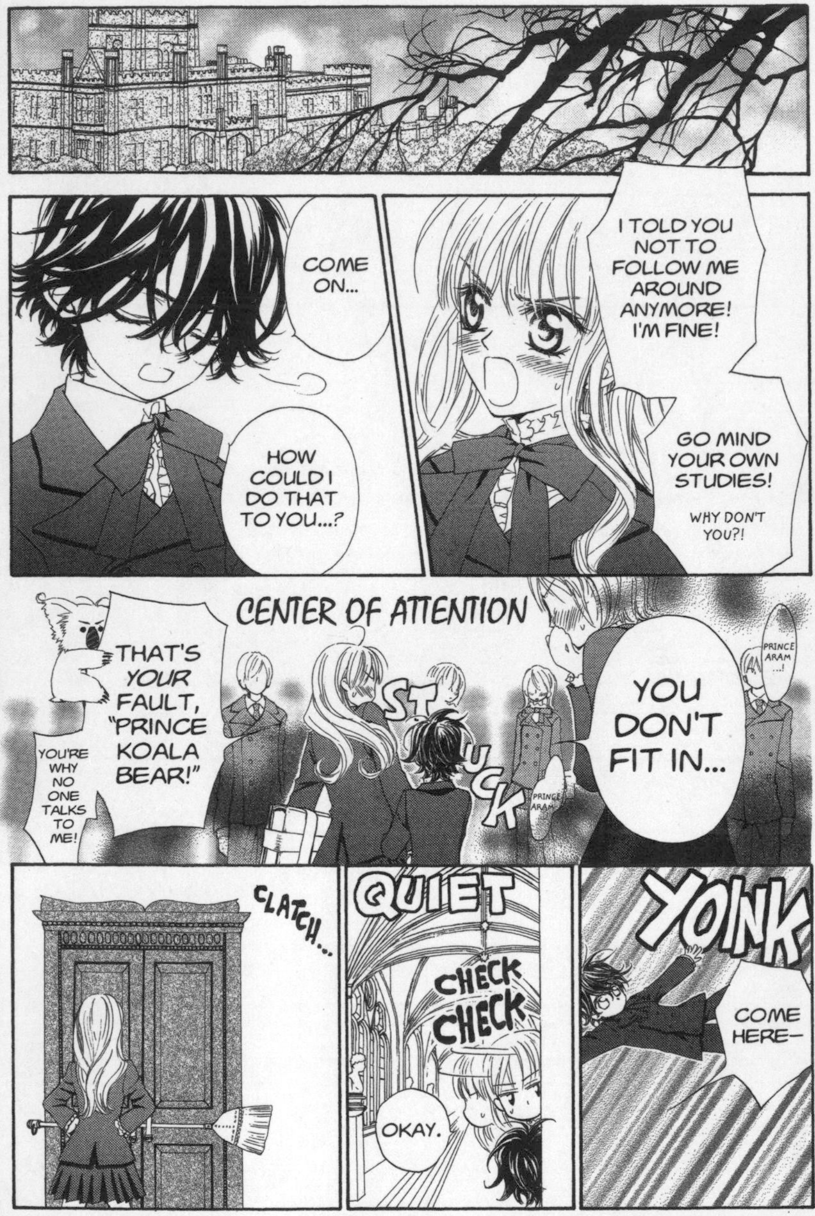
I TOLD YOU NOT TO FOLLOW ME AROUND ANYMORE! I'M FINE!
GO MIND YOUR OWN STUDIES!
WHY DON'T YOU?!
COME ON...
HOW COULD I DO THAT TO YOU...?
PRINCE ARAM ...!
YOU DON'T FIT IN...
PRINCE ARAM
STUCK
CENTER OF ATTENTION
THAT'S YOUR FAULT, "PRINCE KOALA BEAR!"
YOU'RE WHY NO ONE TALKS TO ME!
YOINK
COME HERE—
QUIET
CHECK CHECK
OKAY.
CLATCH...

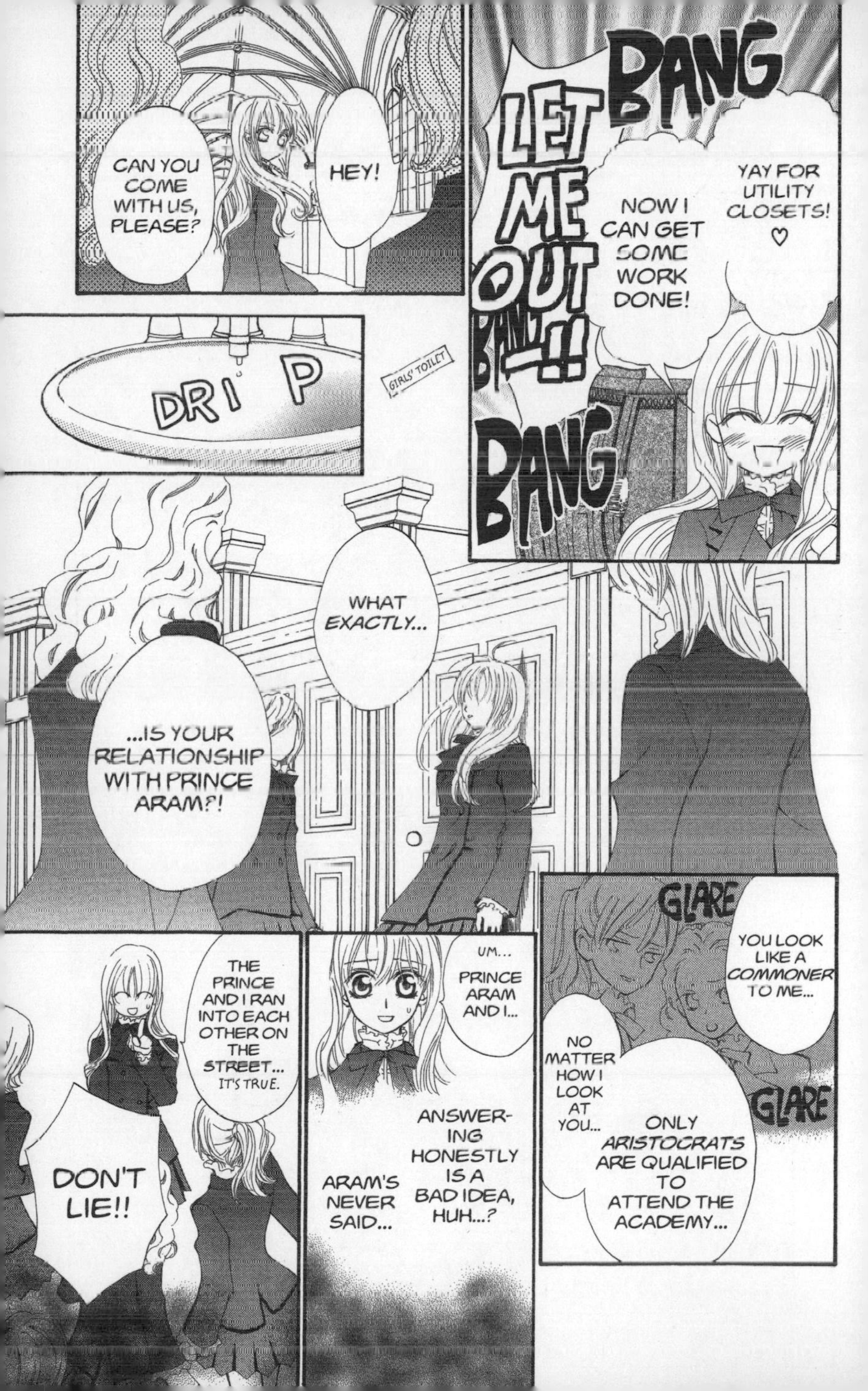
BANG
LET ME OUT
YAY FOR UTILITY CLOSETS! ♡
NOW I CAN GET SOME WORK DONE!
BANG
HEY!
CAN YOU COME WITH US, PLEASE?
DRIP
GIRLS' TOILET
WHAT EXACTLY...
...IS YOUR RELATIONSHIP WITH PRINCE ARAM?!
GLARE
YOU LOOK LIKE A COMMONER TO ME...
NO MATTER HOW I LOOK AT YOU...
GLARE
ONLY ARISTOCRATS ARE QUALIFIED TO ATTEND THE ACADEMY...
UM... PRINCE ARAM AND I...
ANSWERING HONESTLY IS A BAD IDEA, HUH...?
ARAM'S NEVER SAID...
THE PRINCE AND I RAN INTO EACH OTHER ON THE STREET...
IT'S TRUE.
DON'T LIE!!

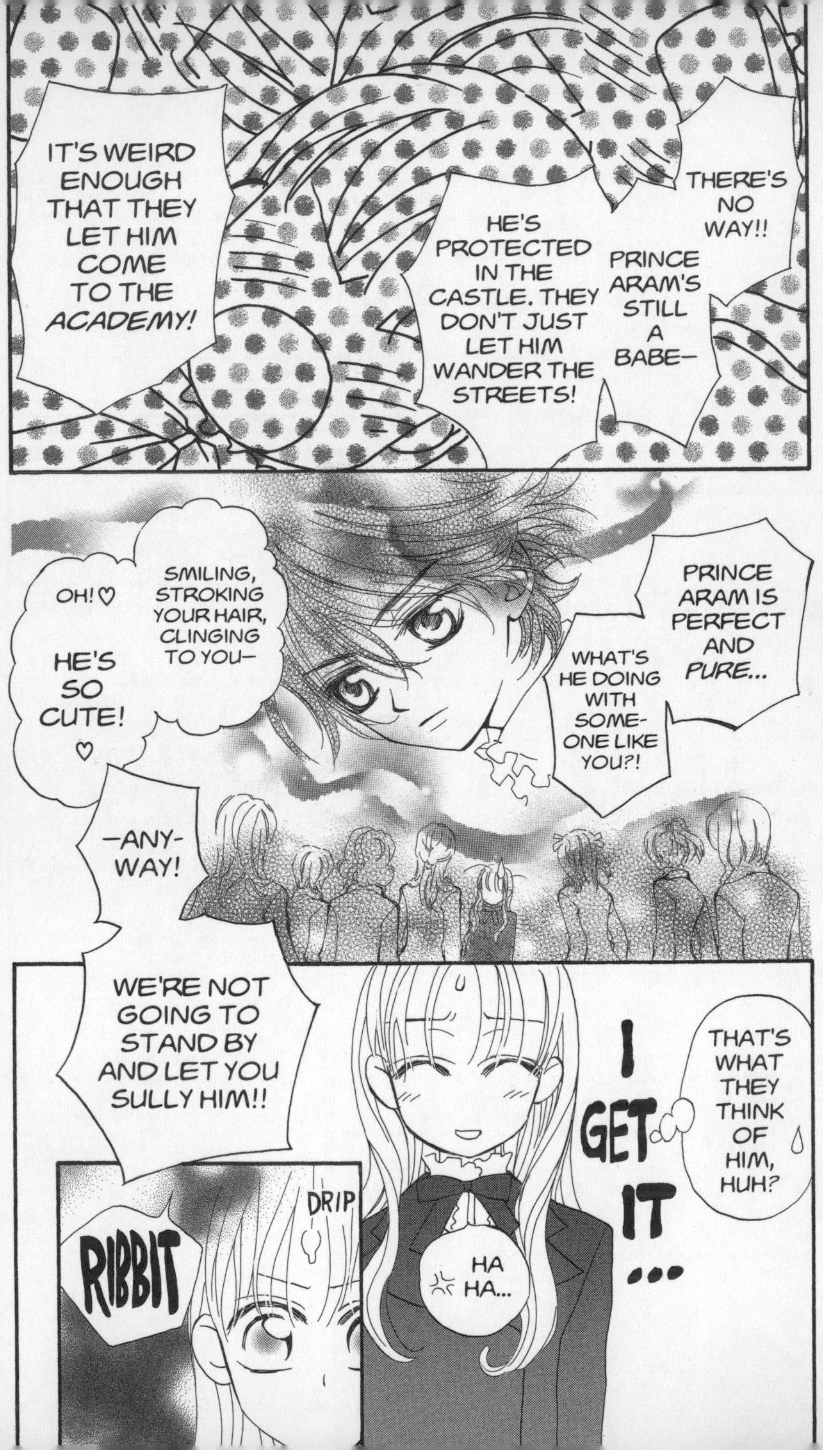
THERE'S NO WAY!! PRINCE ARAM'S STILL A BABE—
HE'S PROTECTED IN THE CASTLE. THEY DON'T JUST LET HIM WANDER THE STREETS!
IT'S WEIRD ENOUGH THAT THEY LET HIM COME TO THE *ACADEMY!*
PRINCE ARAM IS PERFECT AND *PURE*...
WHAT'S HE DOING WITH SOME-ONE LIKE YOU?!
SMILING, STROKING YOUR HAIR, CLINGING TO YOU—
OH! ♡ HE'S SO CUTE! ♡
—ANY-WAY!
WE'RE NOT GOING TO STAND BY AND LET YOU SULLY HIM!!
THAT'S WHAT THEY THINK OF HIM, HUH?
I GET IT...
HA HA...
DRIP
RIBBIT

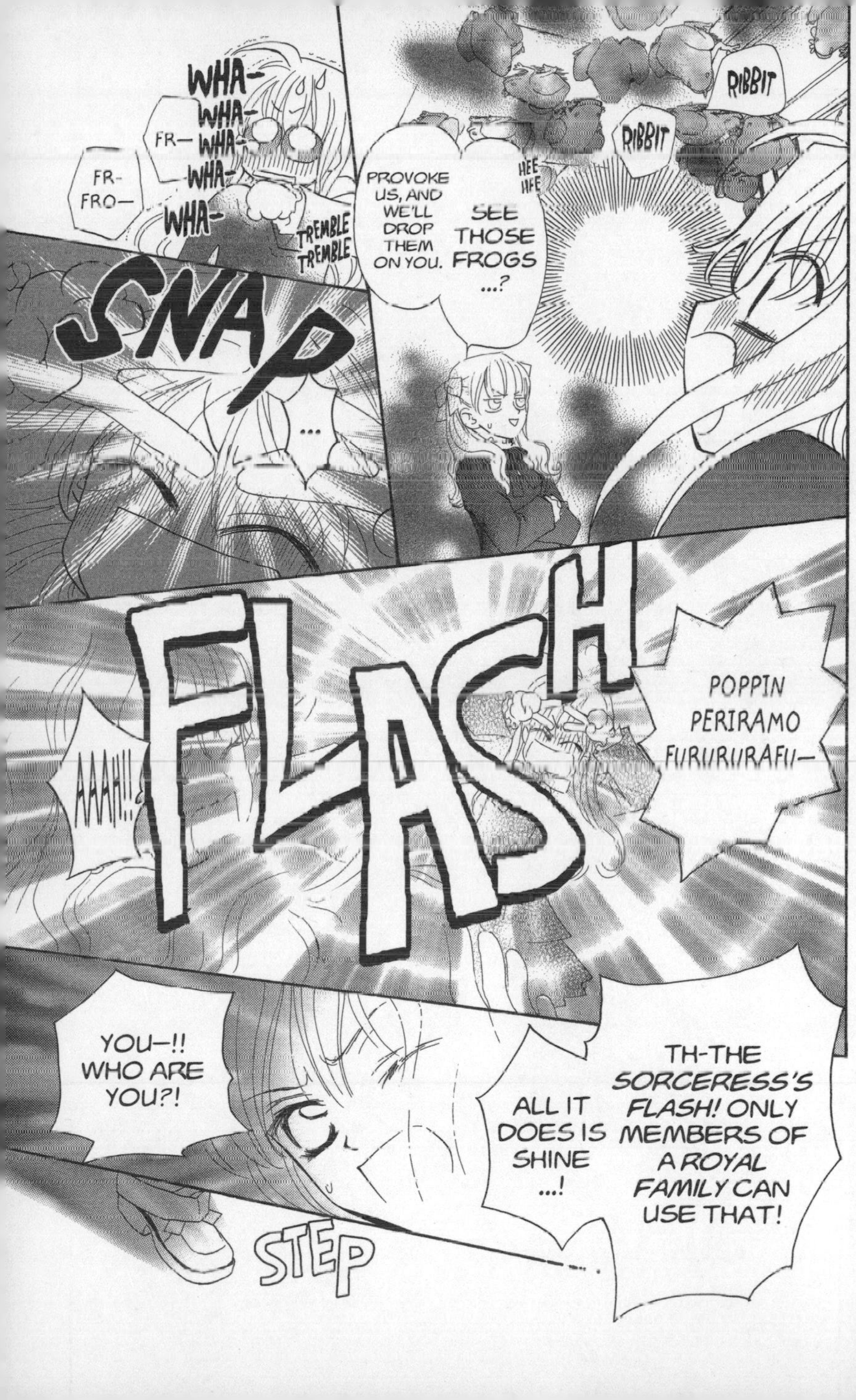
RIBBIT
RIBBIT
HEE HEE
SEE THOSE FROGS ...?
PROVOKE US, AND WE'LL DROP THEM ON YOU.
WHA- WHA- WHA- WHA- WHA-
FR—
FR- FRO—
TREMBLE TREMBLE
SNAP
...
POPPIN PERIRAMO FURURURAFU—
FLASH
AAAH!!
TH-THE SORCERESS'S FLASH! ONLY MEMBERS OF A ROYAL FAMILY CAN USE THAT!
ALL IT DOES IS SHINE ...!
YOU—!! WHO ARE YOU?!
STEP

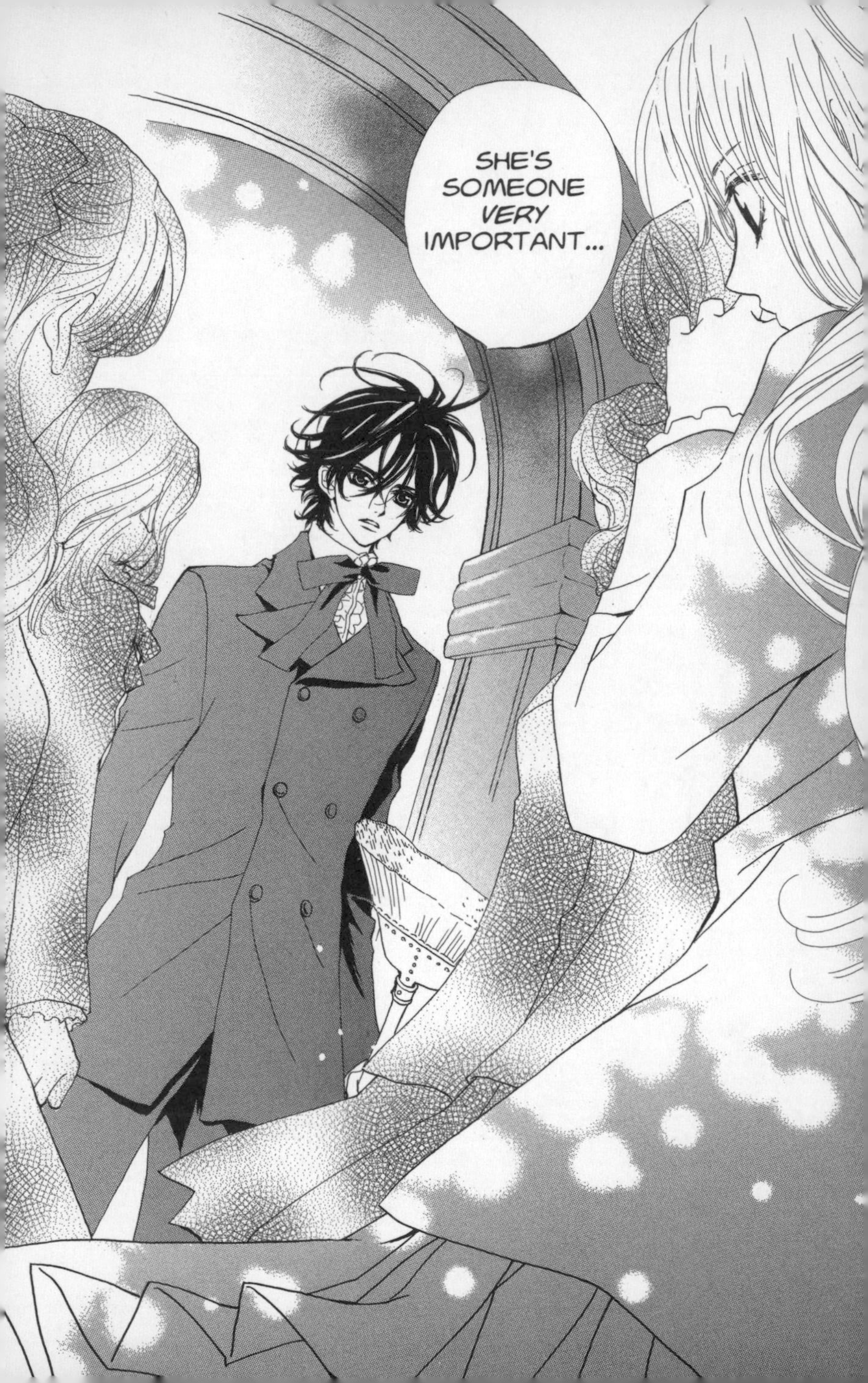
SHE'S SOMEONE VERY IMPORTANT...

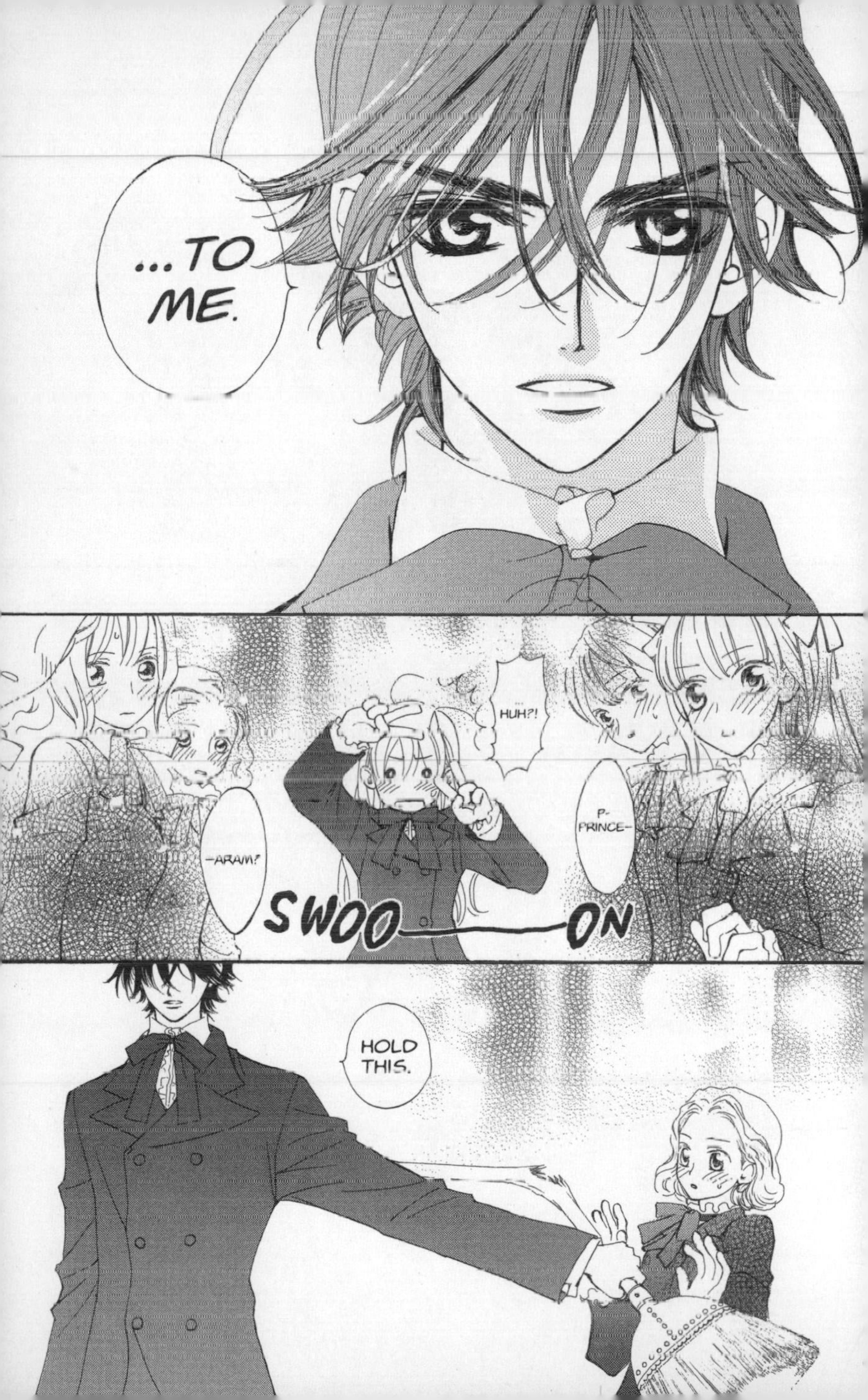
...TO ME.
P-PRINCE-
...HUH?!
-ARAM?
SWOO——ON
HOLD THIS.

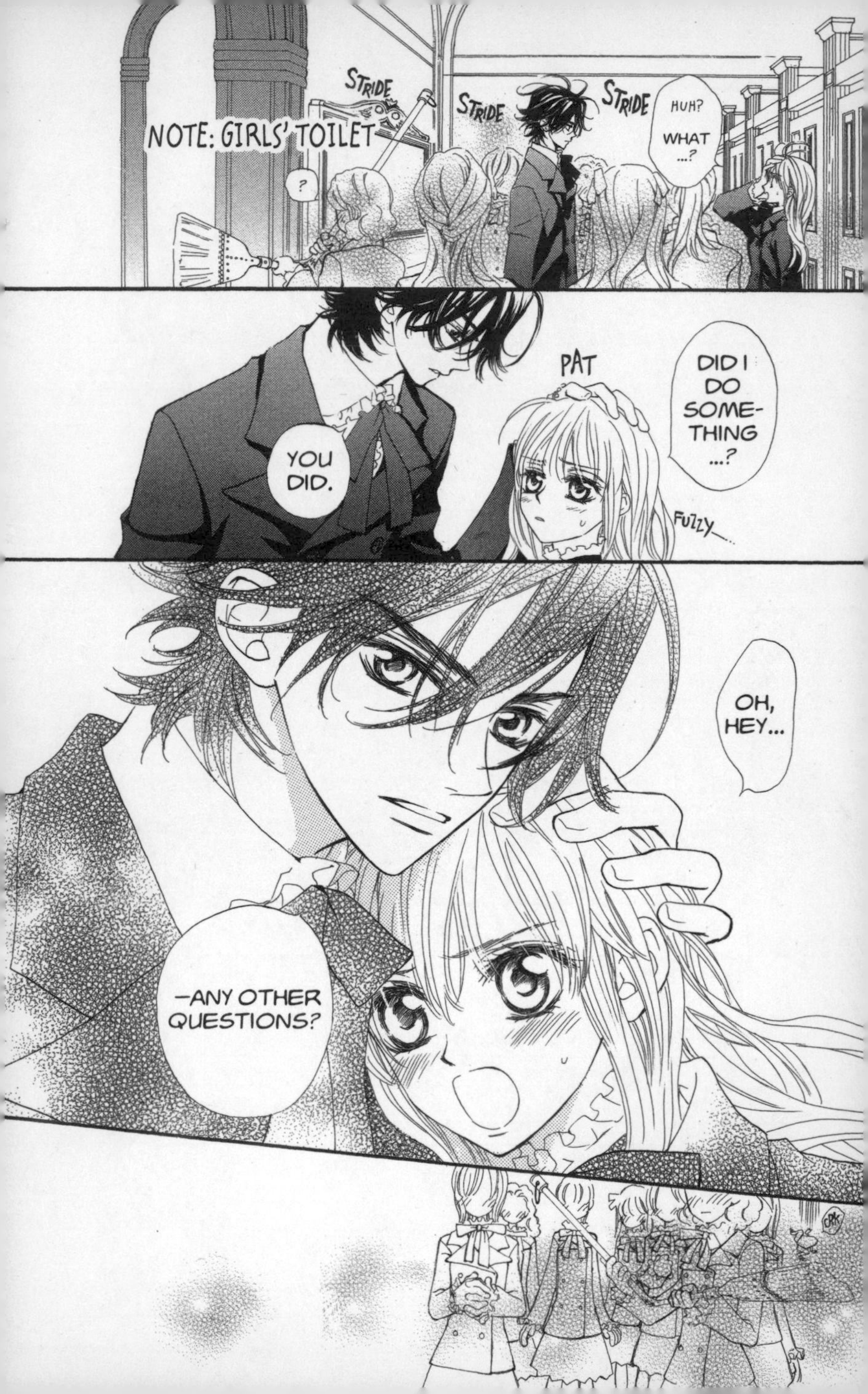
HUH? WHAT ...?
STRIDE
STRIDE
STRIDE
NOTE: GIRLS' TOILET
?
DID I DO SOME-THING ...?
PAT
FUZZY...
YOU DID.
OH, HEY...
—ANY OTHER QUESTIONS?

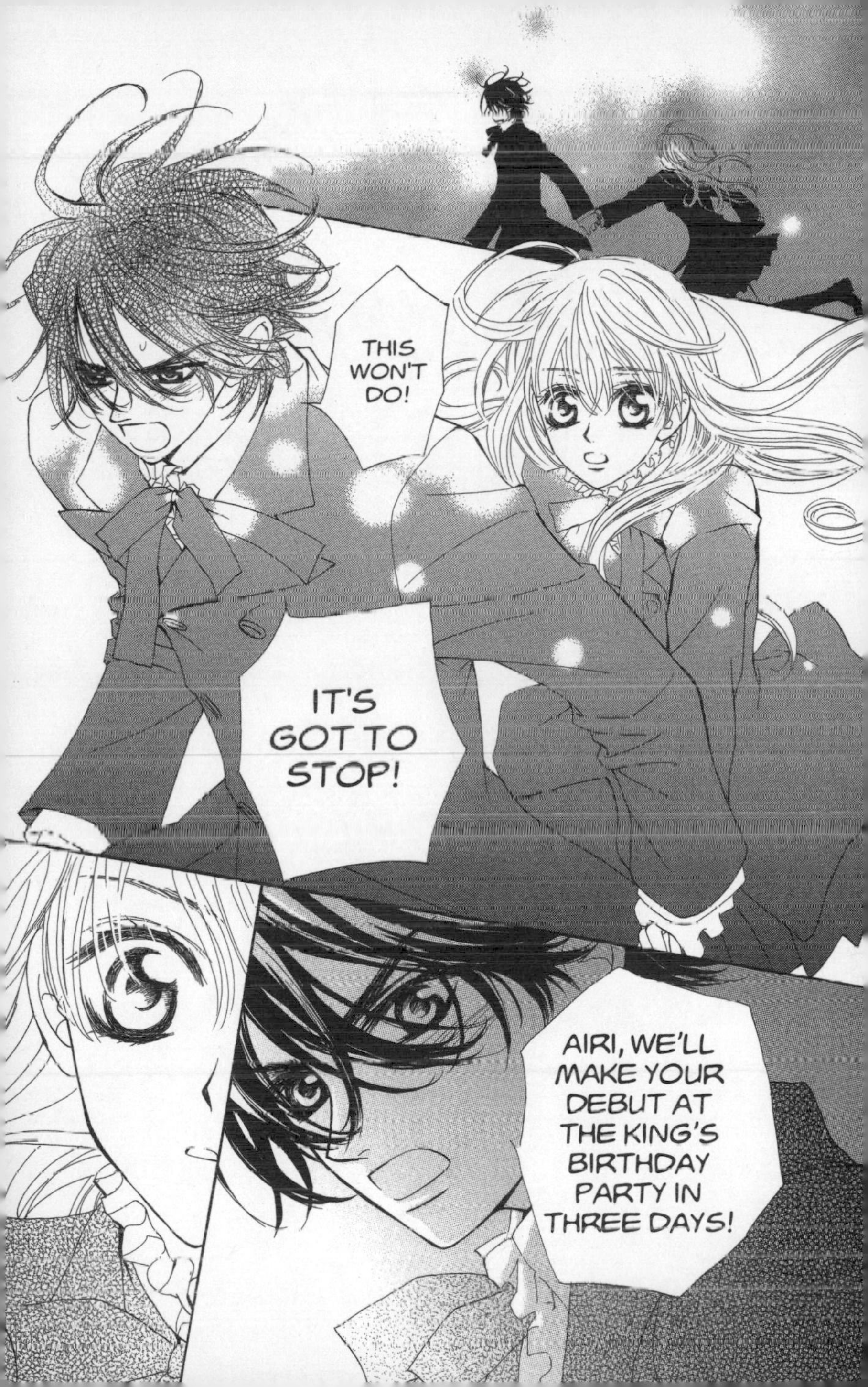
THIS WON'T DO!
IT'S GOT TO STOP!
AIRI, WE'LL MAKE YOUR DEBUT AT THE KING'S BIRTHDAY PARTY IN THREE DAYS!

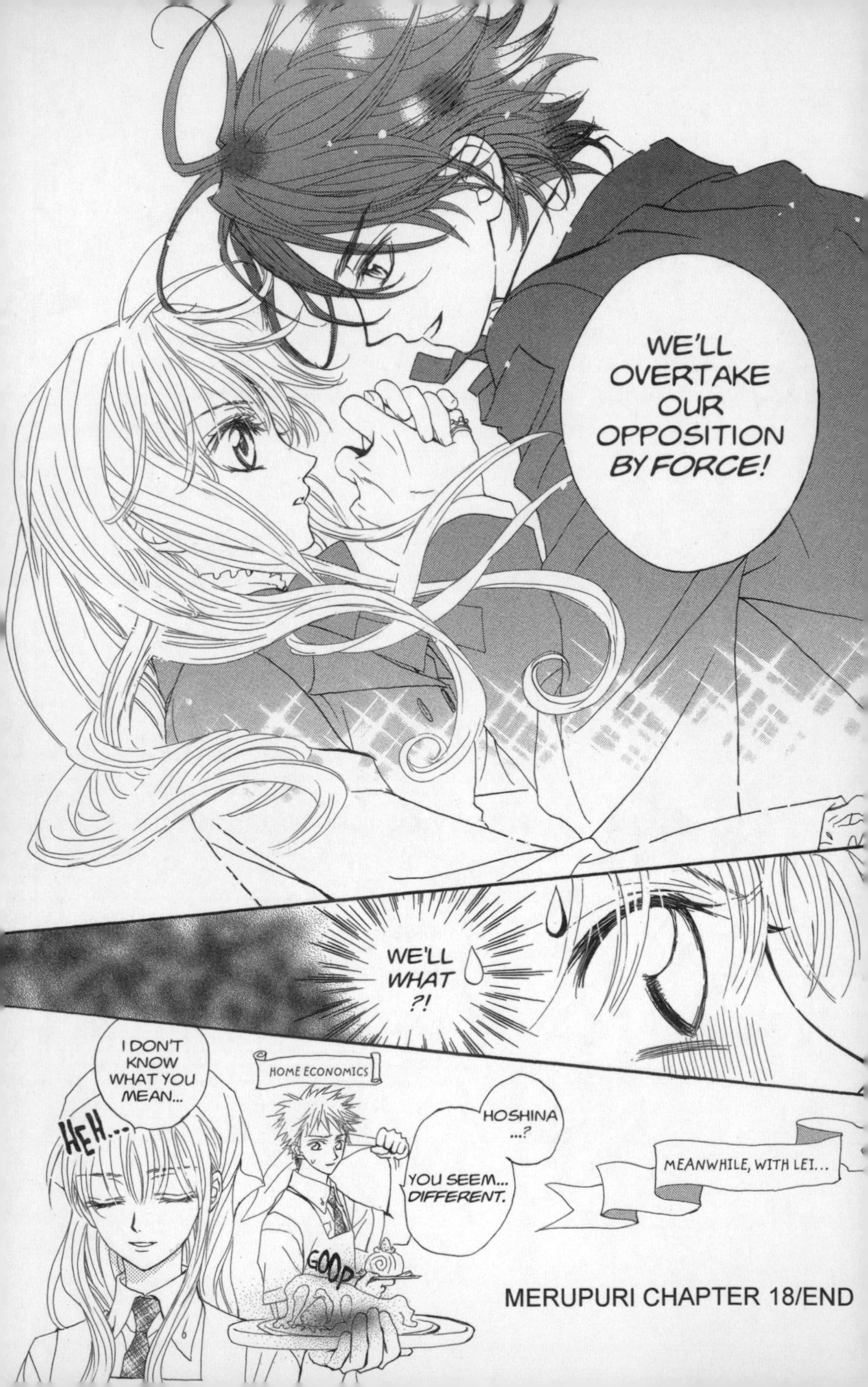
WE'LL OVERTAKE OUR OPPOSITION BY FORCE!
WE'LL WHAT ?!
MEANWHILE, WITH LEI...
HOME ECONOMICS
HOSHINA ...?
YOU SEEM... DIFFERENT.
GOOP
I DON'T KNOW WHAT YOU MEAN...
HEH...

MERUPURI CHAPTER 18/END

# CHAPTER 19

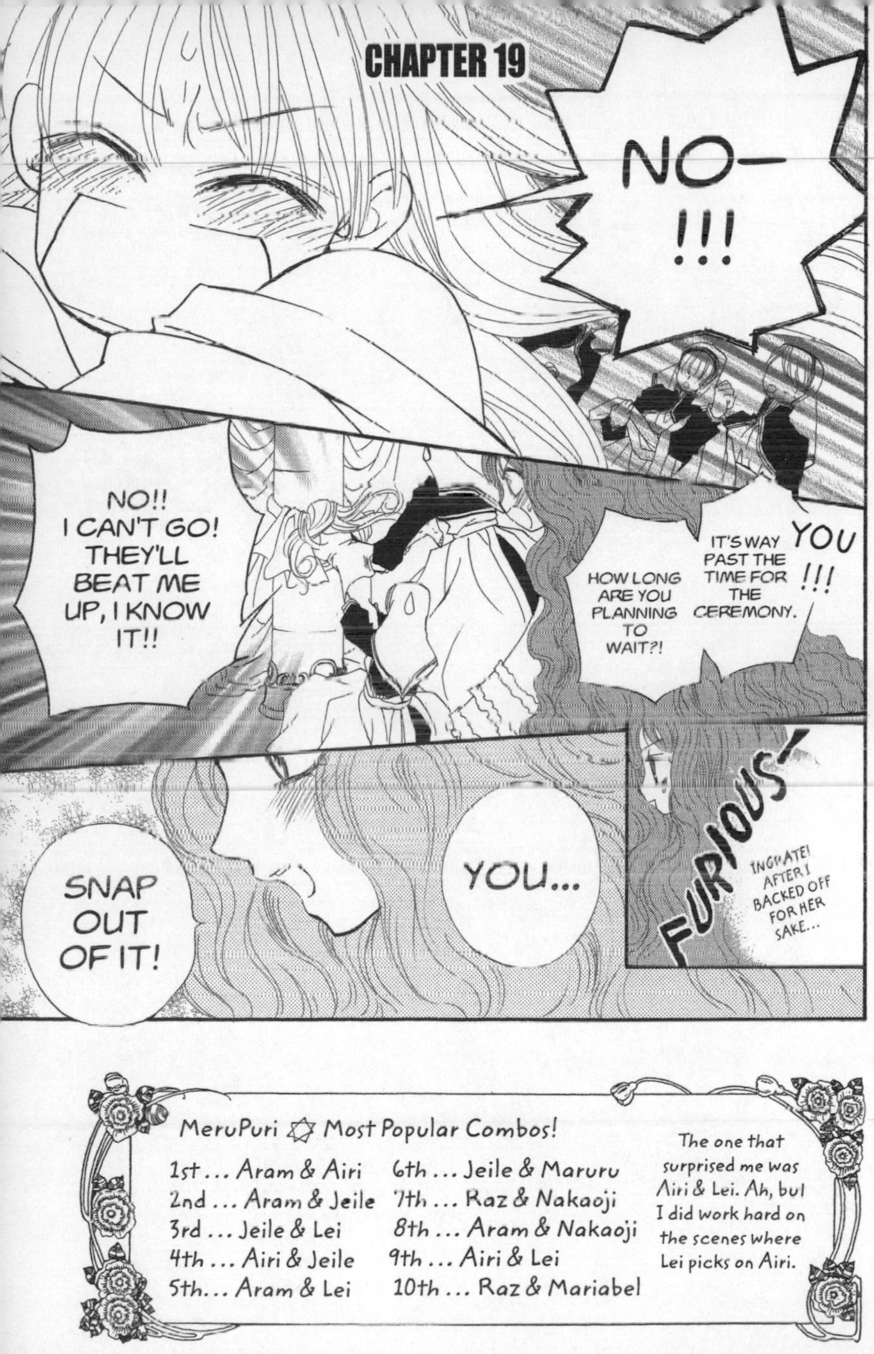
NO—!!!
YOU!!!
IT'S WAY PAST THE TIME FOR THE CEREMONY.
HOW LONG ARE YOU PLANNING TO WAIT?!
NO!! I CAN'T GO! THEY'LL BEAT ME UP, I KNOW IT!!
FURIOUS!
INGRATE! AFTER I BACKED OFF FOR HER SAKE...
YOU...
SNAP OUT OF IT!

MeruPuri ✡ Most Popular Combos!

1st . . . Aram & Airi
2nd . . . Aram & Jeile
3rd . . . Jeile & Lei
4th . . . Airi & Jeile
5th. . . Aram & Lei
6th . . . Jeile & Maruru
7th . . . Raz & Nakaoji
8th . . . Aram & Nakaoji
9th . . . Airi & Lei
10th . . . Raz & Mariabel

The one that surprised me was Airi & Lei. Ah, but I did work hard on the scenes where Lei picks on Airi.

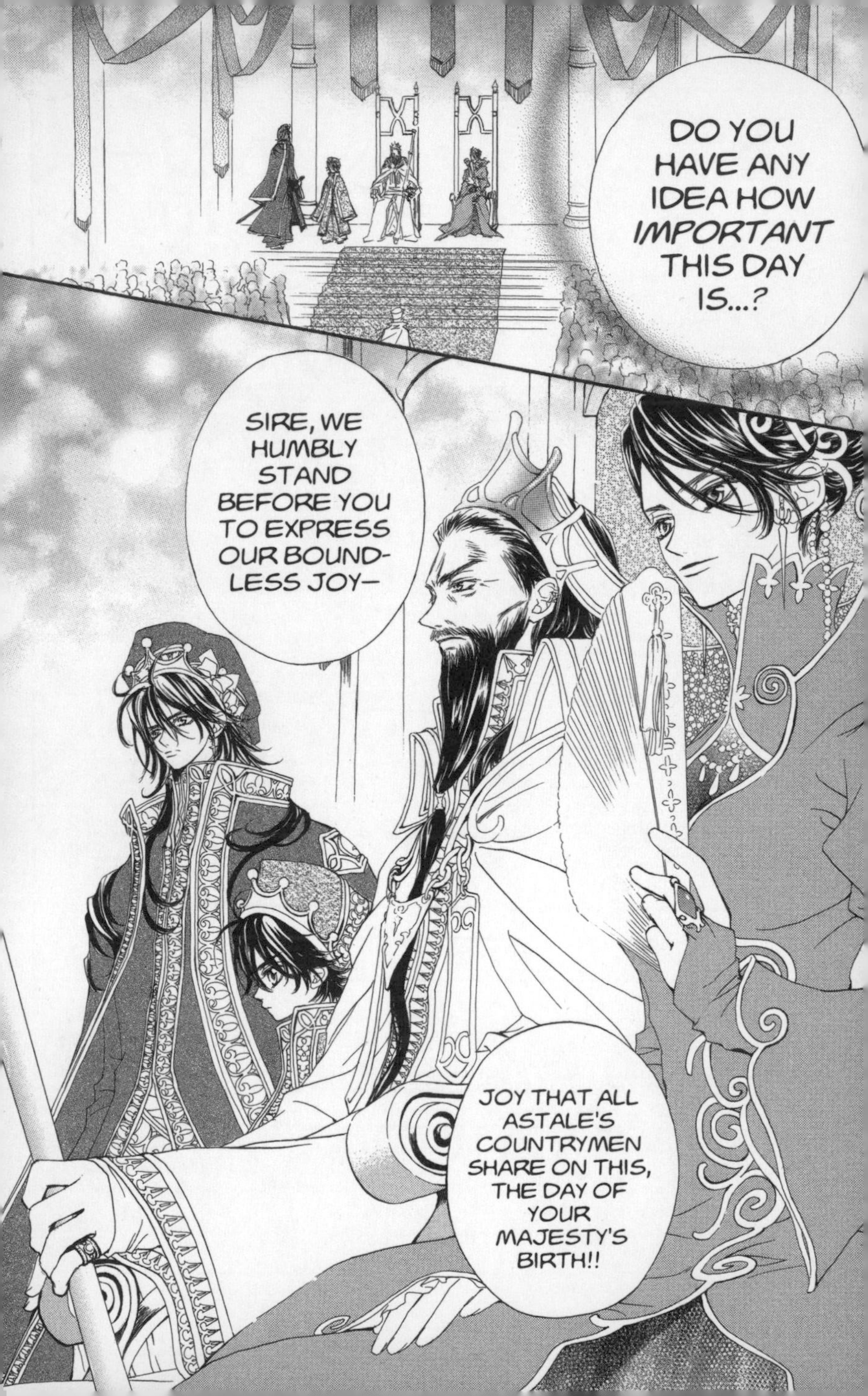
DO YOU HAVE ANY IDEA HOW IMPORTANT THIS DAY IS...?
SIRE, WE HUMBLY STAND BEFORE YOU TO EXPRESS OUR BOUNDLESS JOY–
JOY THAT ALL ASTALE'S COUNTRYMEN SHARE ON THIS, THE DAY OF YOUR MAJESTY'S BIRTH!!

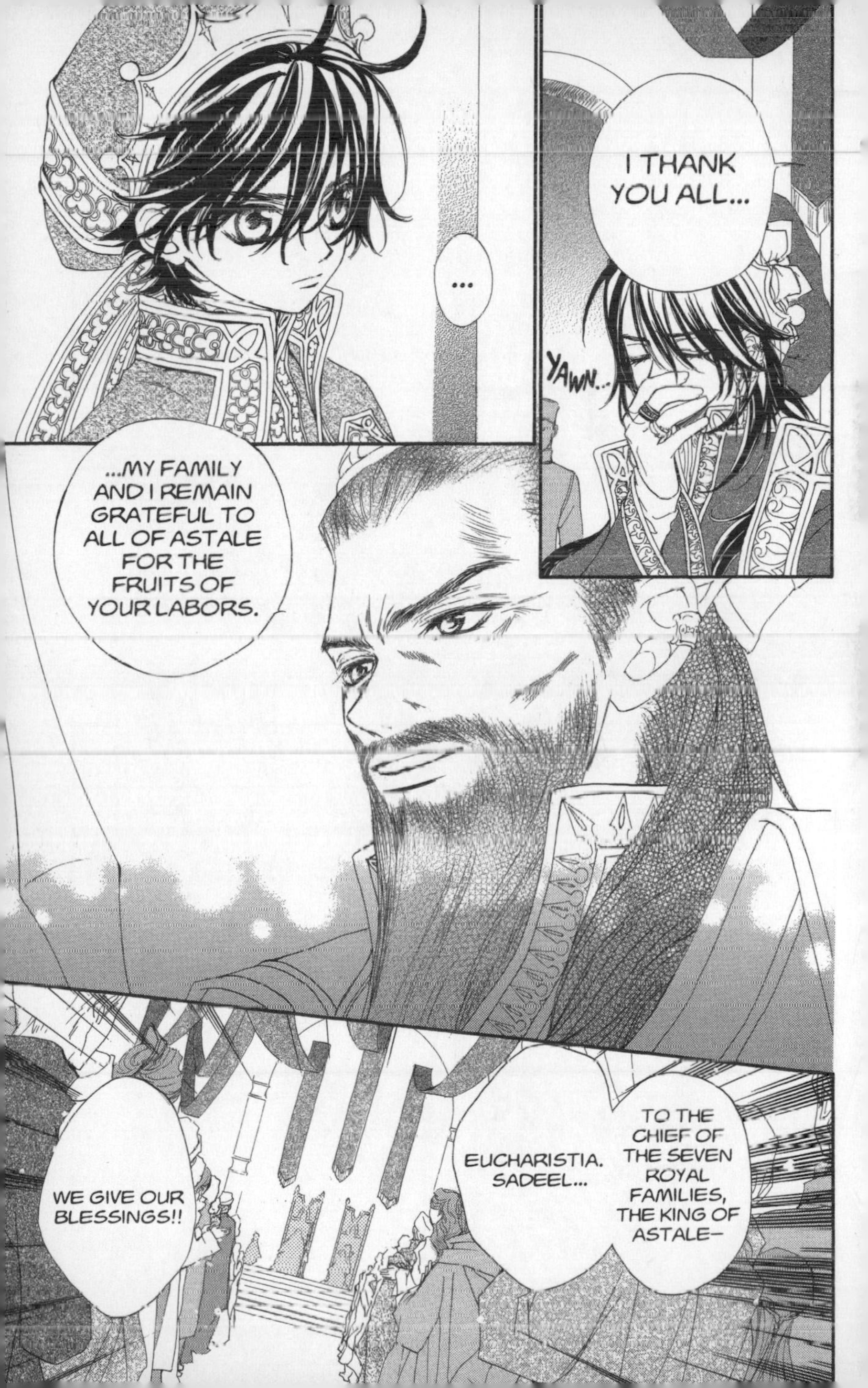
I THANK YOU ALL...
YAWN...
...
...MY FAMILY AND I REMAIN GRATEFUL TO ALL OF ASTALE FOR THE FRUITS OF YOUR LABORS.
TO THE CHIEF OF THE SEVEN ROYAL FAMILIES, THE KING OF ASTALE—
EUCHARISTIA. SADEEL...
WE GIVE OUR BLESSINGS!!

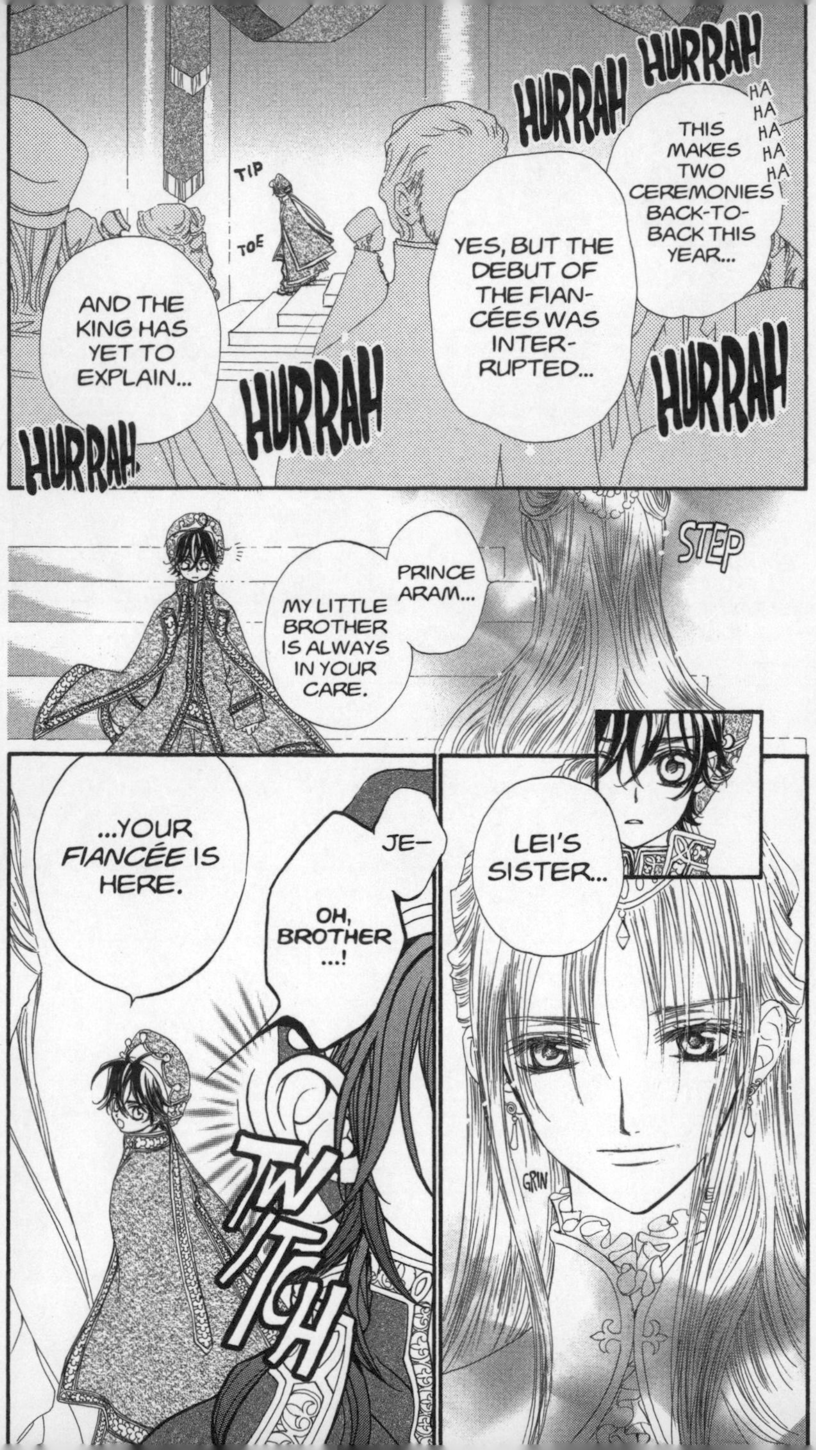
HURRAH HURRAH
THIS MAKES TWO CEREMONIES BACK-TO-BACK THIS YEAR...
HA HA HA HA HA
HURRAH
YES, BUT THE DEBUT OF THE FIANCÉES WAS INTERRUPTED...
TIP
TOE
AND THE KING HAS YET TO EXPLAIN...
HURRAH
HURRAH
HURRAH
STEP
PRINCE ARAM...
MY LITTLE BROTHER IS ALWAYS IN YOUR CARE.
LEI'S SISTER...
GRIN
JE—
OH, BROTHER ...!
...YOUR FIANCÉE IS HERE.
TWITCH

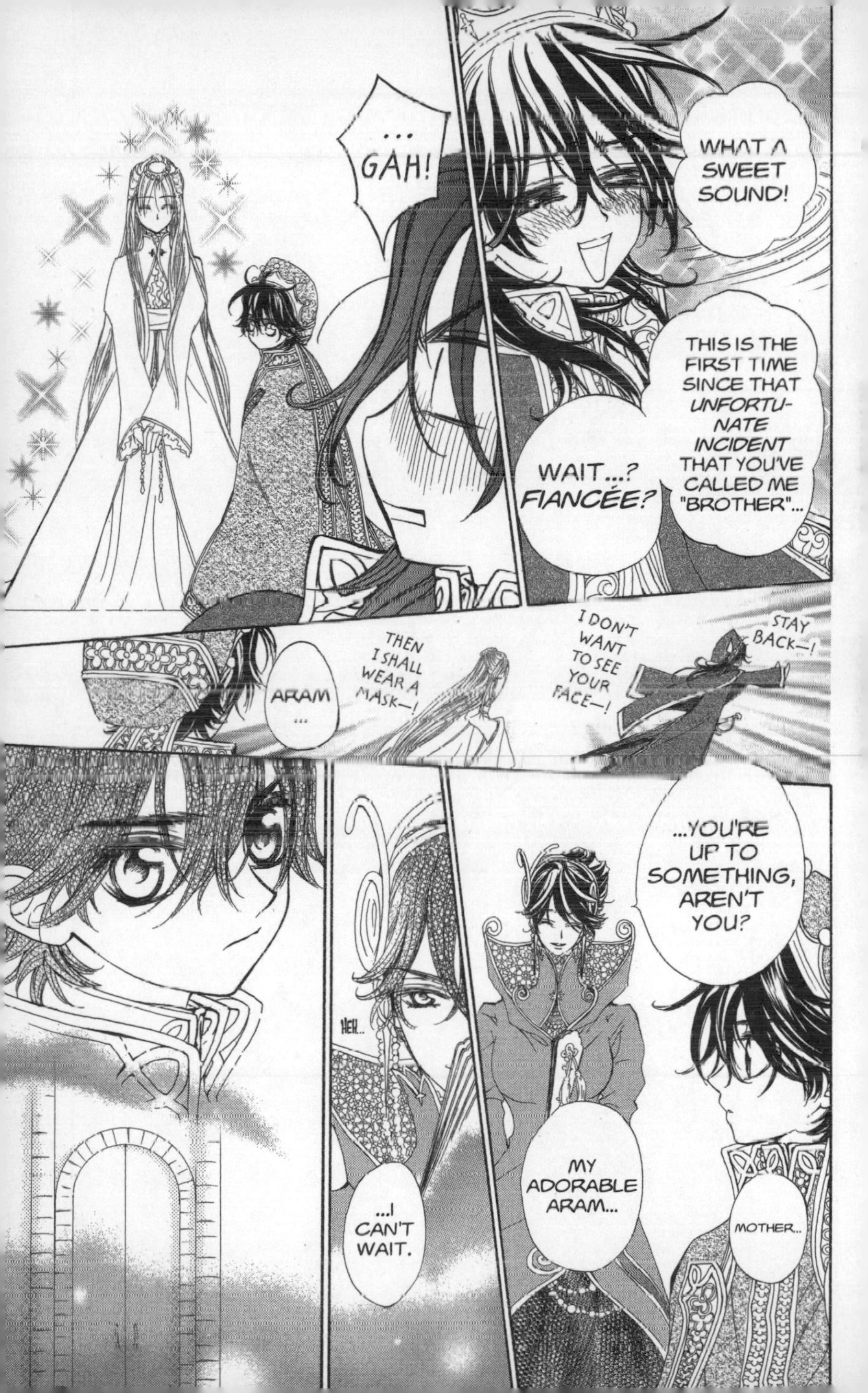
WHAT A SWEET SOUND!
THIS IS THE FIRST TIME SINCE THAT UNFORTUNATE INCIDENT THAT YOU'VE CALLED ME "BROTHER"...
...GAH!
WAIT...? FIANCÉE?
STAY BACK—!
I DON'T WANT TO SEE YOUR FACE—!
THEN I SHALL WEAR A MASK—!
ARAM...
...YOU'RE UP TO SOMETHING, AREN'T YOU?
MY ADORABLE ARAM...
MOTHER...
HEH..
...I CAN'T WAIT.

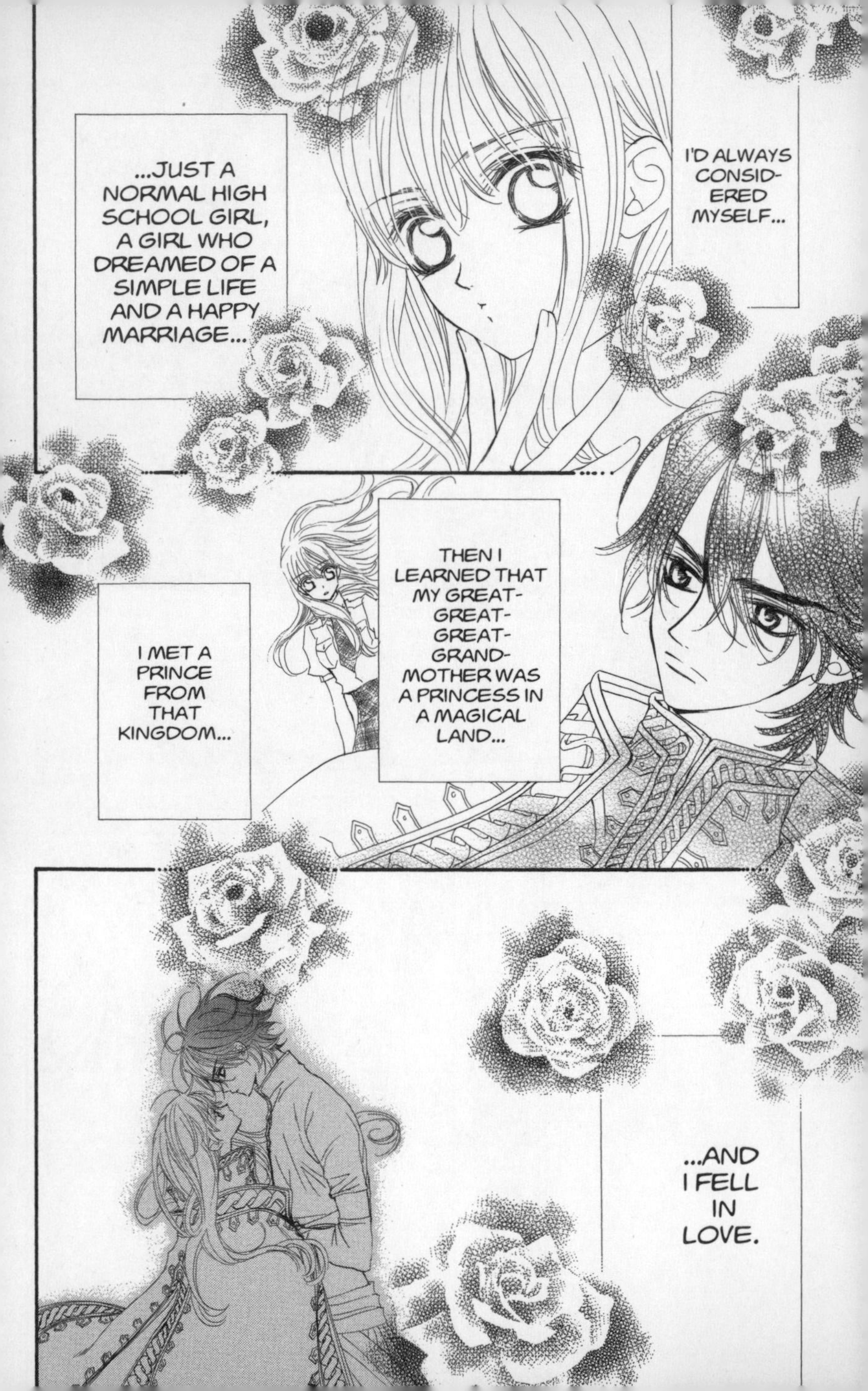
I'D ALWAYS CONSIDERED MYSELF...
...JUST A NORMAL HIGH SCHOOL GIRL, A GIRL WHO DREAMED OF A SIMPLE LIFE AND A HAPPY MARRIAGE...
THEN I LEARNED THAT MY GREAT-GREAT-GREAT-GRANDMOTHER WAS A PRINCESS IN A MAGICAL LAND...
I MET A PRINCE FROM THAT KINGDOM...
...AND I FELL IN LOVE.

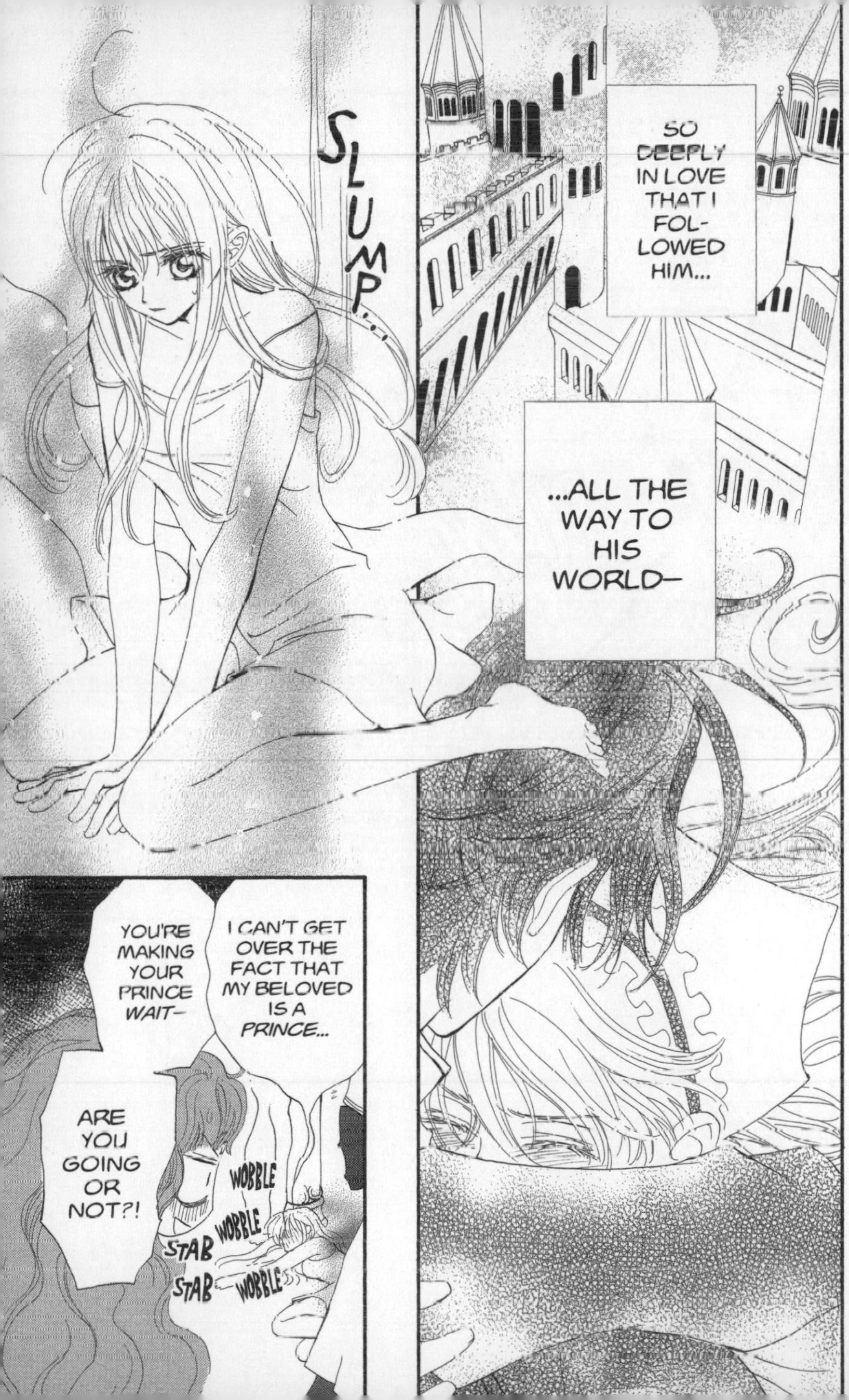
SO DEEPLY IN LOVE THAT I FOL-LOWED HIM...
...ALL THE WAY TO HIS WORLD—
SLUMP...
I CAN'T GET OVER THE FACT THAT MY BELOVED IS A PRINCE...
YOU'RE MAKING YOUR PRINCE WAIT—
ARE YOU GOING OR NOT?!
WOBBLE
WOBBLE
STAB
STAB
WOBBLE

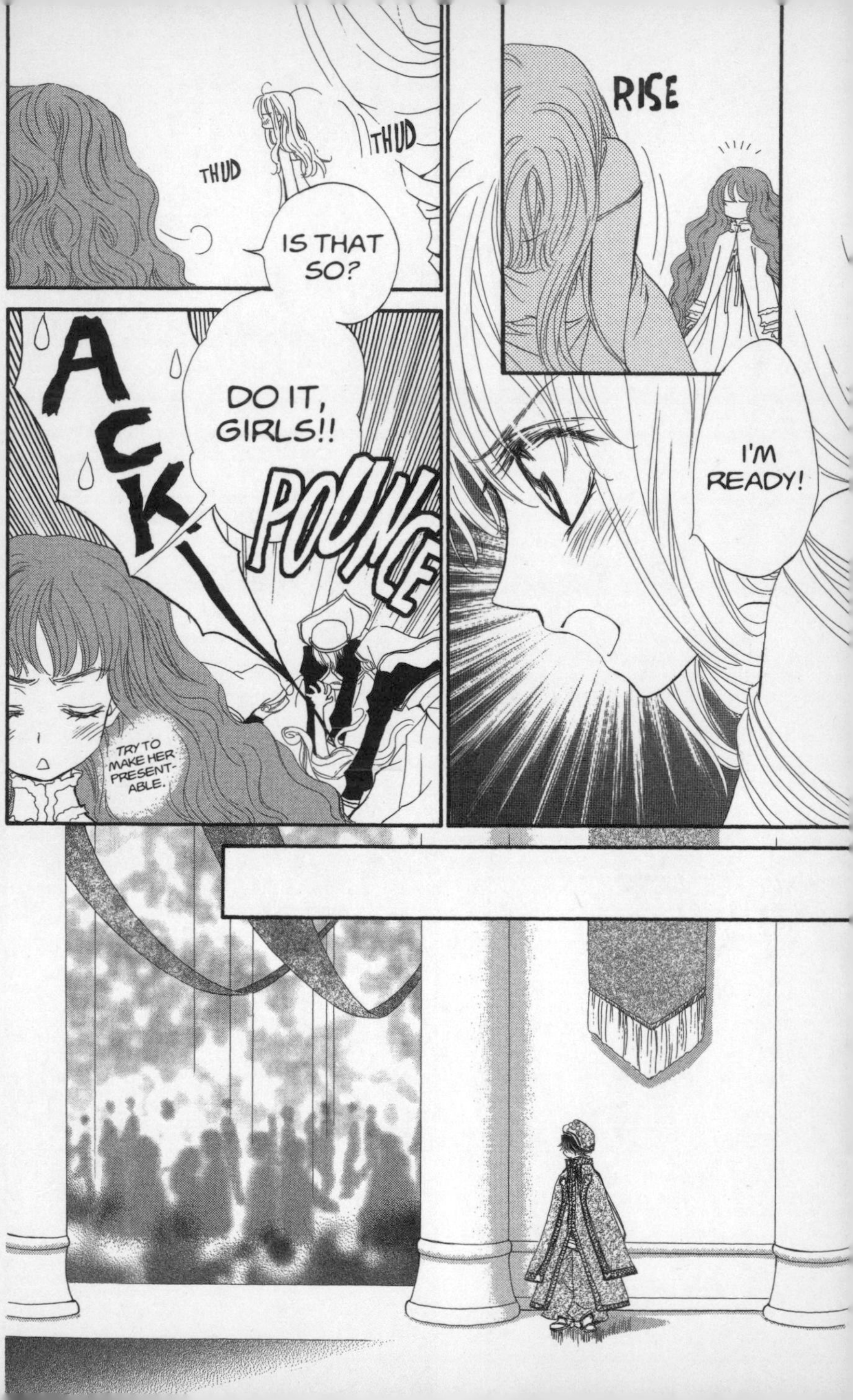
RISE
I'M READY!
THUD
THUD
IS THAT SO?
DO IT, GIRLS!!
ACK
POUNCE
TRY TO MAKE HER PRESENTABLE.

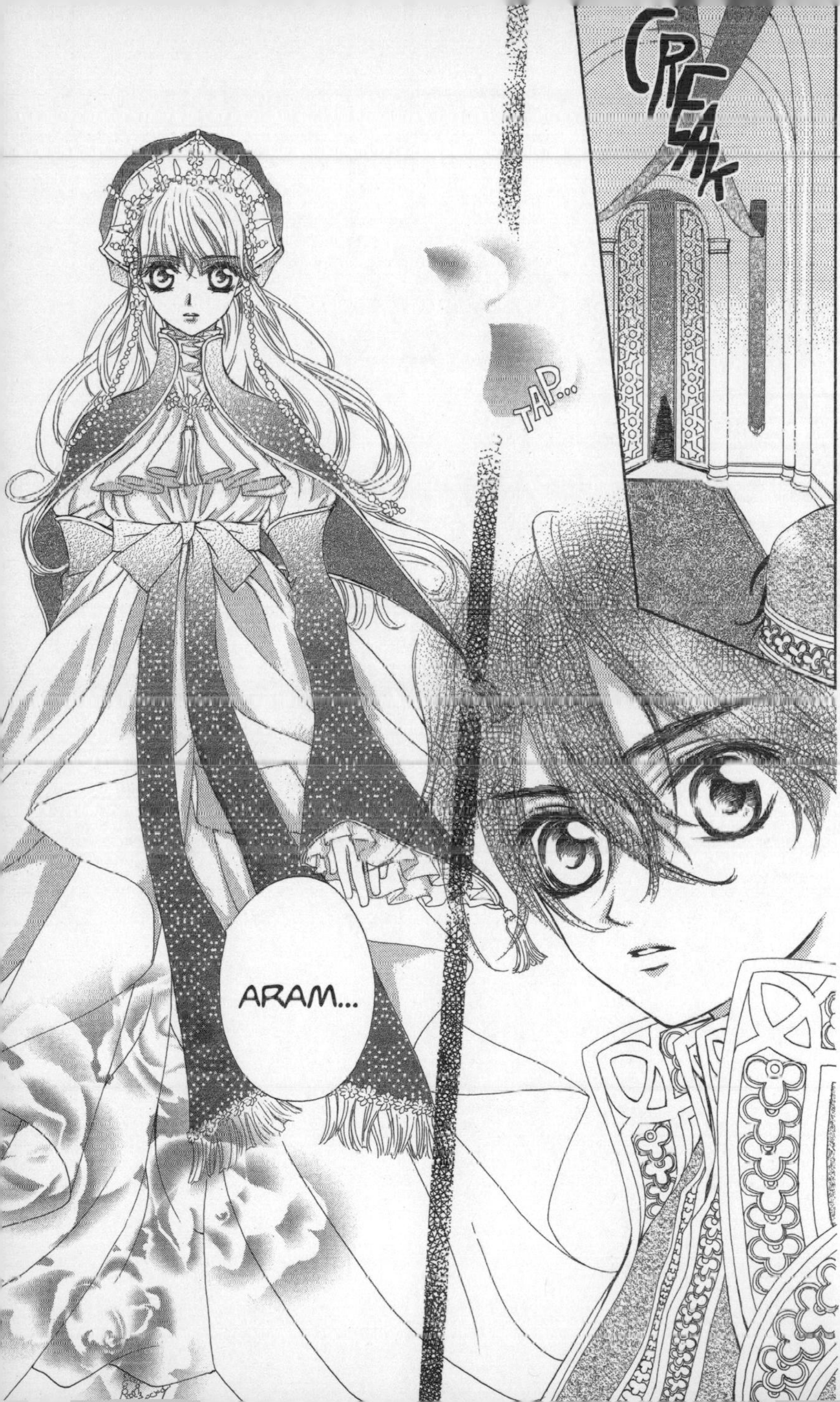

CREAK
TAP...
ARAM...

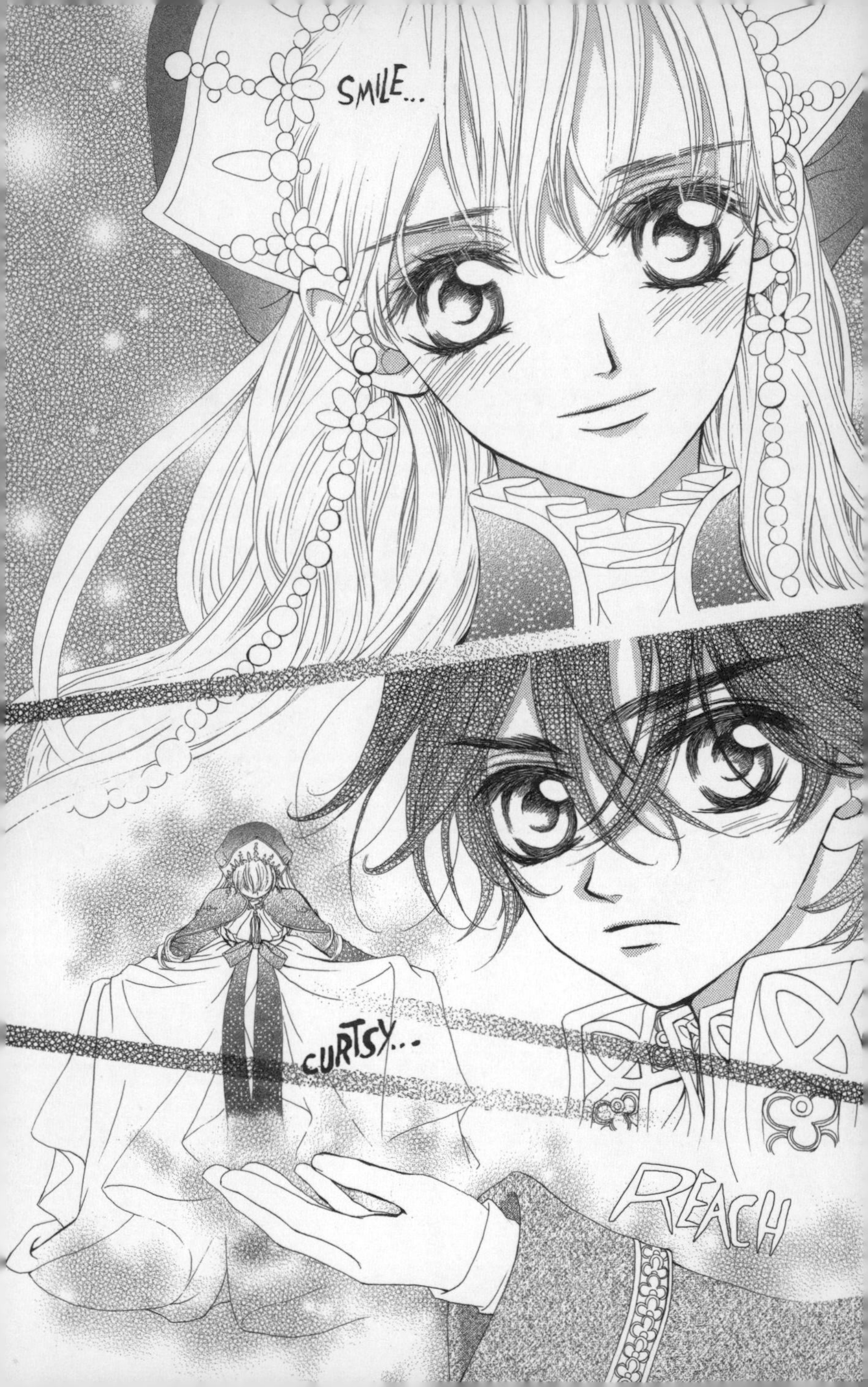
SMILE...
CURTSY...
REACH

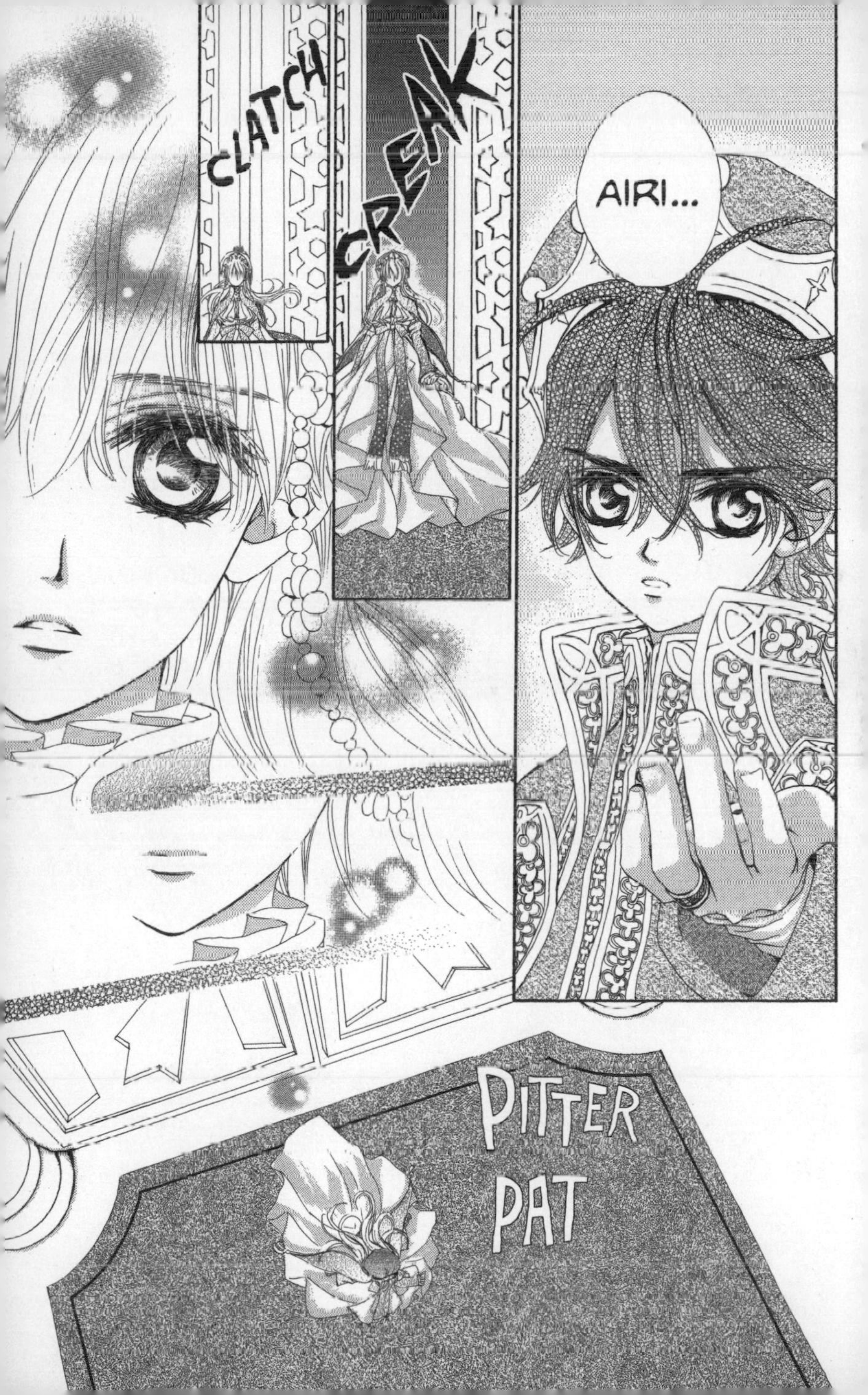
AIRI...
CREAK
CLATCH
PITTER PAT

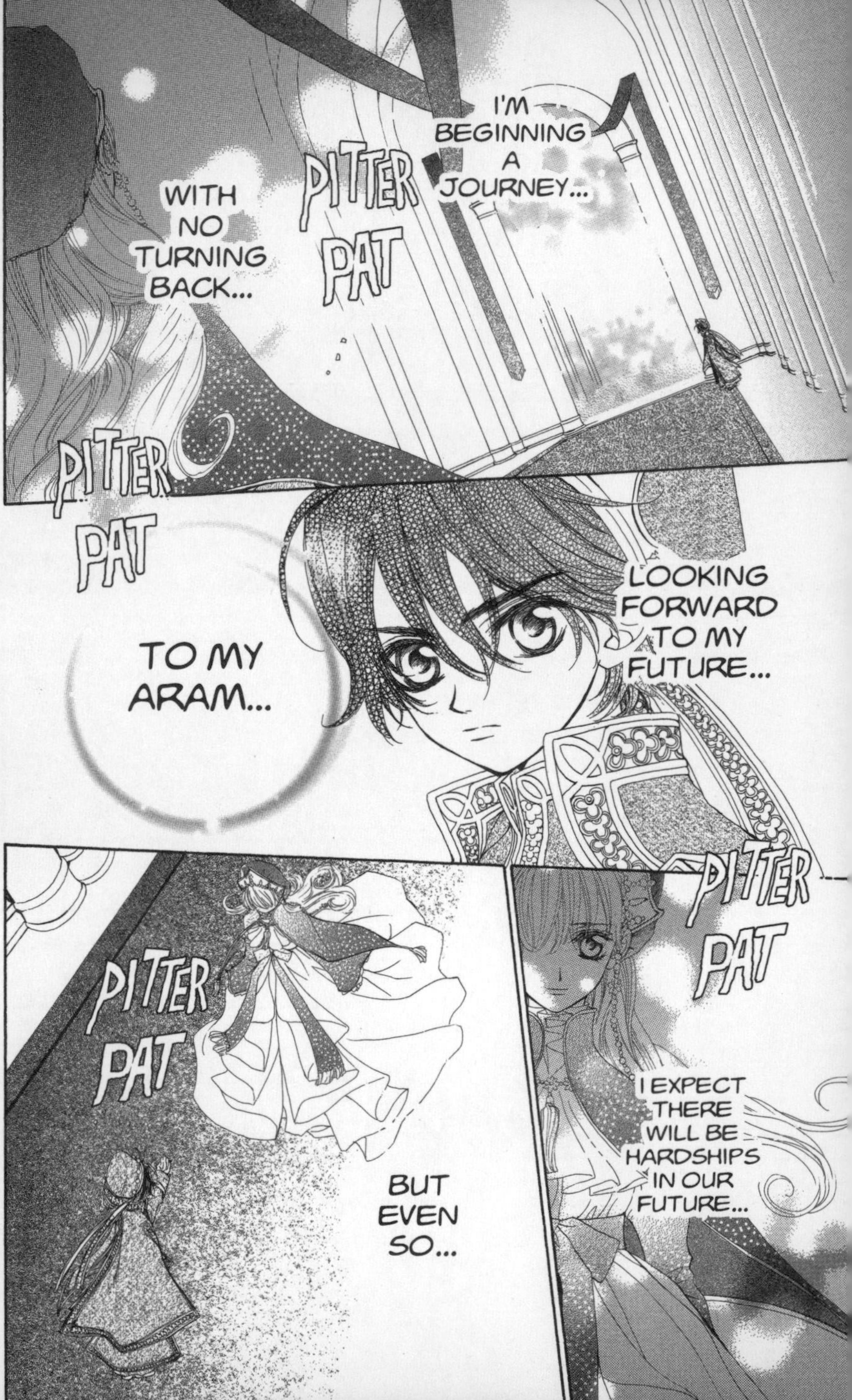
I'M BEGINNING A JOURNEY...
PITTER PAT
WITH NO TURNING BACK...
PITTER PAT
LOOKING FORWARD TO MY FUTURE...
TO MY ARAM...
PITTER PAT
I EXPECT THERE WILL BE HARDSHIPS IN OUR FUTURE...
PITTER PAT
BUT EVEN SO...

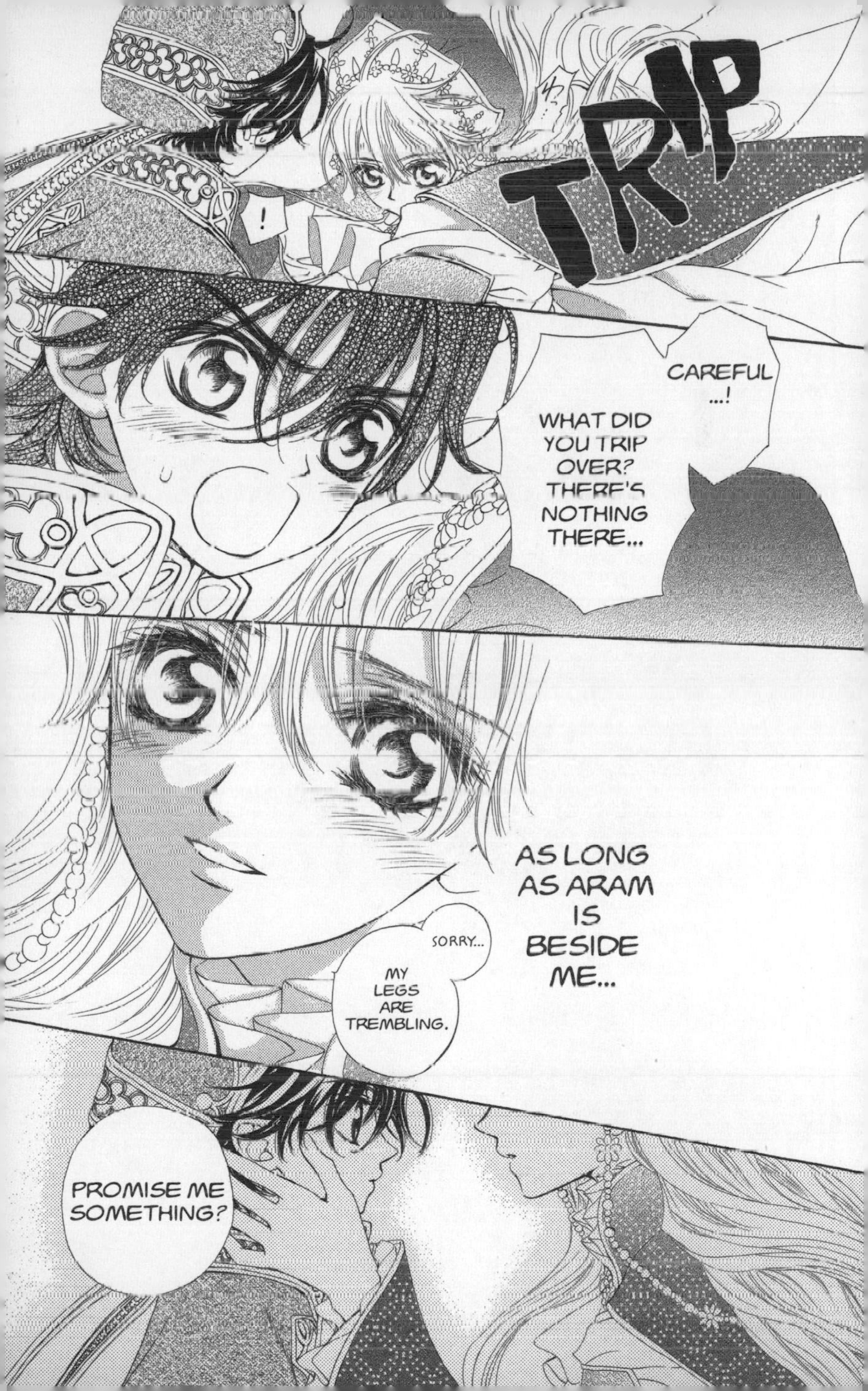
TRIP
!
CAREFUL ...!
WHAT DID YOU TRIP OVER? THERE'S NOTHING THERE...
AS LONG AS ARAM IS BESIDE ME...
SORRY...
MY LEGS ARE TREMBLING.
PROMISE ME SOMETHING?

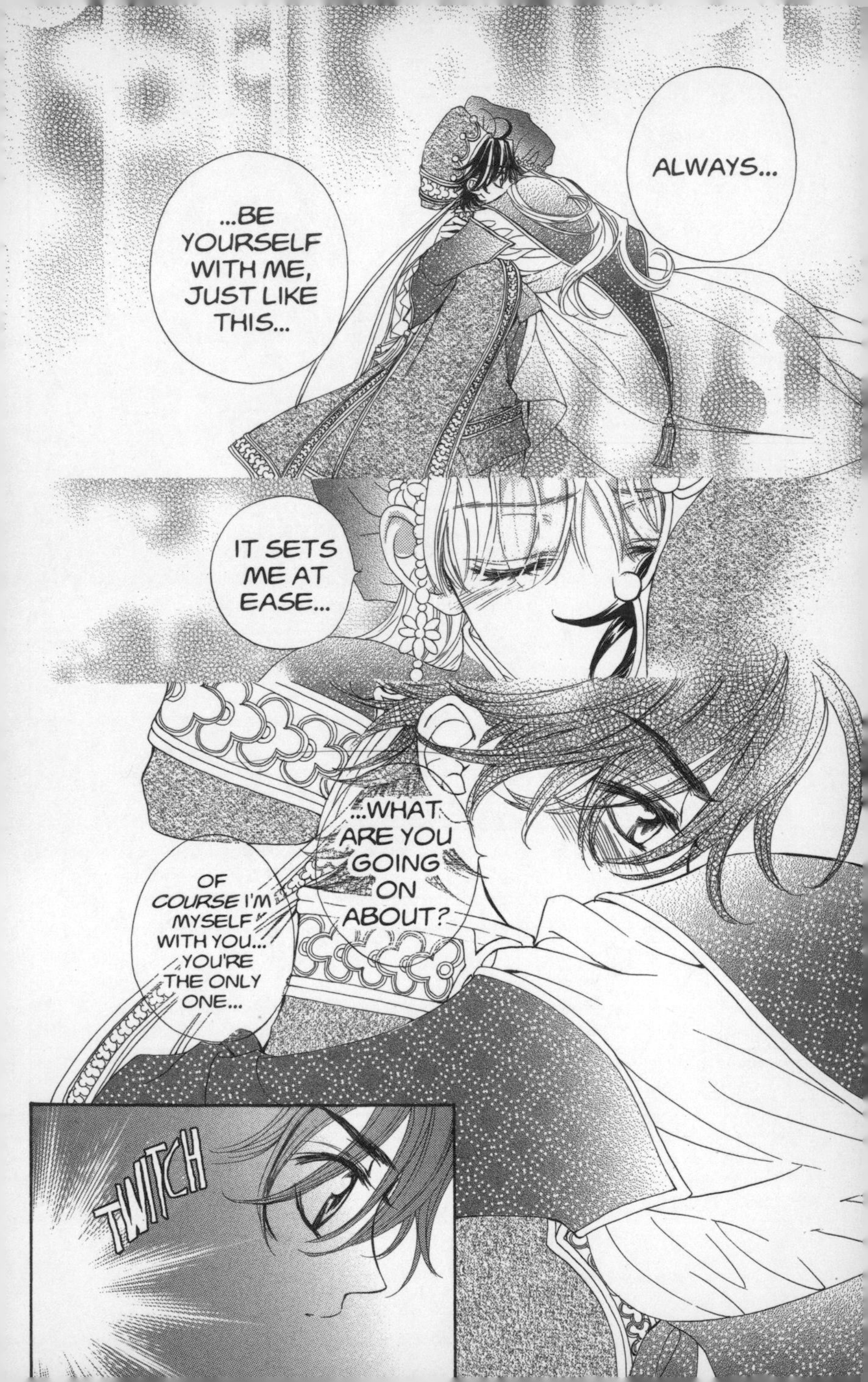
ALWAYS...
...BE YOURSELF WITH ME, JUST LIKE THIS...
IT SETS ME AT EASE...
...WHAT ARE YOU GOING ON ABOUT?
OF COURSE I'M MYSELF WITH YOU... YOU'RE THE ONLY ONE...
TWITCH

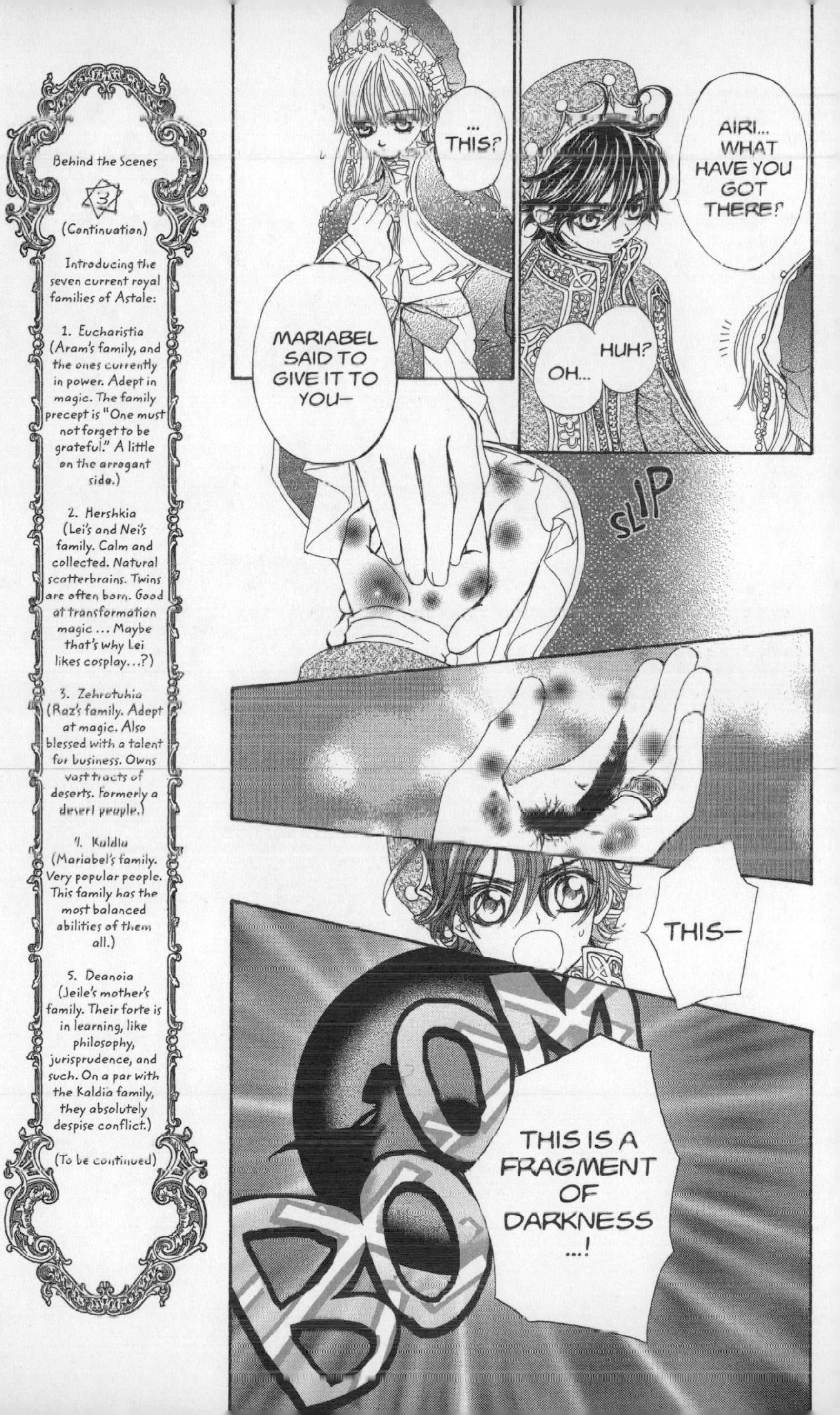
AIRI... WHAT HAVE YOU GOT THERE?
... THIS?
MARIABEL SAID TO GIVE IT TO YOU—
HUH?
OH...
SLIP
THIS—
BOOM
THIS IS A FRAGMENT OF DARKNESS ...!

Behind the Scenes

3

(Continuation)

Introducing the seven current royal families of Astale:

1. Eucharistia (Aram's family, and the ones currently in power. Adept in magic. The family precept is "One must not forget to be grateful." A little on the arrogant side.)

2. Hershkia (Lei's and Nei's family. Calm and collected. Natural scatterbrains. Twins are often born. Good at transformation magic . . . Maybe that's why Lei likes cosplay. . .?)

3. Zehrotuhia (Raz's family. Adept at magic. Also blessed with a talent for business. Owns vast tracts of deserts. Formerly a desert people.)

4. Kaldia (Mariabel's family. Very popular people. This family has the most balanced abilities of them all.)

5. Deanoia (Jeile's mother's family. Their forte is in learning, like philosophy, jurisprudence, and such. On a par with the Kaldia family, they absolutely despise conflict.)

(To be continued)

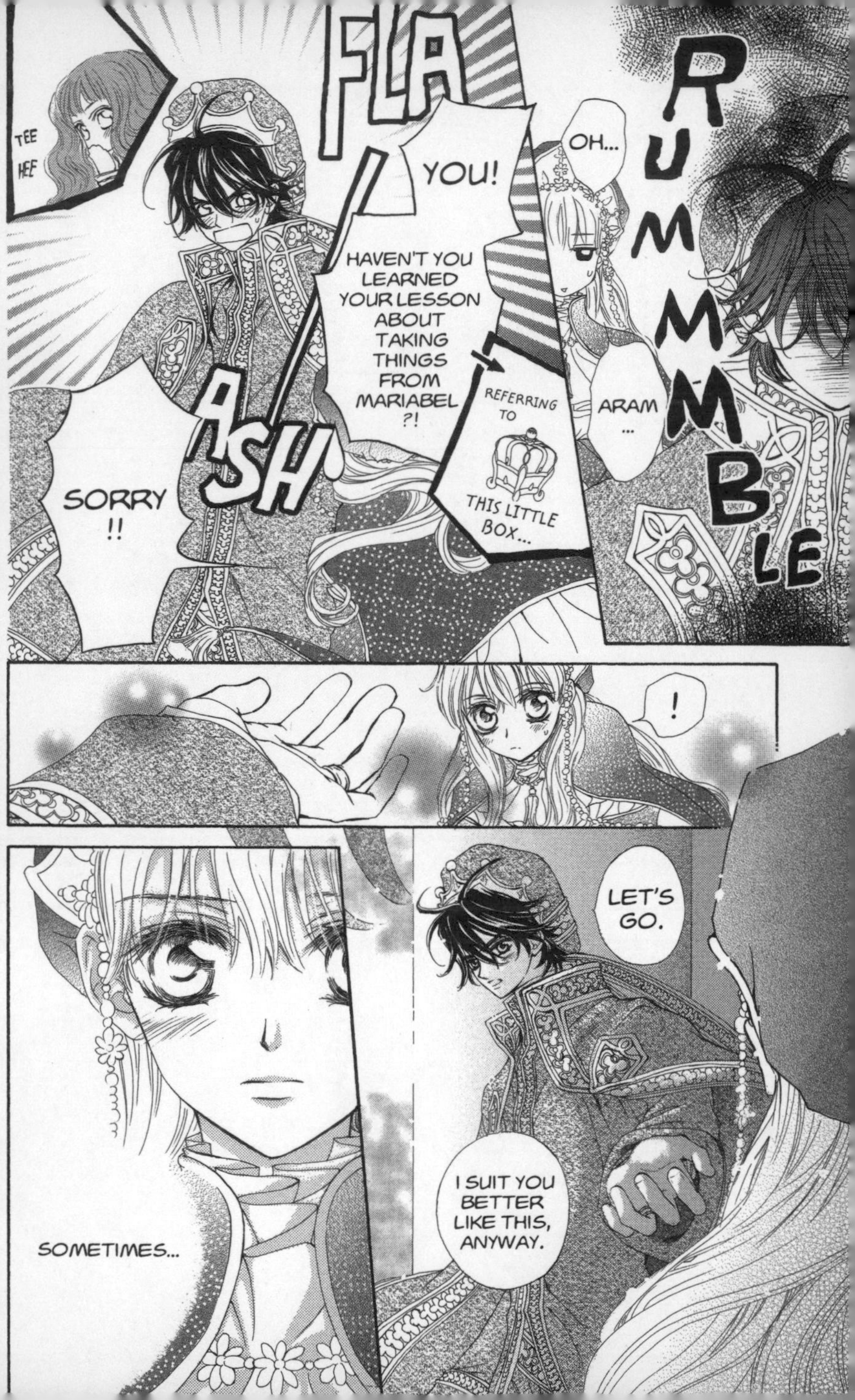
OH...
RUMMMMBLE
ARAM...
FLASH
YOU!
HAVEN'T YOU LEARNED YOUR LESSON ABOUT TAKING THINGS FROM MARIABEL?!
REFERRING TO THIS LITTLE BOX...
TEE HEE
SORRY!!
!
LET'S GO.
I SUIT YOU BETTER LIKE THIS, ANYWAY.
SOMETIMES...

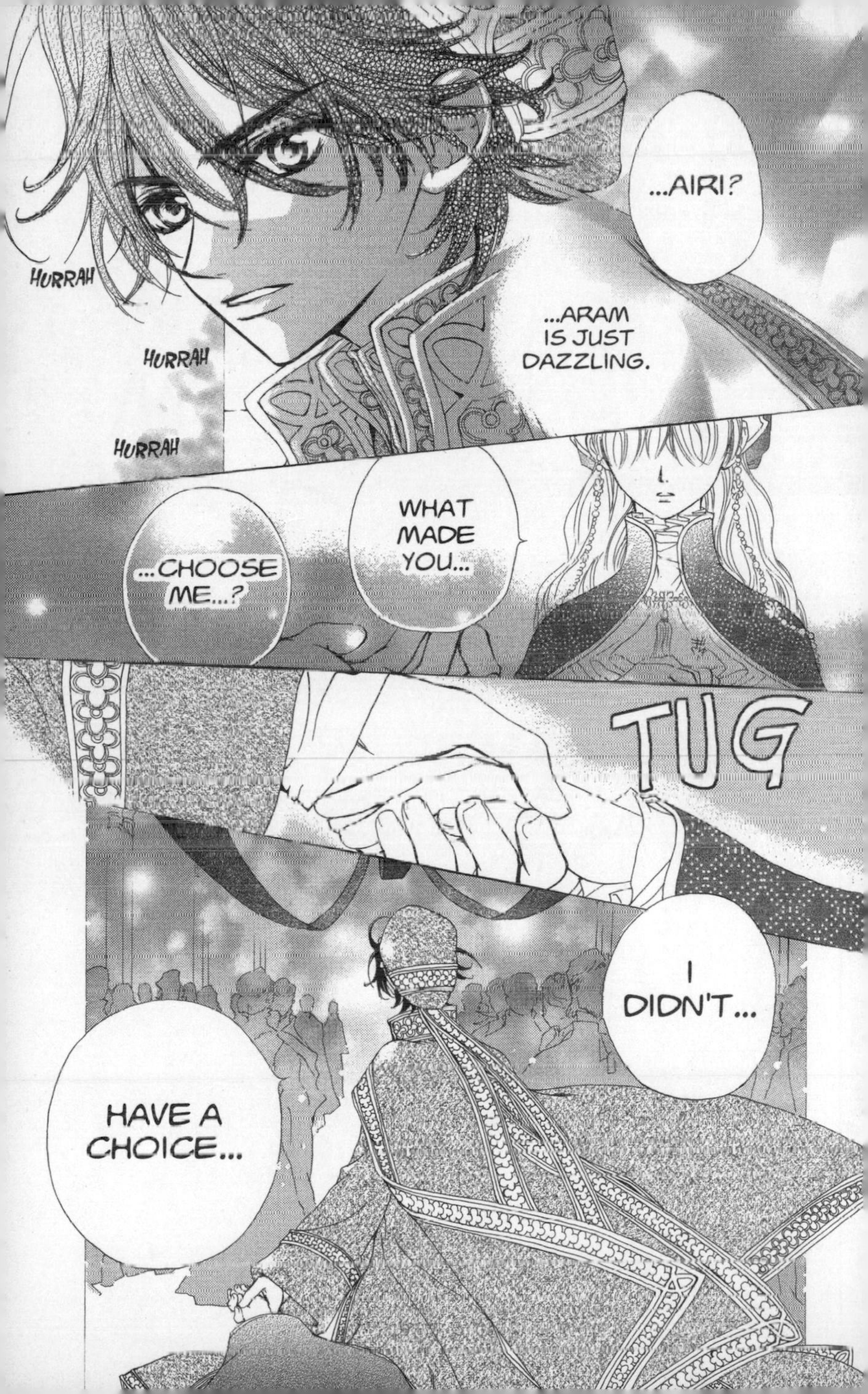
...AIRI?
...ARAM IS JUST DAZZLING.
HURRAH
HURRAH
HURRAH
WHAT MADE YOU...
...CHOOSE ME...?
TUG
I DIDN'T...
HAVE A CHOICE...

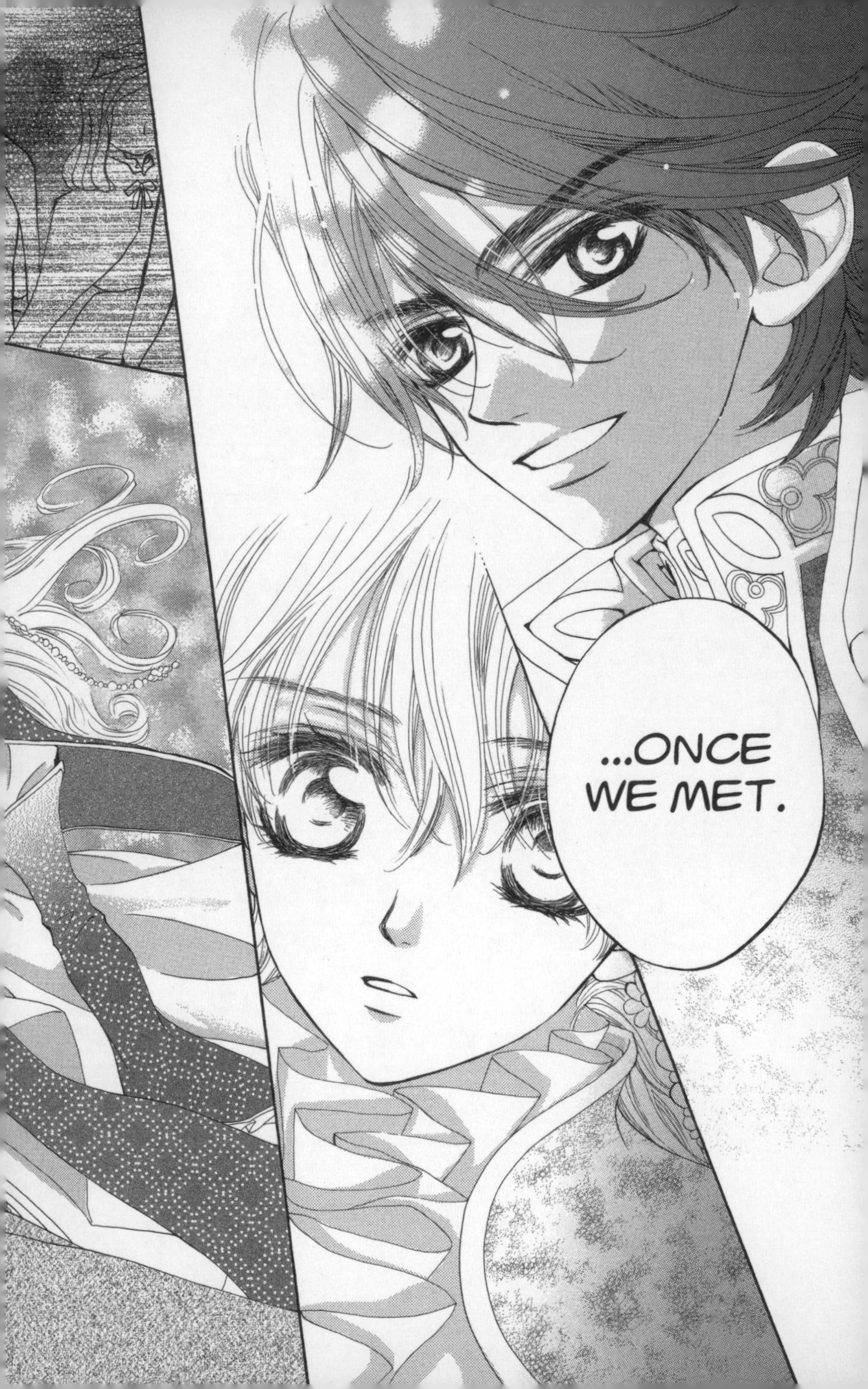
...ONCE WE MET.

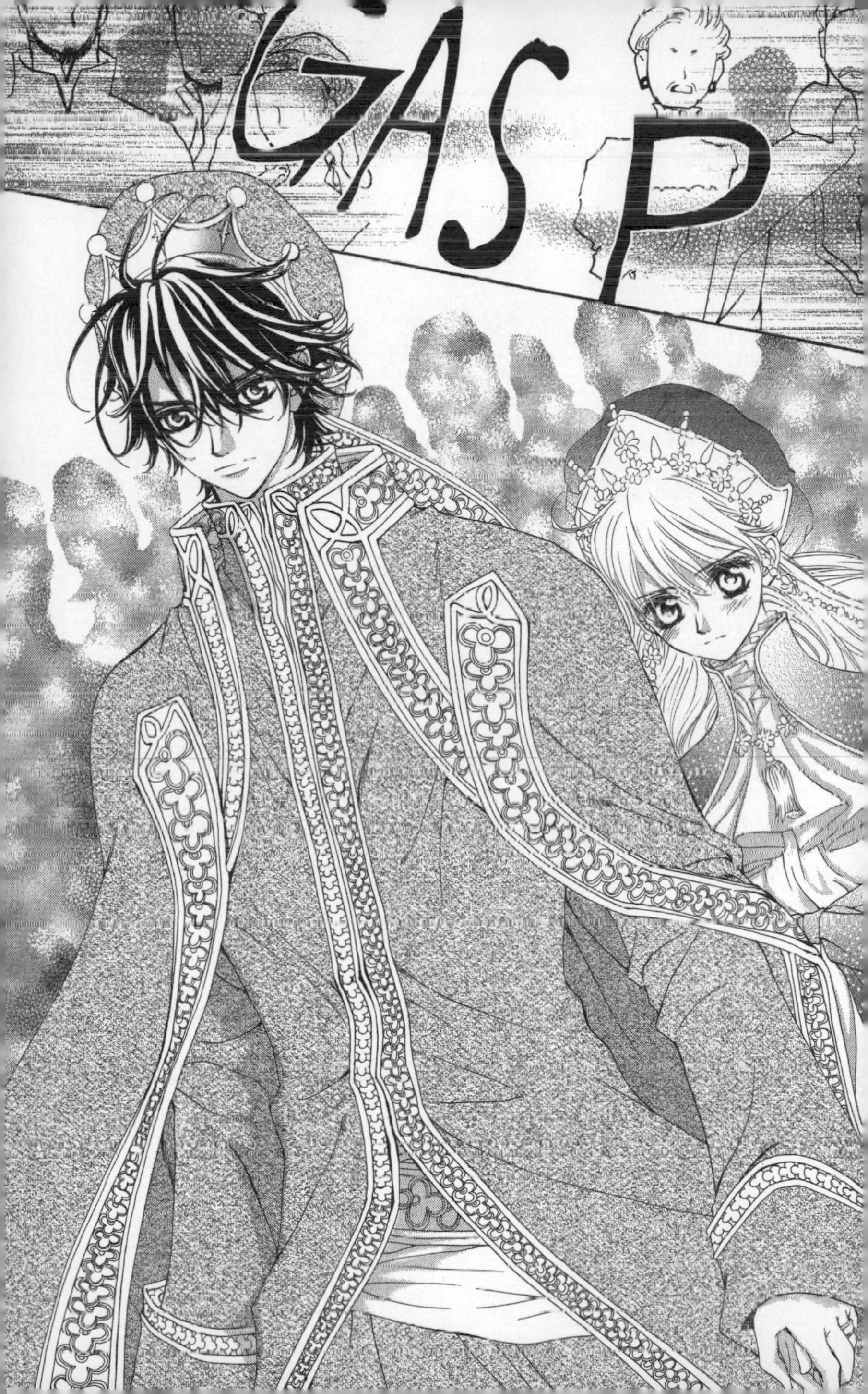
GASP

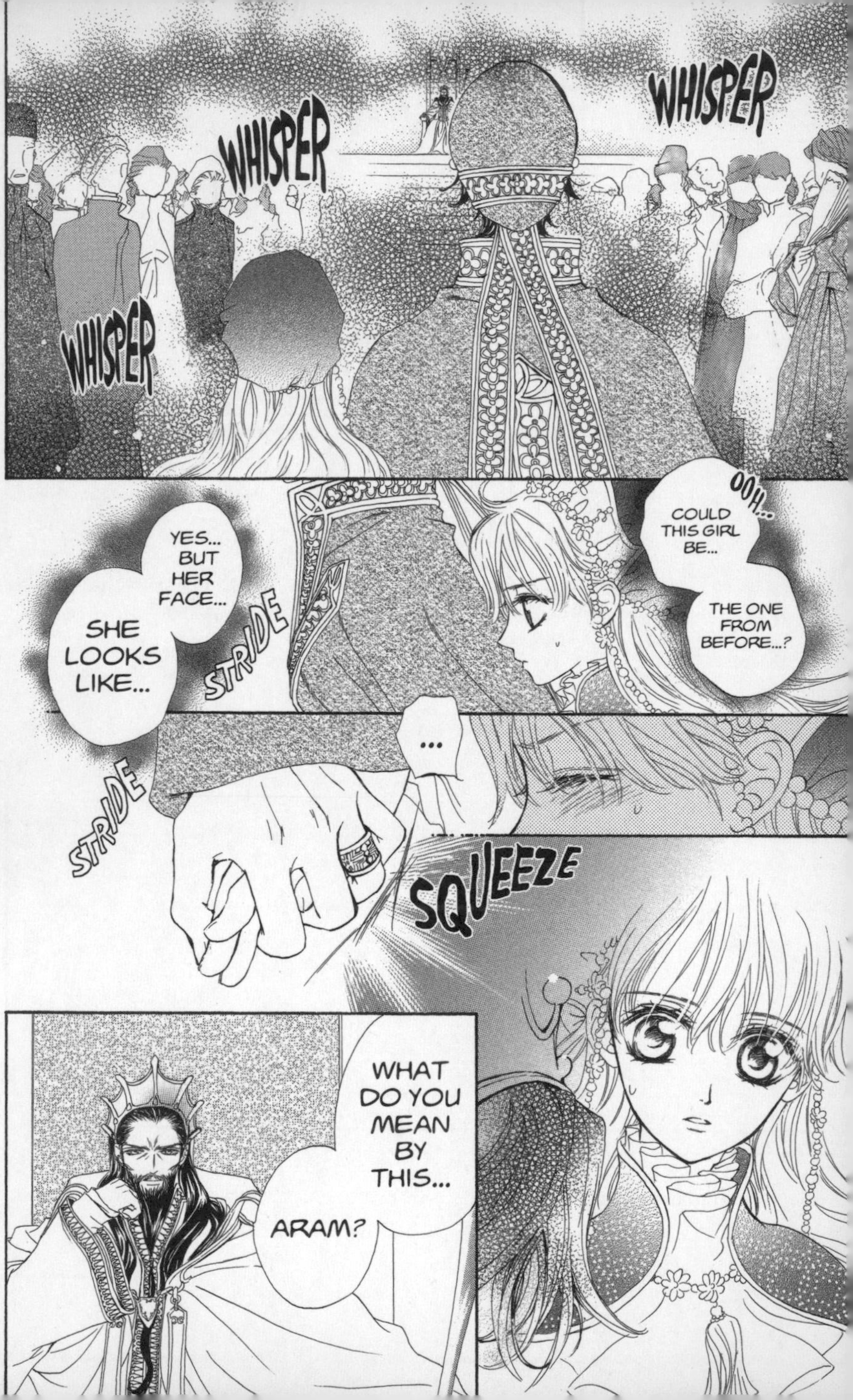
WHISPER
WHISPER
WHISPER
OOH...
COULD THIS GIRL BE...
THE ONE FROM BEFORE...?
YES... BUT HER FACE...
STRIDE
SHE LOOKS LIKE...
...
STRIDE
SQUEEZE
WHAT DO YOU MEAN BY THIS...
ARAM?

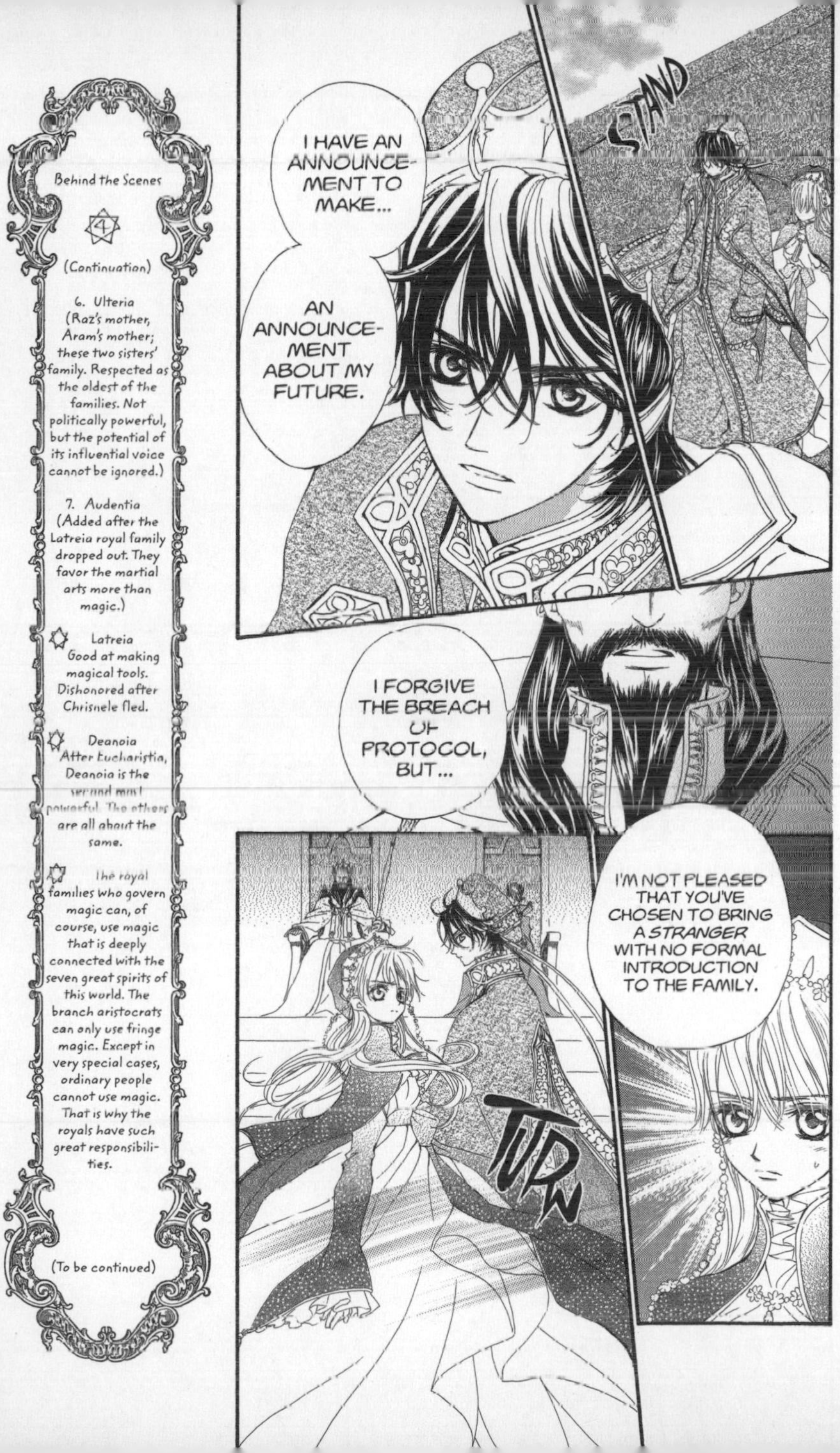
STAND
I HAVE AN ANNOUNCEMENT TO MAKE...
AN ANNOUNCEMENT ABOUT MY FUTURE.
I FORGIVE THE BREACH OF PROTOCOL, BUT...
I'M NOT PLEASED THAT YOU'VE CHOSEN TO BRING A *STRANGER* WITH NO FORMAL INTRODUCTION TO THE FAMILY.
TURN

Behind the Scenes

4

(Continuation)

6. Ulteria
(Raz's mother, Aram's mother; these two sisters' family. Respected as the oldest of the families. Not politically powerful, but the potential of its influential voice cannot be ignored.)

7. Audentia
(Added after the Latreia royal family dropped out. They favor the martial arts more than magic.)

✡ Latreia
Good at making magical tools. Dishonored after Chrisnele fled.

✡ Deanoia
After Eucharistia, Deanoia is the second most powerful. The others are all about the same.

✡ The royal families who govern magic can, of course, use magic that is deeply connected with the seven great spirits of this world. The branch aristocrats can only use fringe magic. Except in very special cases, ordinary people cannot use magic. That is why the royals have such great responsibilities.

(To be continued)

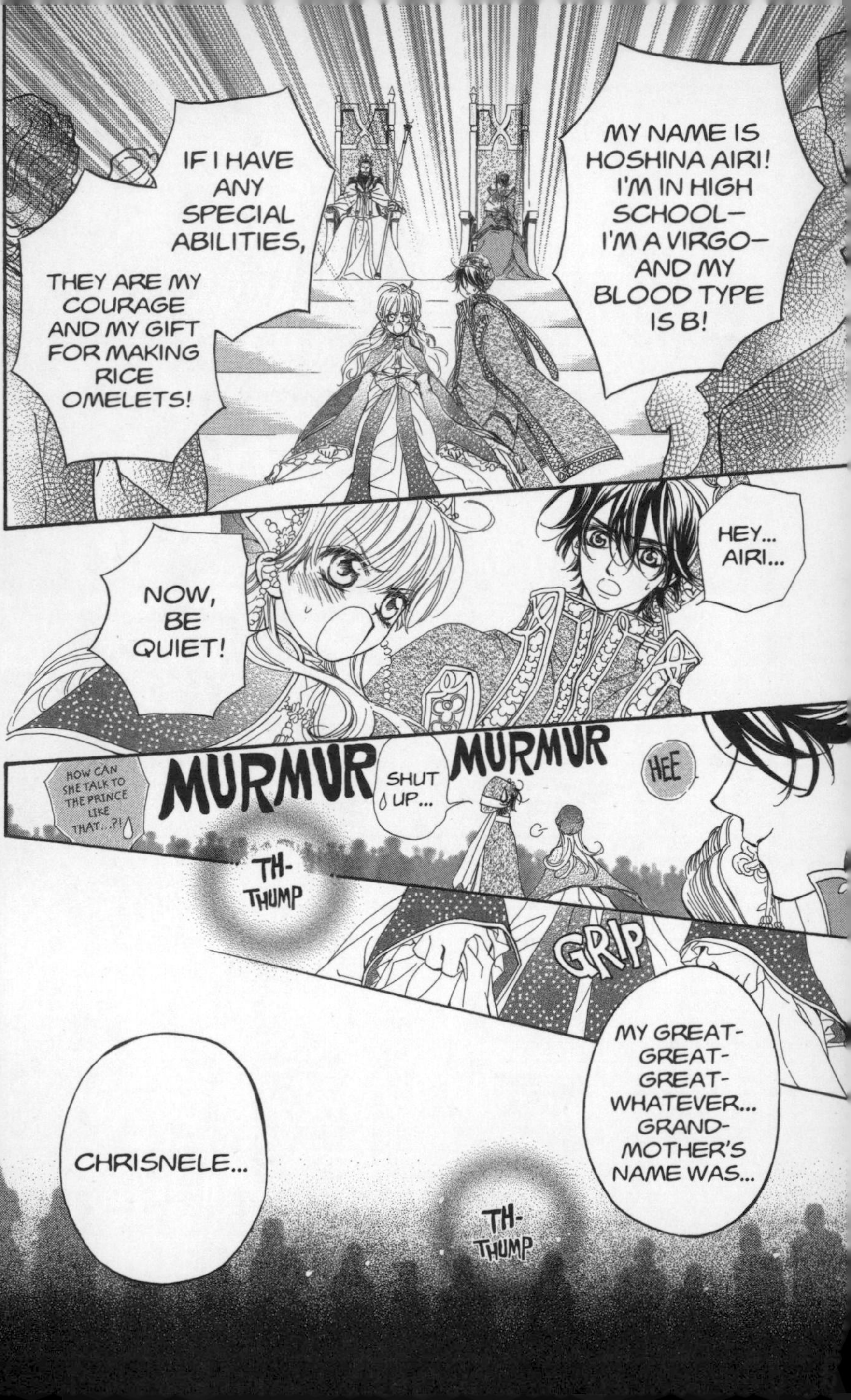
MY NAME IS HOSHINA AIRI! I'M IN HIGH SCHOOL— I'M A VIRGO— AND MY BLOOD TYPE IS B!
IF I HAVE ANY SPECIAL ABILITIES,
THEY ARE MY COURAGE AND MY GIFT FOR MAKING RICE OMELETS!
HEY... AIRI...
NOW, BE QUIET!
HEE
MURMUR
SHUT UP...
MURMUR
HOW CAN SHE TALK TO THE PRINCE LIKE THAT...?!
TH-THUMP
GRIP
MY GREAT-GREAT-GREAT-WHATEVER... GRANDMOTHER'S NAME WAS...
CHRISNELE...
TH-THUMP

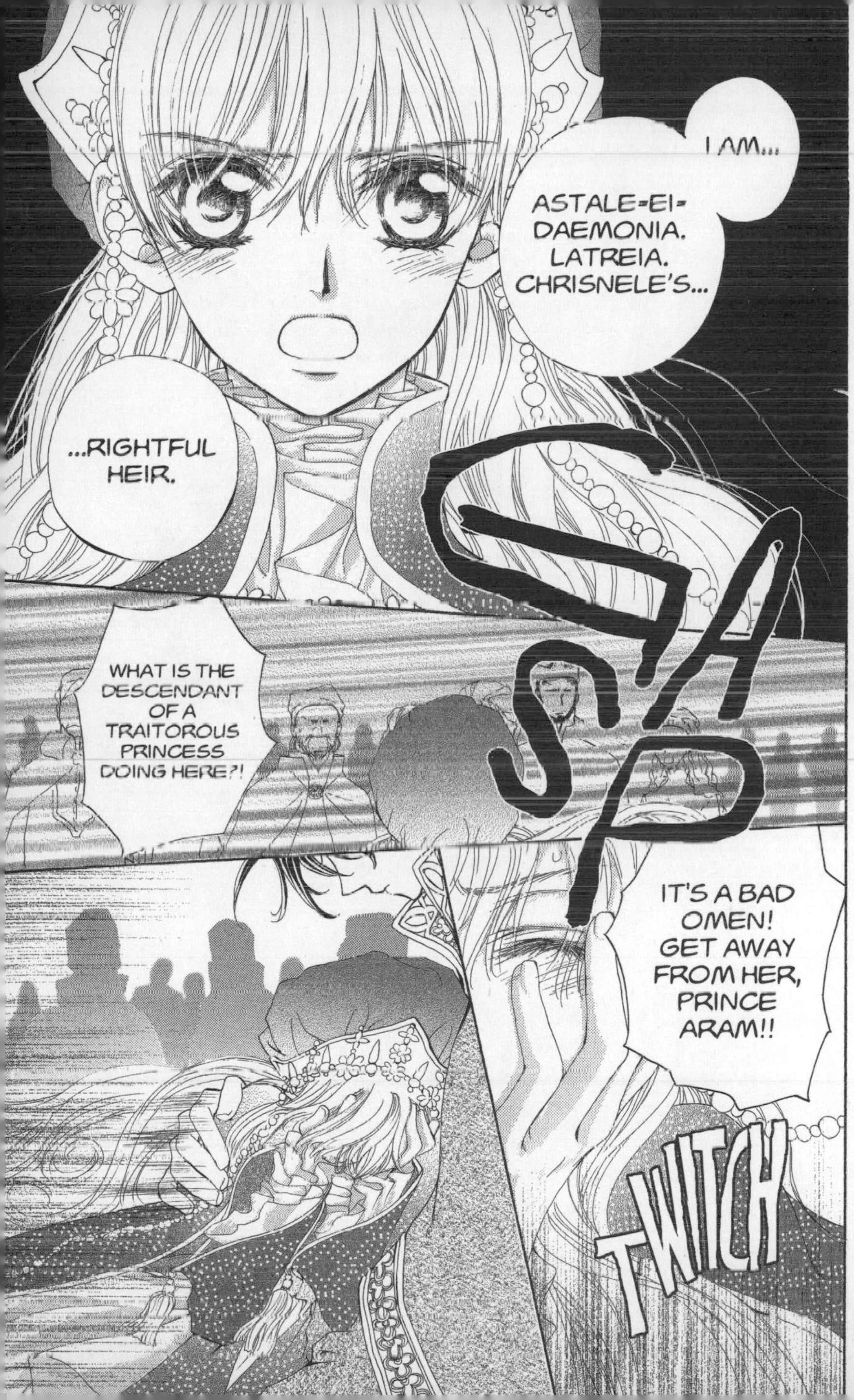
I AM...
ASTALE=EI=DAEMONIA. LATREIA. CHRISNELE'S...
...RIGHTFUL HEIR.
GASP
WHAT IS THE DESCENDANT OF A TRAITOROUS PRINCESS DOING HERE?!
IT'S A BAD OMEN! GET AWAY FROM HER, PRINCE ARAM!!
TWITCH

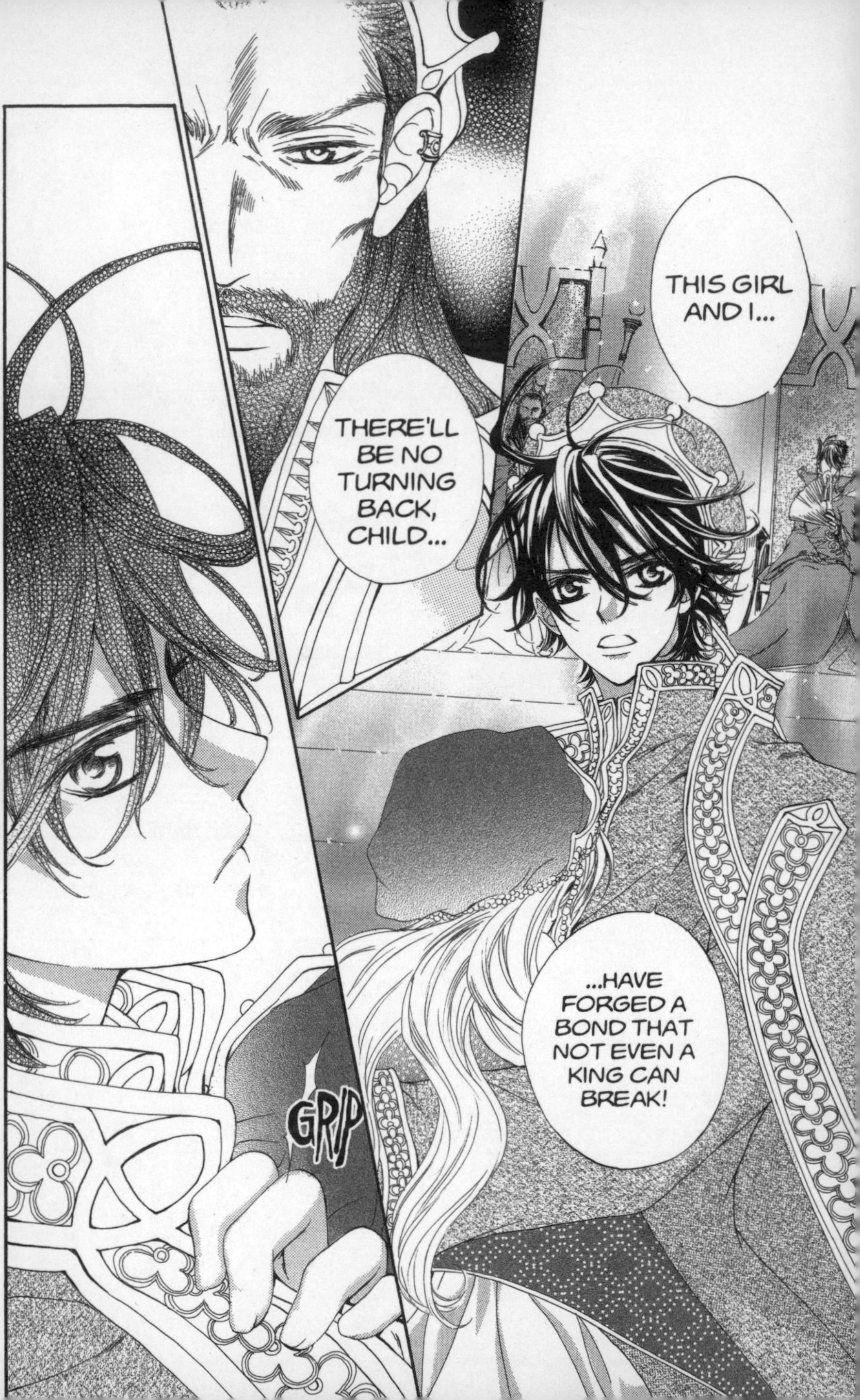
THIS GIRL AND I...
...HAVE FORGED A BOND THAT NOT EVEN A KING CAN BREAK!
THERE'LL BE NO TURNING BACK, CHILD...
GRIP

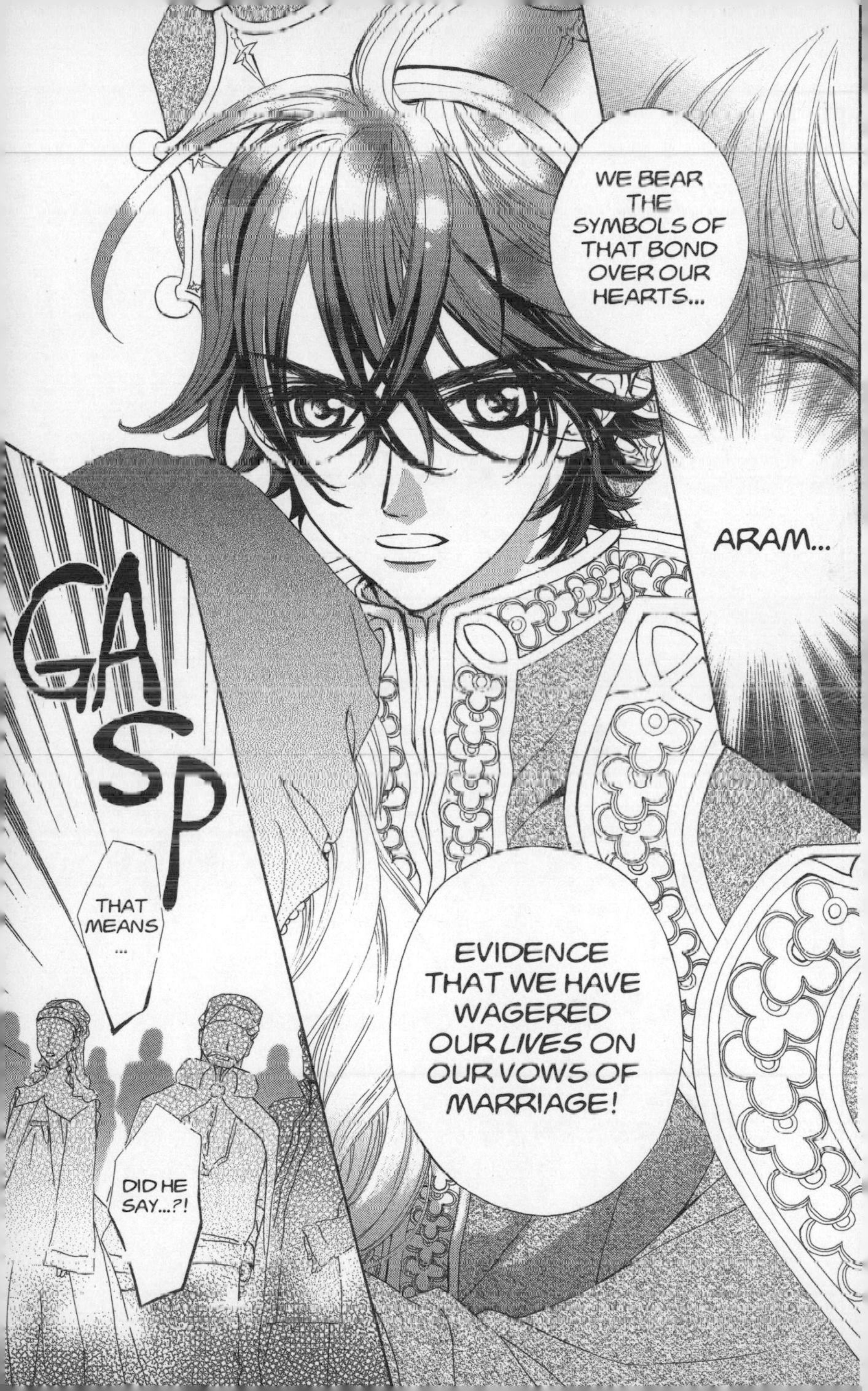
WE BEAR THE SYMBOLS OF THAT BOND OVER OUR HEARTS...
ARAM...
EVIDENCE THAT WE HAVE WAGERED OUR *LIVES* ON OUR VOWS OF MARRIAGE!
GASP
THAT MEANS...
DID HE SAY...?!

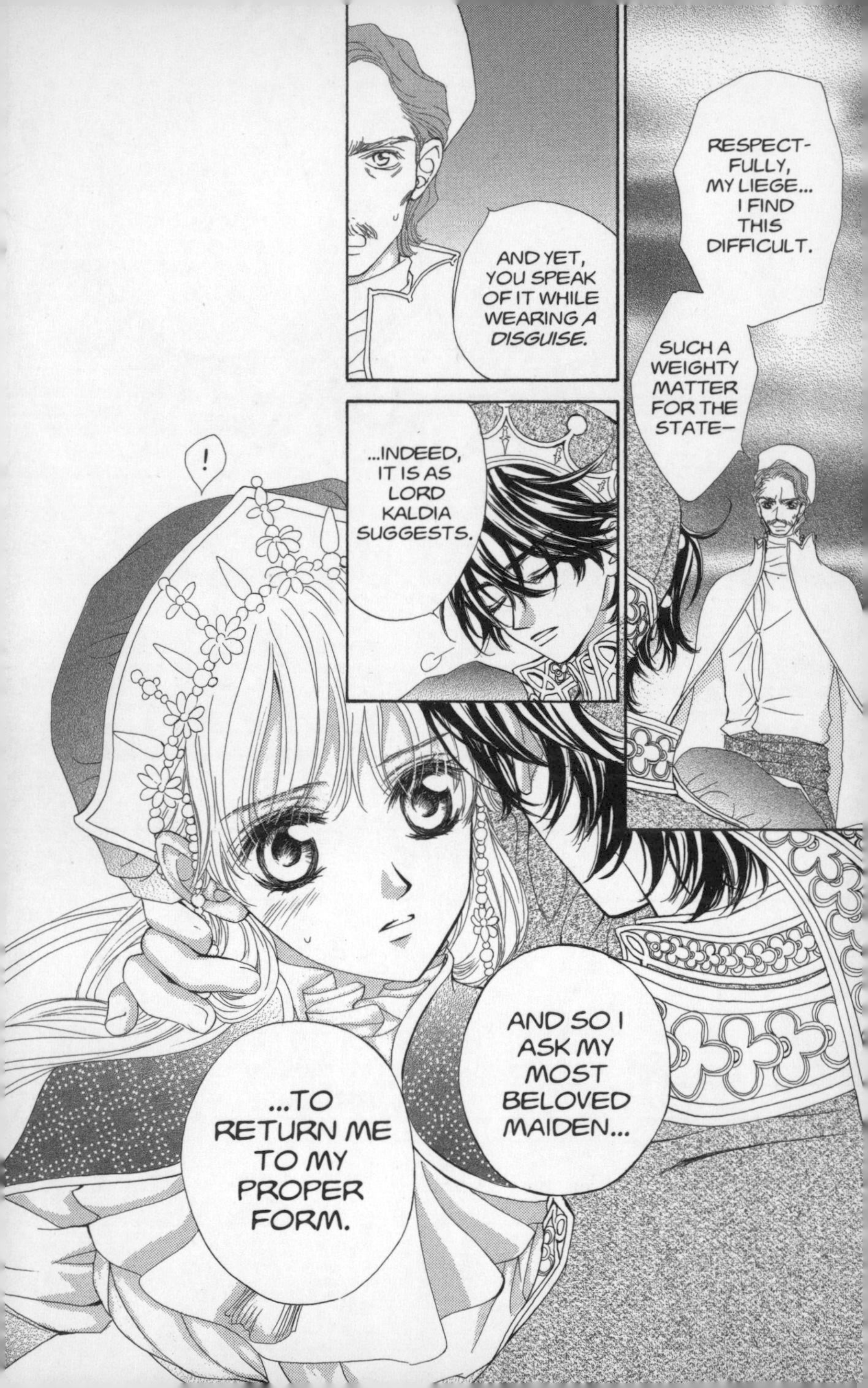
RESPECT-FULLY, MY LIEGE... I FIND THIS DIFFICULT.
SUCH A WEIGHTY MATTER FOR THE STATE–
AND YET, YOU SPEAK OF IT WHILE WEARING A *DISGUISE.*
...INDEED, IT IS AS LORD KALDIA SUGGESTS.
!
AND SO I ASK MY MOST BELOVED MAIDEN...
...TO RETURN ME TO MY PROPER FORM.

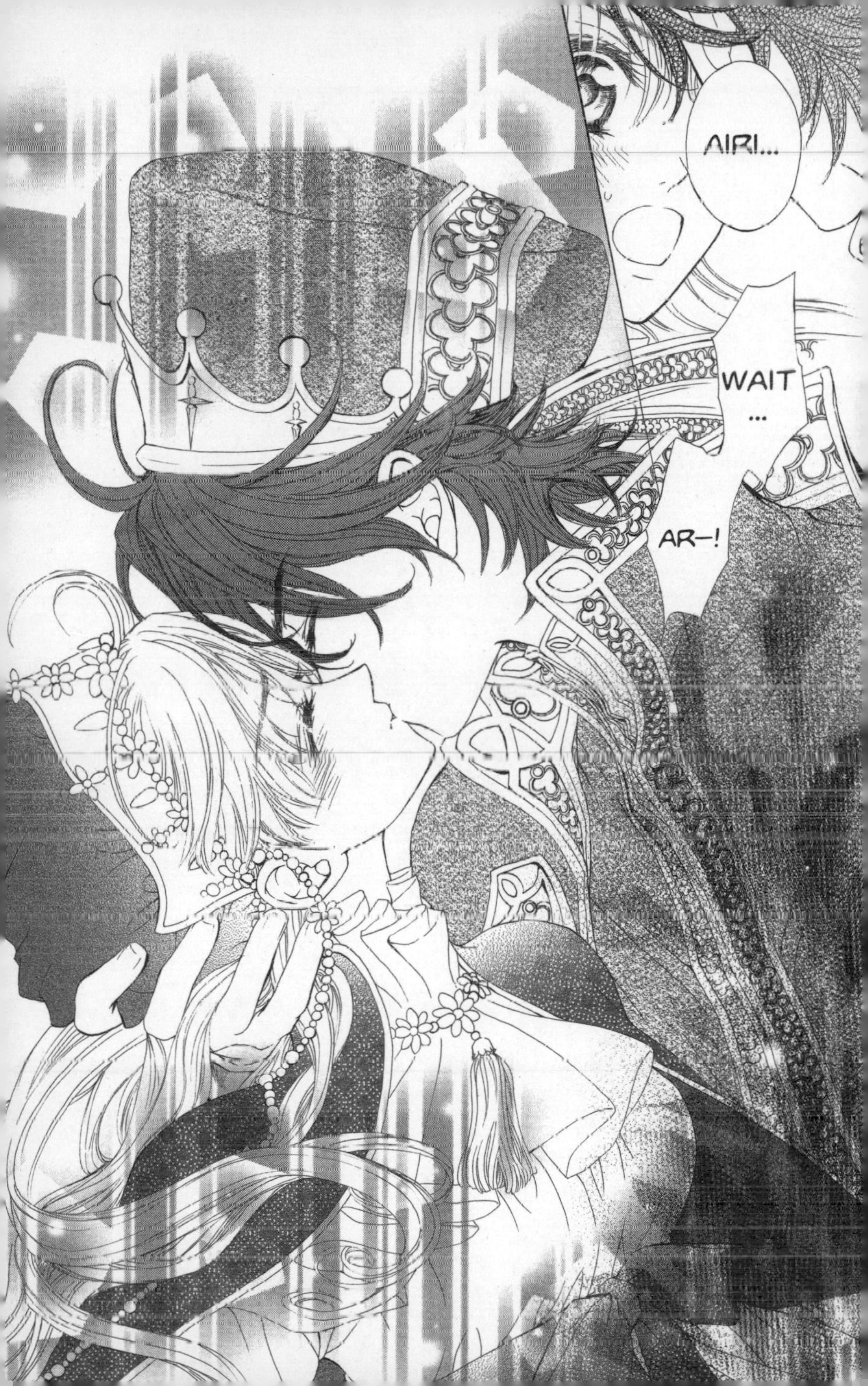
AIRI...
WAIT
...
AR-!

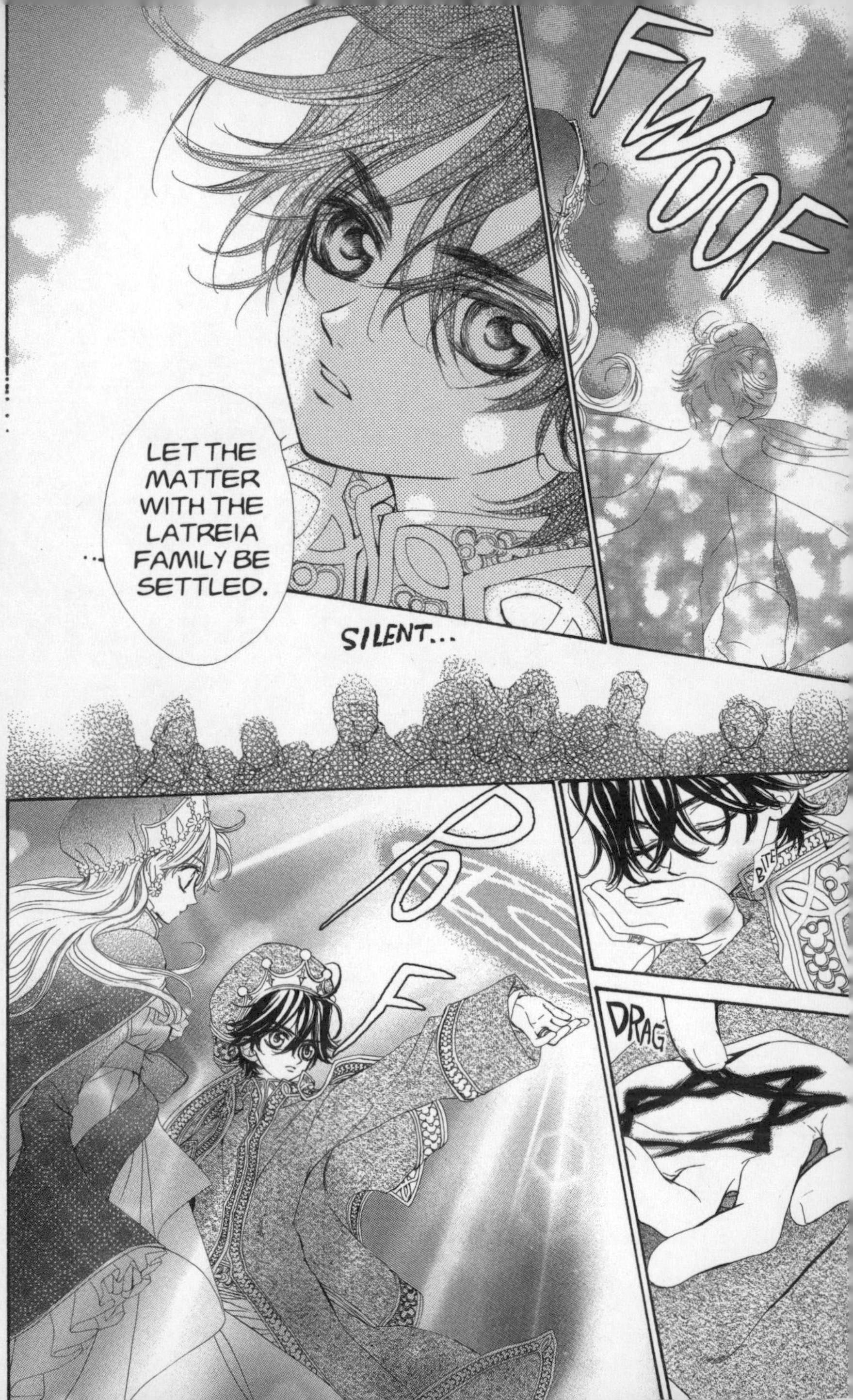
FWOOF
...LET THE MATTER WITH THE LATREIA FAMILY BE SETTLED.
SILENT...
BITE
DRAG
POF

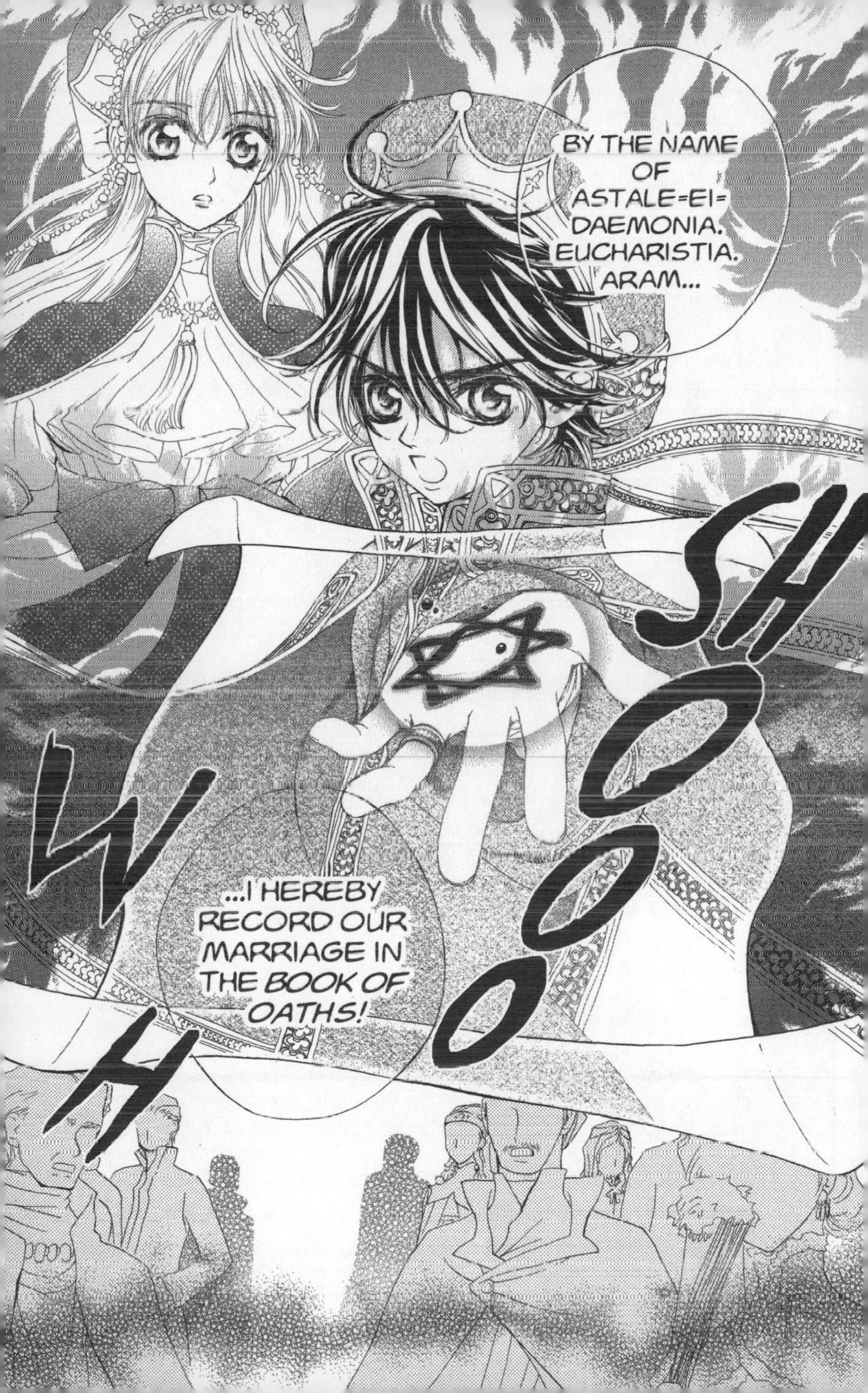
BY THE NAME OF ASTALE=EI=DAEMONIA. EUCHARISTIA. ARAM...
SHOOOSH
...I HEREBY RECORD OUR MARRIAGE IN THE *BOOK OF OATHS!*

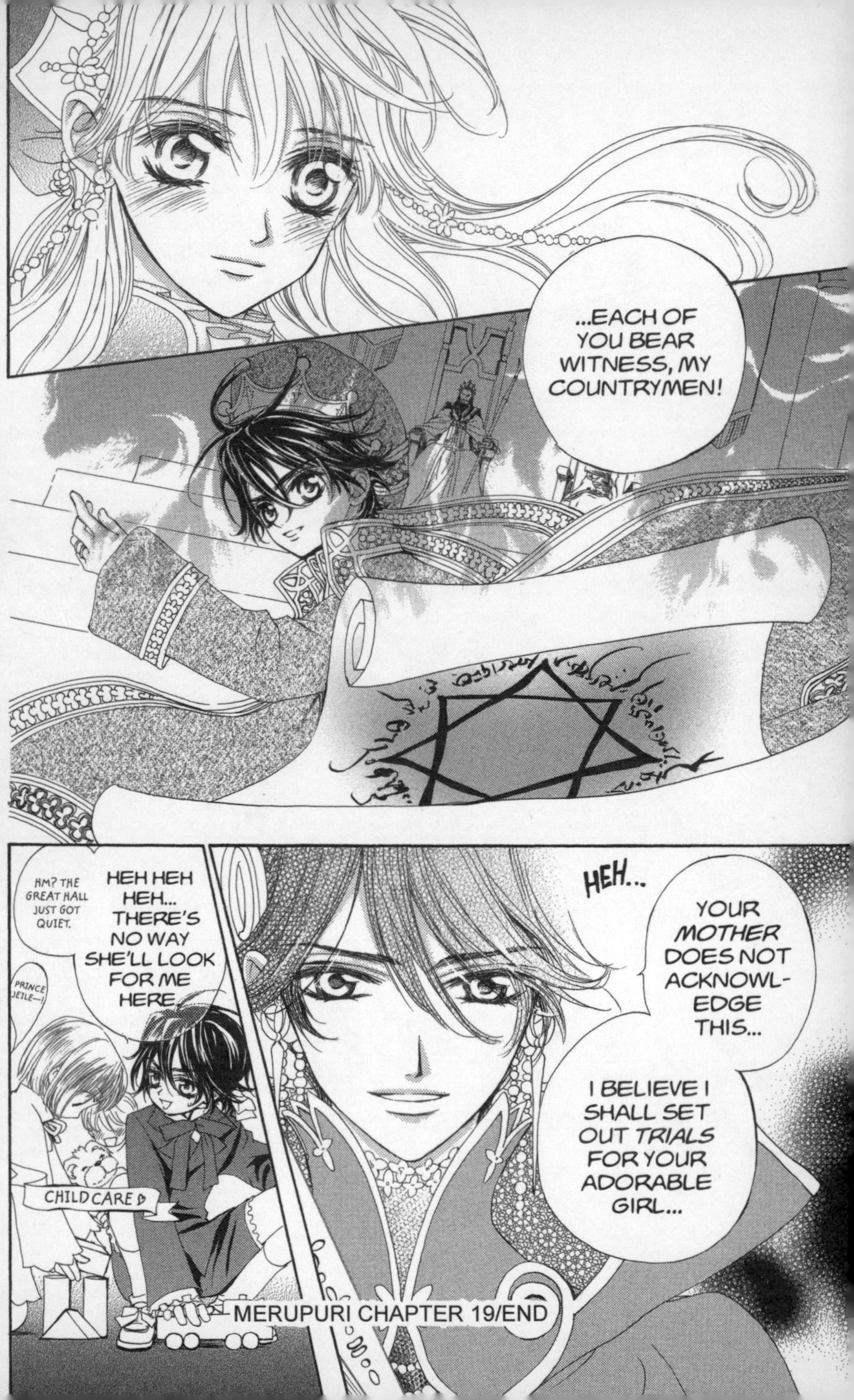
...EACH OF YOU BEAR WITNESS, MY COUNTRYMEN!
HEH...
YOUR *MOTHER* DOES NOT ACKNOWLEDGE THIS...
I BELIEVE I SHALL SET OUT *TRIALS* FOR YOUR ADORABLE GIRL...
HEH HEH HEH... THERE'S NO WAY SHE'LL LOOK FOR ME HERE.
HM? THE GREAT HALL JUST GOT QUIET.
PRINCE JEILE--!
CHILD CARE ♡
MERUPURI CHAPTER 19/END

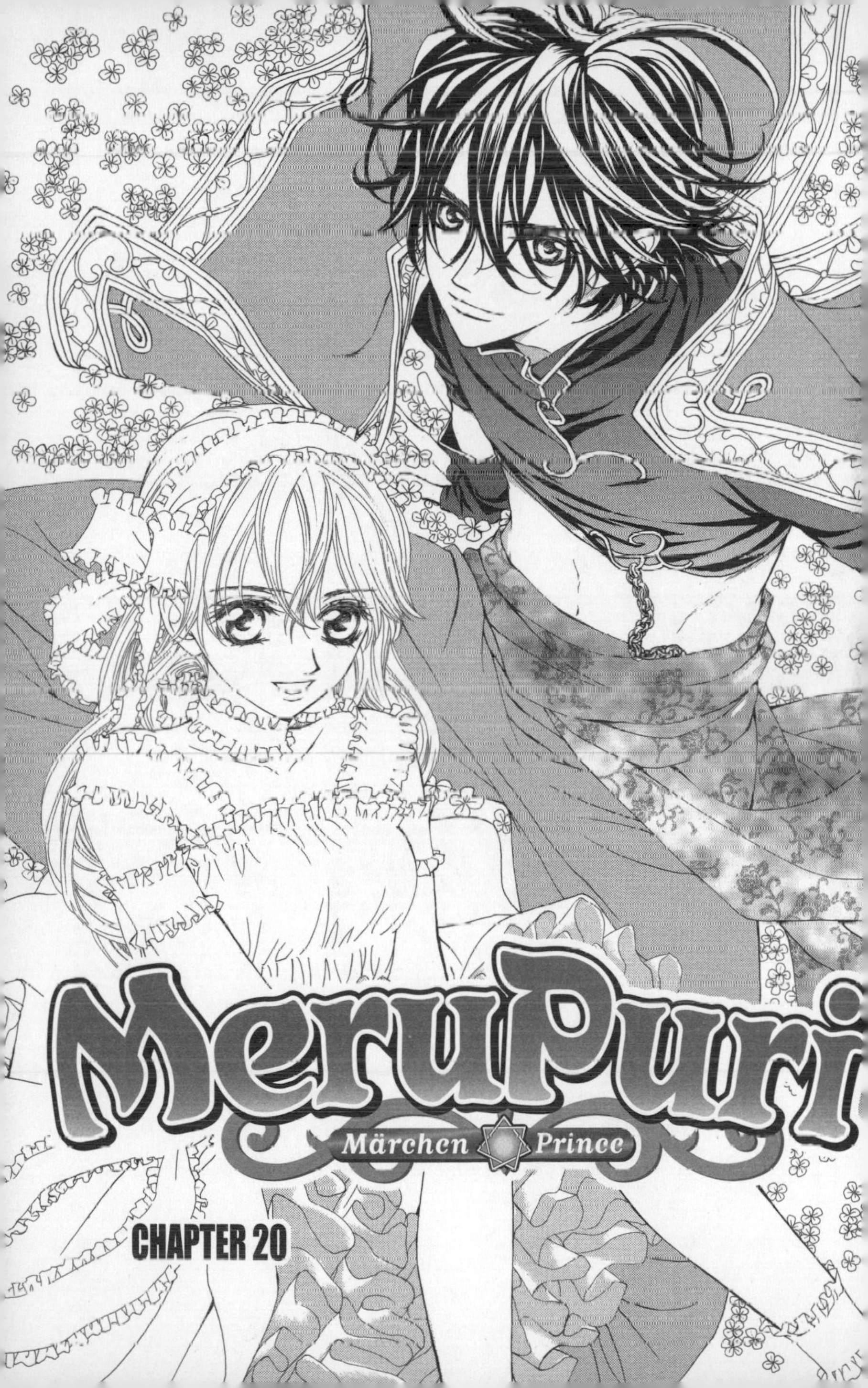
MeruPuri
Märchen Prince
CHAPTER 20

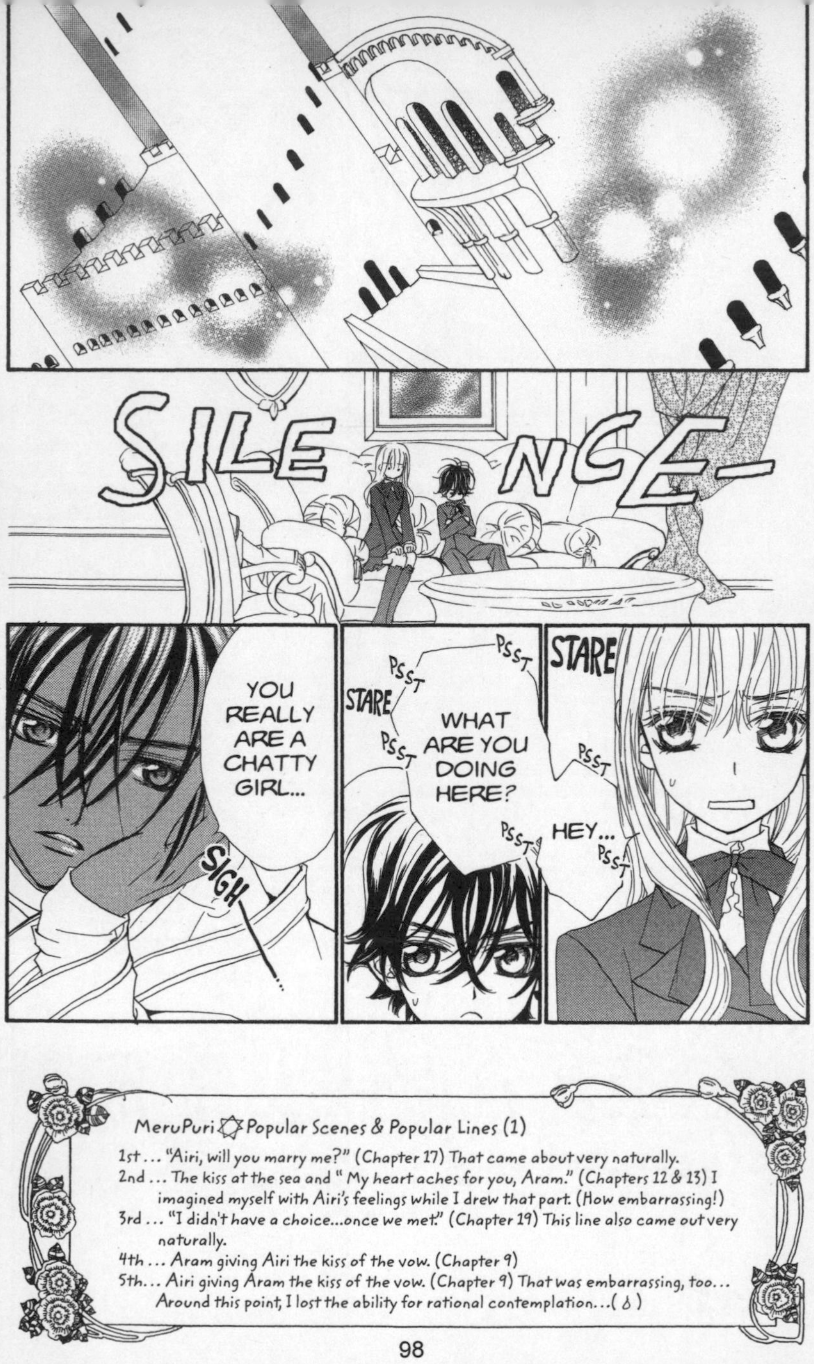
SILENCE-
STARE
PSST
HEY...
PSST
PSST
STARE
PSST
WHAT ARE YOU DOING HERE?
PSST
YOU REALLY ARE A CHATTY GIRL...
SIGH

MeruPuri ✡ Popular Scenes & Popular Lines (1)

1st ... "Airi, will you marry me?" (Chapter 17) That came about very naturally.
2nd ... The kiss at the sea and " My heart aches for you, Aram." (Chapters 12 & 13) I imagined myself with Airi's feelings while I drew that part. (How embarrassing!)
3rd ... "I didn't have a choice...once we met." (Chapter 19) This line also came out very naturally.
4th ... Aram giving Airi the kiss of the vow. (Chapter 9)
5th... Airi giving Aram the kiss of the vow. (Chapter 9) That was embarrassing, too... Around this point, I lost the ability for rational contemplation...( ♪ )

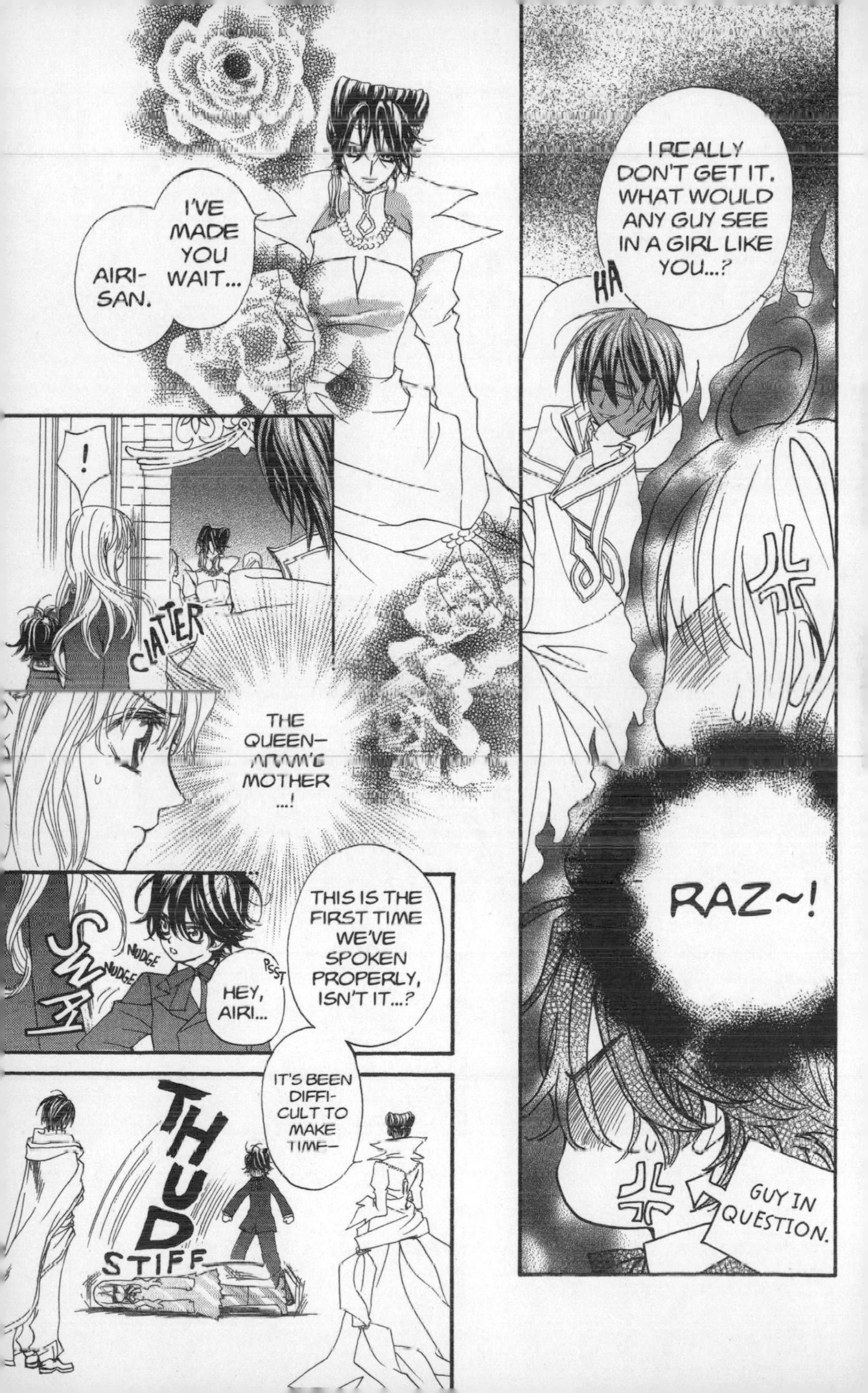
I REALLY DON'T GET IT. WHAT WOULD ANY GUY SEE IN A GIRL LIKE YOU...?
HA
RAZ~!
GUY IN QUESTION.
I'VE MADE YOU WAIT... AIRI-SAN.
!
CLATTER
THE QUEEN— ARAM'S MOTHER ...!
THIS IS THE FIRST TIME WE'VE SPOKEN PROPERLY, ISN'T IT...?
PSSST
HEY, AIRI...
NUDGE NUDGE
SWAH
IT'S BEEN DIFFI-CULT TO MAKE TIME—
THUD
STIFF

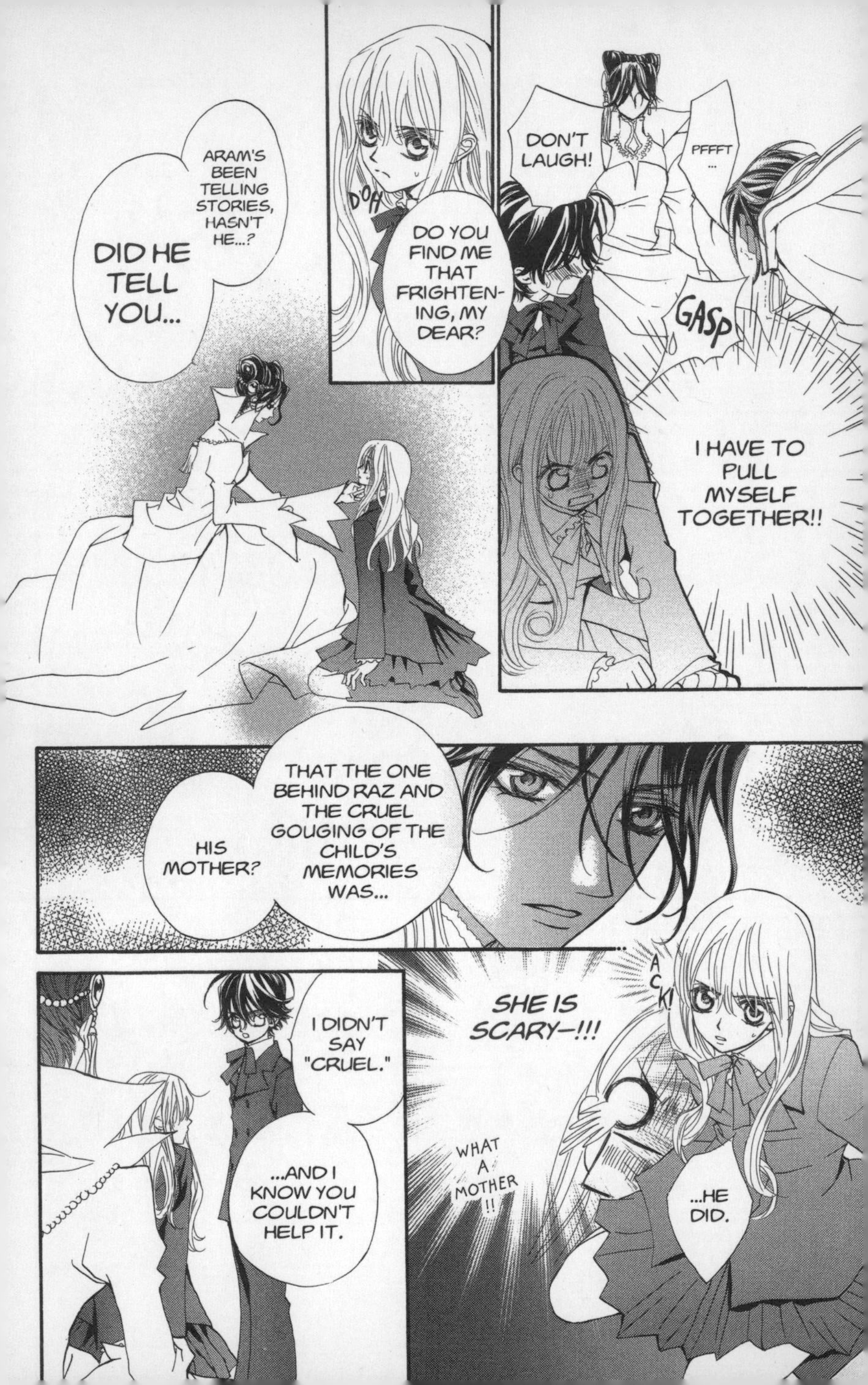
DON'T LAUGH!
PFFFT ...
GASP
I HAVE TO PULL MYSELF TOGETHER!!
D'OH
DO YOU FIND ME THAT FRIGHTEN-ING, MY DEAR?
ARAM'S BEEN TELLING STORIES, HASN'T HE...?
DID HE TELL YOU...
THAT THE ONE BEHIND RAZ AND THE CRUEL GOUGING OF THE CHILD'S MEMORIES WAS...
HIS MOTHER?
ACK!
SHE IS SCARY–!!!
WHAT A MOTHER !!
...HE DID.
I DIDN'T SAY "CRUEL."
...AND I KNOW YOU COULDN'T HELP IT.

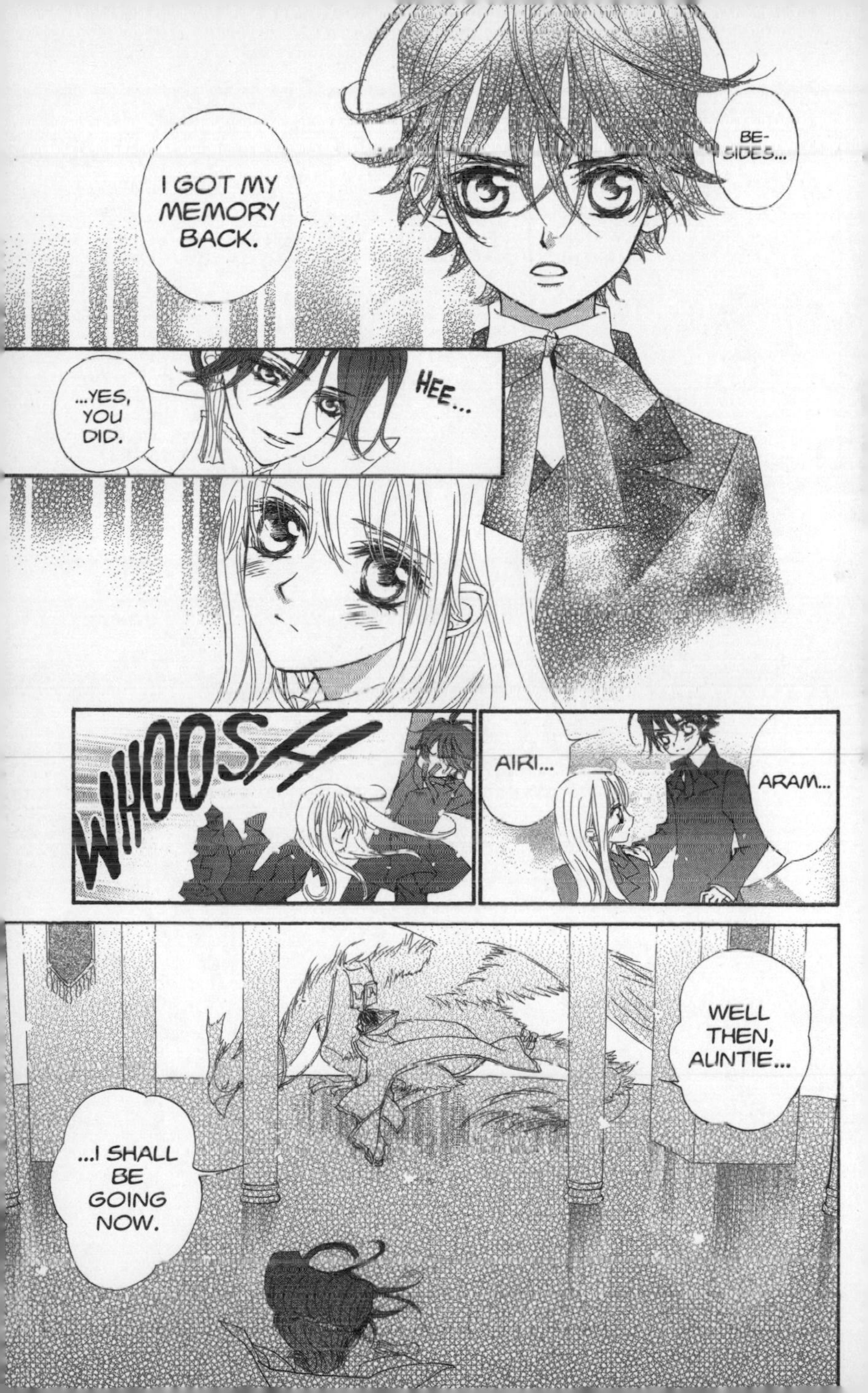
BE-SIDES...
I GOT MY MEMORY BACK.
HEE...
...YES, YOU DID.
ARAM...
AIRI...
WHOOSH
WELL THEN, AUNTIE...
...I SHALL BE GOING NOW.

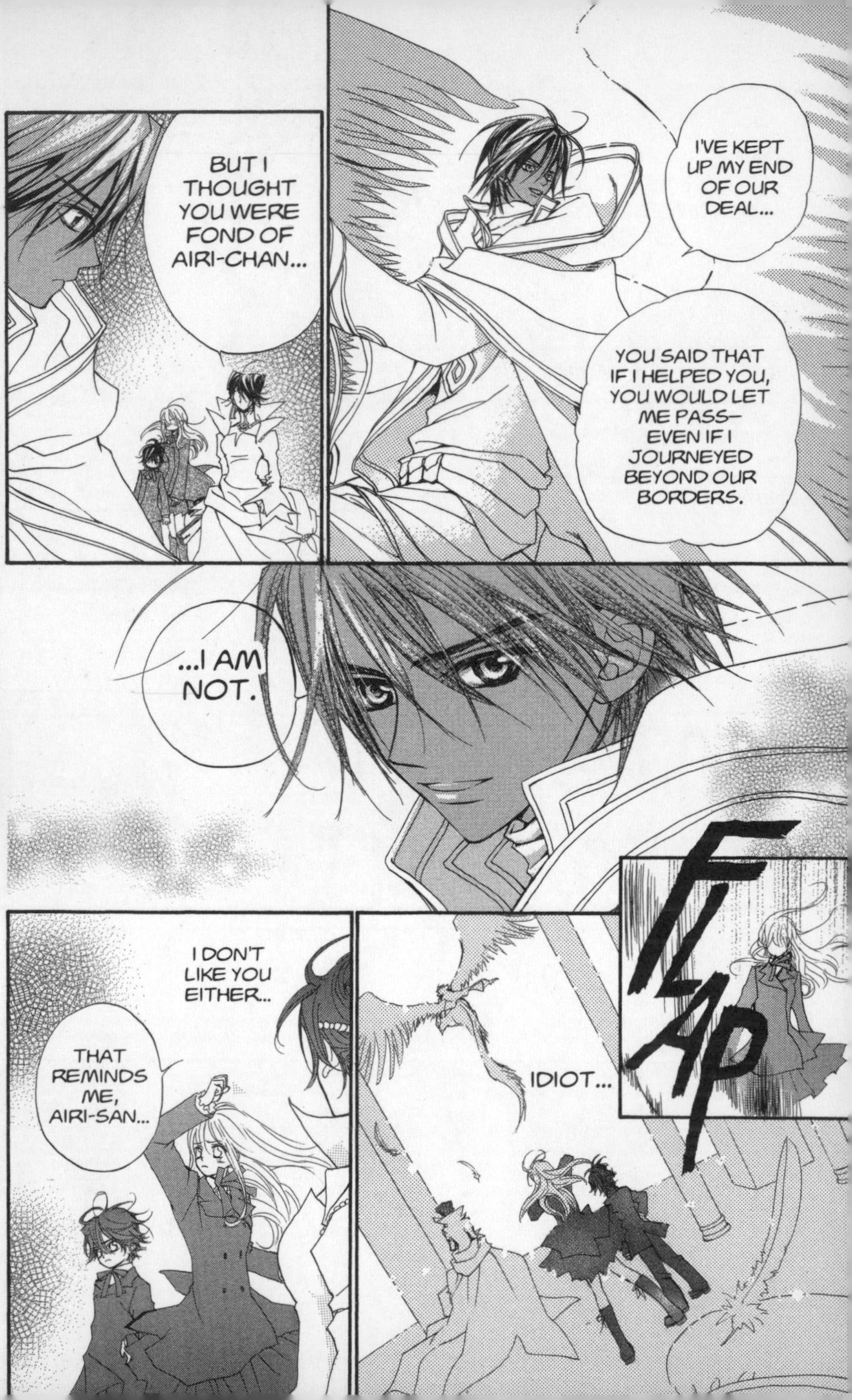
I'VE KEPT UP MY END OF OUR DEAL...
YOU SAID THAT IF I HELPED YOU, YOU WOULD LET ME PASS—EVEN IF I JOURNEYED BEYOND OUR BORDERS.
BUT I THOUGHT YOU WERE FOND OF AIRI-CHAN...
...I AM NOT.
FLAP
IDIOT...
I DON'T LIKE YOU EITHER..
THAT REMINDS ME, AIRI-SAN...

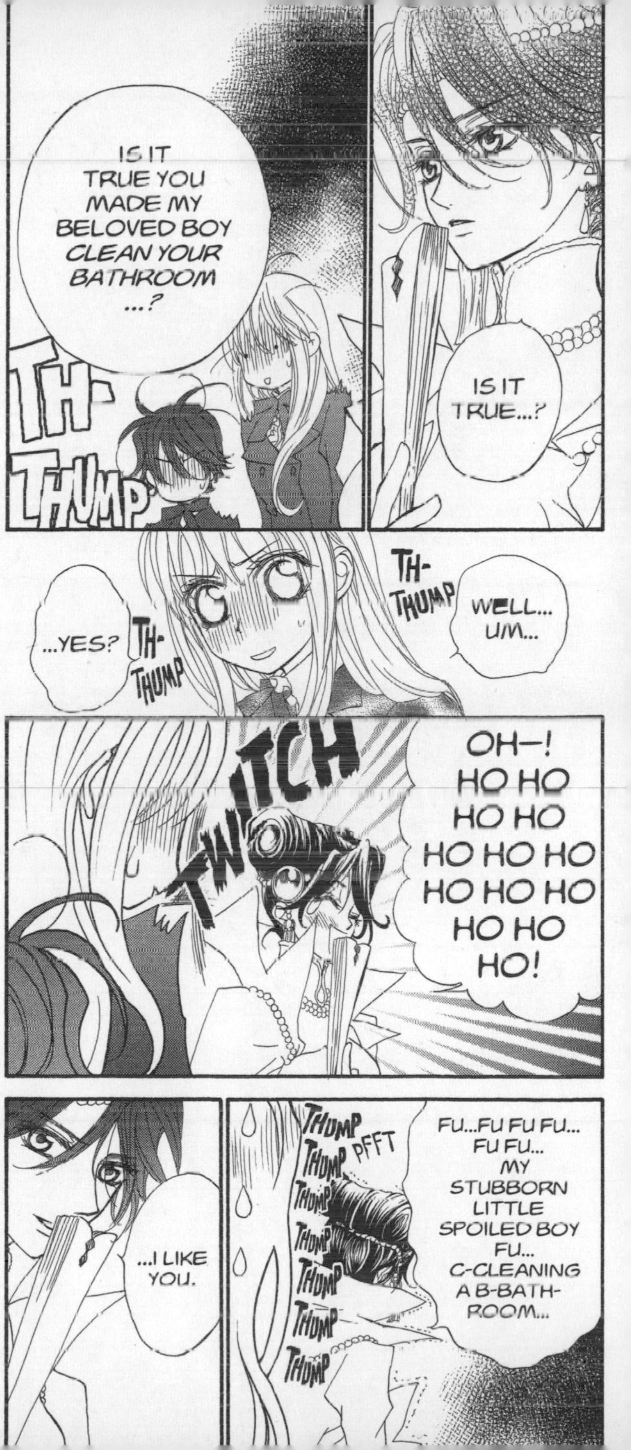
IS IT TRUE...?
IS IT TRUE YOU MADE MY BELOVED BOY CLEAN YOUR BATHROOM ...?
TH-THUMP
TH-THUMP
WELL... UM...
...YES?
TH-THUMP
OH—! HO HO HO HO HO HO HO HO HO HO HO HO HO!
TWITCH
FU...FU FU FU... FU FU... MY STUBBORN LITTLE SPOILED BOY FU... C-CLEANING A B-BATH-ROOM...
THUMP THUMP THUMP THUMP THUMP THUMP THUMP
PFFT
...I LIKE YOU.

Behind the Scenes

5

(Continuation)

Chapter 20. The chapter cover is an image of the two of them, laid back and happy. I was glad I finally got to draw them like that. At first, I thought it might be the last chapter. Now I wish I'd been able to draw more of Airi while she was still learning to use magic.

Chapter 21 + α
A side story. I really like the chapter cover. It reminds me of waiting for Cinderella. In this section I gave Lei, Raz, and Jeile monologues, and they proved to be surprisingly normal in their heads...
+α (plus alpha)'s "Secret Story I" came about in response to a number of letters wanting to know what happened to Raz. I thought I'd give a few hints...

(To be continued)

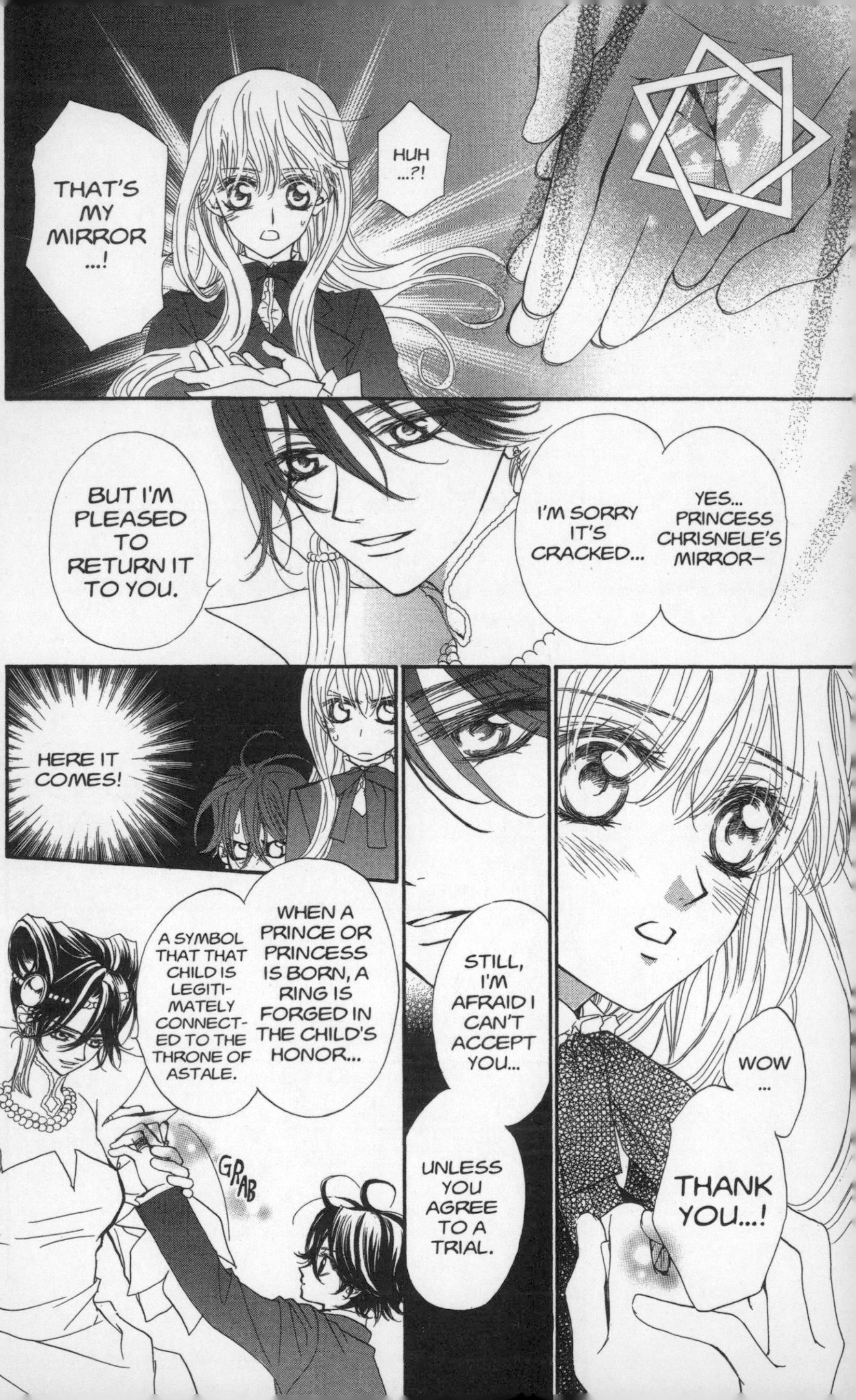
HUH ...?!
THAT'S MY MIRROR ...!
YES... PRINCESS CHRISNELE'S MIRROR—
I'M SORRY IT'S CRACKED...
BUT I'M PLEASED TO RETURN IT TO YOU.
WOW ...
THANK YOU...!
STILL, I'M AFRAID I CAN'T ACCEPT YOU...
UNLESS YOU AGREE TO A TRIAL.
HERE IT COMES!
WHEN A PRINCE OR PRINCESS IS BORN, A RING IS FORGED IN THE CHILD'S HONOR...
A SYMBOL THAT THAT CHILD IS LEGITI-MATELY CONNECT-ED TO THE THRONE OF ASTALE.
GRAB

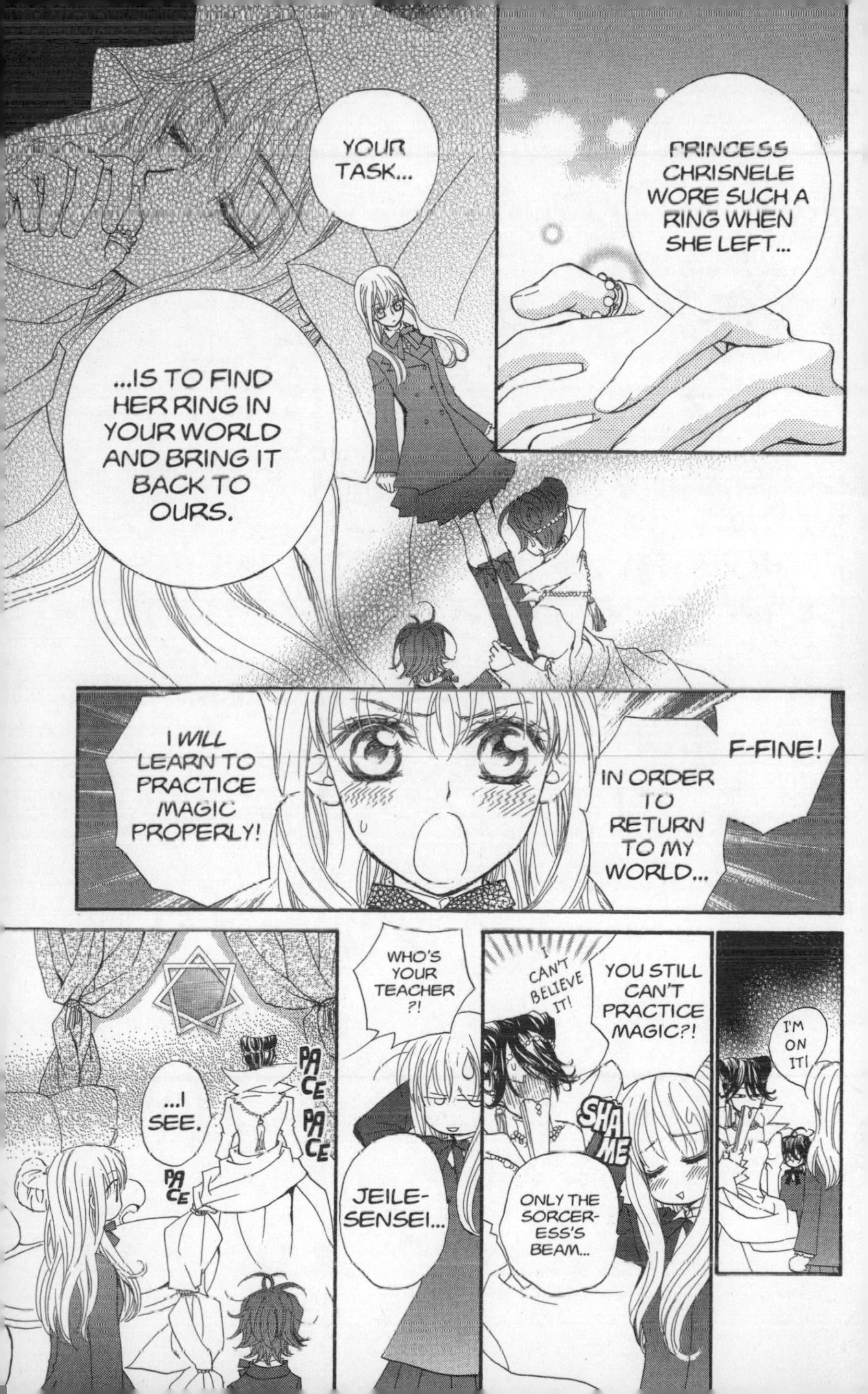
PRINCESS CHRISNELE WORE SUCH A RING WHEN SHE LEFT...
YOUR TASK...
...IS TO FIND HER RING IN YOUR WORLD AND BRING IT BACK TO OURS.
F-FINE!
IN ORDER TO RETURN TO MY WORLD...
I WILL LEARN TO PRACTICE MAGIC PROPERLY!
I'M ON IT!
YOU STILL CAN'T PRACTICE MAGIC?!
I CAN'T BELIEVE IT!
SHAME
ONLY THE SORCERESS'S BEAM...
WHO'S YOUR TEACHER?!
JEILE-SENSEI...
PACE PACE
...I SEE.
PACE

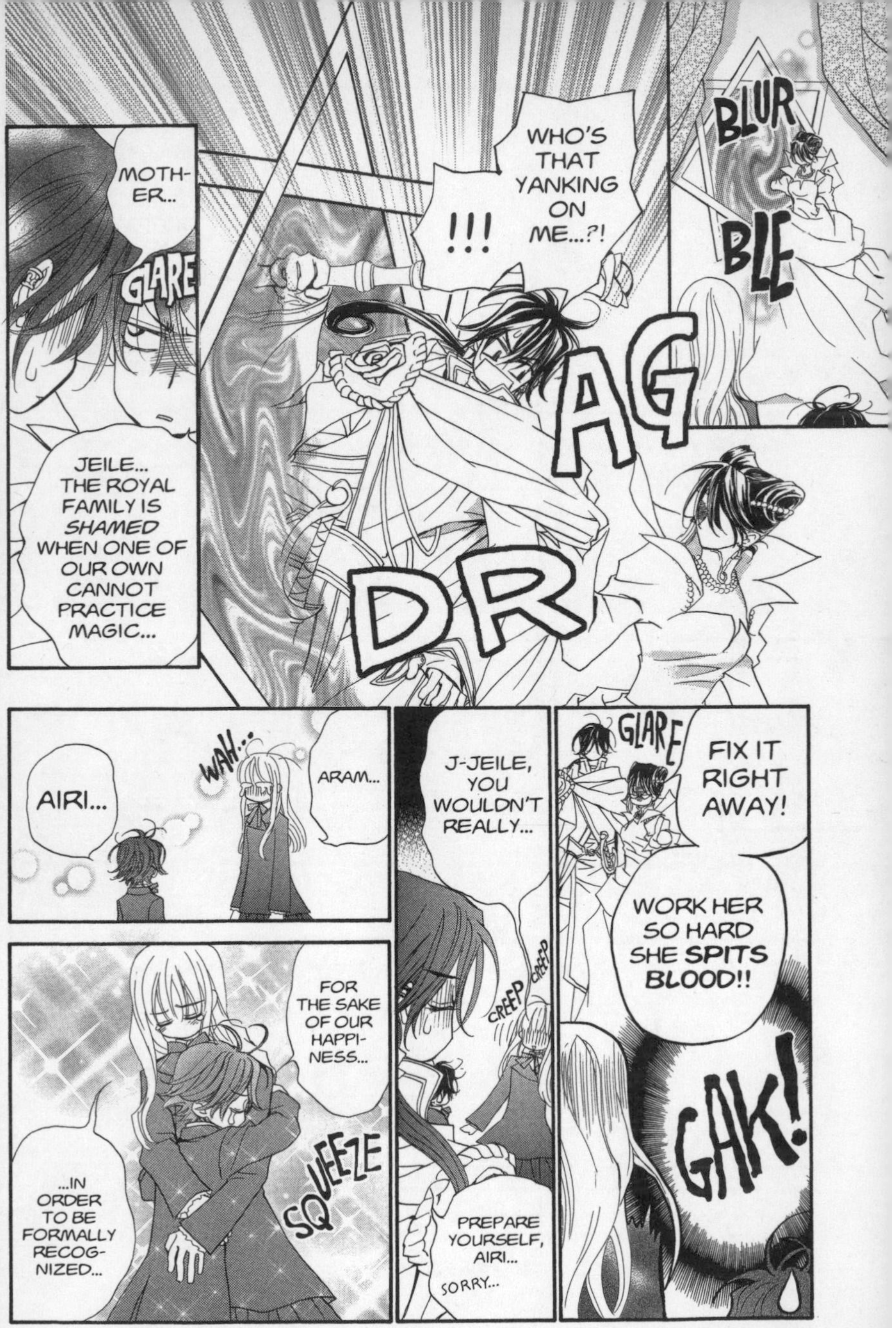
BLUR
BLE
WHO'S THAT YANKING ON ME...?!
!!!
AG
DR
MOTHER...
GLARE
JEILE... THE ROYAL FAMILY IS *SHAMED* WHEN ONE OF OUR OWN CANNOT PRACTICE MAGIC...
GLARE
FIX IT RIGHT AWAY!
WORK HER SO HARD SHE **SPITS BLOOD**!!
GAK!
J-JEILE, YOU WOULDN'T REALLY...
CREEP
CREEP
PREPARE YOURSELF, AIRI...
SORRY...
ARAM...
WAH...
AIRI...
FOR THE SAKE OF OUR HAPPINESS...
SQUEEZE
...IN ORDER TO BE FORMALLY RECOGNIZED...

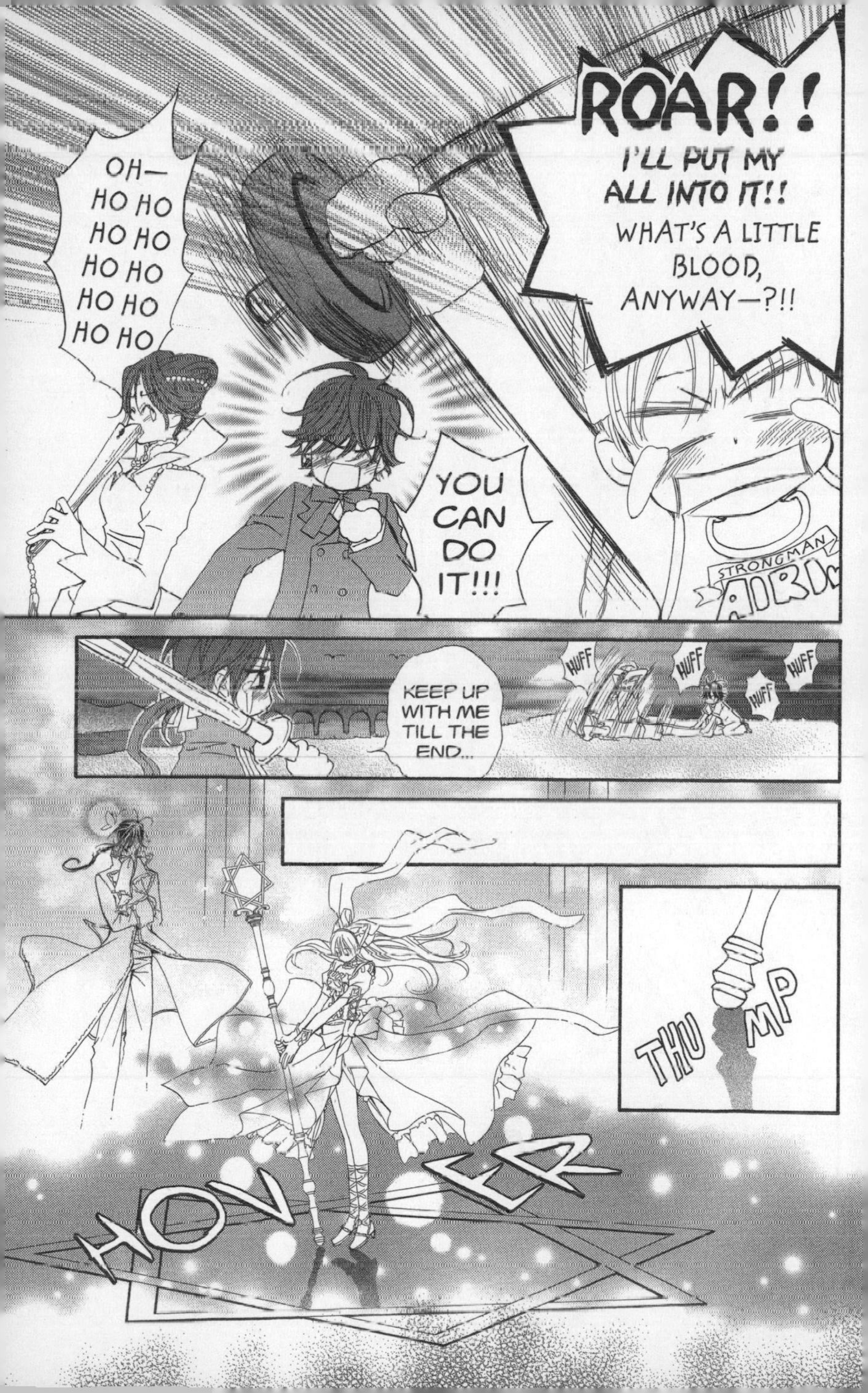
ROAR!!
I'LL PUT MY ALL INTO IT!! WHAT'S A LITTLE BLOOD, ANYWAY—?!!
STRONGMAN AIRI
YOU CAN DO IT!!!
OH—HO HO HO HO HO HO HO HO HO HO
HUFF
HUFF
HUFF
HUFF
KEEP UP WITH ME TILL THE END...
THUMP
HOVER

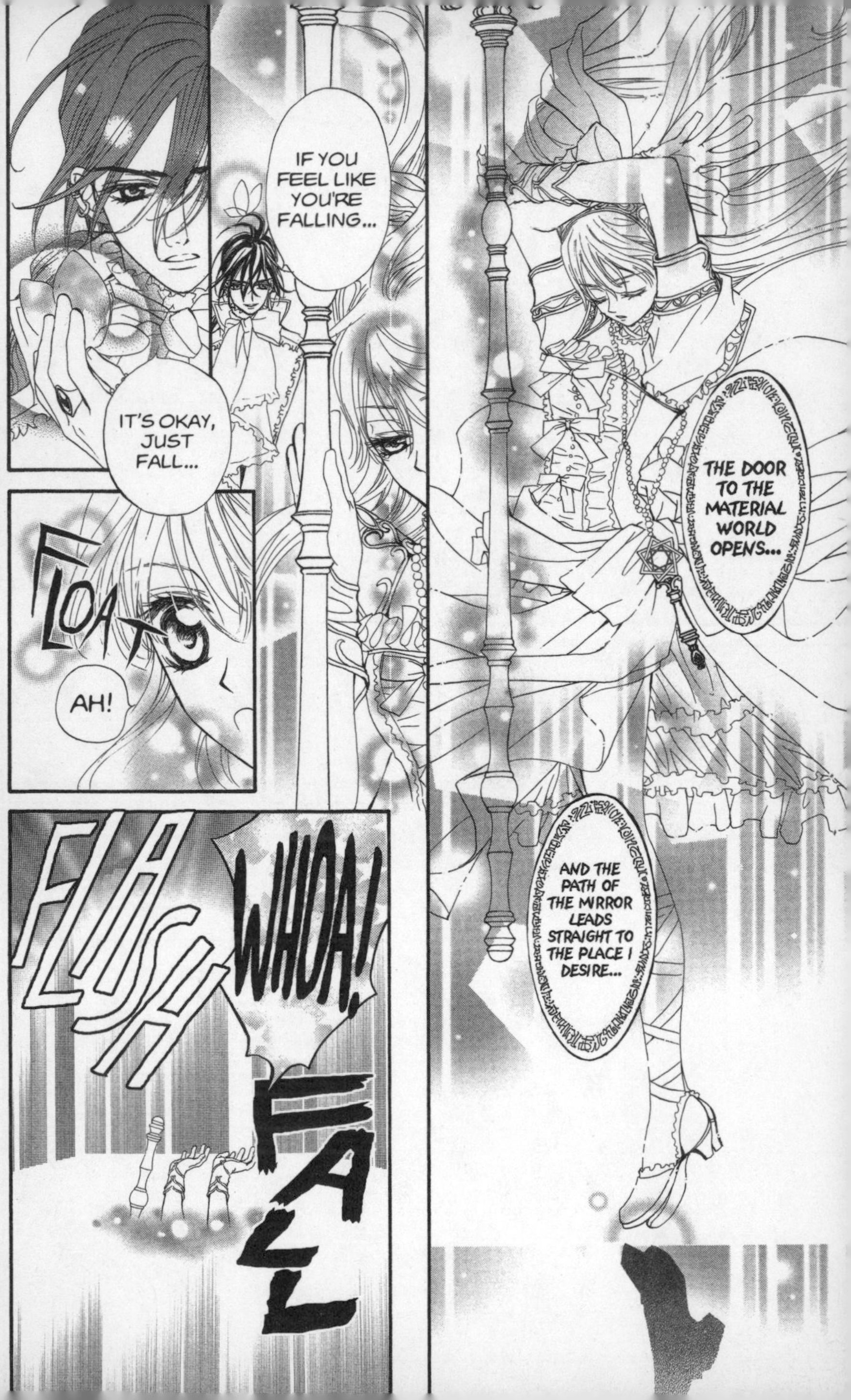
THE DOOR TO THE MATERIAL WORLD OPENS...
AND THE PATH OF THE MIRROR LEADS STRAIGHT TO THE PLACE I DESIRE...
IF YOU FEEL LIKE YOU'RE FALLING...
IT'S OKAY, JUST FALL...
FLOAT
AH!
FLASH
WHOA!
FALL

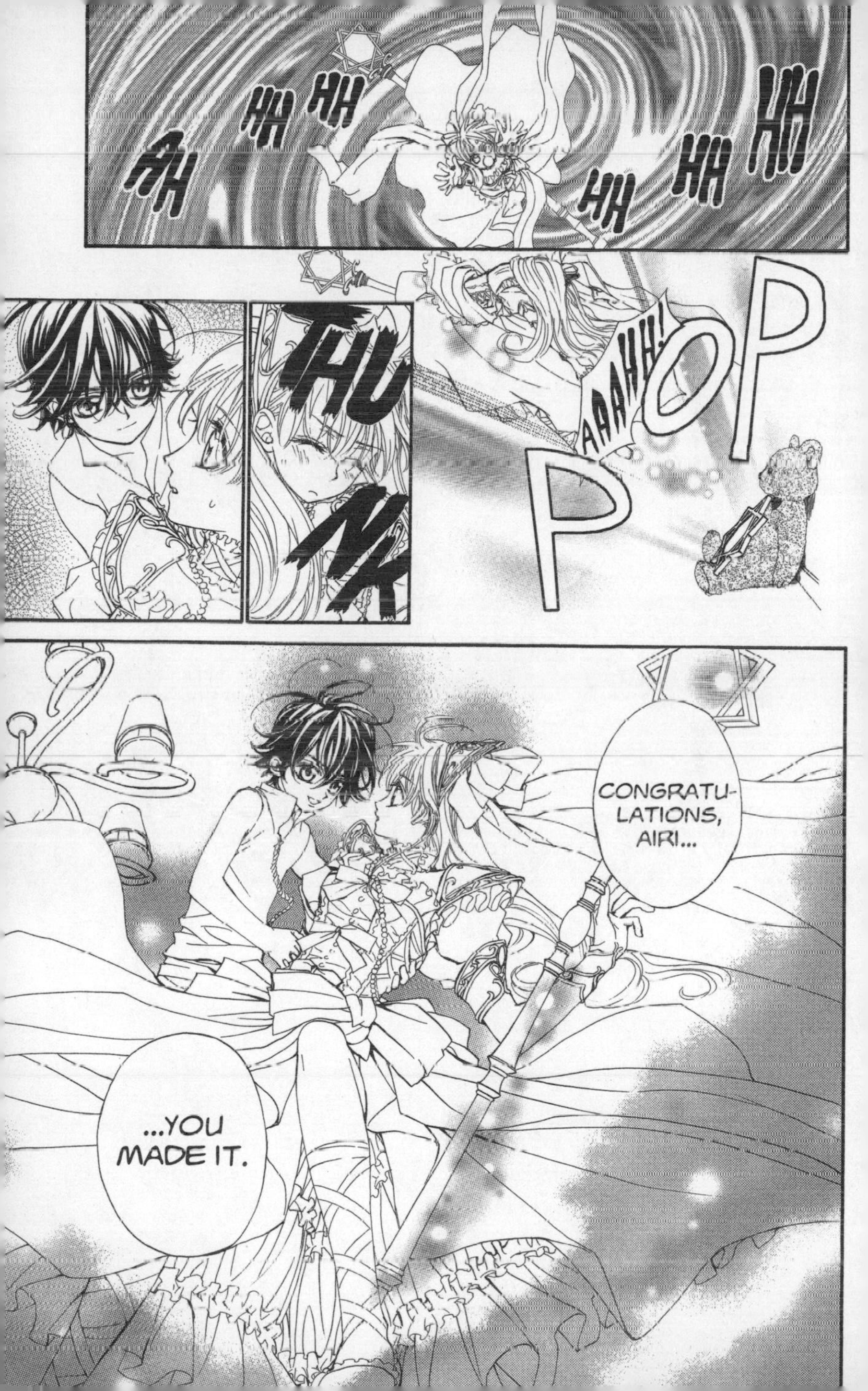
HH
HH
HH
HH
AH
HH
HH
HH
AAAHH!
POP
THUNK
CONGRATU-
LATIONS,
AIRI...
...YOU
MADE IT.

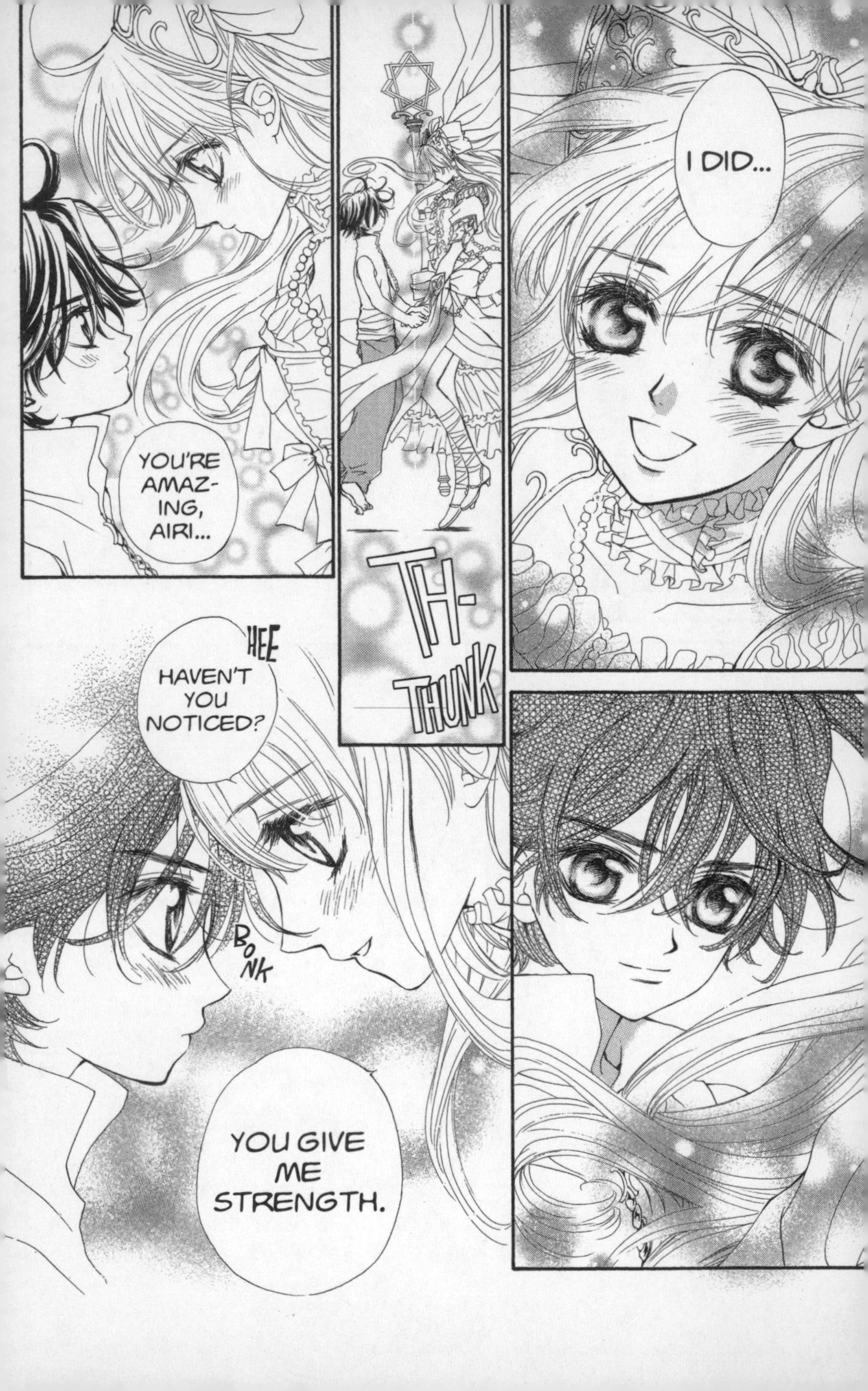
I DID...
TH-THUNK
YOU'RE AMAZ-ING, AIRI...
HEE
HAVEN'T YOU NOTICED?
BONK
YOU GIVE ME STRENGTH.

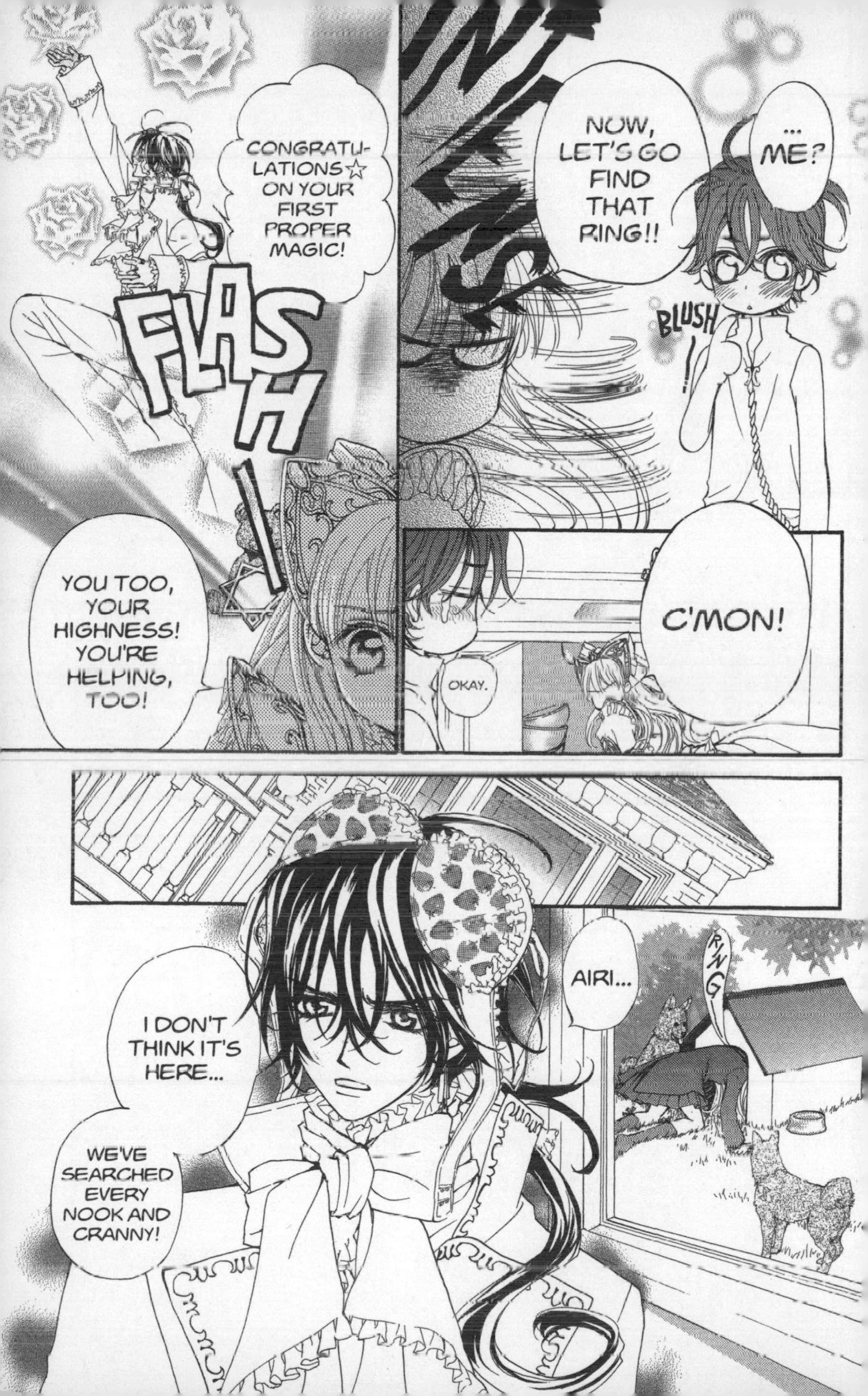
NOW, LET'S GO FIND THAT RING!!
... ME?
BLUSH
C'MON!
OKAY.
CONGRATULATIONS☆ ON YOUR FIRST PROPER MAGIC!
FLASH
YOU TOO, YOUR HIGHNESS! YOU'RE HELPING, TOO!
AIRI...
RING
I DON'T THINK IT'S HERE...
WE'VE SEARCHED EVERY NOOK AND CRANNY!

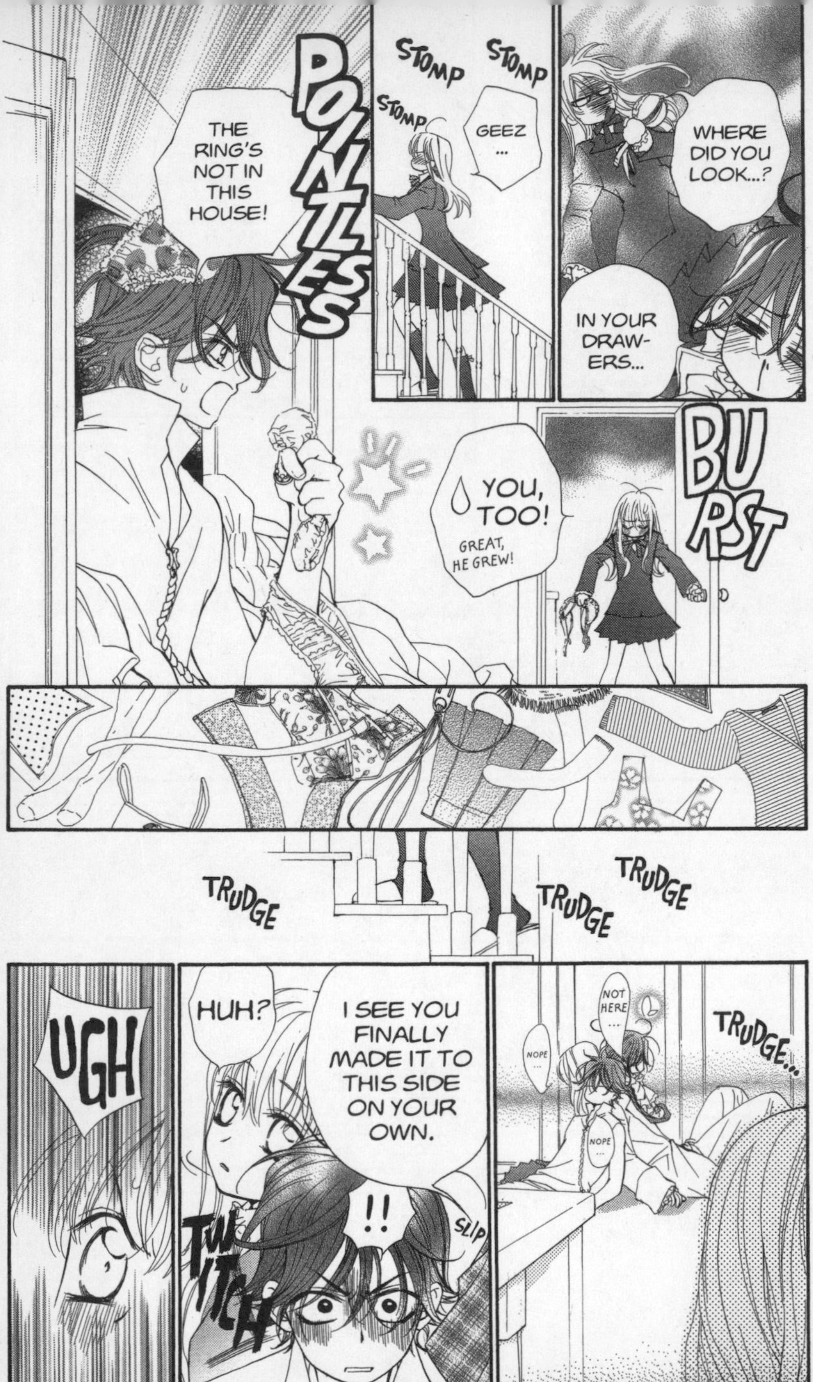
WHERE DID YOU LOOK...?
IN YOUR DRAW-ERS...
STOMP
STOMP
STOMP
GEEZ ...
BURST
YOU, TOO!
GREAT, HE GREW!
THE RING'S NOT IN THIS HOUSE!
POINTLESS
TRUDGE
TRUDGE
TRUDGE
TRUDGE...
NOT HERE ...
NOPE ...
NOPE ...
HUH?
I SEE YOU FINALLY MADE IT TO THIS SIDE ON YOUR OWN.
!!
SLIP
TWITCH
UGH

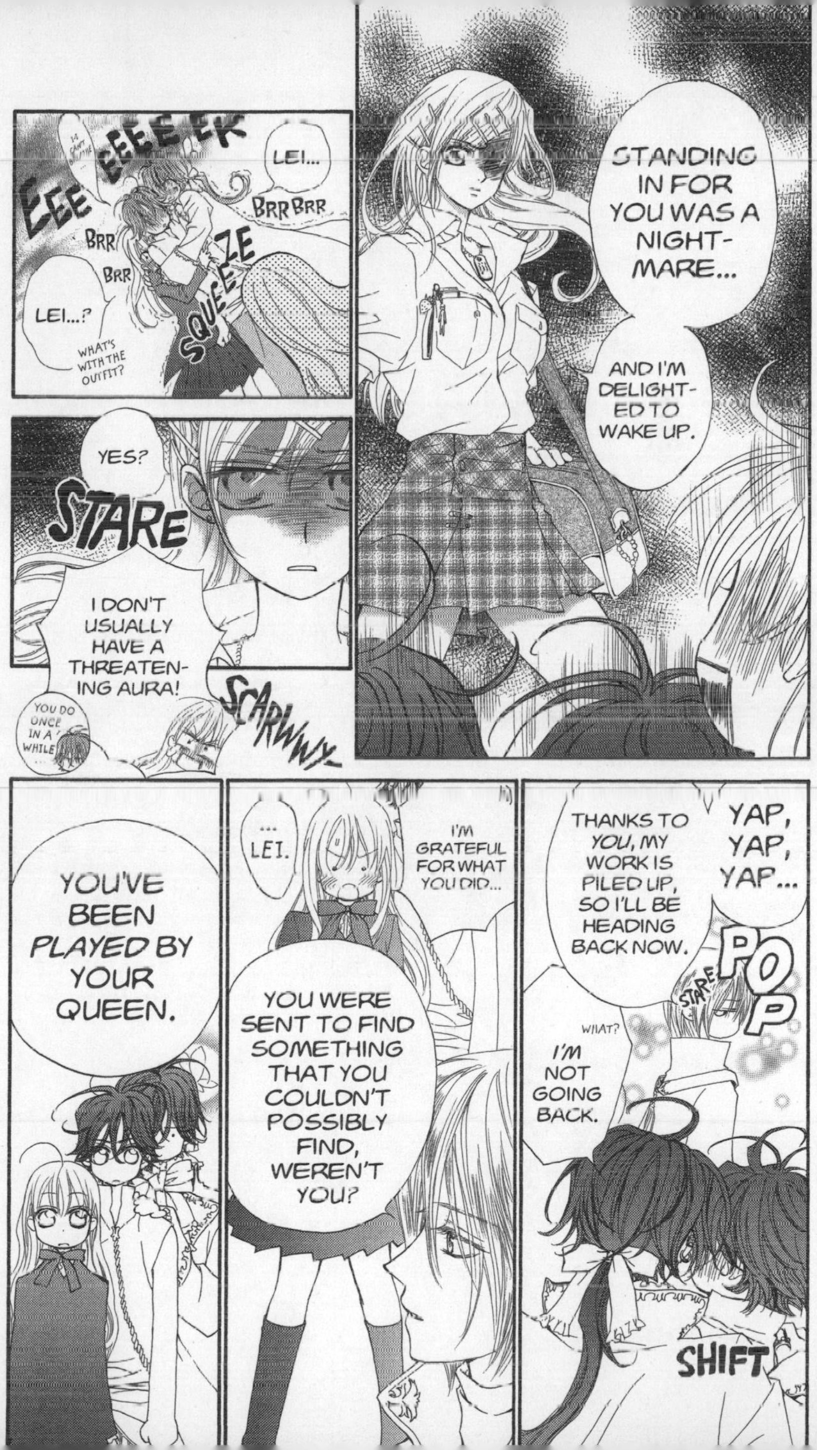
STANDING IN FOR YOU WAS A NIGHT-MARE...
AND I'M DELIGHT-ED TO WAKE UP.
EEE EEEEEEK
LEI...
BRR BRR
BRR
BRR
SQUEEZE
LEI...?
WHAT'S WITH THE OUTFIT?
YES?
STARE
I DON'T USUALLY HAVE A THREATEN-ING AURA!
YOU DO ONCE IN A WHILE...
SCARWWY
THANKS TO *YOU*, MY WORK IS PILED UP, SO I'LL BE HEADING BACK NOW.
YAP, YAP, YAP...
POP
STARE
WHAT?
I'M NOT GOING BACK.
SHIFT
...LEI.
I'M GRATEFUL FOR WHAT YOU DID...
YOU WERE SENT TO FIND SOMETHING THAT YOU COULDN'T POSSIBLY FIND, WEREN'T YOU?
YOU'VE BEEN *PLAYED* BY YOUR QUEEN.

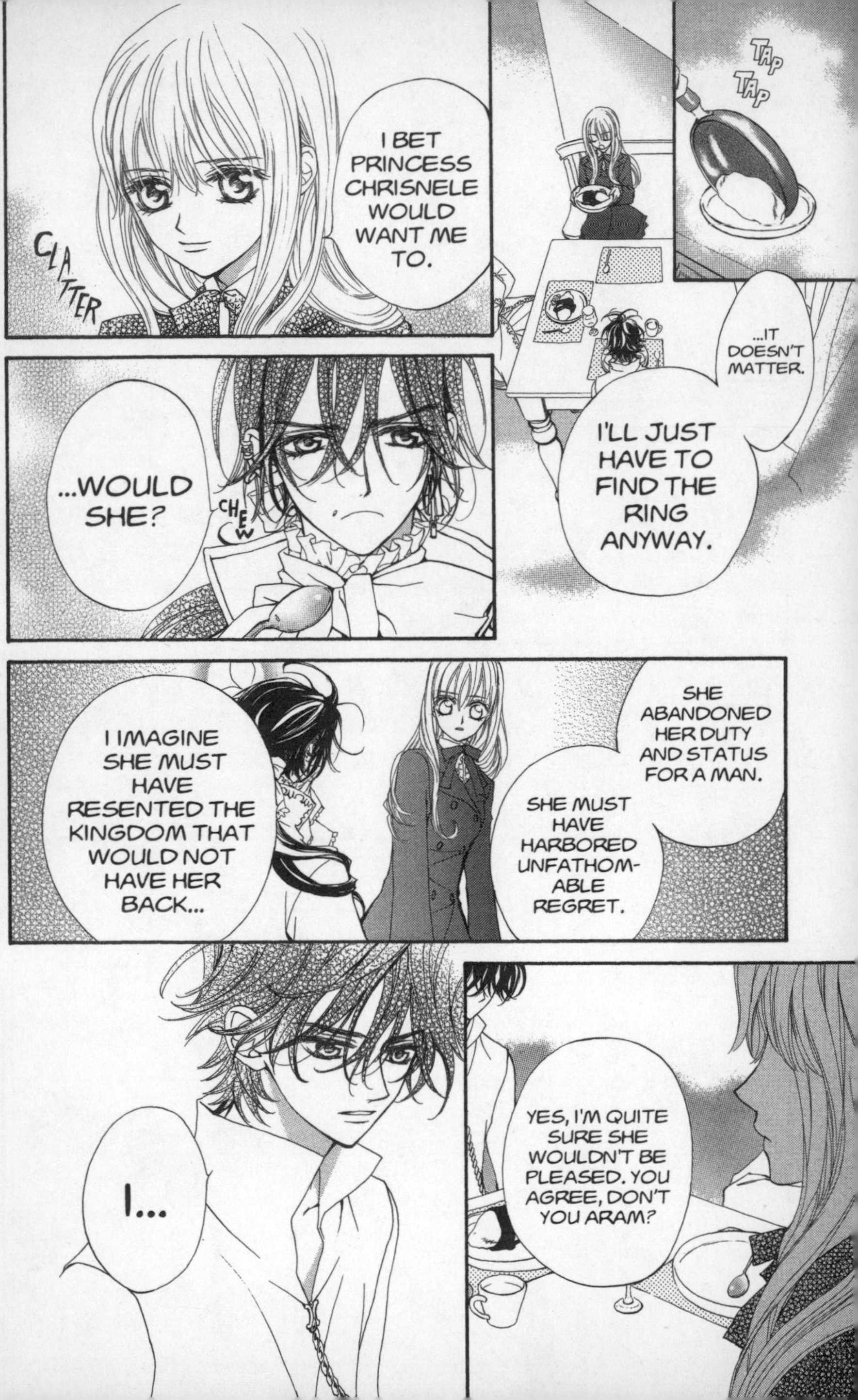
TAP
TAP
...IT DOESN'T MATTER.
I'LL JUST HAVE TO FIND THE RING ANYWAY.
I BET PRINCESS CHRISNELE WOULD WANT ME TO.
CLATTER
...WOULD SHE?
CHEW
SHE ABANDONED HER DUTY AND STATUS FOR A MAN.
SHE MUST HAVE HARBORED UNFATHOM-ABLE REGRET.
I IMAGINE SHE MUST HAVE RESENTED THE KINGDOM THAT WOULD NOT HAVE HER BACK...
YES, I'M QUITE SURE SHE WOULDN'T BE PLEASED. YOU AGREE, DON'T YOU ARAM?
I...

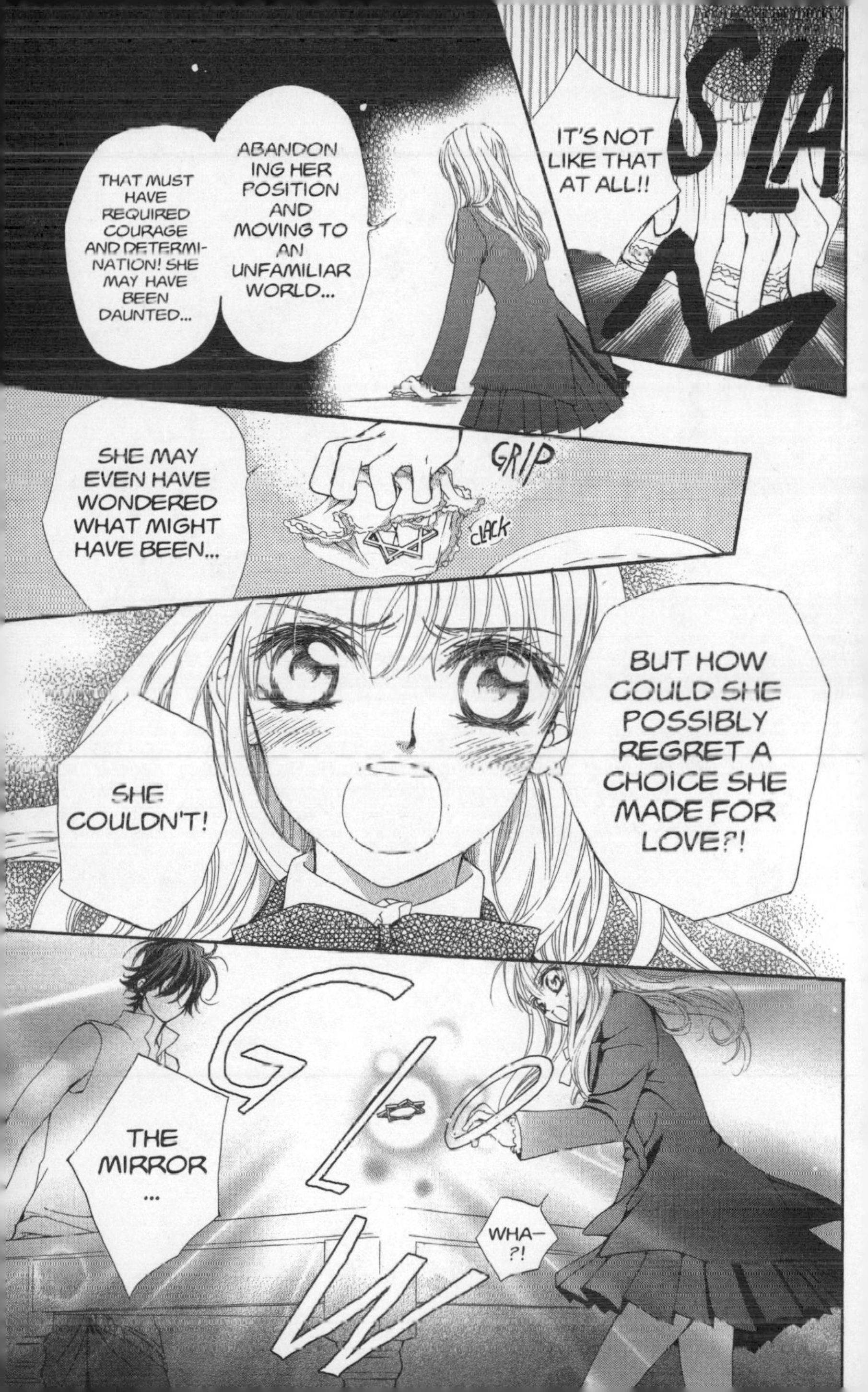
IT'S NOT LIKE THAT AT ALL!!
SLAM
ABANDONING HER POSITION AND MOVING TO AN UNFAMILIAR WORLD...
THAT MUST HAVE REQUIRED COURAGE AND DETERMINATION! SHE MAY HAVE BEEN DAUNTED...
GRIP
CLACK
SHE MAY EVEN HAVE WONDERED WHAT MIGHT HAVE BEEN...
BUT HOW COULD SHE POSSIBLY REGRET A CHOICE SHE MADE FOR LOVE?!
SHE COULDN'T!
WHA-?!
GLOW
THE MIRROR ...

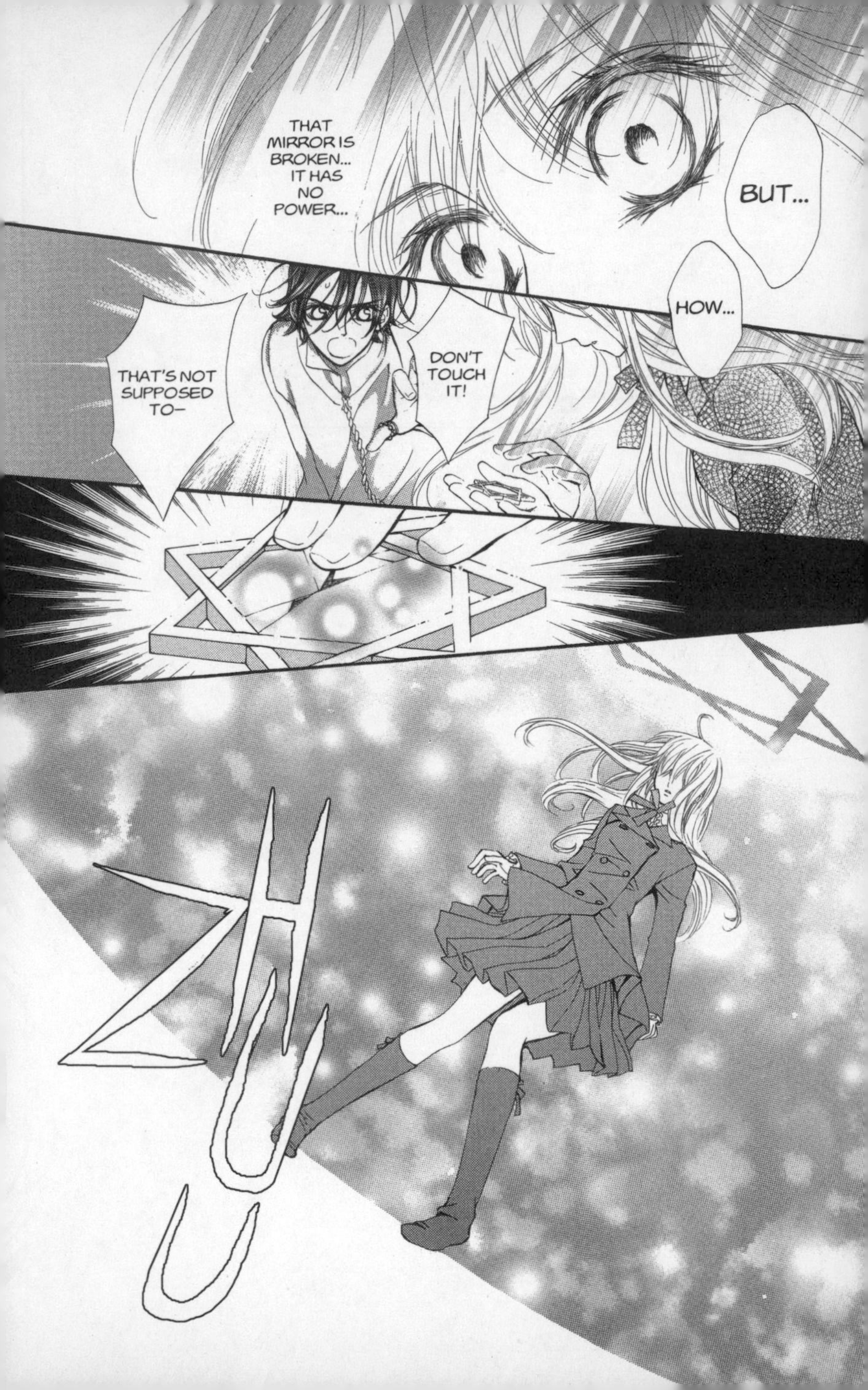
BUT...
HOW...
THAT MIRROR IS BROKEN... IT HAS NO POWER...
DON'T TOUCH IT!
THAT'S NOT SUPPOSED TO–

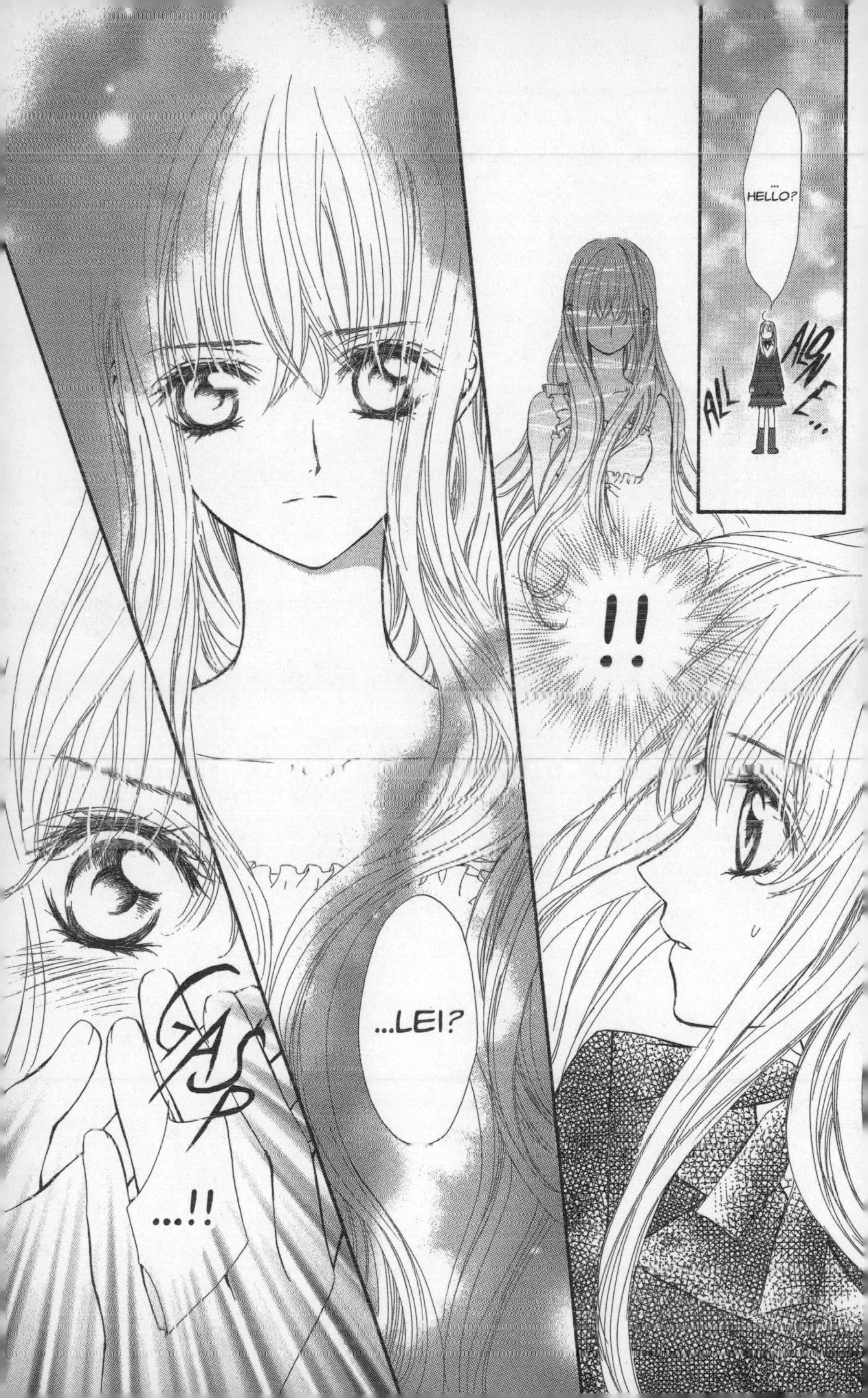

...HELLO?
ALL ALONE...
!!
...LEI?
GASP
...!!

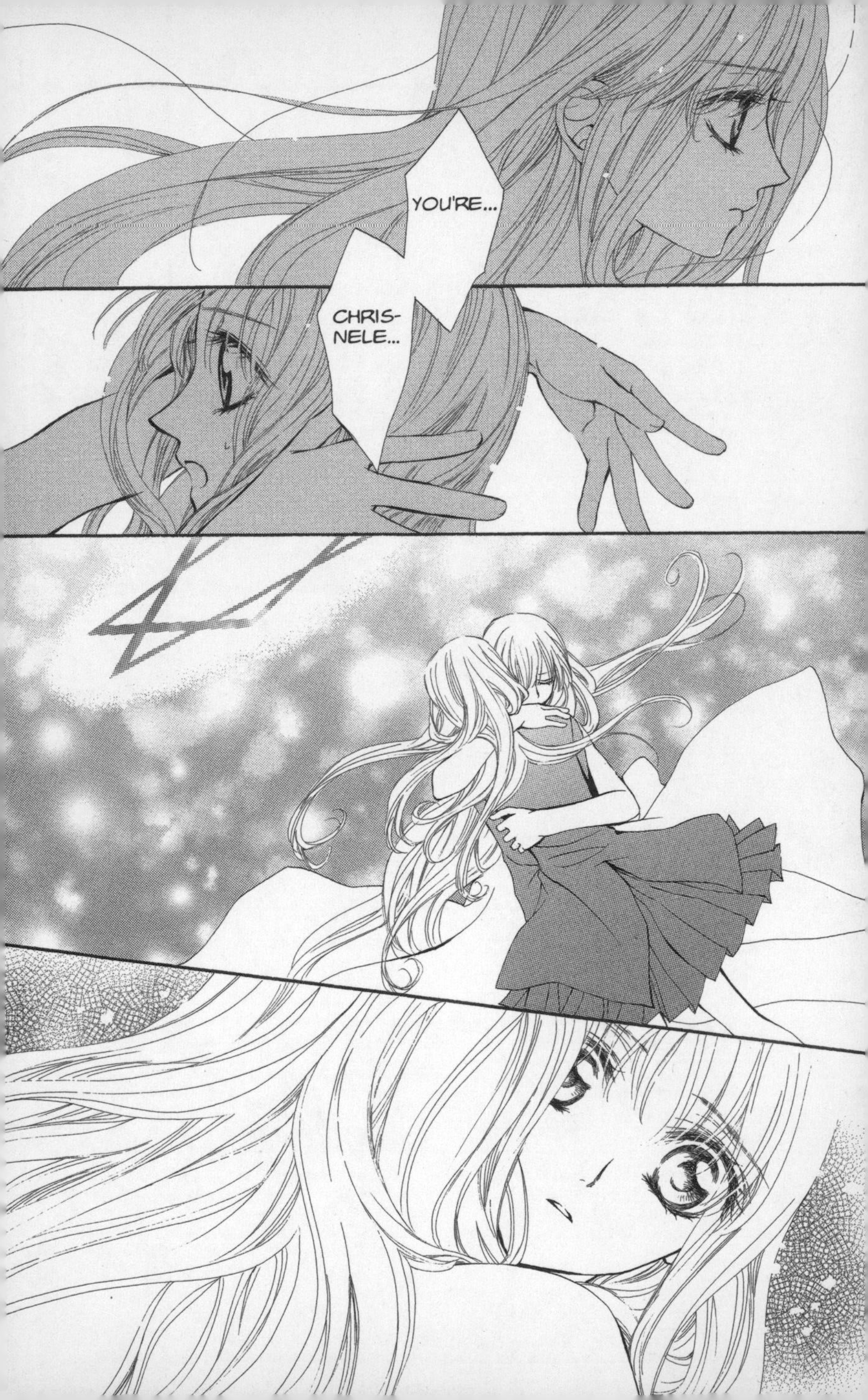
YOU'RE...
CHRIS-NELE...

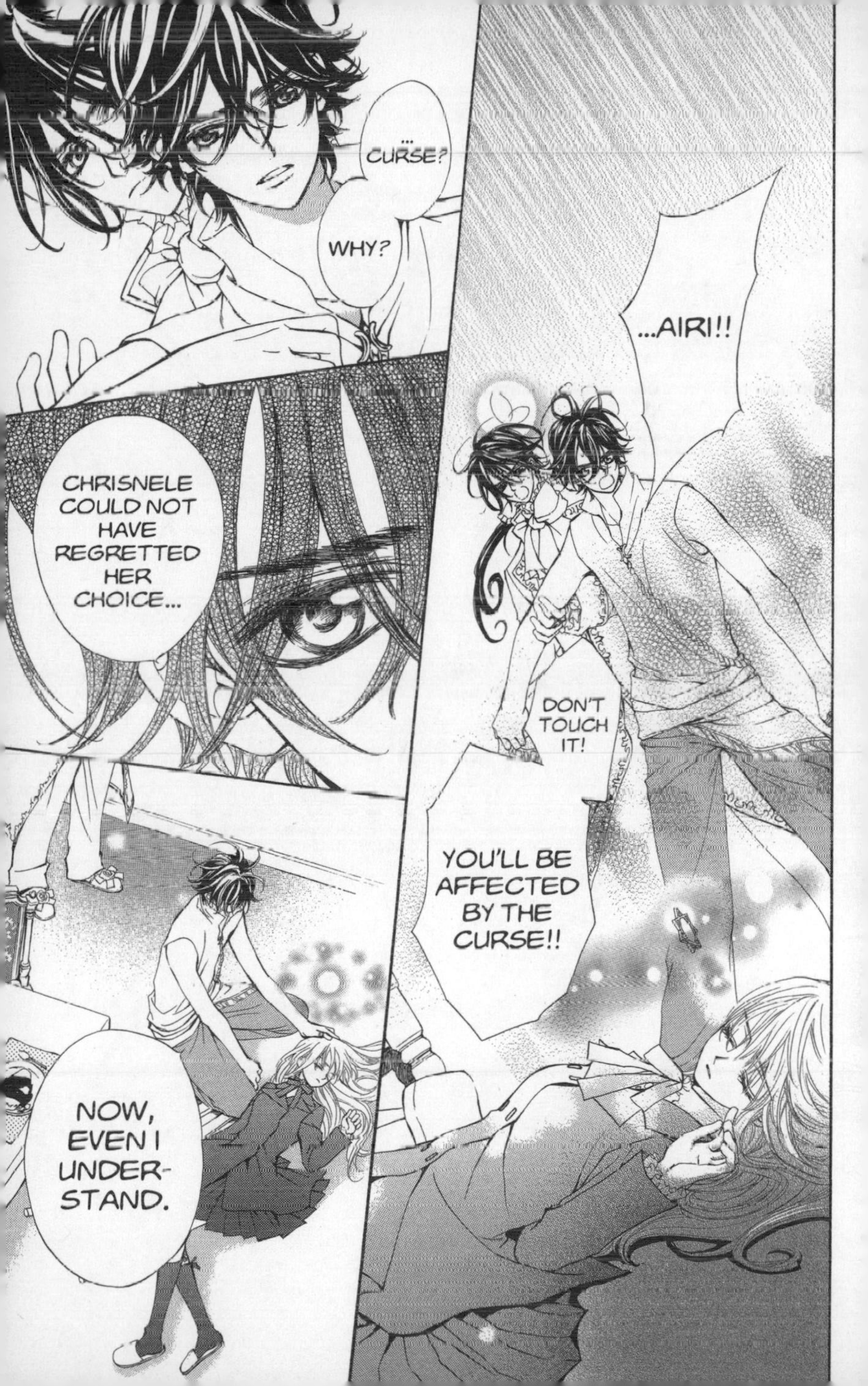
...AIRI!!
DON'T TOUCH IT!
YOU'LL BE AFFECTED BY THE CURSE!!
...CURSE?
WHY?
CHRISNELE COULD NOT HAVE REGRETTED HER CHOICE...
NOW, EVEN I UNDER-STAND.

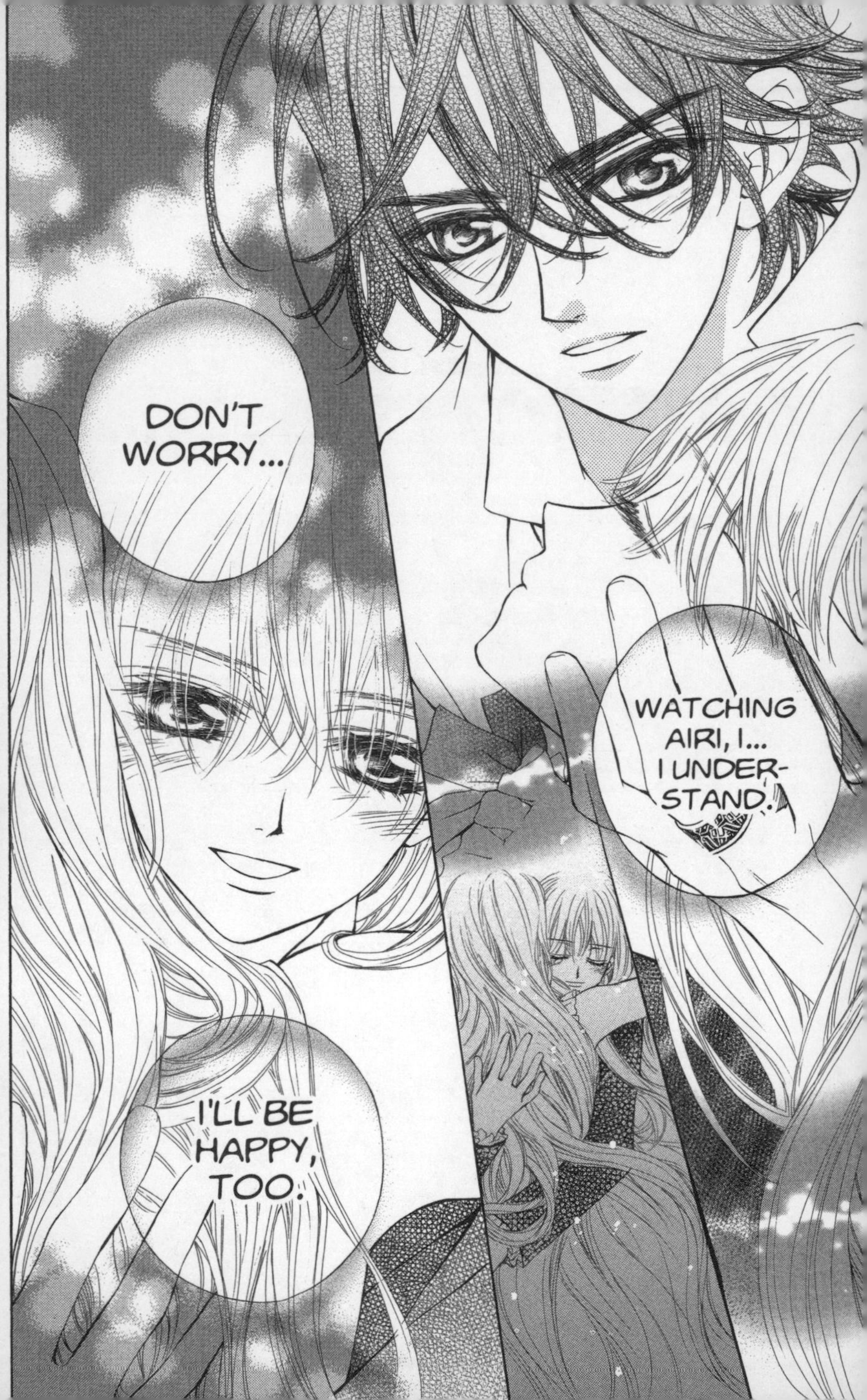
WATCHING AIRI, I... I UNDERSTAND.
DON'T WORRY...
I'LL BE HAPPY, TOO.

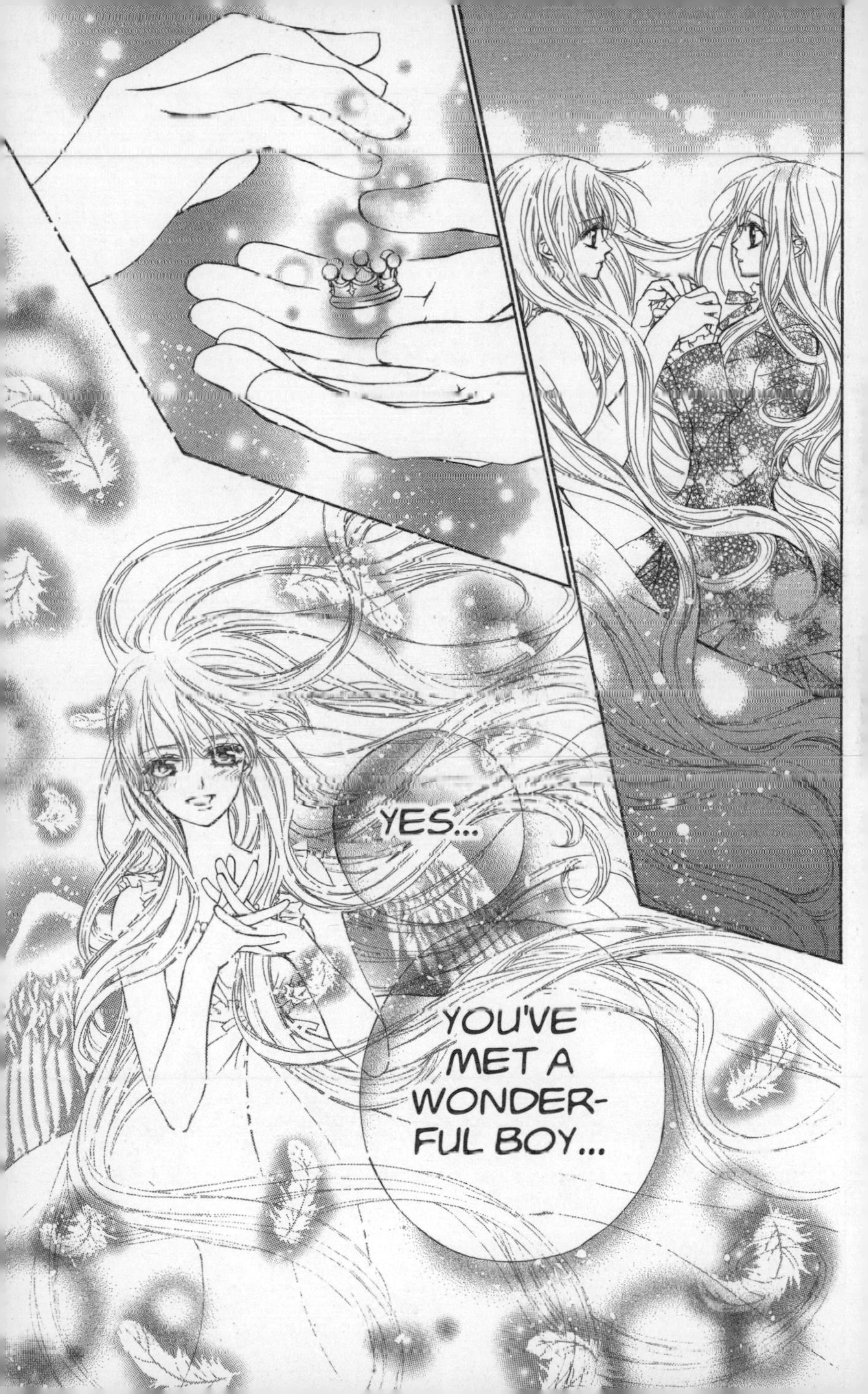
YES...
YOU'VE MET A WONDER-FUL BOY...

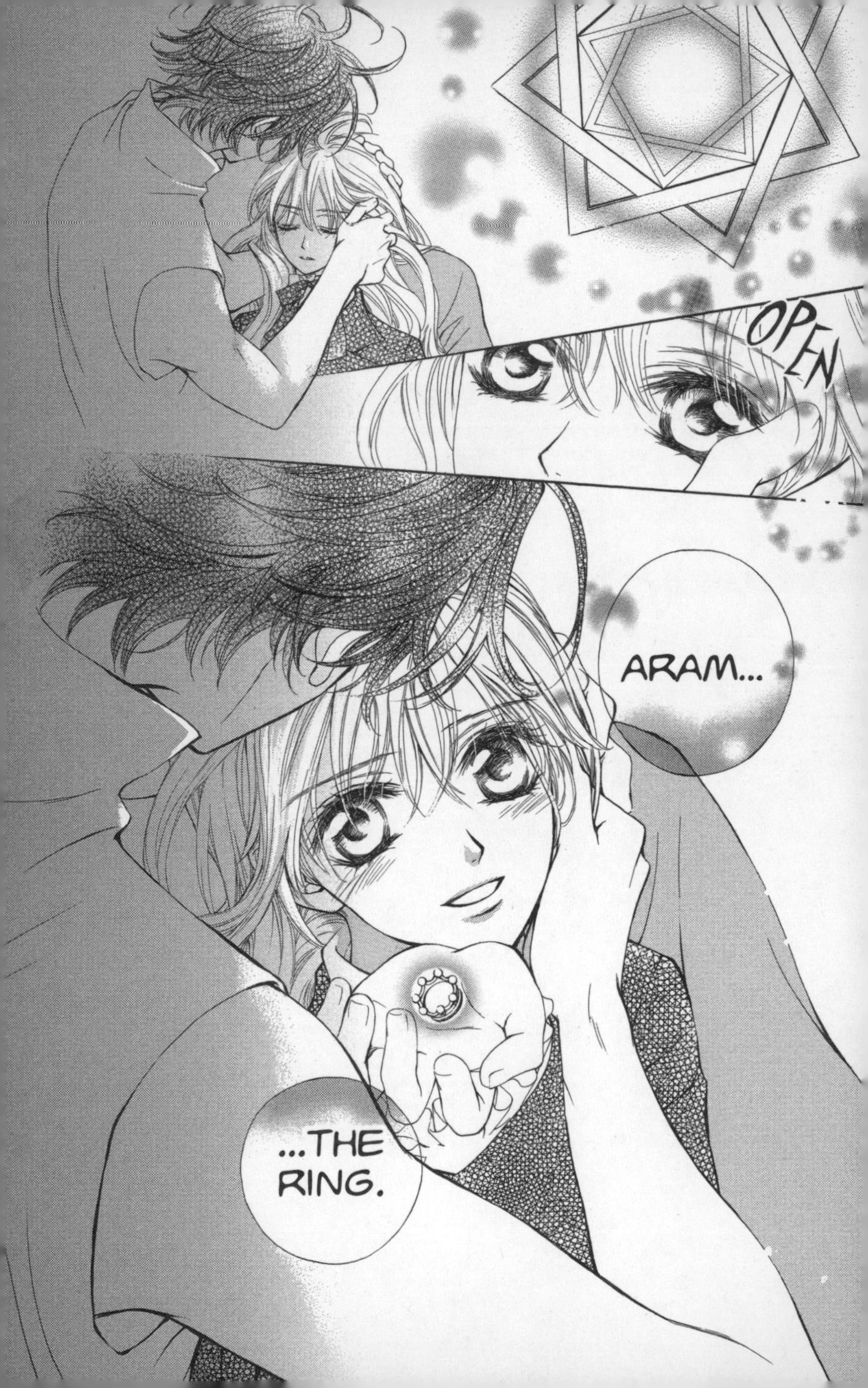
OPEN
ARAM...
...THE RING.

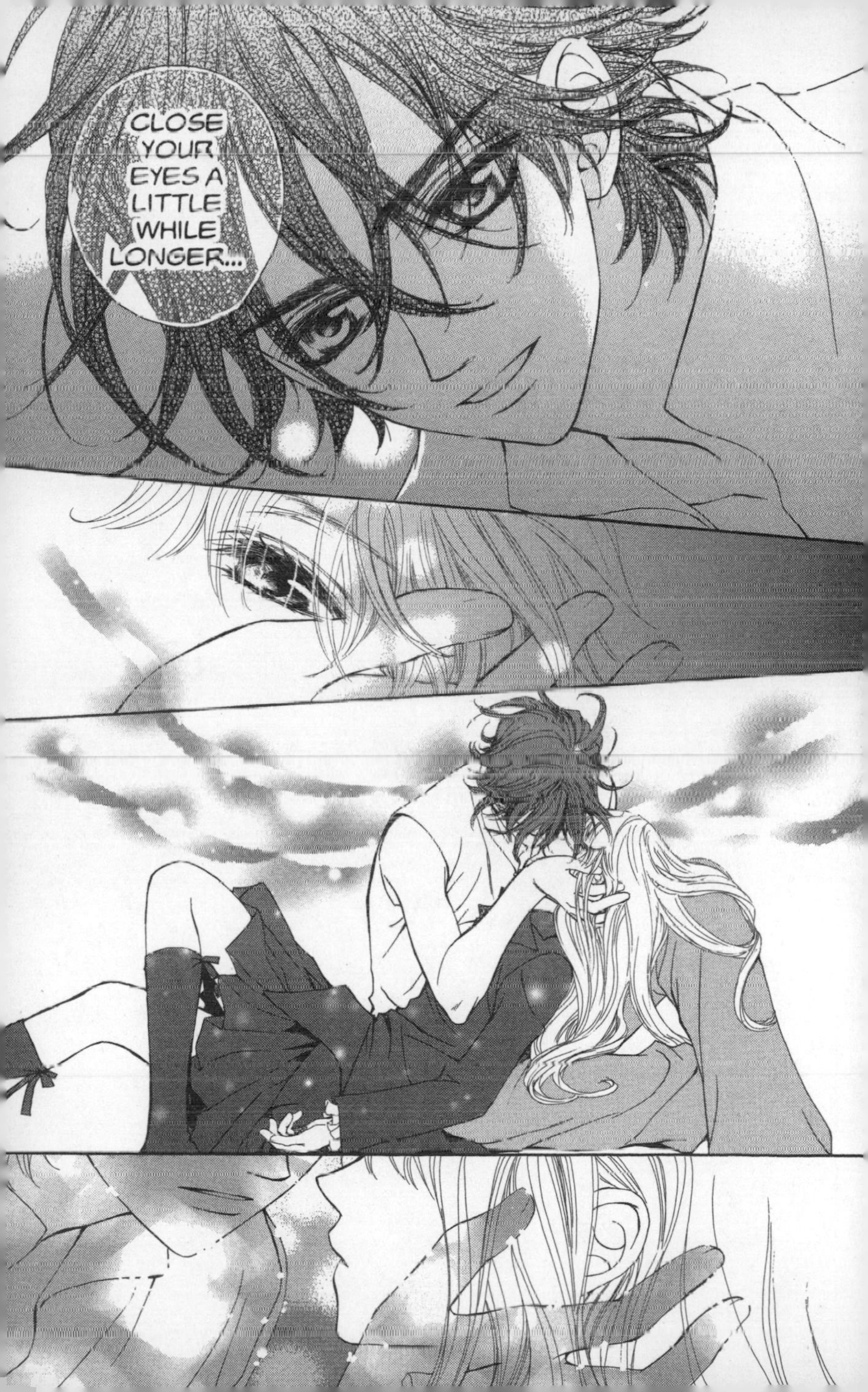
CLOSE YOUR EYES A LITTLE WHILE LONGER...

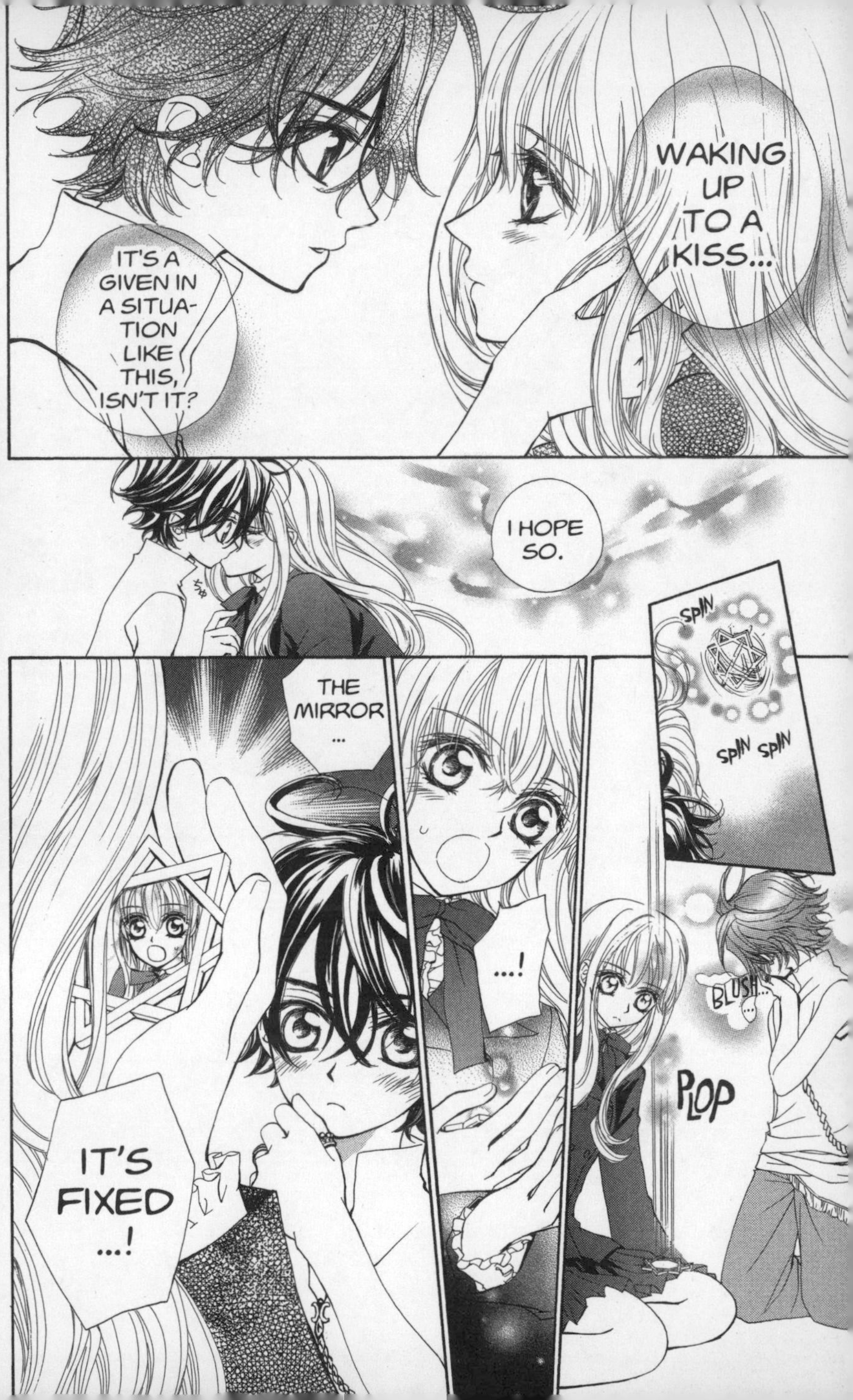
WAKING UP TO A KISS...
IT'S A GIVEN IN A SITUATION LIKE THIS, ISN'T IT?
I HOPE SO.
SPIN
SPIN SPIN
BLUSH...
...
PLOP
THE MIRROR ...
...!
IT'S FIXED ...!

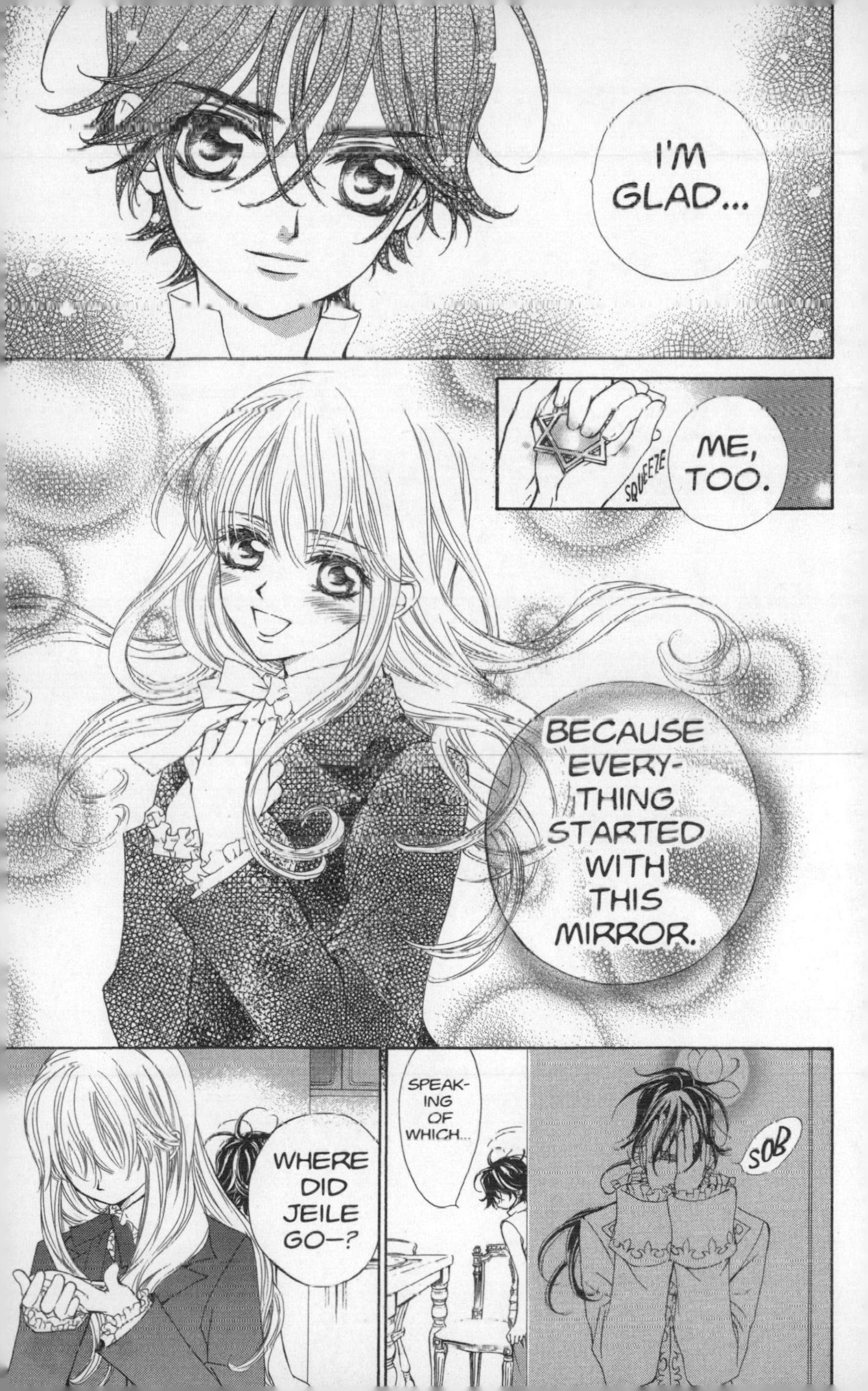
I'M GLAD...
ME, TOO.
SQUEEZE
BECAUSE EVERY-THING STARTED WITH THIS MIRROR.
SOB
SPEAK-ING OF WHICH...
WHERE DID JEILE GO--?

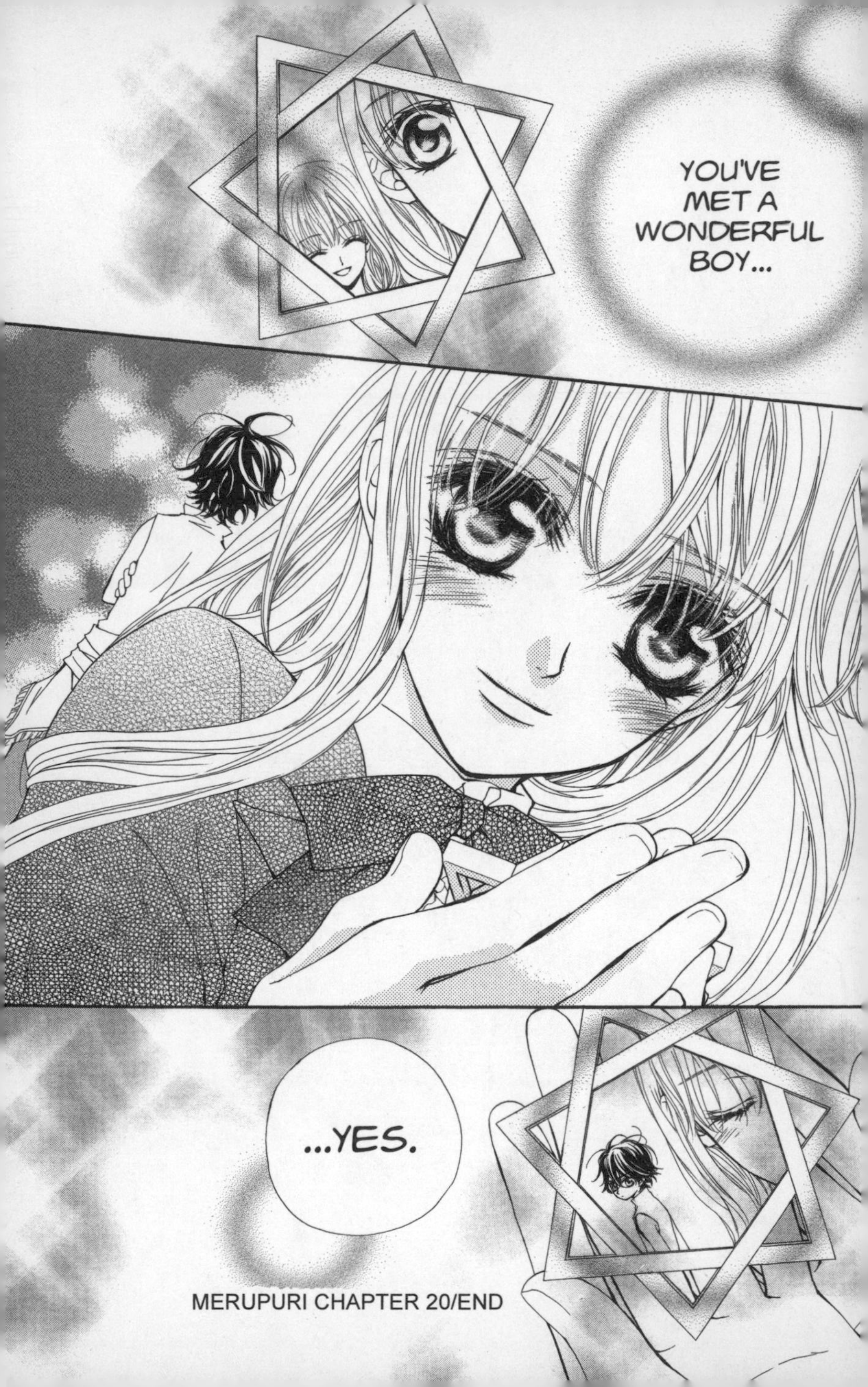
YOU'VE MET A WONDERFUL BOY...
...YES.
MERUPURI CHAPTER 20/END

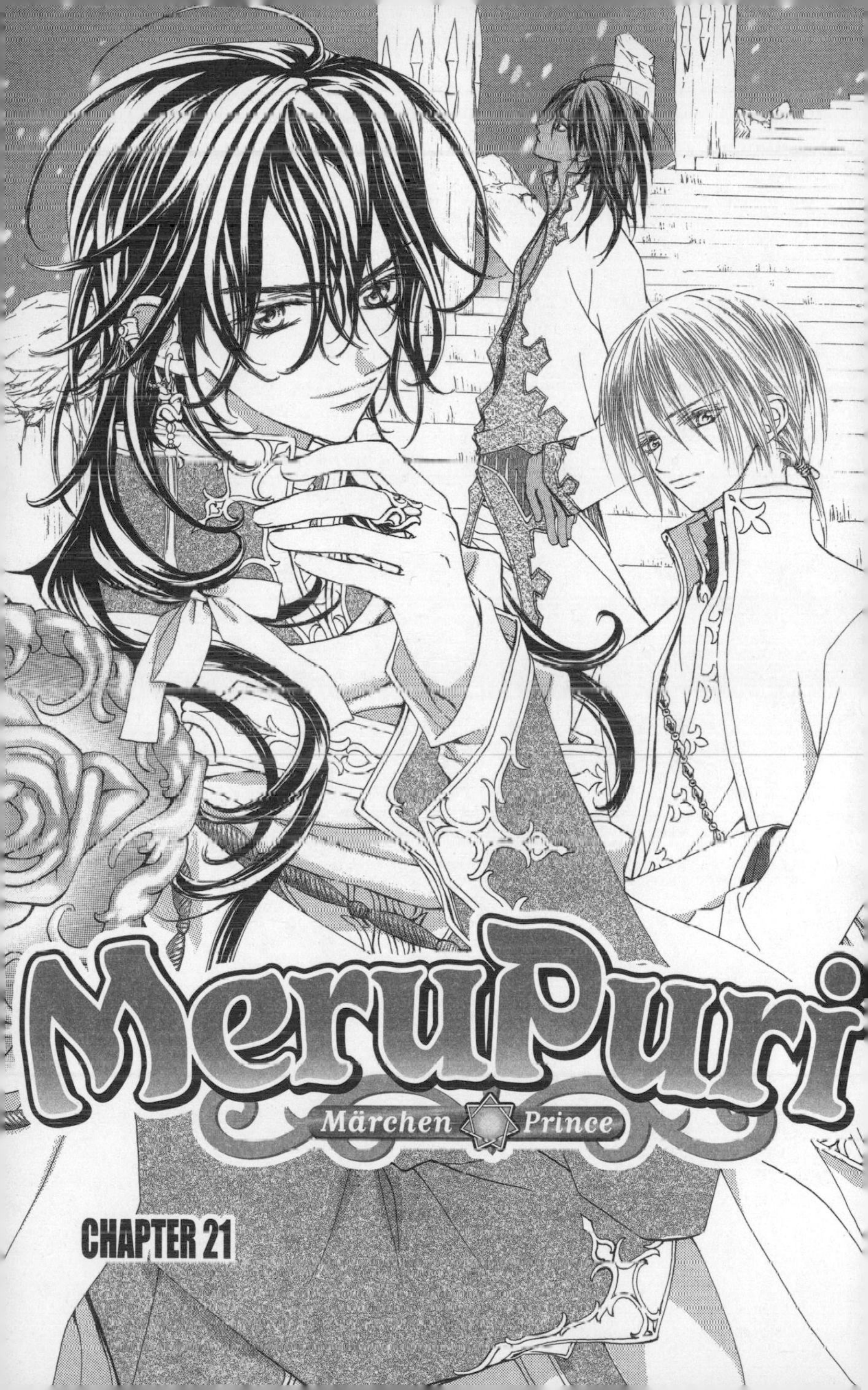
MeruPuri
Märchen Prince
CHAPTER 21

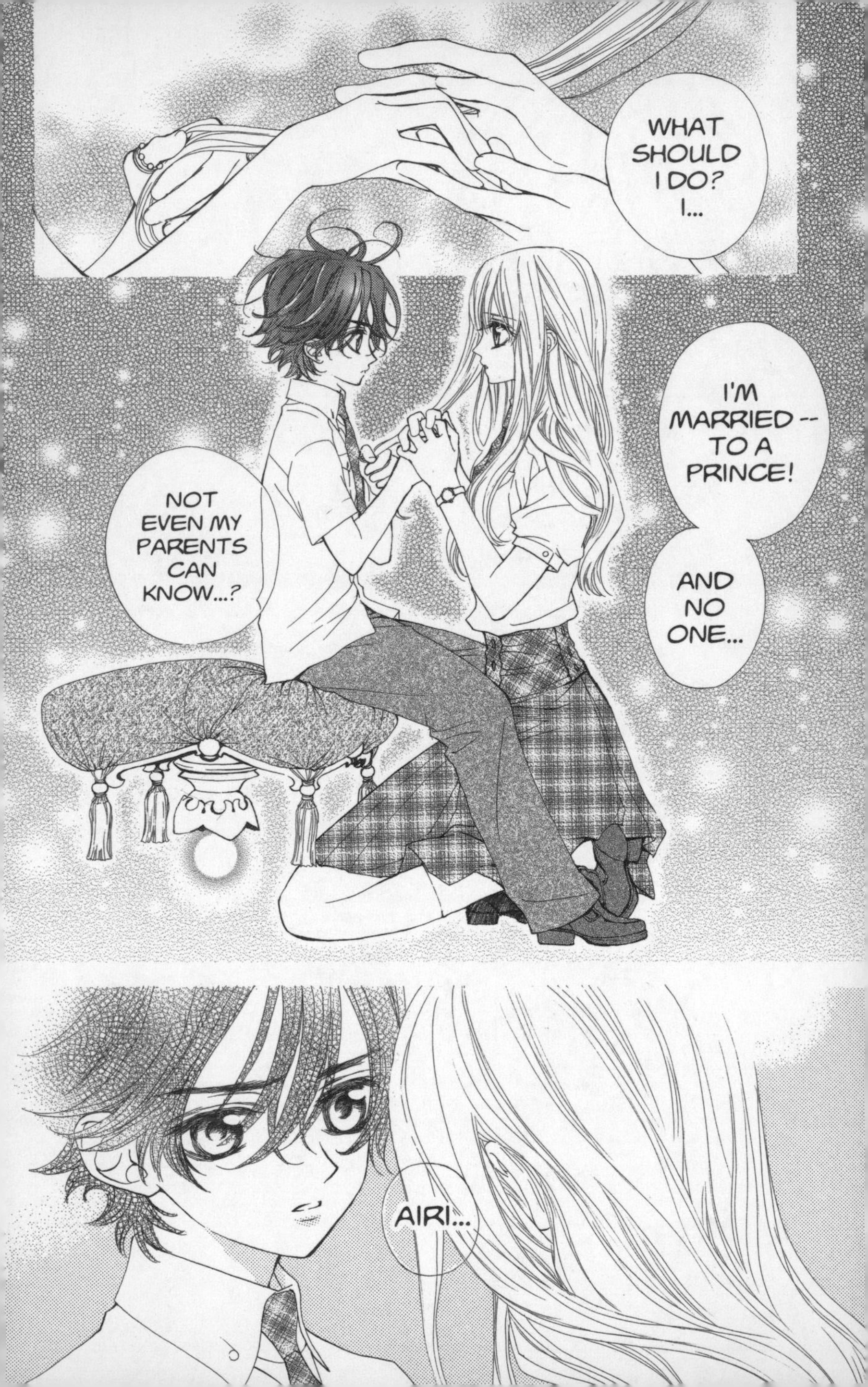
WHAT SHOULD I DO? I...
I'M MARRIED -- TO A PRINCE!
AND NO ONE...
NOT EVEN MY PARENTS CAN KNOW...?
AIRI...

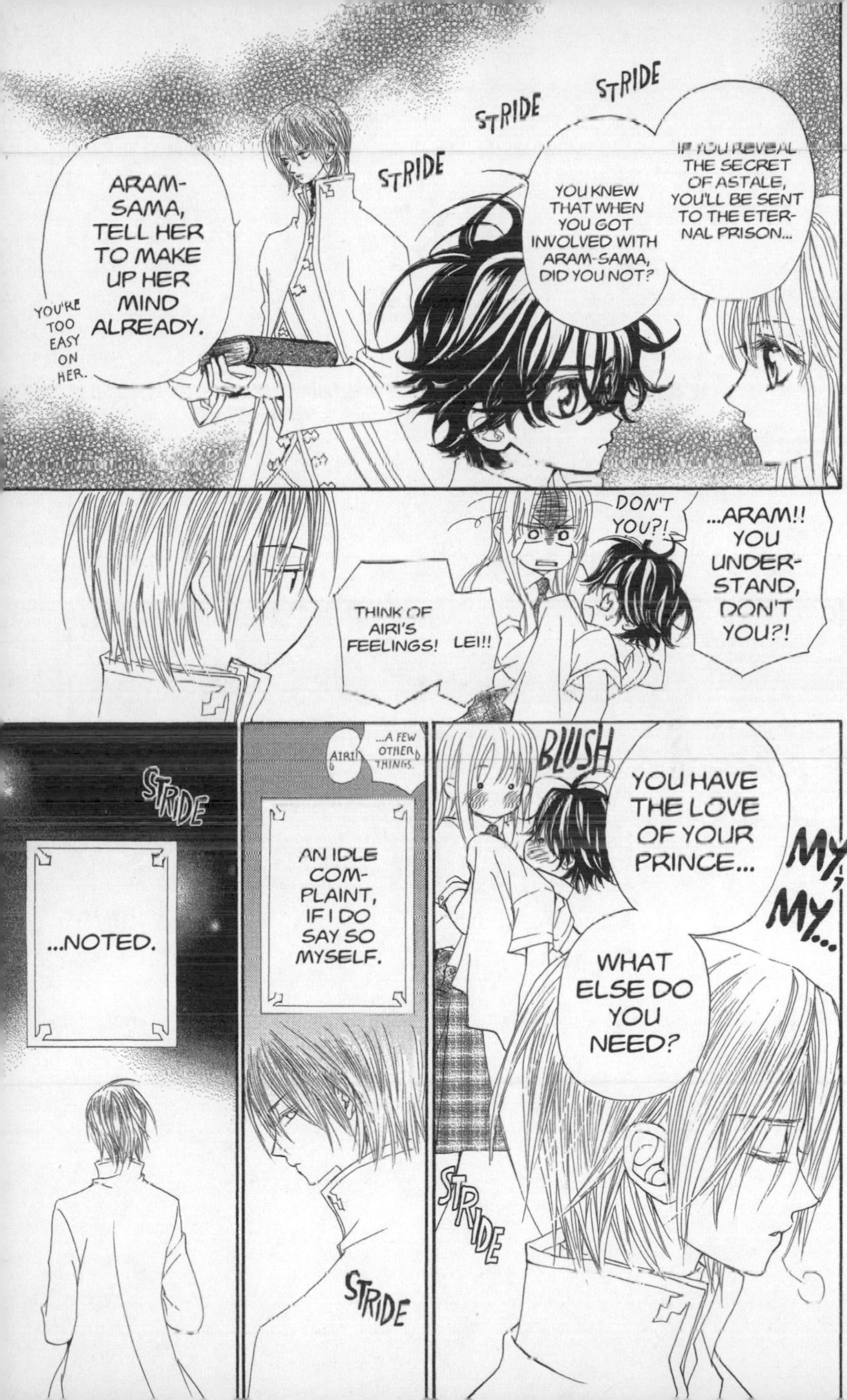

IF YOU REVEAL THE SECRET OF ASTALE, YOU'LL BE SENT TO THE ETERNAL PRISON...
YOU KNEW THAT WHEN YOU GOT INVOLVED WITH ARAM-SAMA, DID YOU NOT?
STRIDE
STRIDE
STRIDE
ARAM-SAMA, TELL HER TO MAKE UP HER MIND ALREADY.
YOU'RE TOO EASY ON HER.
...ARAM!! YOU UNDERSTAND, DON'T YOU?!
DON'T YOU?!
LEI!!
THINK OF AIRI'S FEELINGS!
YOU HAVE THE LOVE OF YOUR PRINCE...
MY, MY...
BLUSH
WHAT ELSE DO YOU NEED?
STRIDE
AIRI!
...A FEW OTHER THINGS.
AN IDLE COMPLAINT, IF I DO SAY SO MYSELF.
STRIDE
STRIDE
...NOTED.

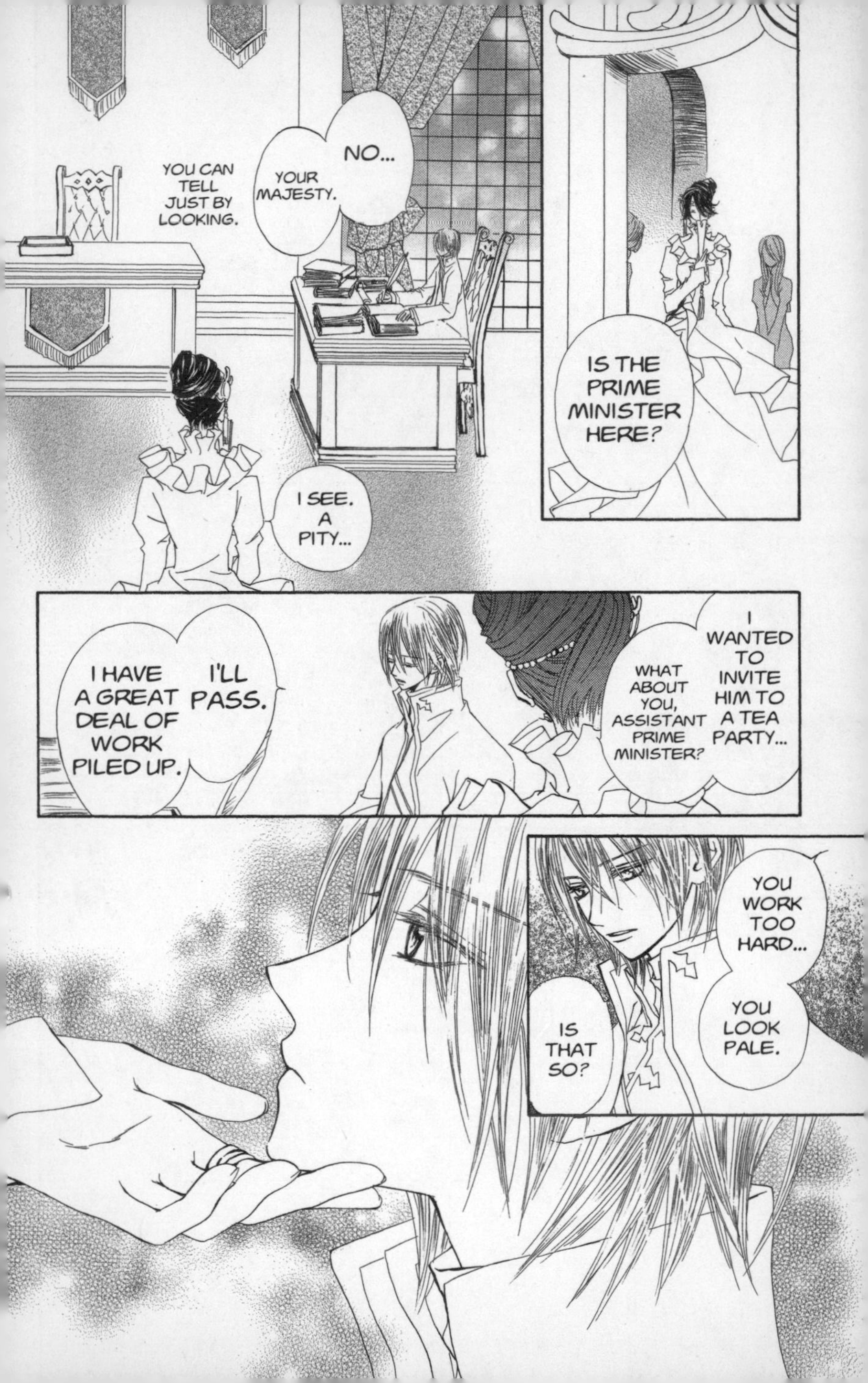
IS THE PRIME MINISTER HERE?
NO... YOUR MAJESTY.
YOU CAN TELL JUST BY LOOKING.
I SEE. A PITY...
I WANTED TO INVITE HIM TO A TEA PARTY...
WHAT ABOUT YOU, ASSISTANT PRIME MINISTER?
I'LL PASS.
I HAVE A GREAT DEAL OF WORK PILED UP.
YOU WORK TOO HARD...
YOU LOOK PALE.
IS THAT SO?

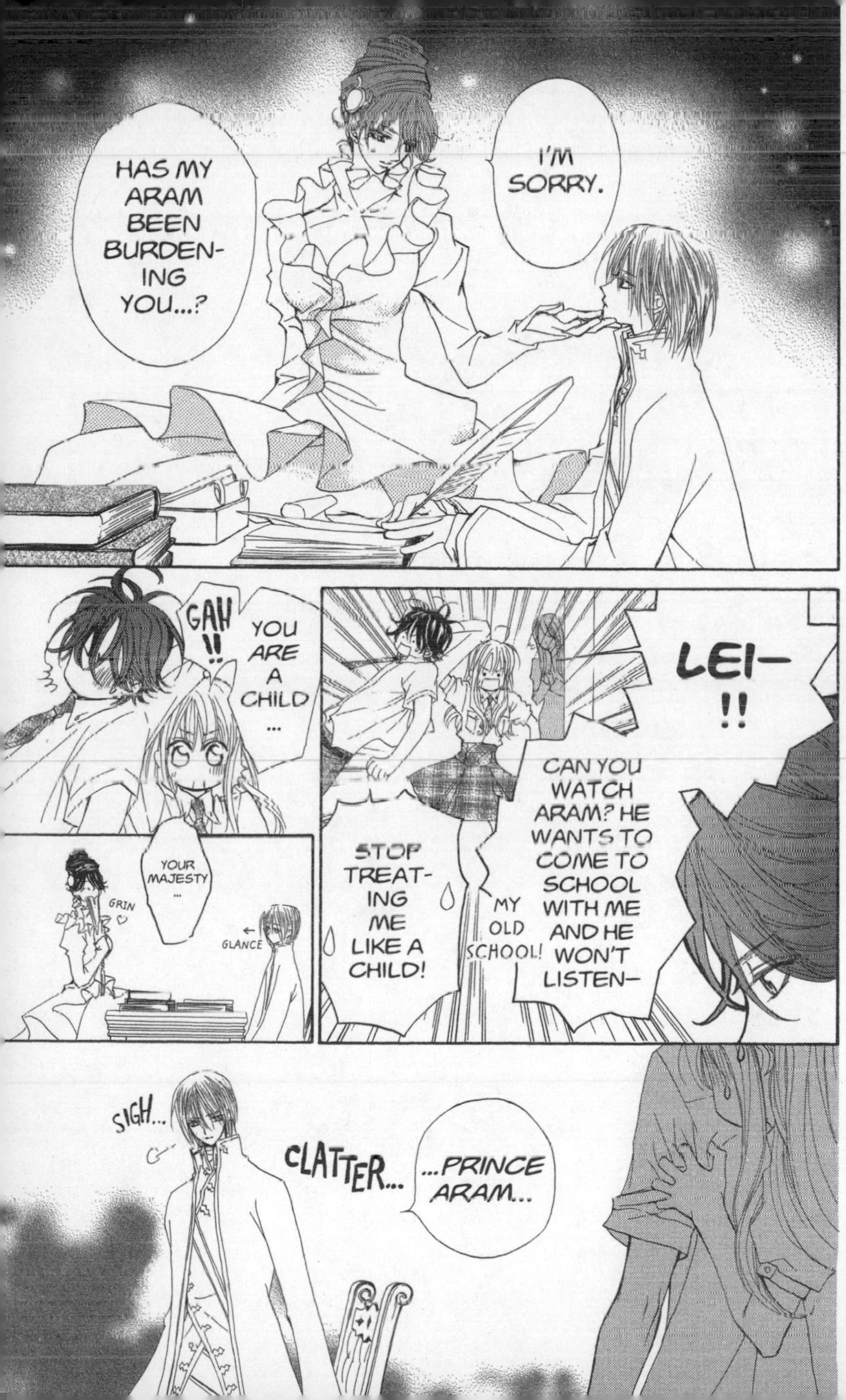
I'M SORRY.
HAS MY ARAM BEEN BURDEN-ING YOU...?
LEI— !!
CAN YOU WATCH ARAM? HE WANTS TO COME TO SCHOOL WITH ME AND HE WON'T LISTEN—
MY OLD SCHOOL!
STOP TREAT-ING ME LIKE A CHILD!
YOU ARE A CHILD ...
GAH !!
YOUR MAJESTY ...
GRIN
GLANCE
...PRINCE ARAM...
CLATTER...
SIGH...

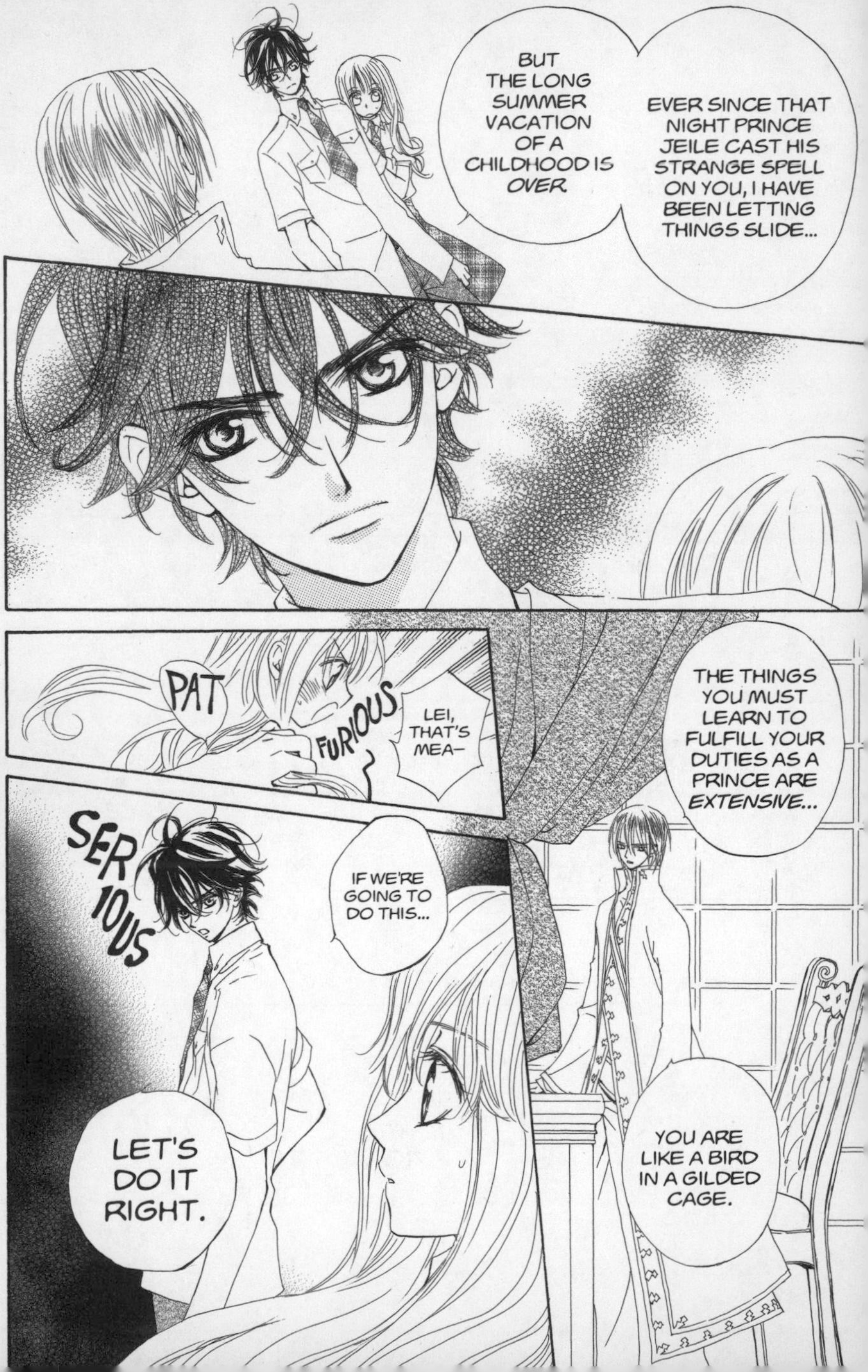
EVER SINCE THAT NIGHT PRINCE JEILE CAST HIS STRANGE SPELL ON YOU, I HAVE BEEN LETTING THINGS SLIDE...
BUT THE LONG SUMMER VACATION OF A CHILDHOOD IS *OVER*.
THE THINGS YOU MUST LEARN TO FULFILL YOUR DUTIES AS A PRINCE ARE *EXTENSIVE*...
PAT
FURIOUS
LEI, THAT'S MEA—
YOU ARE LIKE A BIRD IN A GILDED CAGE.
IF WE'RE GOING TO DO THIS...
SERIOUS
LET'S DO IT RIGHT.

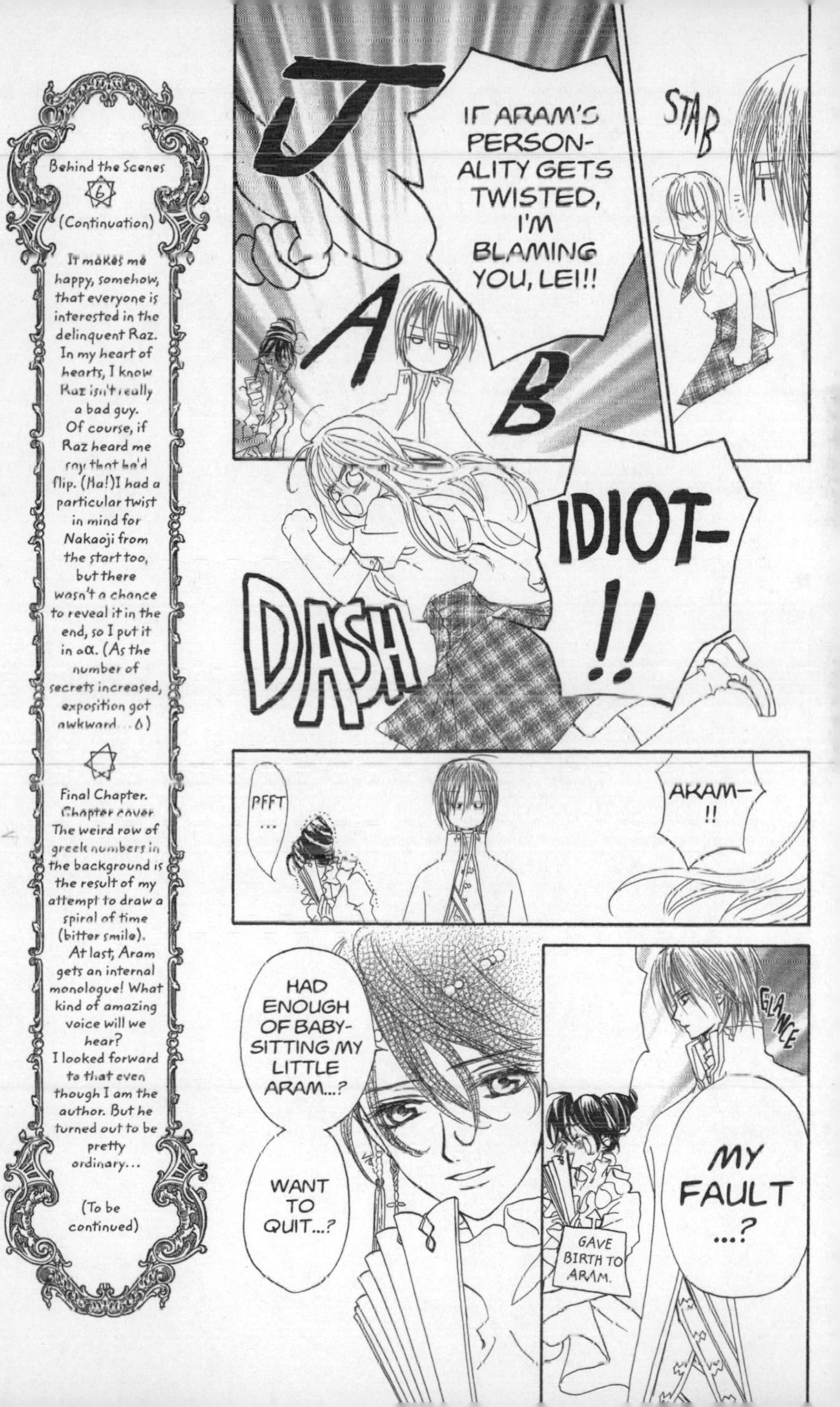
STAB
JAB
IF ARAM'S PERSON-ALITY GETS TWISTED, I'M BLAMING YOU, LEI!!
IDIOT—!!
DASH
ARAM—!!
PFFT...
GLANCE
MY FAULT...?
GAVE BIRTH TO ARAM.
HAD ENOUGH OF BABY-SITTING MY LITTLE ARAM...?
WANT TO QUIT...?

Behind the Scenes 6 (Continuation)

It makes me happy, somehow, that everyone is interested in the delinquent Raz. In my heart of hearts, I know Raz isn't really a bad guy. Of course, if Raz heard me say that he'd flip. (Ha!) I had a particular twist in mind for Nakaoji from the start too, but there wasn't a chance to reveal it in the end, so I put it in aα. (As the number of secrets increased, exposition got awkward...)

Final Chapter. Chapter cover. The weird row of greek numbers in the background is the result of my attempt to draw a spiral of time (bitter smile). At last, Aram gets an internal monologue! What kind of amazing voice will we hear? I looked forward to that even though I am the author. But he turned out to be pretty ordinary...

(To be continued)

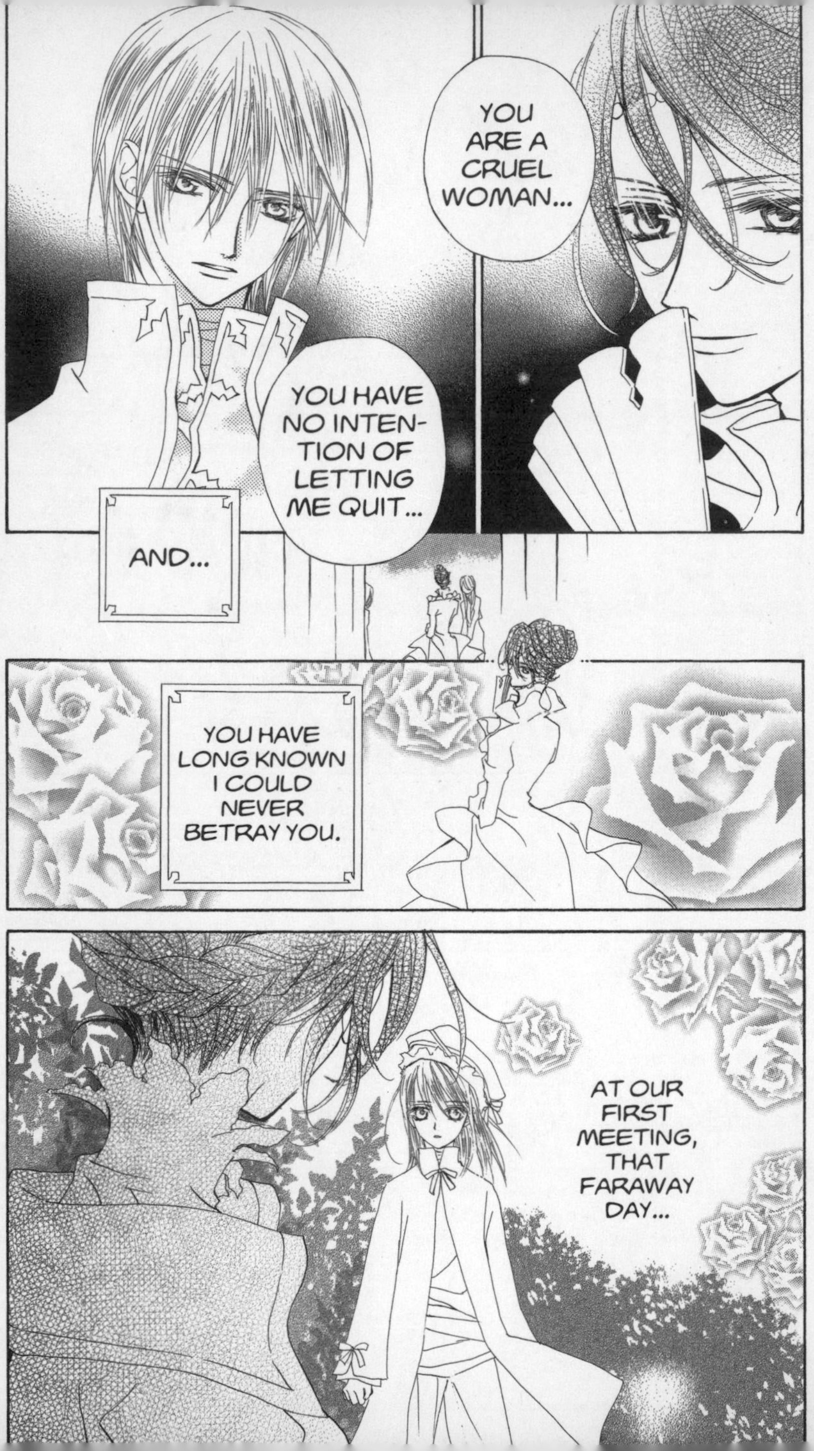
YOU ARE A CRUEL WOMAN...
YOU HAVE NO INTEN-TION OF LETTING ME QUIT...
AND...
YOU HAVE LONG KNOWN I COULD NEVER BETRAY YOU.
AT OUR FIRST MEETING, THAT FARAWAY DAY...

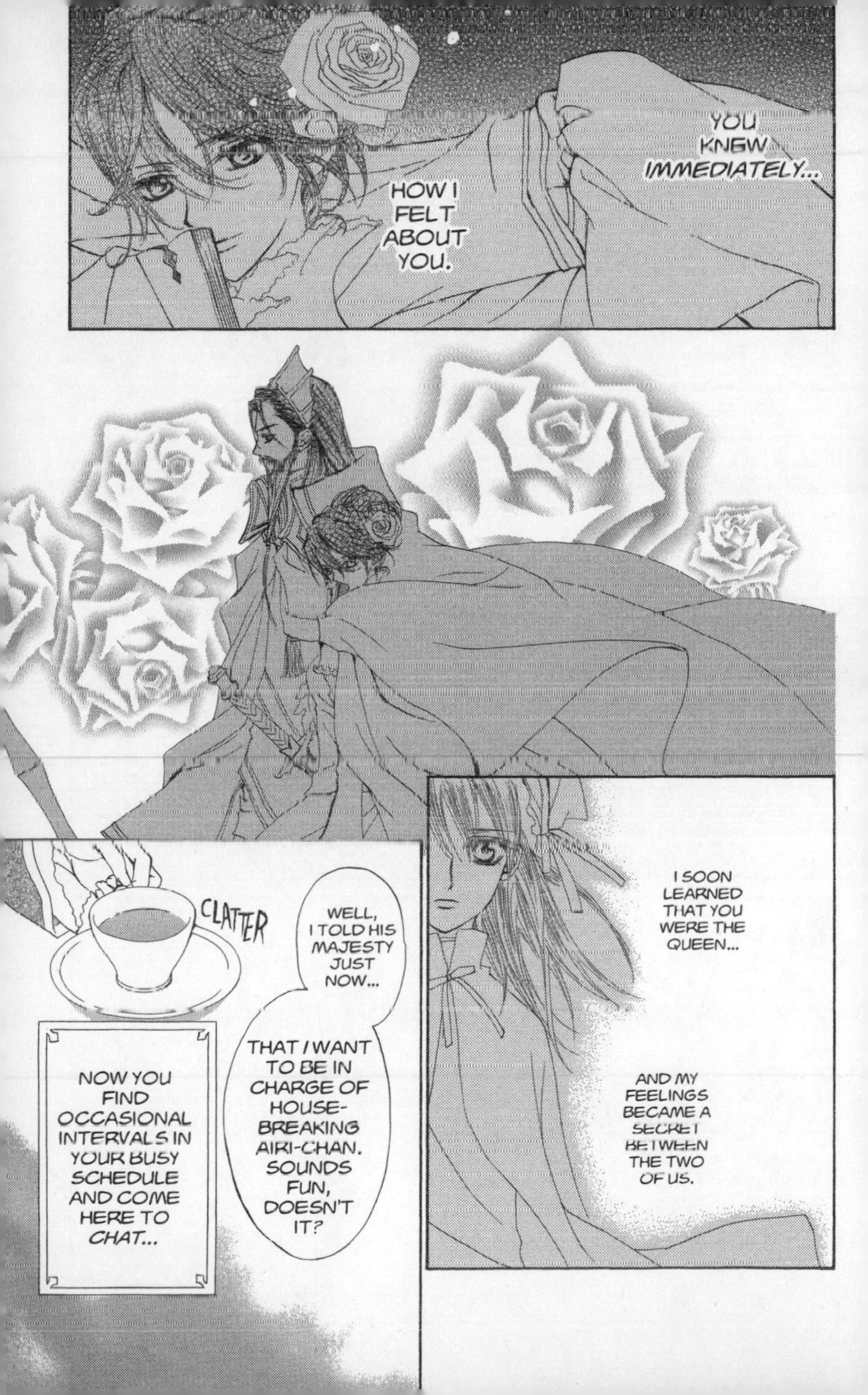
YOU KNEW IMMEDIATELY...
HOW I FELT ABOUT YOU.
I SOON LEARNED THAT YOU WERE THE QUEEN...
AND MY FEELINGS BECAME A SECRET BETWEEN THE TWO OF US.
WELL, I TOLD HIS MAJESTY JUST NOW...
THAT I WANT TO BE IN CHARGE OF HOUSE-BREAKING AIRI-CHAN. SOUNDS FUN, DOESN'T IT?
CLATTER
NOW YOU FIND OCCASIONAL INTERVALS IN YOUR BUSY SCHEDULE AND COME HERE TO CHAT...

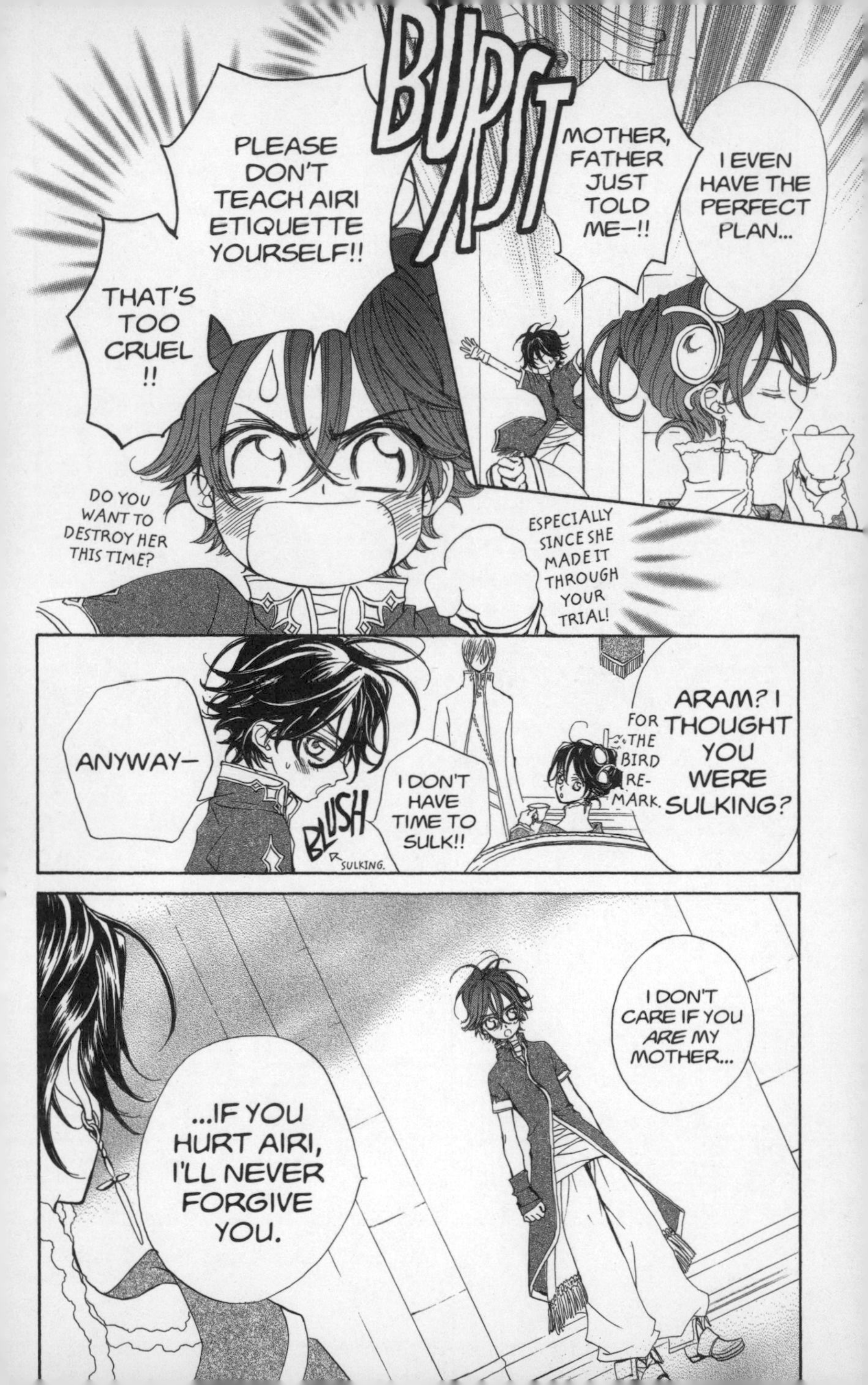
I EVEN HAVE THE PERFECT PLAN...
BURST
MOTHER, FATHER JUST TOLD ME—!!
PLEASE DON'T TEACH AIRI ETIQUETTE YOURSELF!!
THAT'S TOO CRUEL!!
ESPECIALLY SINCE SHE MADE IT THROUGH YOUR TRIAL!
DO YOU WANT TO DESTROY HER THIS TIME?
ARAM? I THOUGHT YOU WERE SULKING?
FOR THE BIRD RE-MARK.
I DON'T HAVE TIME TO SULK!!
BLUSH
SULKING.
ANYWAY—
I DON'T CARE IF YOU ARE MY MOTHER...
...IF YOU HURT AIRI, I'LL NEVER FORGIVE YOU.

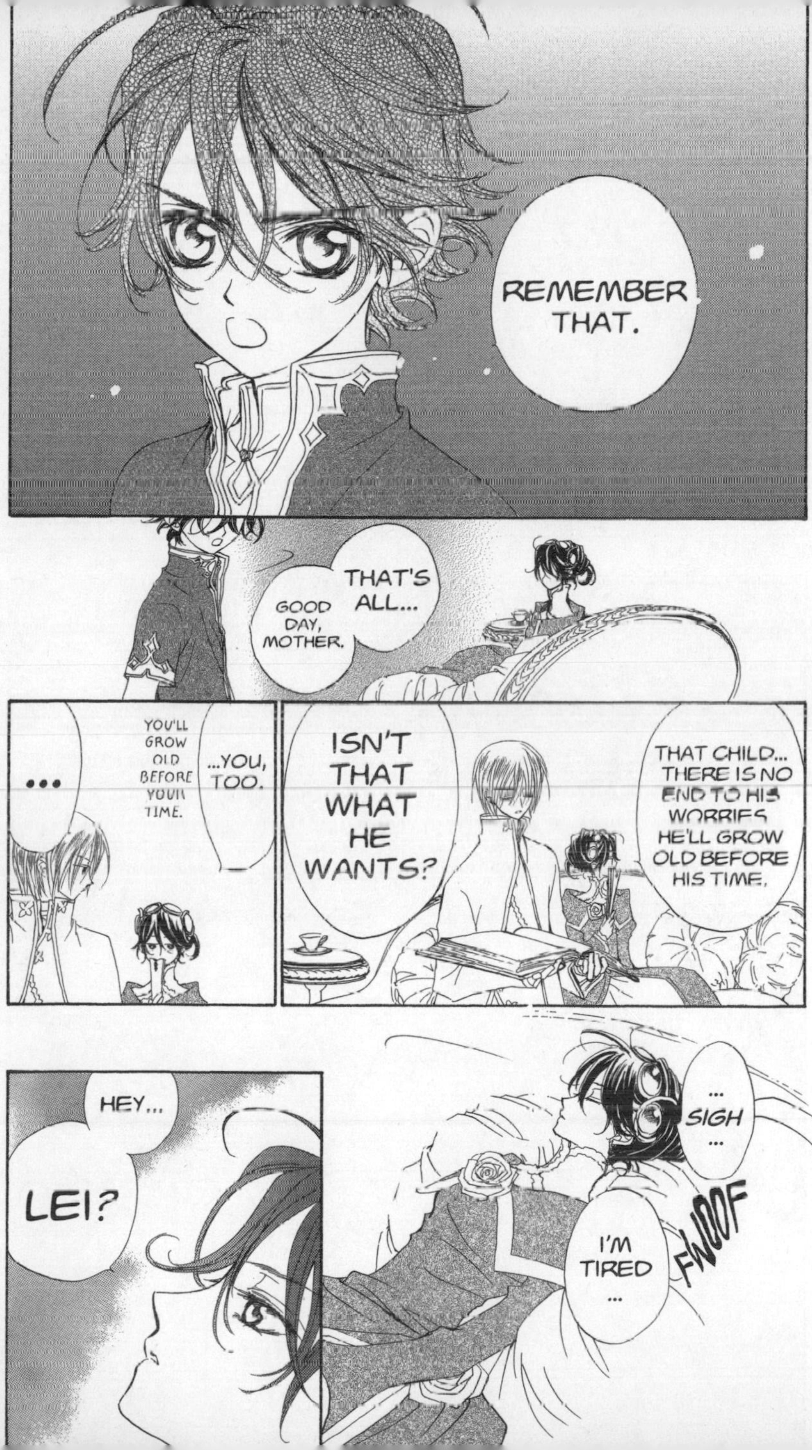
REMEMBER THAT.
THAT'S ALL...
GOOD DAY, MOTHER.
THAT CHILD... THERE IS NO END TO HIS WORRIES. HE'LL GROW OLD BEFORE HIS TIME.
ISN'T THAT WHAT HE WANTS?
...YOU, TOO.
YOU'LL GROW OLD BEFORE YOUR TIME.
...
... SIGH ...
I'M TIRED ...
FWOOF
HEY...
LEI?

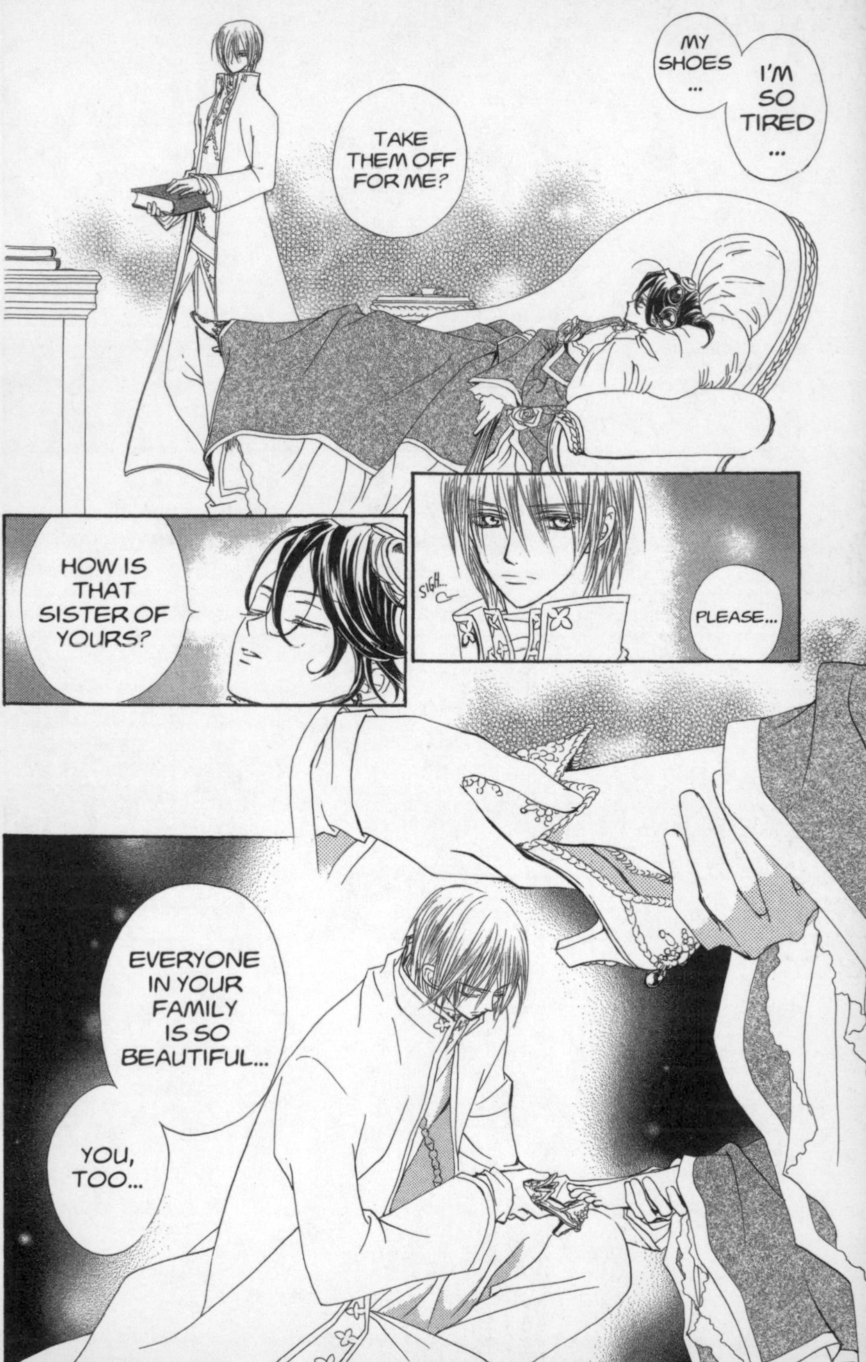
I'M SO TIRED ...
MY SHOES ...
TAKE THEM OFF FOR ME?
SIGH...
PLEASE...
HOW IS THAT SISTER OF YOURS?
EVERYONE IN YOUR FAMILY IS SO BEAUTIFUL...
YOU, TOO...

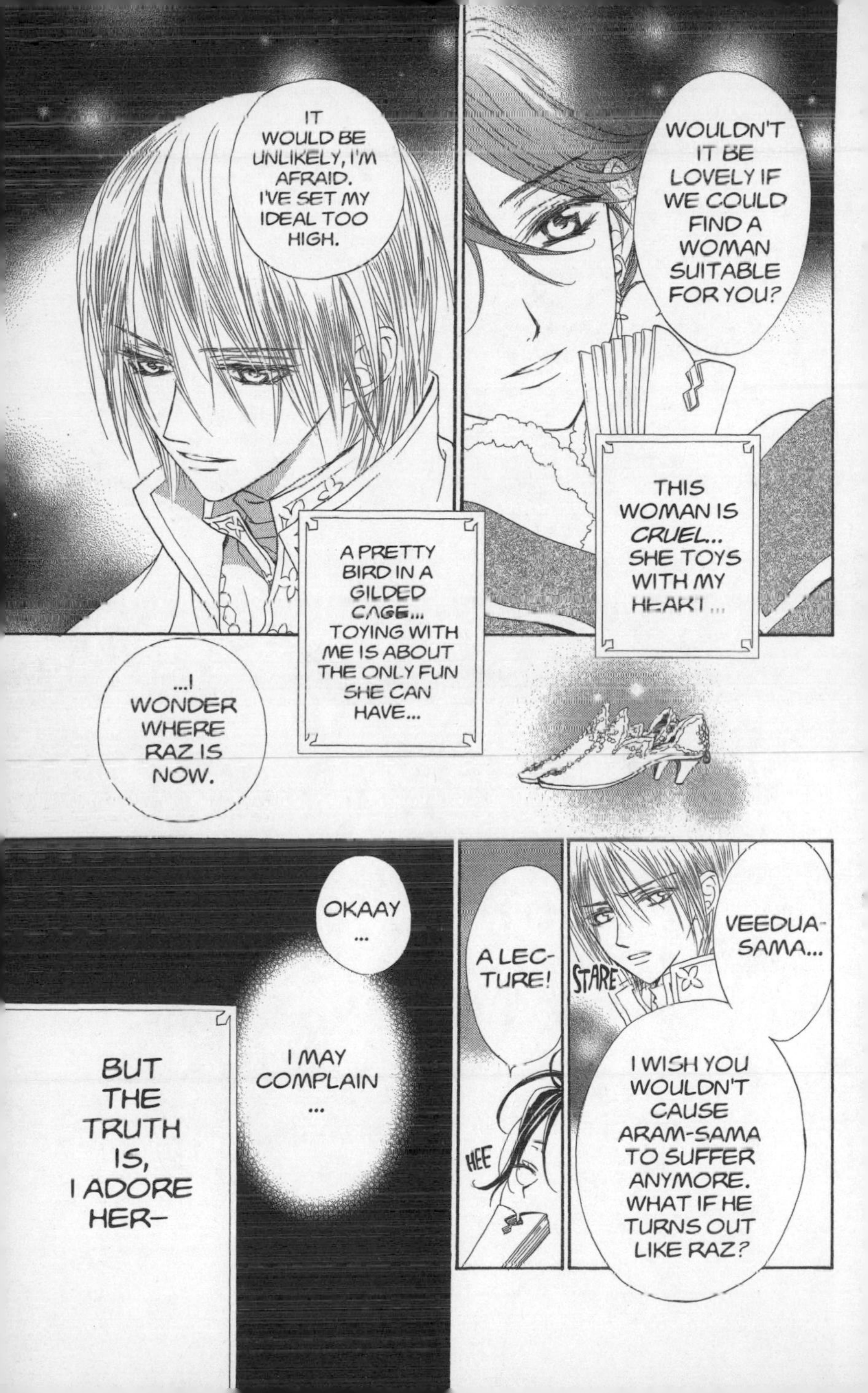
WOULDN'T IT BE LOVELY IF WE COULD FIND A WOMAN SUITABLE FOR YOU?
THIS WOMAN IS *CRUEL*... SHE TOYS WITH MY HEART...
IT WOULD BE UNLIKELY, I'M AFRAID. I'VE SET MY IDEAL TOO HIGH.
A PRETTY BIRD IN A GILDED CAGE... TOYING WITH ME IS ABOUT THE ONLY FUN SHE CAN HAVE...
...I WONDER WHERE RAZ IS NOW.
VEEDUA-SAMA...
STARE
I WISH YOU WOULDN'T CAUSE ARAM-SAMA TO SUFFER ANYMORE. WHAT IF HE TURNS OUT LIKE RAZ?
A LEC-TURE!
HEE
OKAAY...
I MAY COMPLAIN...
BUT THE TRUTH IS, I ADORE HER-

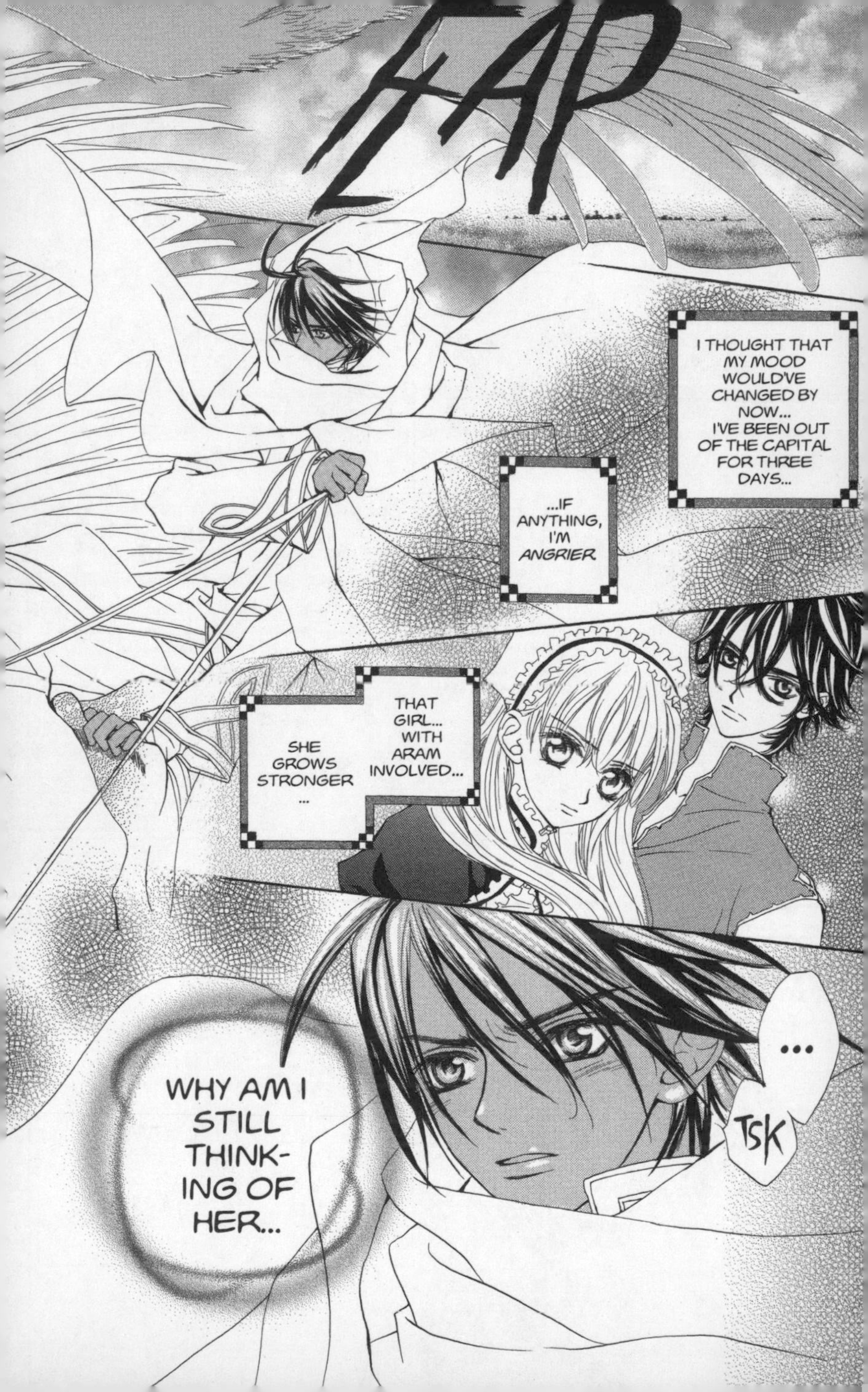
FAP
I THOUGHT THAT MY MOOD WOULD'VE CHANGED BY NOW... I'VE BEEN OUT OF THE CAPITAL FOR THREE DAYS...
...IF ANYTHING, I'M ANGRIER
THAT GIRL... WITH ARAM INVOLVED...
SHE GROWS STRONGER ...
...
TSK
WHY AM I STILL THINK-ING OF HER...

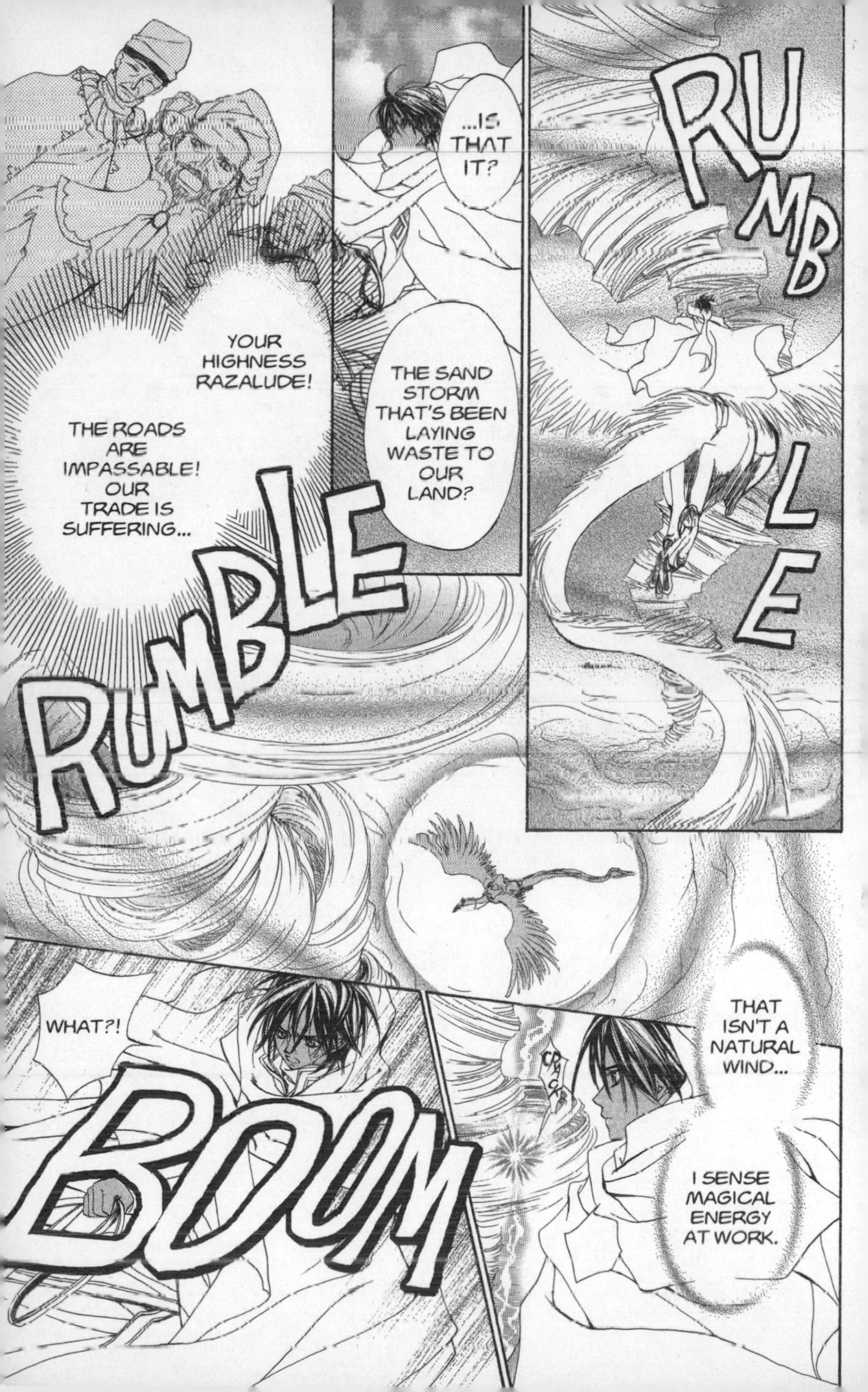
RUMBLE
...IS THAT IT?
THE SAND STORM THAT'S BEEN LAYING WASTE TO OUR LAND?
YOUR HIGHNESS RAZALUDE!
THE ROADS ARE IMPASSABLE! OUR TRADE IS SUFFERING...
RUMBLE
THAT ISN'T A NATURAL WIND...
I SENSE MAGICAL ENERGY AT WORK.
CRACK
WHAT?!
BOOM

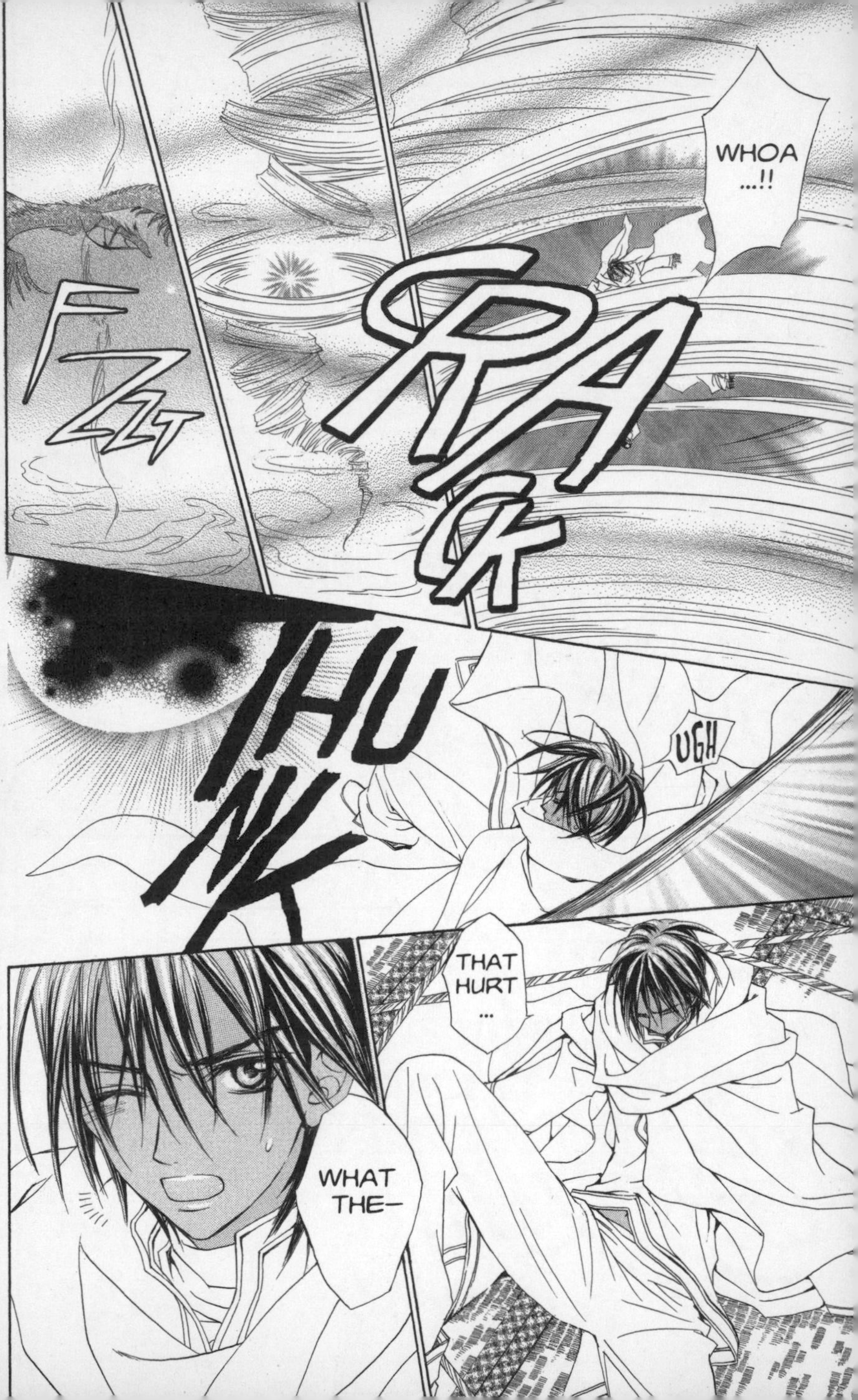
WHOA ...!!
CRACK
FZZT
UGH
THUNK
THAT HURT ...
WHAT THE—

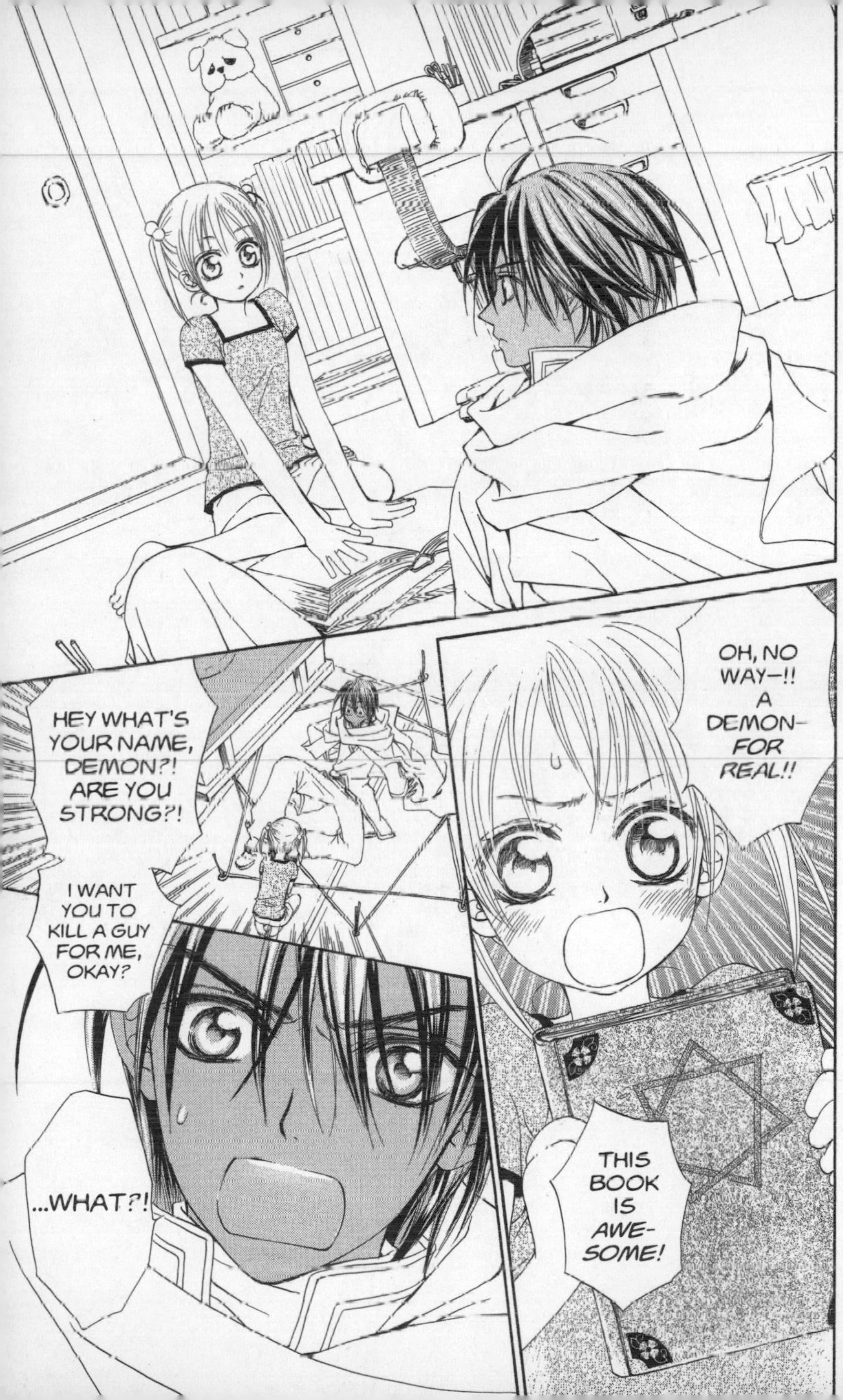
OH, NO WAY—!! A DEMON—FOR REAL!!
THIS BOOK IS AWESOME!
HEY WHAT'S YOUR NAME, DEMON?! ARE YOU STRONG?!
I WANT YOU TO KILL A GUY FOR ME, OKAY?
...WHAT?!

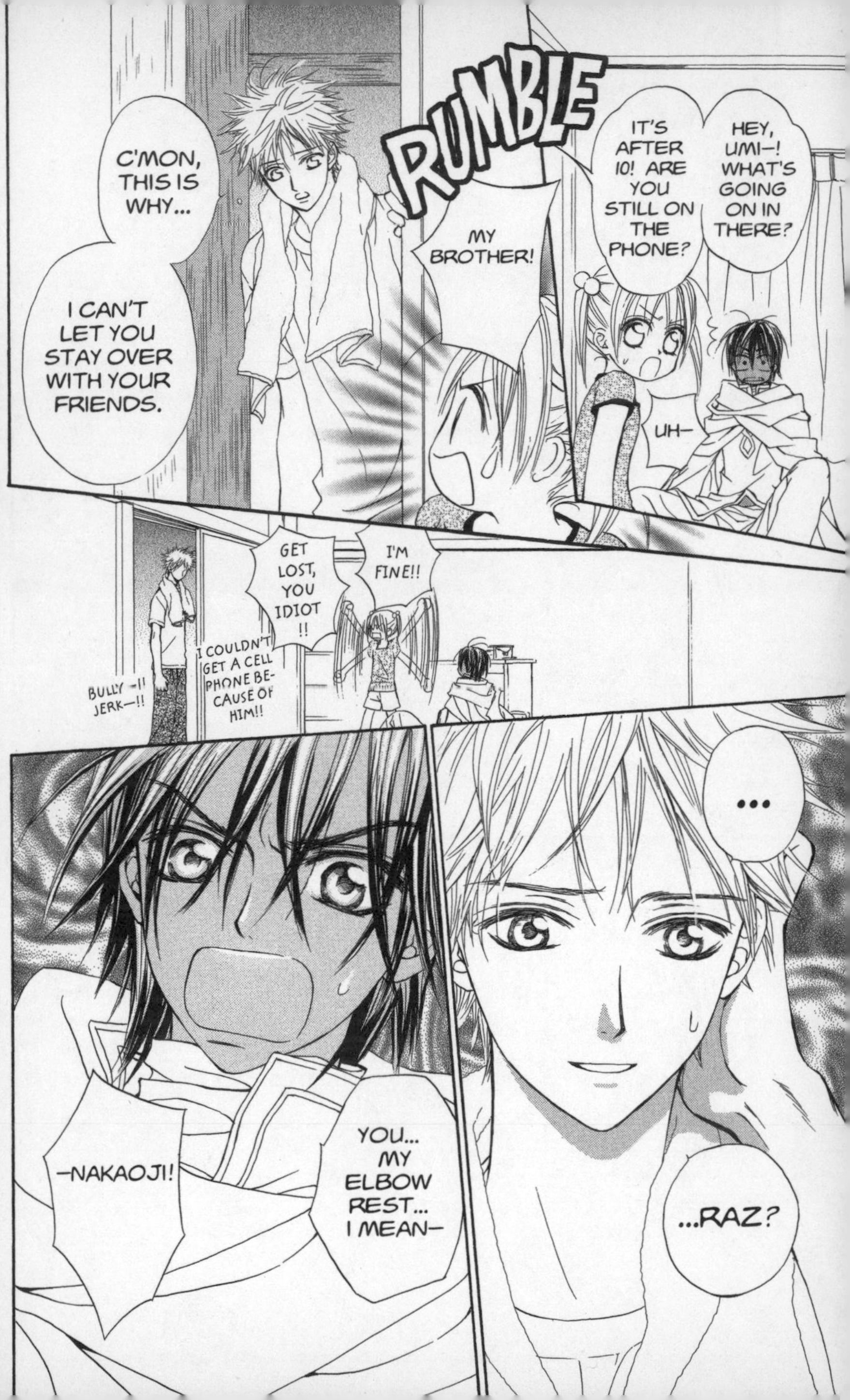
HEY, UMI—! WHAT'S GOING ON IN THERE?
IT'S AFTER 10! ARE YOU STILL ON THE PHONE?
UH—
RUMBLE
MY BROTHER!
C'MON, THIS IS WHY...
I CAN'T LET YOU STAY OVER WITH YOUR FRIENDS.
I'M FINE!!
GET LOST, YOU IDIOT !!
I COULDN'T GET A CELL PHONE BE-CAUSE OF HIM!!
BULLY—!! JERK—!!
...
...RAZ?
YOU... MY ELBOW REST... I MEAN—
—NAKAOJI!

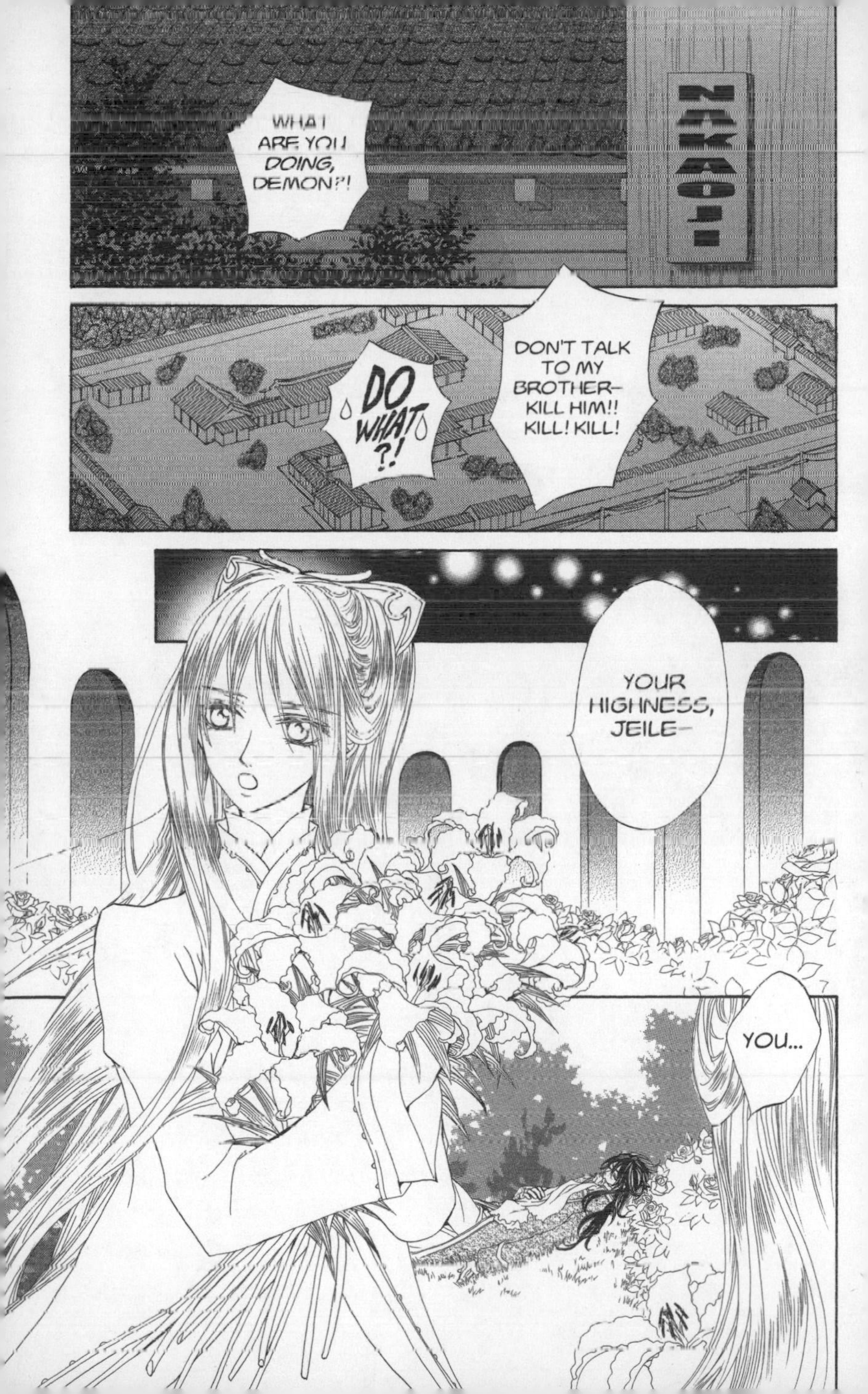
WHAT ARE YOU DOING, DEMON?!
DON'T TALK TO MY BROTHER— KILL HIM!! KILL! KILL!
DO WHAT?!
YOUR HIGHNESS, JEILE—
YOU...

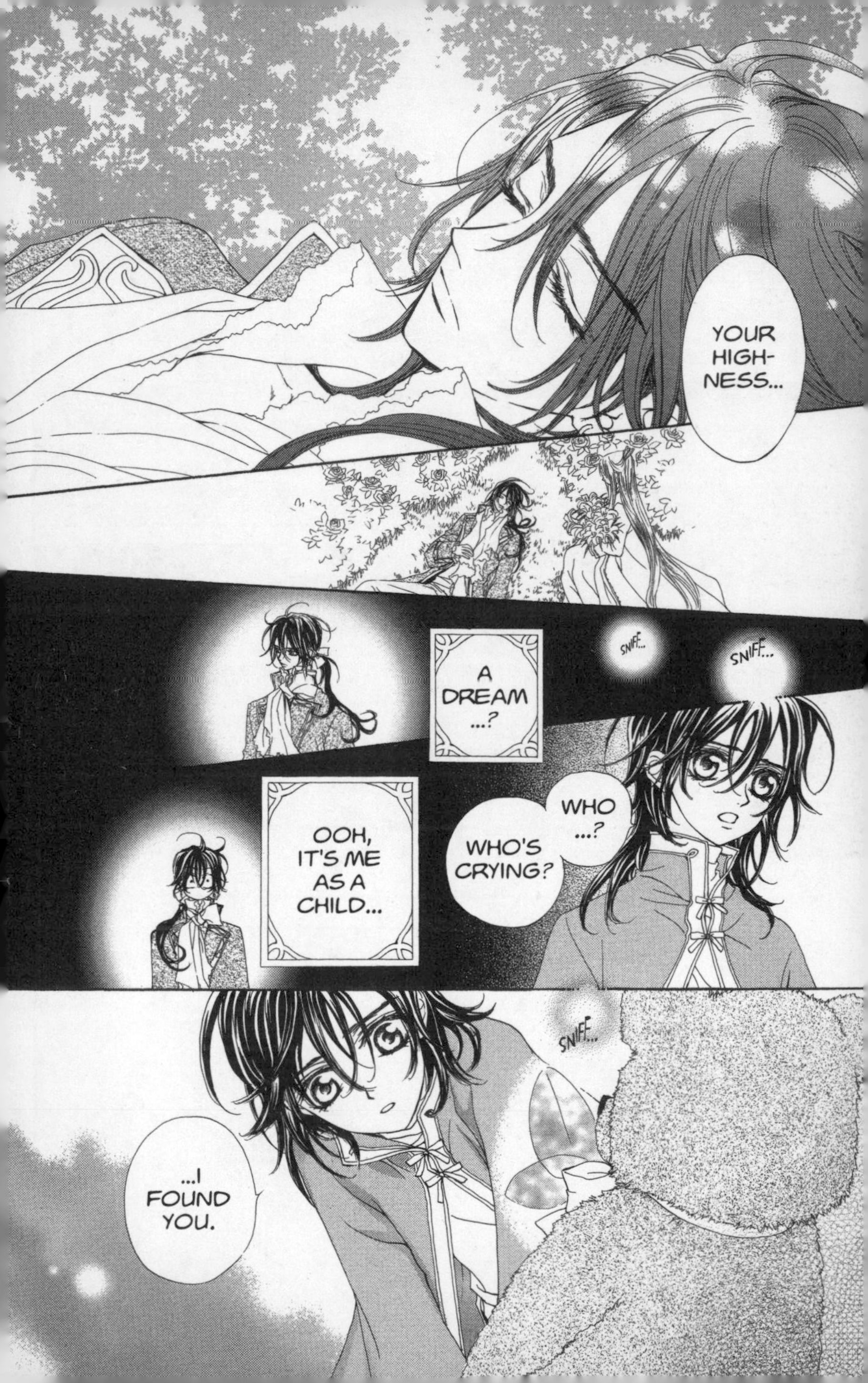
YOUR HIGH-NESS...
SNIFF...
SNIFF...
A DREAM ...?
WHO ...?
WHO'S CRYING?
OOH, IT'S ME AS A CHILD...
SNIFF...
...I FOUND YOU.

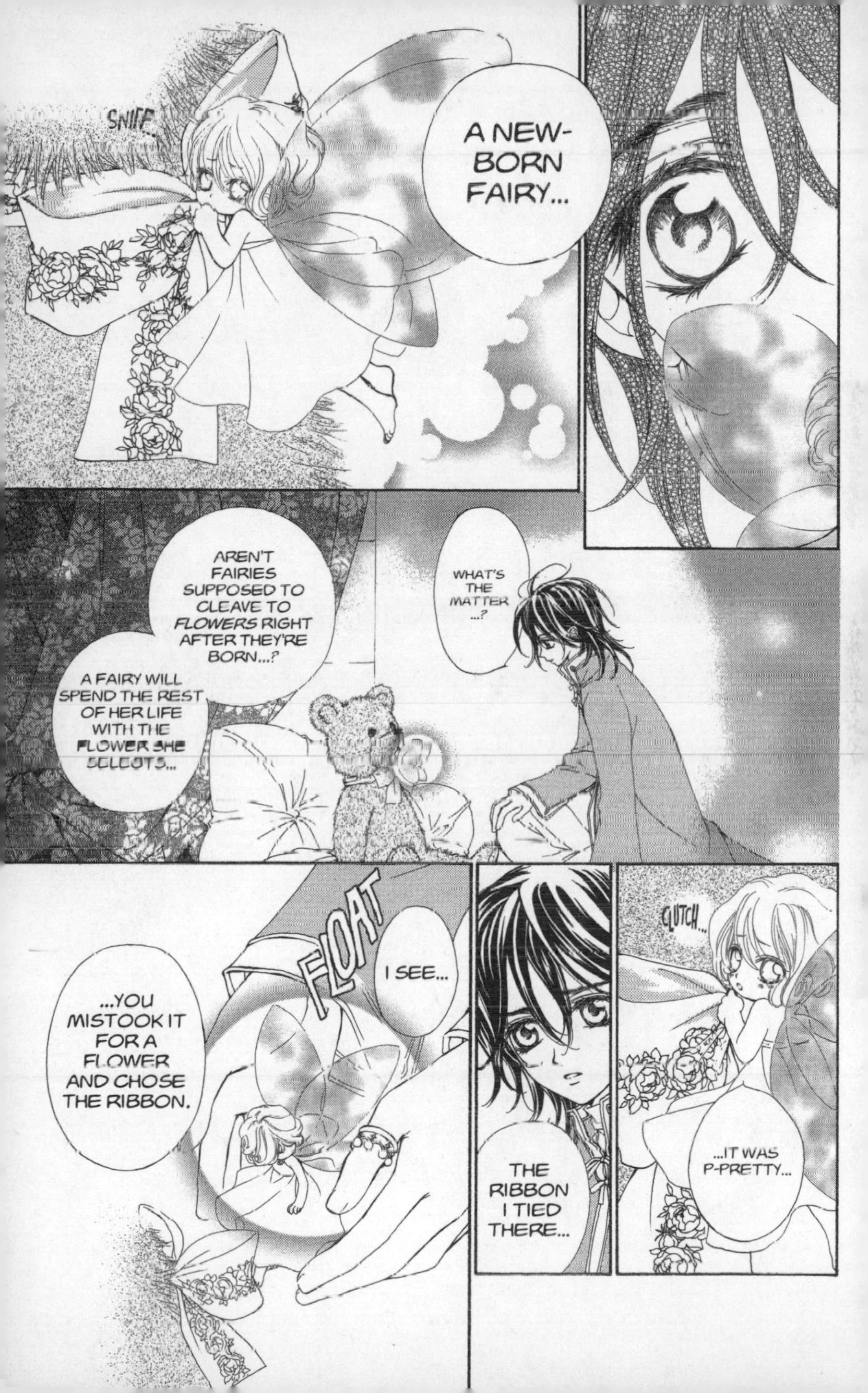
A NEW-BORN FAIRY...
SNIFF...
WHAT'S THE MATTER...?
AREN'T FAIRIES SUPPOSED TO CLEAVE TO *FLOWERS* RIGHT AFTER THEY'RE BORN...?
A FAIRY WILL SPEND THE REST OF HER LIFE WITH THE FLOWER SHE SELECTS...
CLUTCH...
...IT WAS P-PRETTY...
THE RIBBON I TIED THERE...
FLOAT
I SEE...
...YOU MISTOOK IT FOR A FLOWER AND CHOSE THE RIBBON.

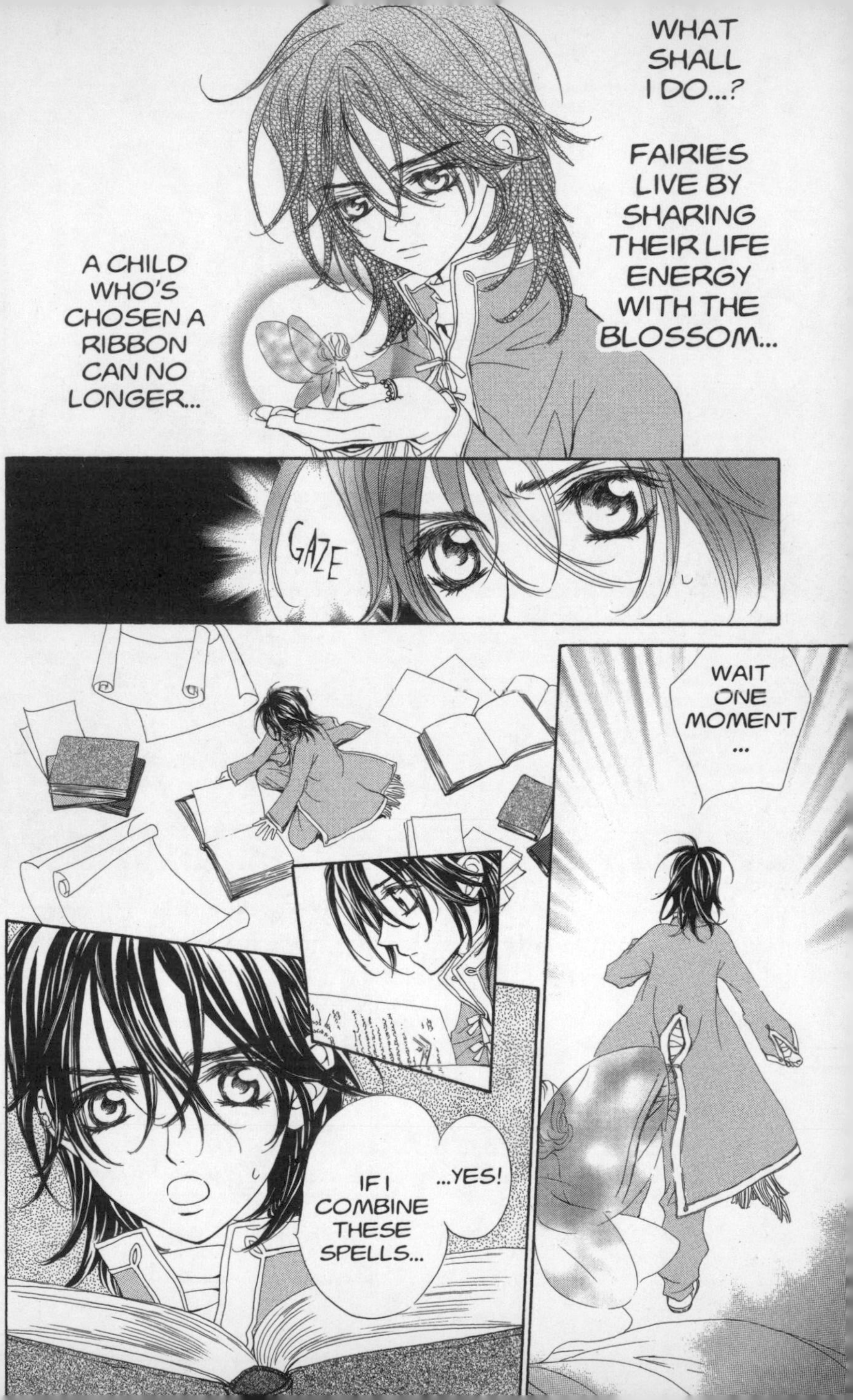
WHAT SHALL I DO...?
FAIRIES LIVE BY SHARING THEIR LIFE ENERGY WITH THE BLOSSOM...
A CHILD WHO'S CHOSEN A RIBBON CAN NO LONGER...
GAZE
WAIT ONE MOMENT ...
...YES!
IF I COMBINE THESE SPELLS...

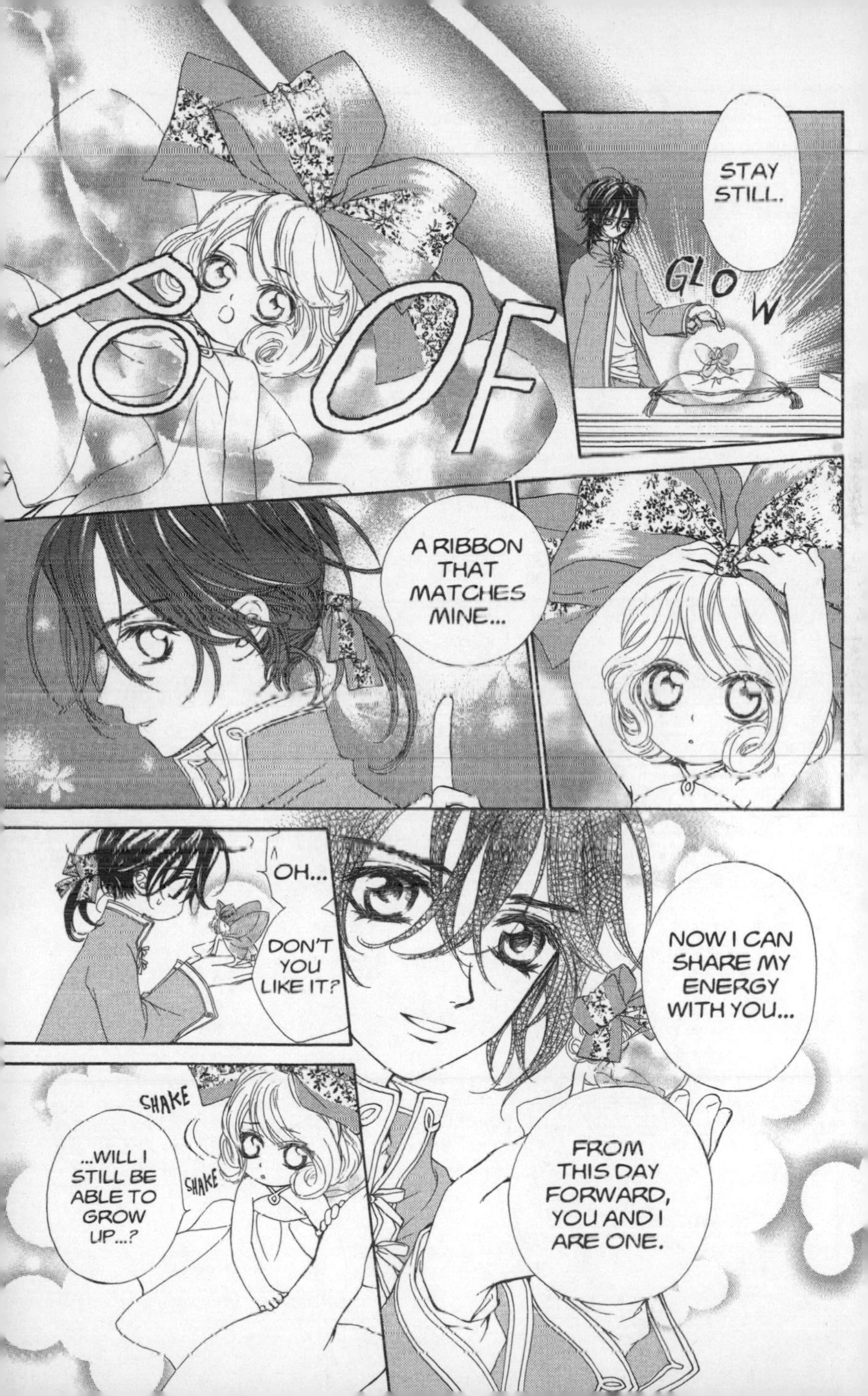
STAY STILL.
GLOW
POOF
A RIBBON THAT MATCHES MINE...
NOW I CAN SHARE MY ENERGY WITH YOU...
FROM THIS DAY FORWARD, YOU AND I ARE ONE.
OH...
DON'T YOU LIKE IT?
SHAKE
SHAKE
...WILL I STILL BE ABLE TO GROW UP...?

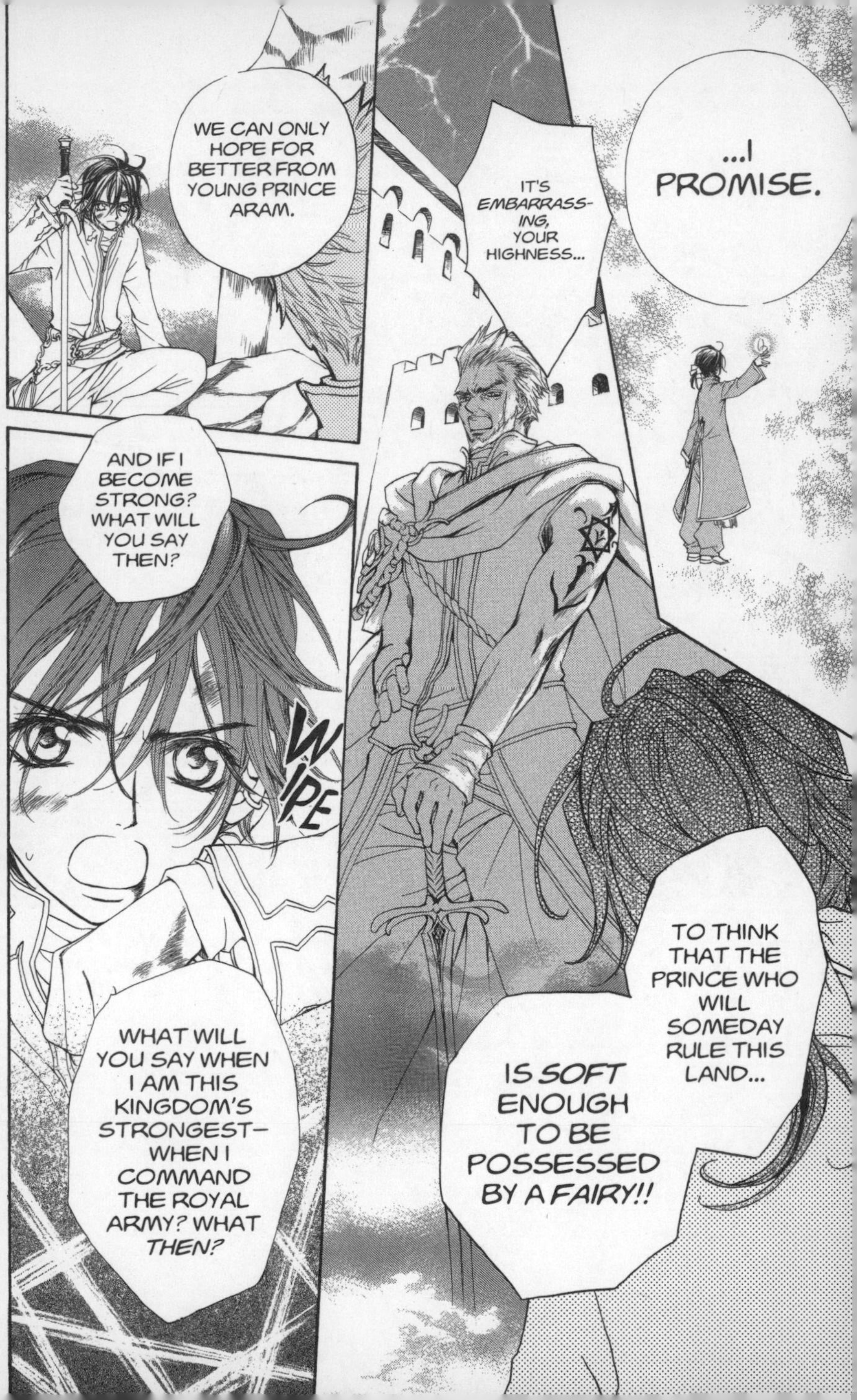
...I PROMISE.
IT'S EMBARRASSING, YOUR HIGHNESS...
TO THINK THAT THE PRINCE WHO WILL SOMEDAY RULE THIS LAND...
IS *SOFT* ENOUGH TO BE POSSESSED BY A *FAIRY!!*
WE CAN ONLY HOPE FOR BETTER FROM YOUNG PRINCE ARAM.
AND IF I BECOME STRONG? WHAT WILL YOU SAY THEN?
WIPE
WHAT WILL YOU SAY WHEN I AM THIS KINGDOM'S STRONGEST—WHEN I COMMAND THE ROYAL ARMY? WHAT *THEN?*

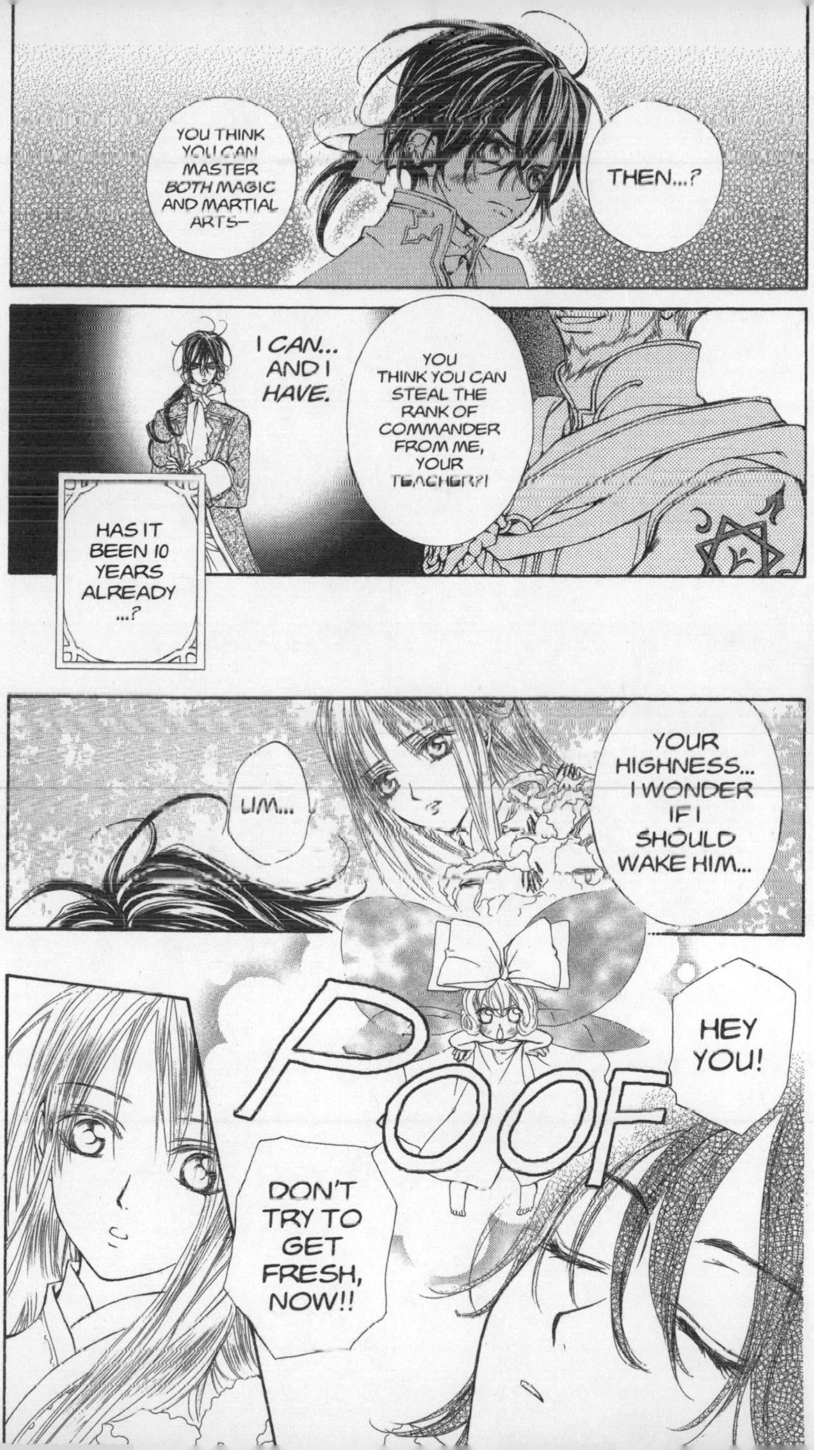
THEN...?
YOU THINK YOU CAN MASTER *BOTH* MAGIC AND MARTIAL ARTS—
YOU THINK YOU CAN STEAL THE RANK OF COMMANDER FROM ME, YOUR TEACHER?!
I *CAN*... AND I *HAVE*.
HAS IT BEEN 10 YEARS ALREADY ...?
YOUR HIGHNESS... I WONDER IF I SHOULD WAKE HIM...
LIM...
HEY YOU!
POOF
DON'T TRY TO GET FRESH, NOW!!

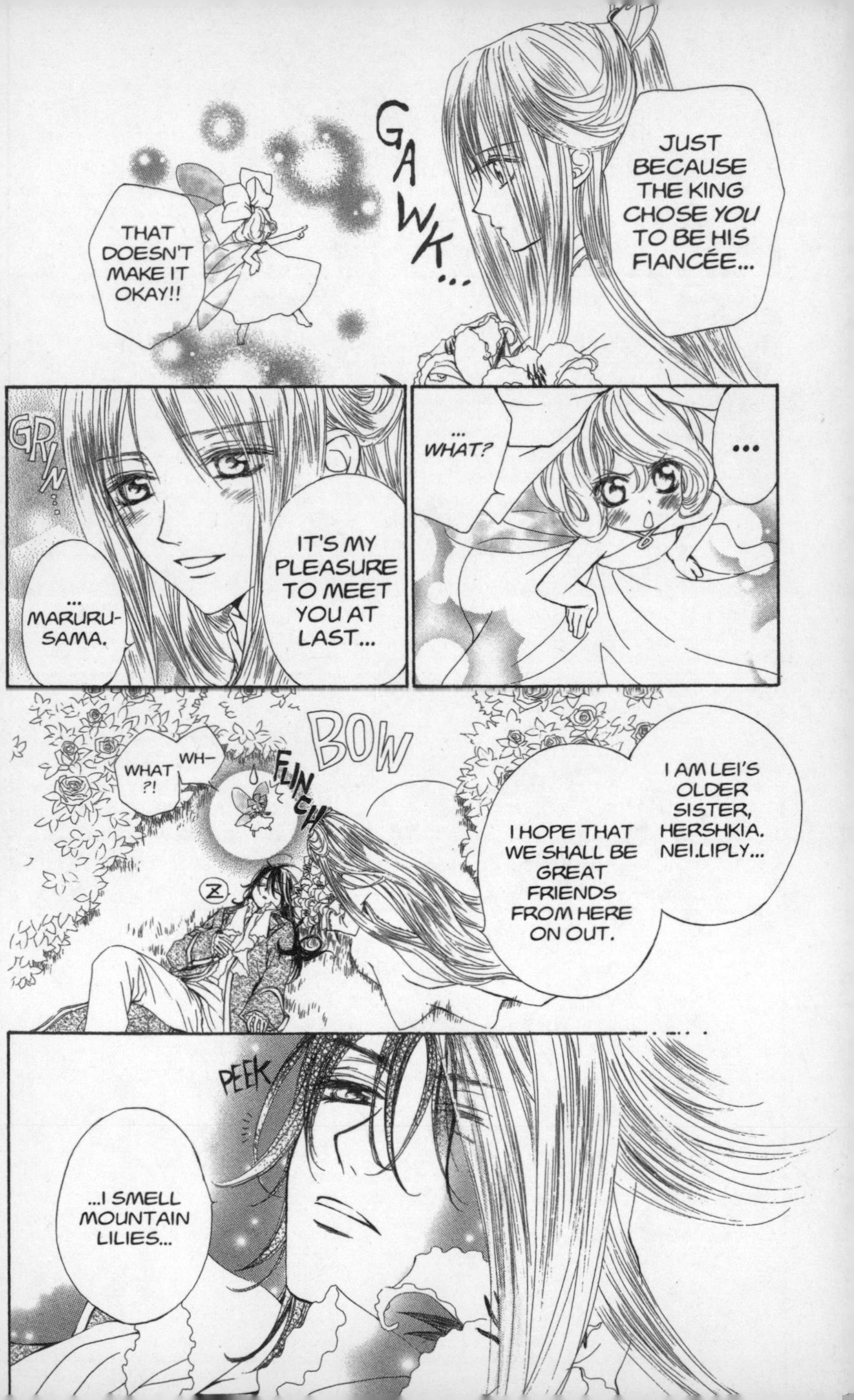
JUST BECAUSE THE KING CHOSE *YOU* TO BE HIS FIANCÉE...
GAWK...
THAT DOESN'T MAKE IT OKAY!!
...
... *WHAT?*
IT'S MY PLEASURE TO MEET YOU AT LAST...
GRIN...
... MARURU-SAMA.
I AM LEI'S OLDER SISTER, HERSHKIA. NEI.LIPLY...
I HOPE THAT WE SHALL BE GREAT FRIENDS FROM HERE ON OUT.
BOW
FLINCH
WH-
WHAT ?!
Z
PEEK
...I SMELL MOUNTAIN LILIES...

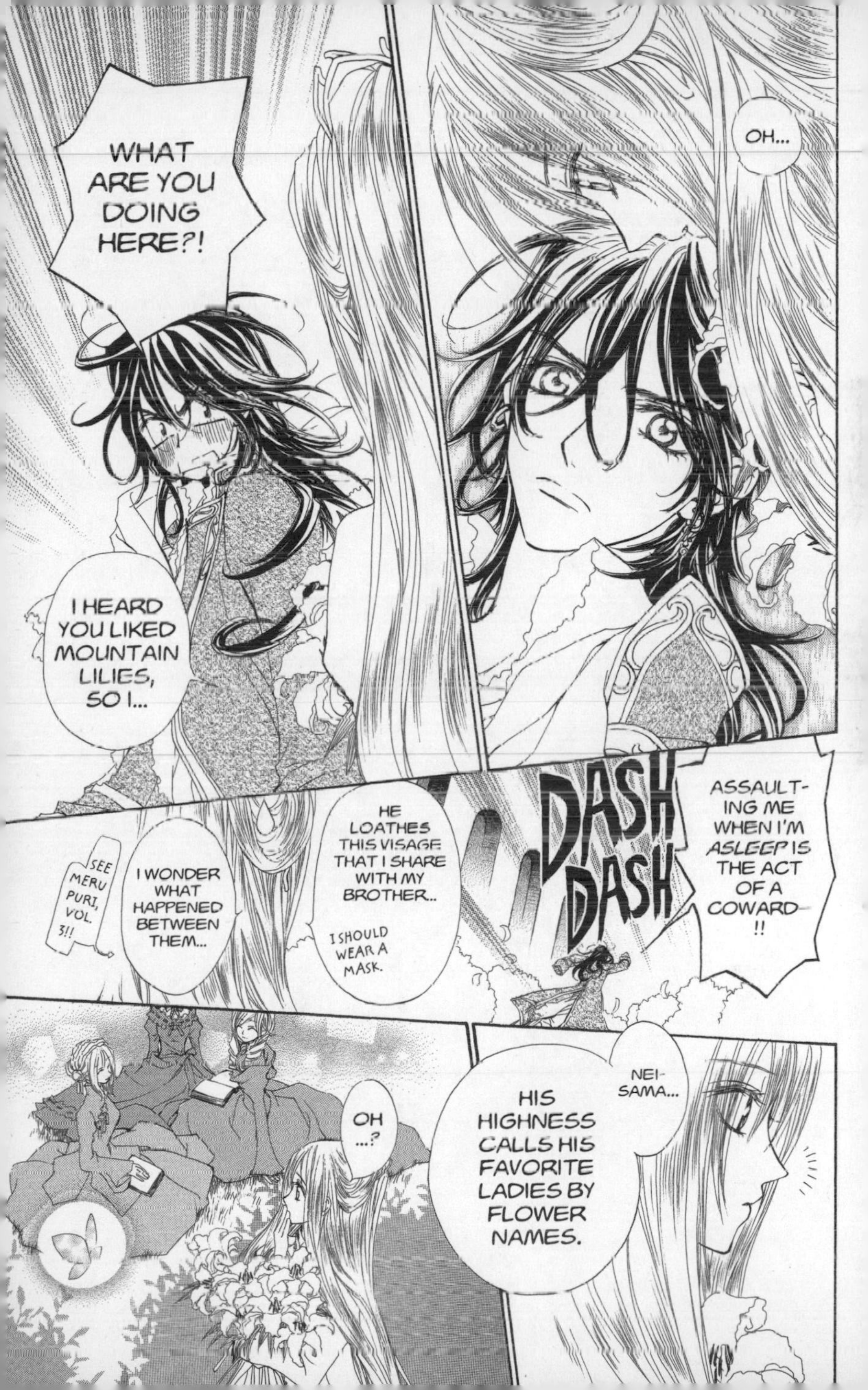
OH...
WHAT ARE YOU DOING HERE?!
I HEARD YOU LIKED MOUNTAIN LILIES, SO I...
ASSAULTING ME WHEN I'M *ASLEEP* IS THE ACT OF A COWARD!!
DASH DASH
HE LOATHES THIS VISAGE THAT I SHARE WITH MY BROTHER...
I SHOULD WEAR A MASK.
I WONDER WHAT HAPPENED BETWEEN THEM...
SEE MERU PURI, VOL. 3!!
NEI-SAMA...
HIS HIGHNESS CALLS HIS FAVORITE LADIES BY FLOWER NAMES.
OH ...?

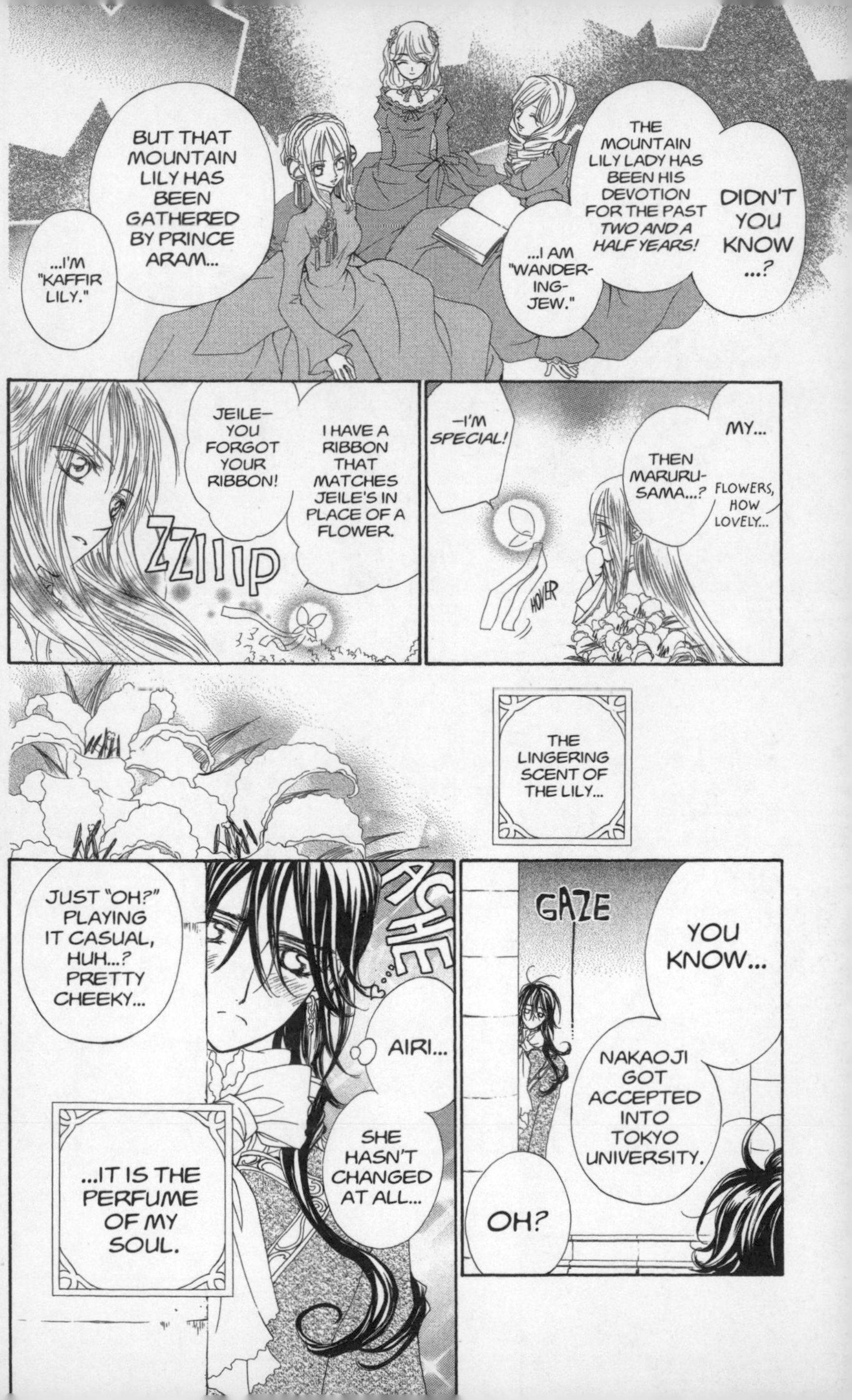
DIDN'T YOU KNOW ...?
THE MOUNTAIN LILY LADY HAS BEEN HIS DEVOTION FOR THE PAST TWO AND A HALF YEARS!
...I AM "WANDERING-JEW."
BUT THAT MOUNTAIN LILY HAS BEEN GATHERED BY PRINCE ARAM...
...I'M "KAFFIR LILY."
MY...
FLOWERS, HOW LOVELY...
THEN MARURU-SAMA...?
—I'M SPECIAL!
HOVER
I HAVE A RIBBON THAT MATCHES JEILE'S IN PLACE OF A FLOWER.
JEILE—YOU FORGOT YOUR RIBBON!
ZZIIIP
THE LINGERING SCENT OF THE LILY...
YOU KNOW...
GAZE
NAKAOJI GOT ACCEPTED INTO TOKYO UNIVERSITY.
OH?
ACHE
AIRI...
SHE HASN'T CHANGED AT ALL...
JUST "OH?" PLAYING IT CASUAL, HUH...? PRETTY CHEEKY...
...IT IS THE PERFUME OF MY SOUL.

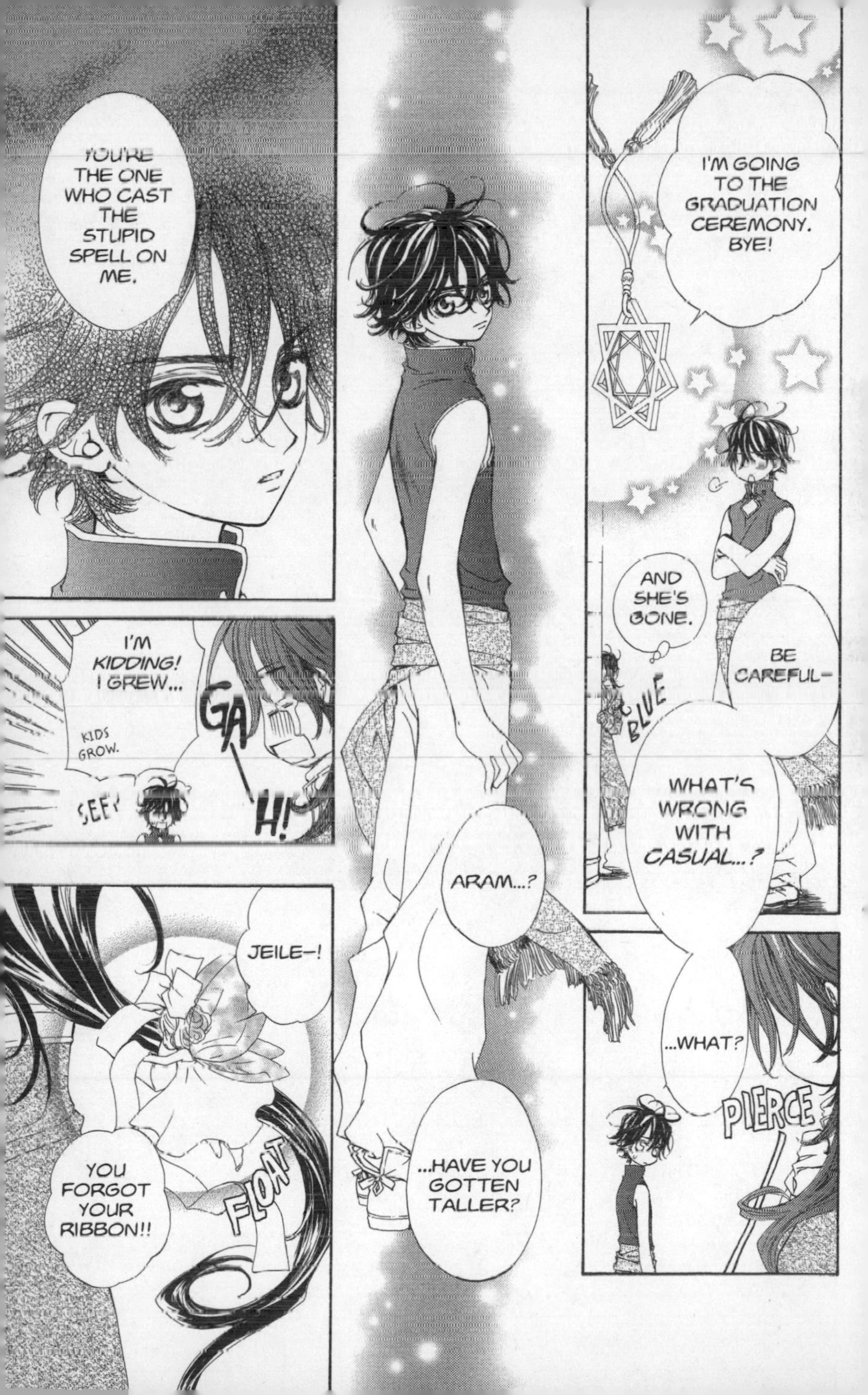
I'M GOING TO THE GRADUATION CEREMONY. BYE!
AND SHE'S GONE.
BE CAREFUL-
BLUE
WHAT'S WRONG WITH CASUAL...?
...WHAT?
PIERCE
ARAM...?
...HAVE YOU GOTTEN TALLER?
YOU'RE THE ONE WHO CAST THE STUPID SPELL ON ME.
I'M KIDDING! I GREW...
KIDS GROW.
GA-H!
JEILE-!
YOU FORGOT YOUR RIBBON!!
FLOAT

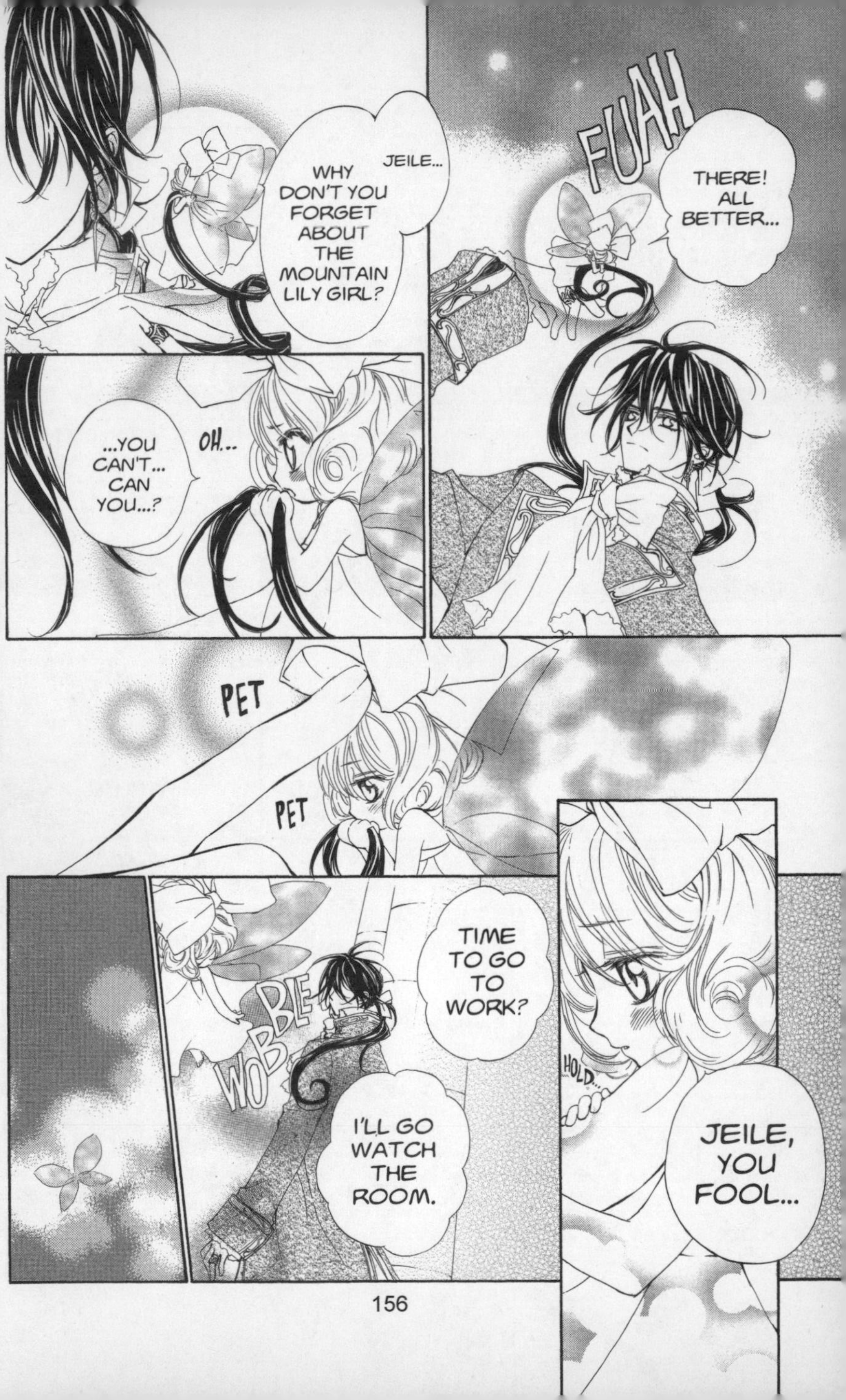
FUAH
THERE! ALL BETTER...
JEILE...
WHY DON'T YOU FORGET ABOUT THE MOUNTAIN LILY GIRL?
OH...
...YOU CAN'T... CAN YOU...?
PET
PET
HOLD...
JEILE, YOU FOOL...
TIME TO GO TO WORK?
WOBBLE
I'LL GO WATCH THE ROOM.

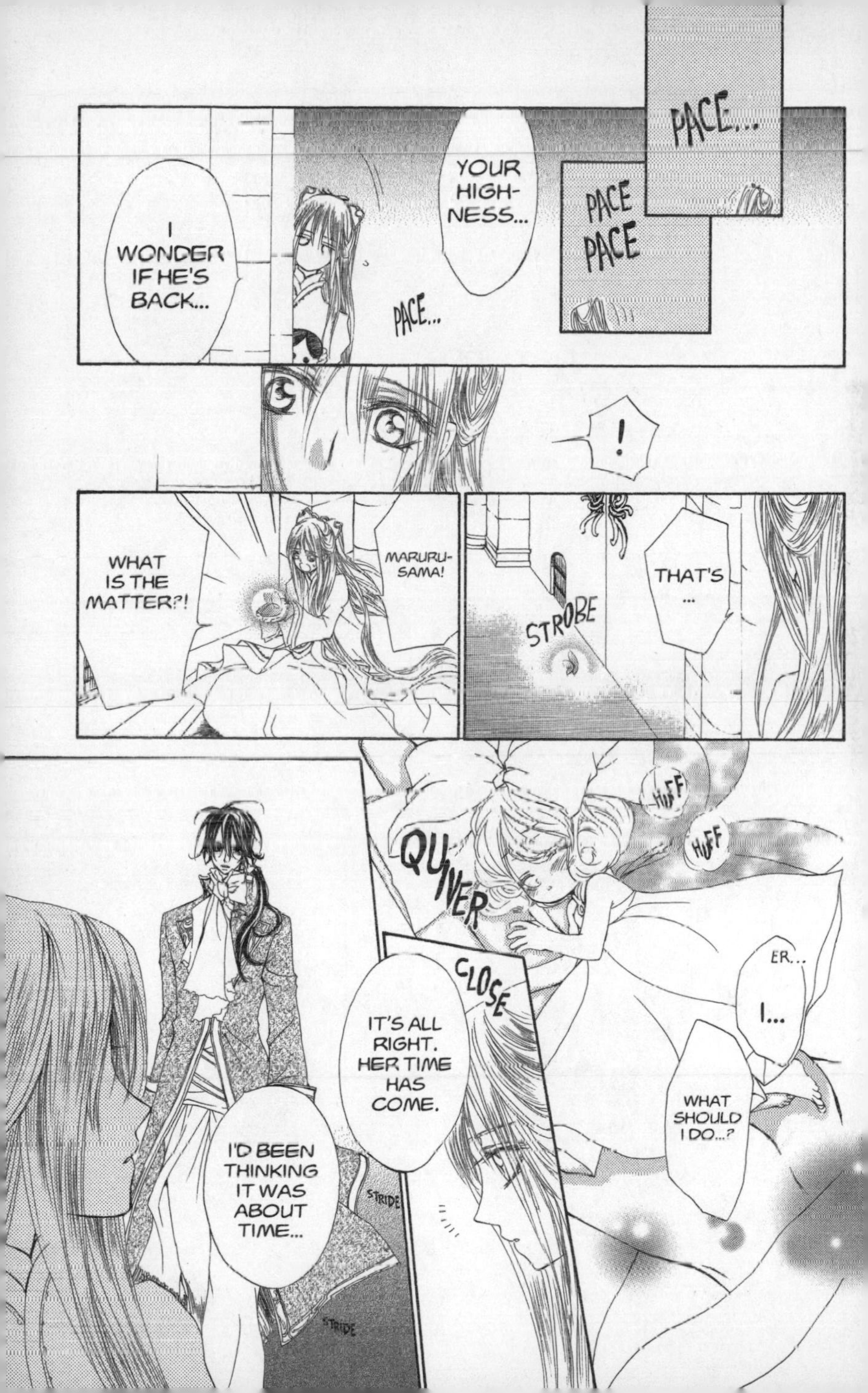
PACE...
PACE
PACE
YOUR HIGHNESS...
PACE...
I WONDER IF HE'S BACK...
!
THAT'S ...
STROBE
MARURU-SAMA!
WHAT IS THE MATTER?!
HUFF
HUFF
QUIVER
ER...
I...
WHAT SHOULD I DO...?
CLOSE
IT'S ALL RIGHT. HER TIME HAS COME.
I'D BEEN THINKING IT WAS ABOUT TIME...
STRIDE
STRIDE

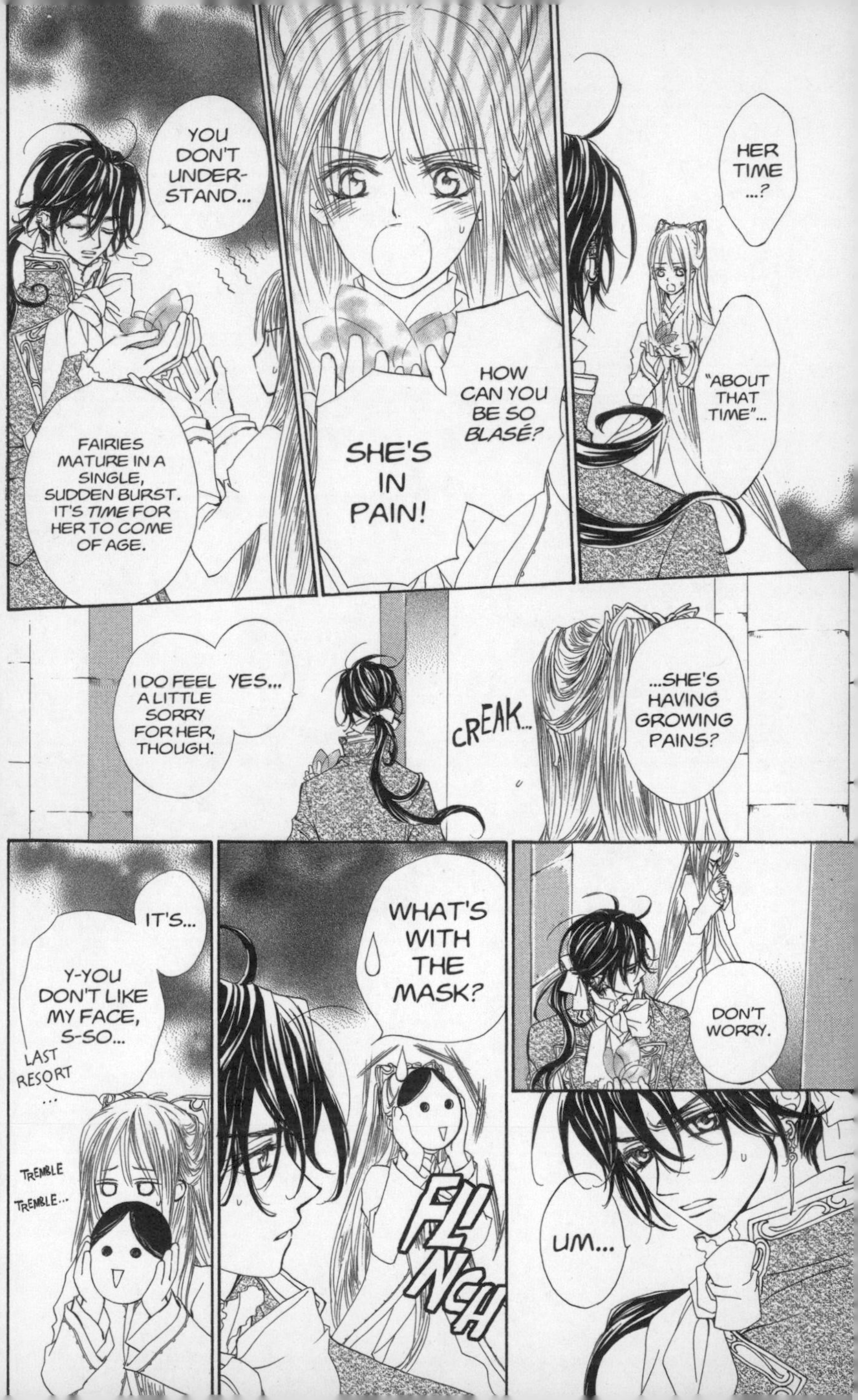
HER TIME ...?
"ABOUT THAT TIME"...
HOW CAN YOU BE SO *BLASÉ*?
SHE'S IN PAIN!
YOU DON'T UNDER-STAND...
FAIRIES MATURE IN A SINGLE, SUDDEN BURST. IT'S *TIME* FOR HER TO COME OF AGE.
...SHE'S HAVING GROWING PAINS?
CREAK...
YES...
I DO FEEL A LITTLE SORRY FOR HER, THOUGH.
DON'T WORRY.
UM...
WHAT'S WITH THE MASK?
FLINCH
IT'S...
Y-YOU DON'T LIKE MY FACE, S-SO...
LAST RESORT...
TREMBLE
TREMBLE...

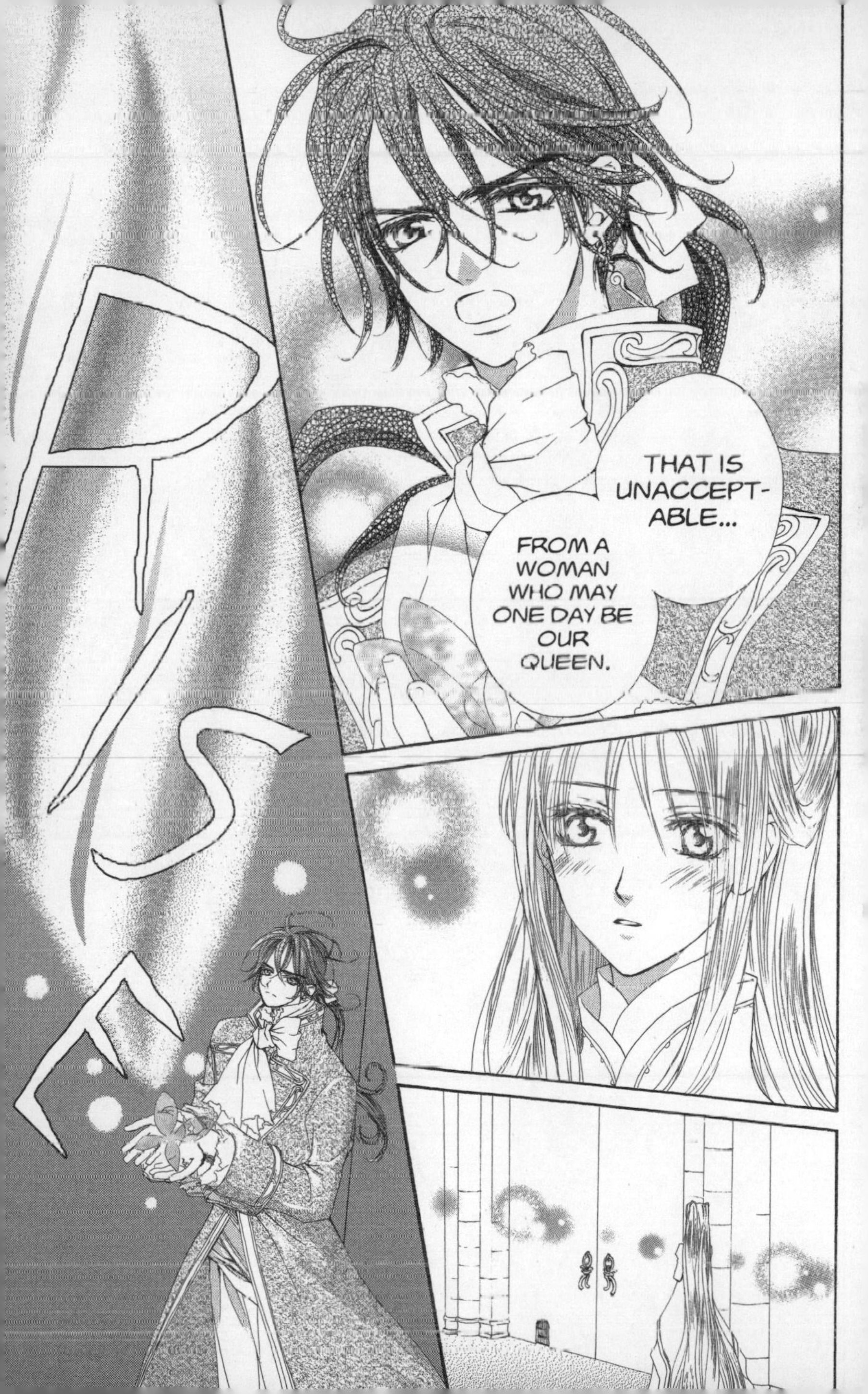
THAT IS UNACCEPT-ABLE...
FROM A WOMAN WHO MAY ONE DAY BE OUR QUEEN.
RISE

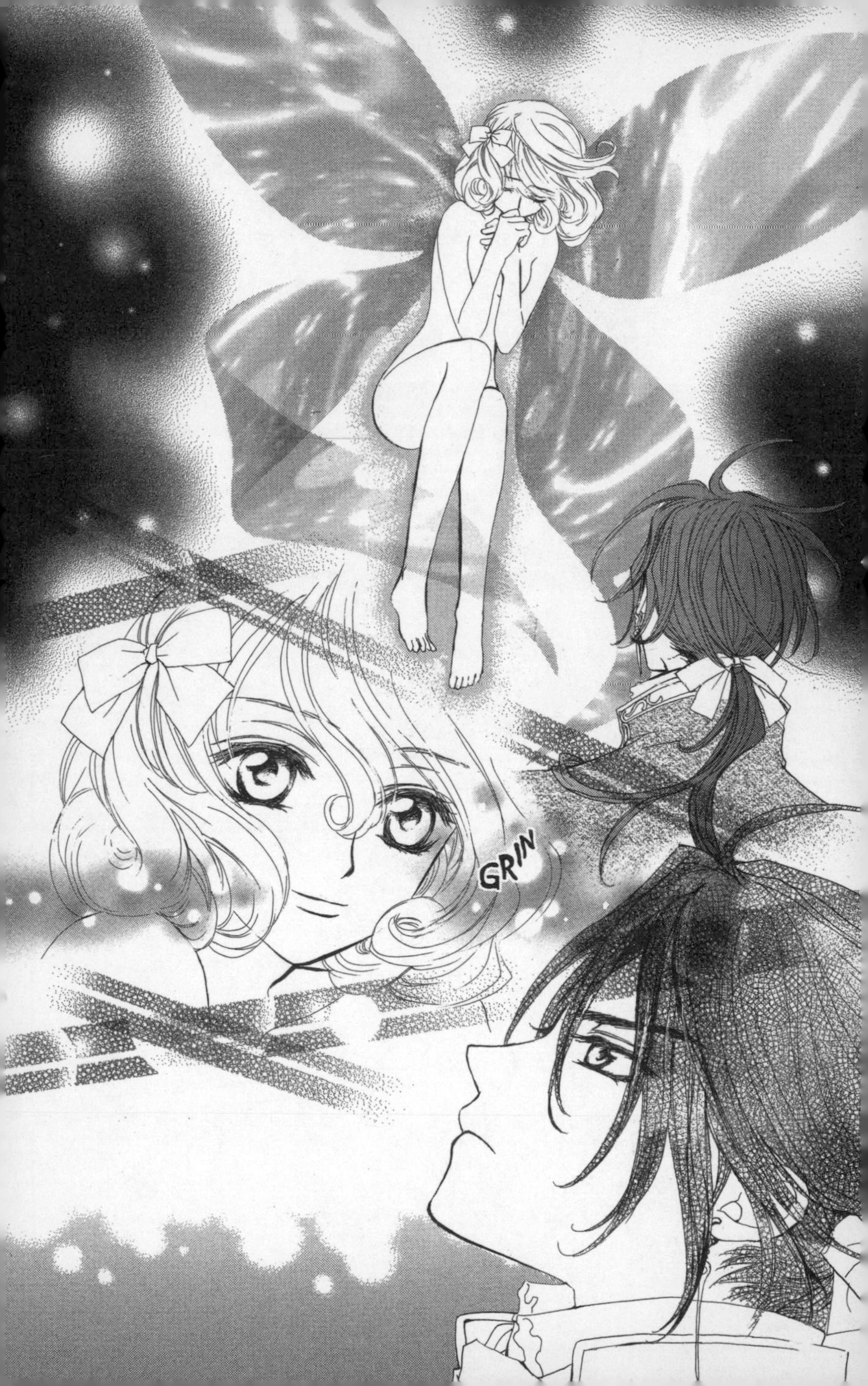
GRIN

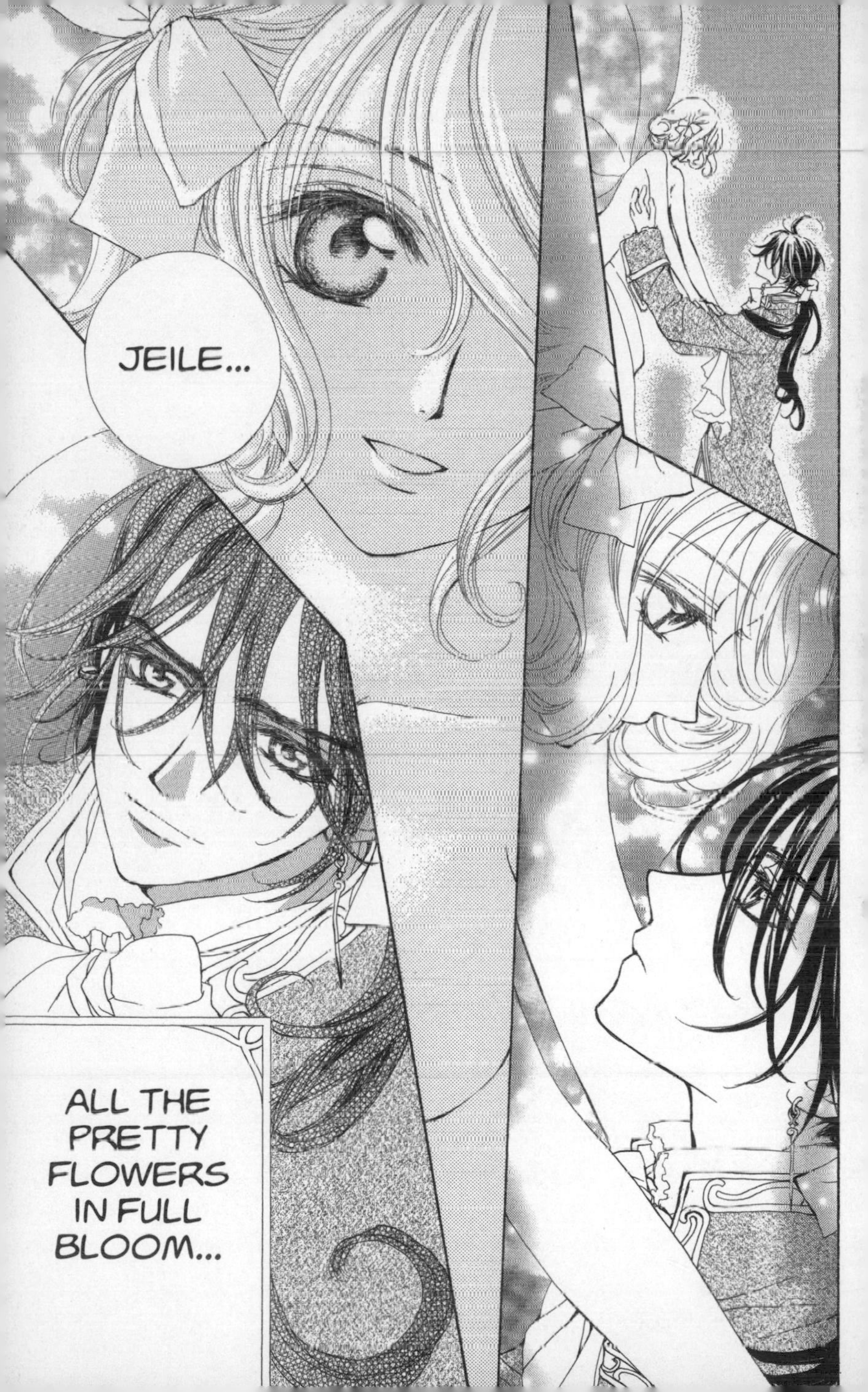
JEILE...
ALL THE PRETTY FLOWERS IN FULL BLOOM...

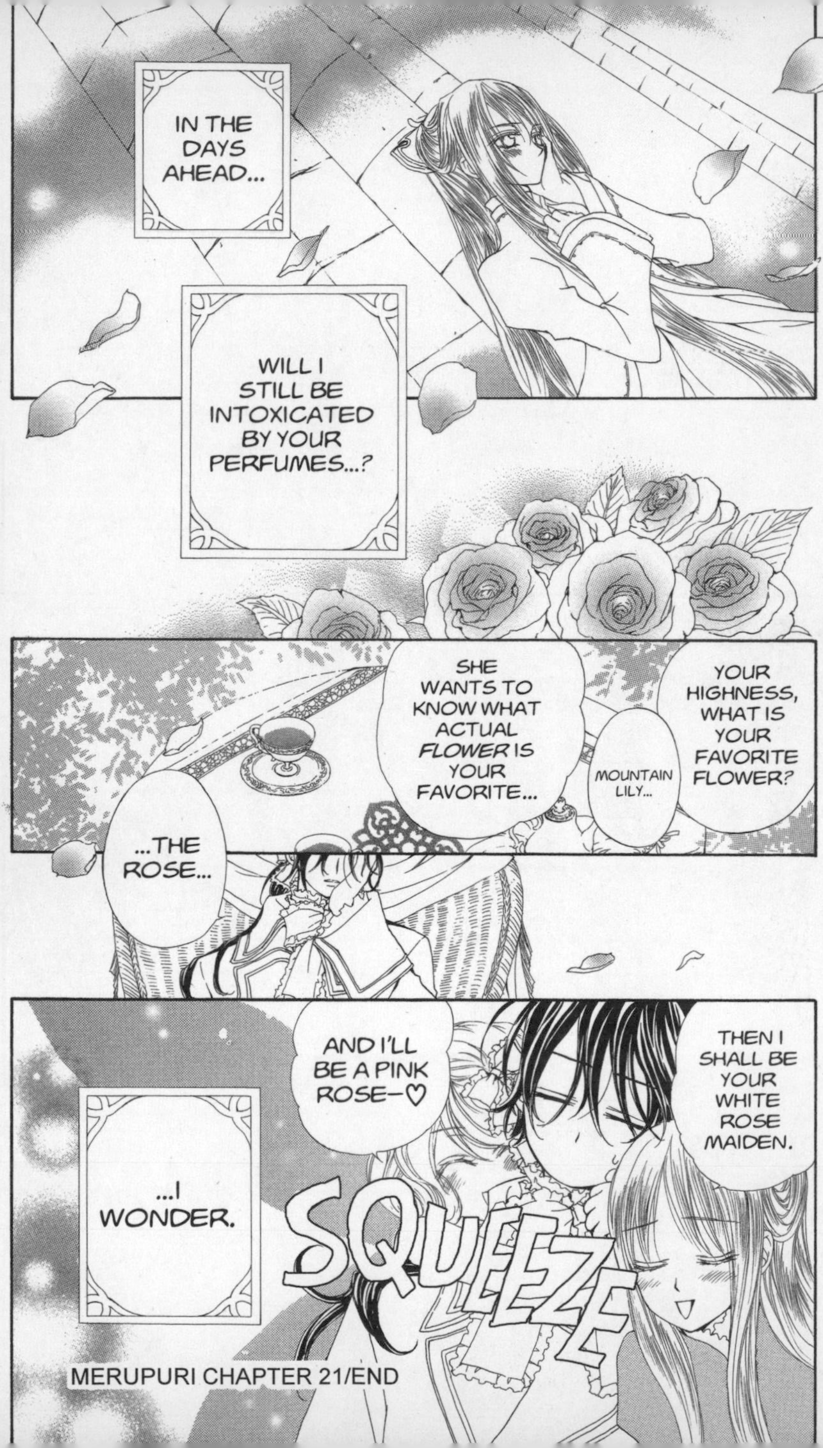
IN THE DAYS AHEAD...
WILL I STILL BE INTOXICATED BY YOUR PERFUMES...?
YOUR HIGHNESS, WHAT IS YOUR FAVORITE FLOWER?
MOUNTAIN LILY...
SHE WANTS TO KNOW WHAT ACTUAL *FLOWER* IS YOUR FAVORITE...
...THE ROSE...
THEN I SHALL BE YOUR WHITE ROSE MAIDEN.
AND I'LL BE A PINK ROSE-♡
SQUEEZE
...I WONDER.
MERUPURI CHAPTER 21/END

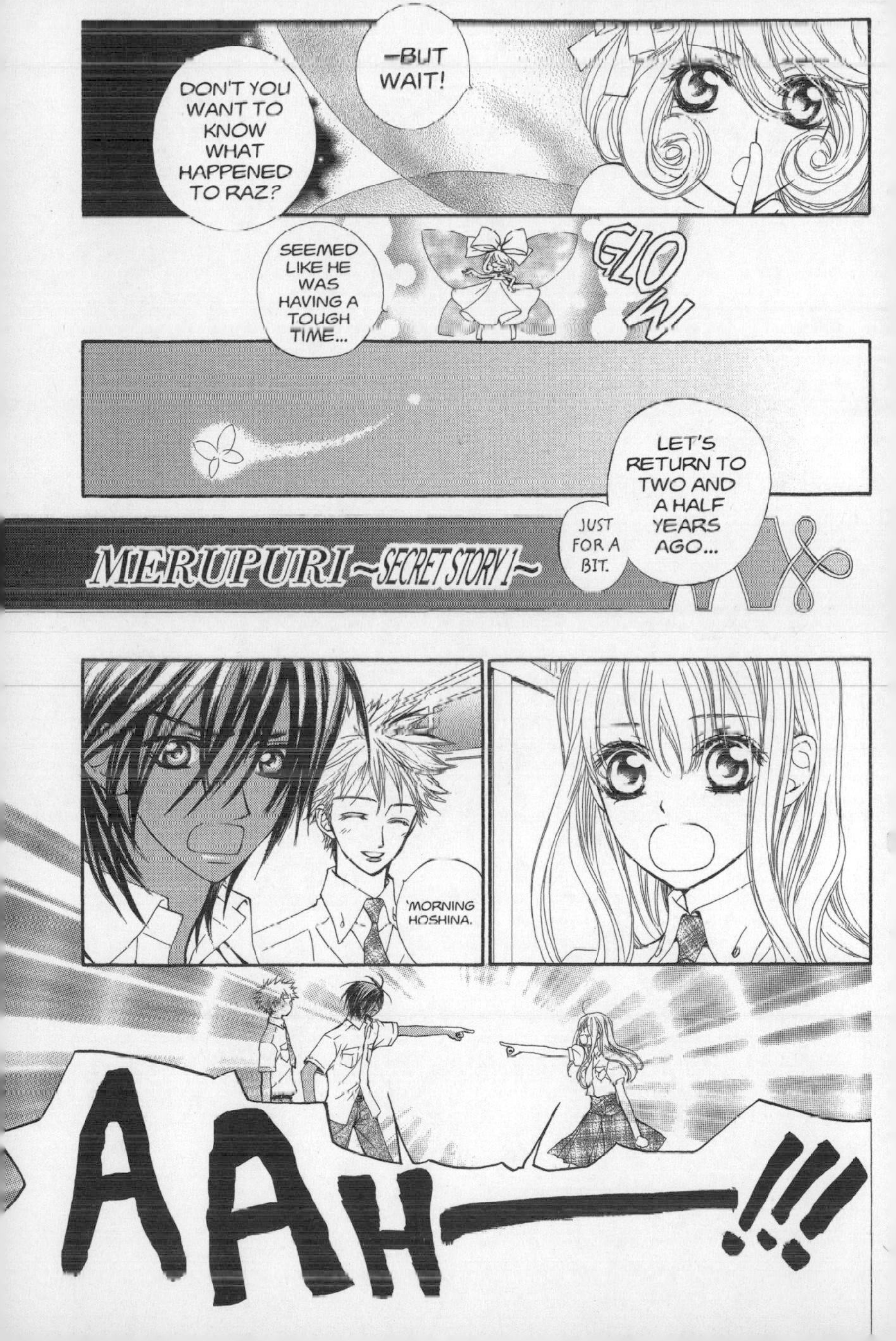
—BUT WAIT!
DON'T YOU WANT TO KNOW WHAT HAPPENED TO RAZ?
GLOW
SEEMED LIKE HE WAS HAVING A TOUGH TIME...
LET'S RETURN TO TWO AND A HALF YEARS AGO...
JUST FOR A BIT.
MERUPURI ~SECRET STORY 1~
'MORNING HOSHINA.
AAH—!!!

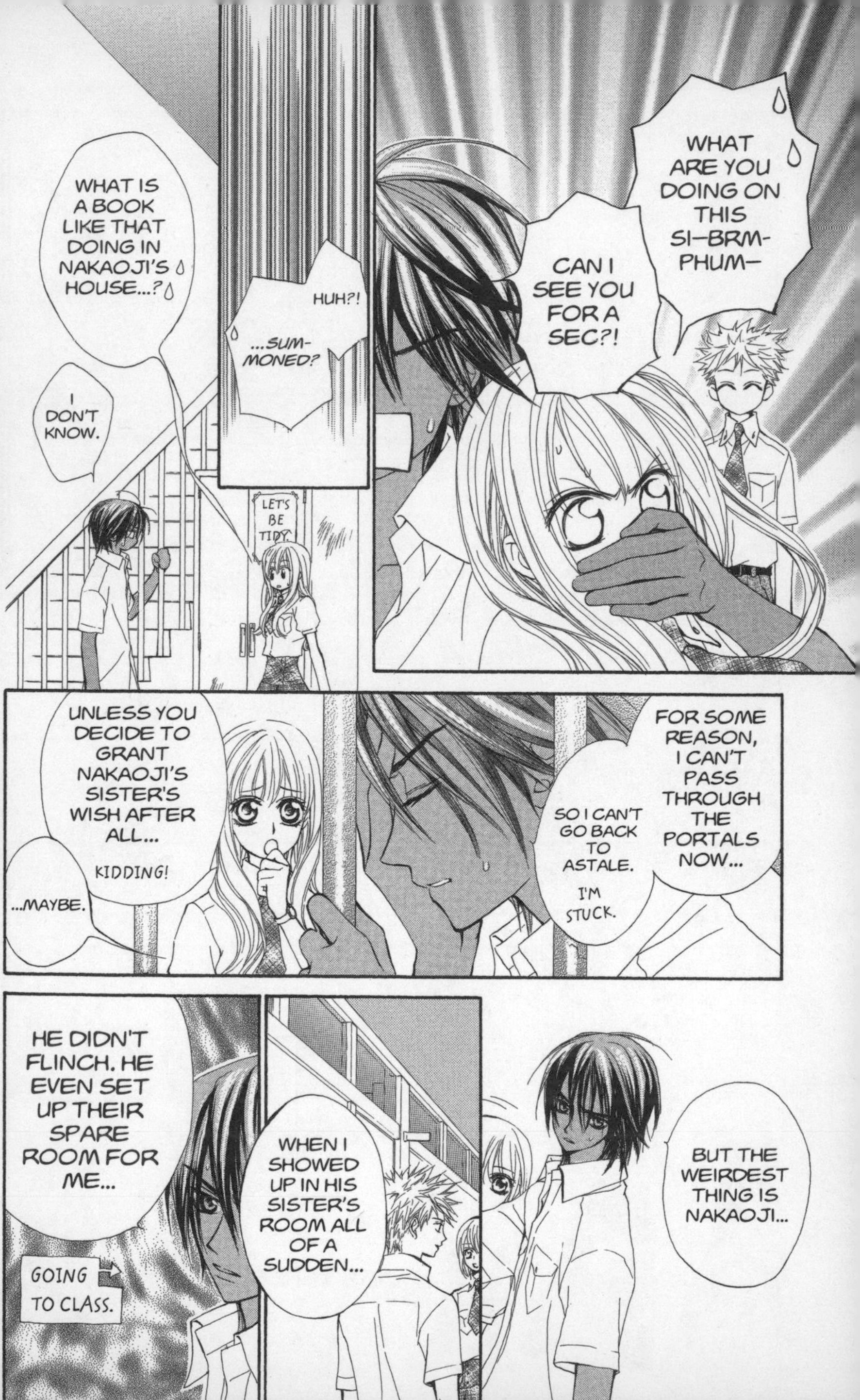
WHAT ARE YOU DOING ON THIS SI—BRM-PHUM—
CAN I SEE YOU FOR A SEC?!
HUH?!
...SUM-MONED?
WHAT IS A BOOK LIKE THAT DOING IN NAKAOJI'S HOUSE...?
I DON'T KNOW.
LET'S BE TIDY.
FOR SOME REASON, I CAN'T PASS THROUGH THE PORTALS NOW...
SO I CAN'T GO BACK TO ASTALE.
I'M STUCK.
UNLESS YOU DECIDE TO GRANT NAKAOJI'S SISTER'S WISH AFTER ALL...
KIDDING!
...MAYBE.
BUT THE WEIRDEST THING IS NAKAOJI...
WHEN I SHOWED UP IN HIS SISTER'S ROOM ALL OF A SUDDEN...
HE DIDN'T FLINCH. HE EVEN SET UP THEIR SPARE ROOM FOR ME...
GOING TO CLASS.

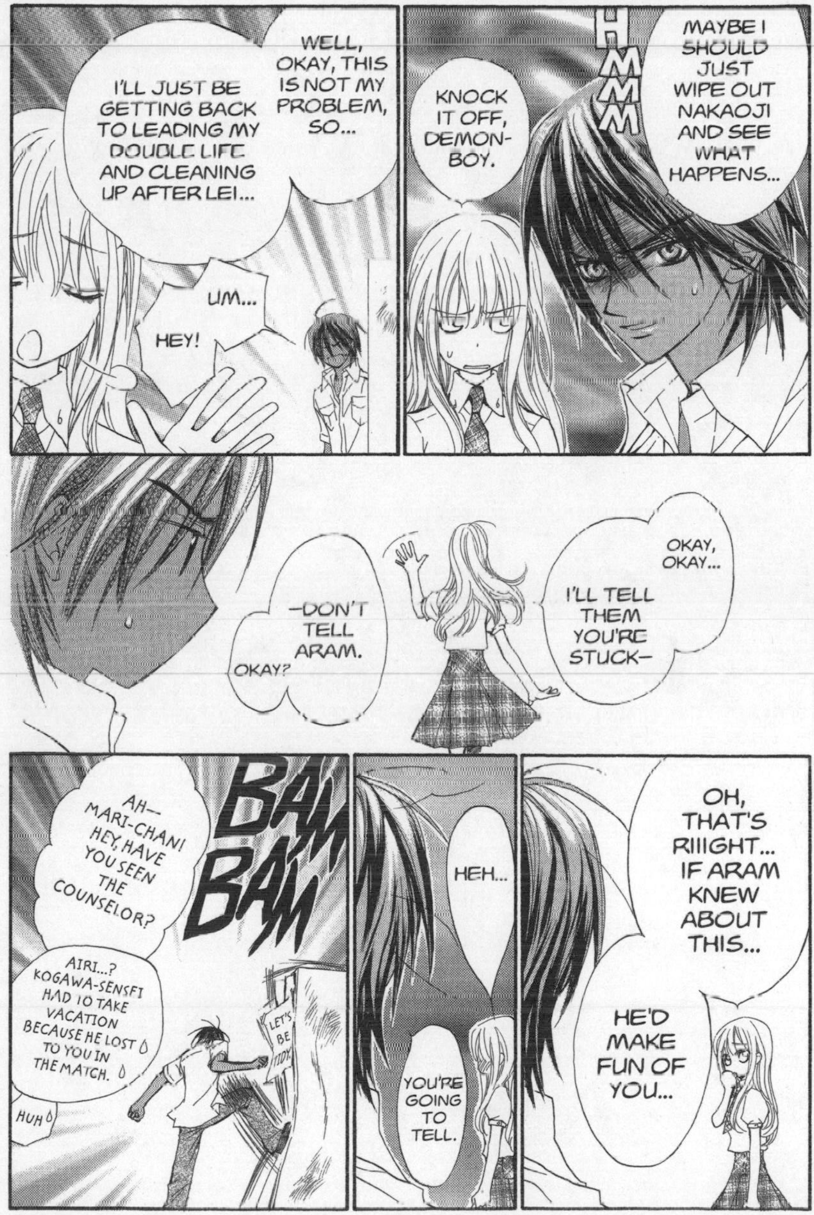
HMMM
MAYBE I SHOULD JUST WIPE OUT NAKAOJI AND SEE WHAT HAPPENS...
KNOCK IT OFF, DEMON-BOY.
WELL, OKAY, THIS IS NOT MY PROBLEM, SO...
I'LL JUST BE GETTING BACK TO LEADING MY DOUBLE LIFE AND CLEANING UP AFTER LEI...
UM...
HEY!
OKAY, OKAY...
I'LL TELL THEM YOU'RE STUCK—
—DON'T TELL ARAM.
OKAY?
OH, THAT'S RIIIGHT... IF ARAM KNEW ABOUT THIS...
HE'D MAKE FUN OF YOU...
HEH...
YOU'RE GOING TO TELL.
BAM BAM
AH— MARI-CHAN! HEY, HAVE YOU SEEN THE COUNSELOR?
AIRI...? KOGAWA-SENSEI HAD TO TAKE VACATION BECAUSE HE LOST TO YOU IN THE MATCH.
HUH
LET'S BE TIDY.

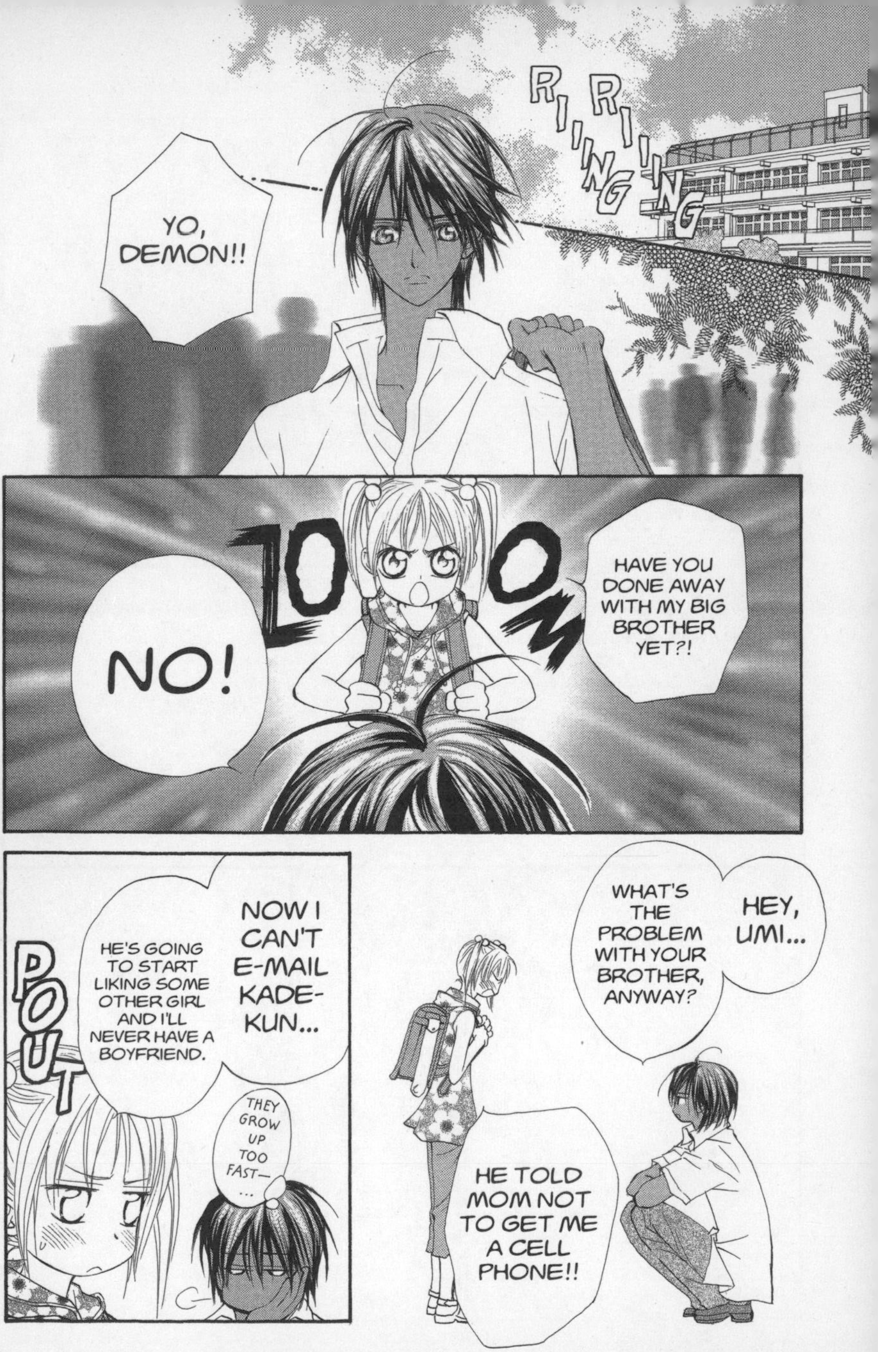
RIIIING RIIIING
YO, DEMON!!
HAVE YOU DONE AWAY WITH MY BIG BROTHER YET?!
ZOOM
NO!
HEY, UMI...
WHAT'S THE PROBLEM WITH YOUR BROTHER, ANYWAY?
HE TOLD MOM NOT TO GET ME A CELL PHONE!!
NOW I CAN'T E-MAIL KADE-KUN...
HE'S GOING TO START LIKING SOME OTHER GIRL AND I'LL NEVER HAVE A BOYFRIEND.
POUT
THEY GROW UP TOO FAST—...

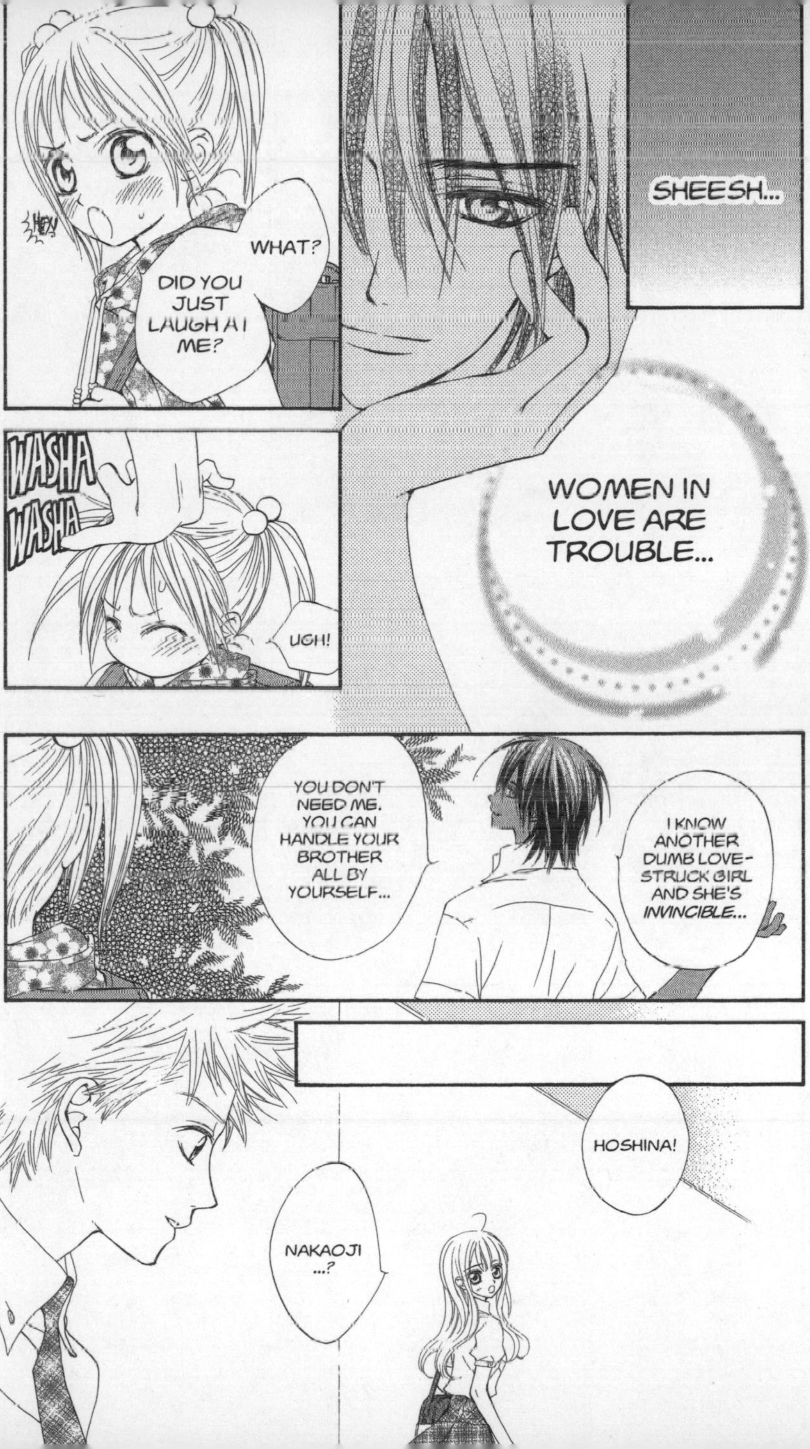
SHEESH...
WOMEN IN LOVE ARE TROUBLE...
HEY!
WHAT? DID YOU JUST LAUGH AT ME?
WASHA WASHA
UGH!
I KNOW ANOTHER DUMB LOVE-STRUCK GIRL AND SHE'S INVINCIBLE...
YOU DON'T NEED ME. YOU CAN HANDLE YOUR BROTHER ALL BY YOURSELF...
HOSHINA!
NAKAOJI ...?

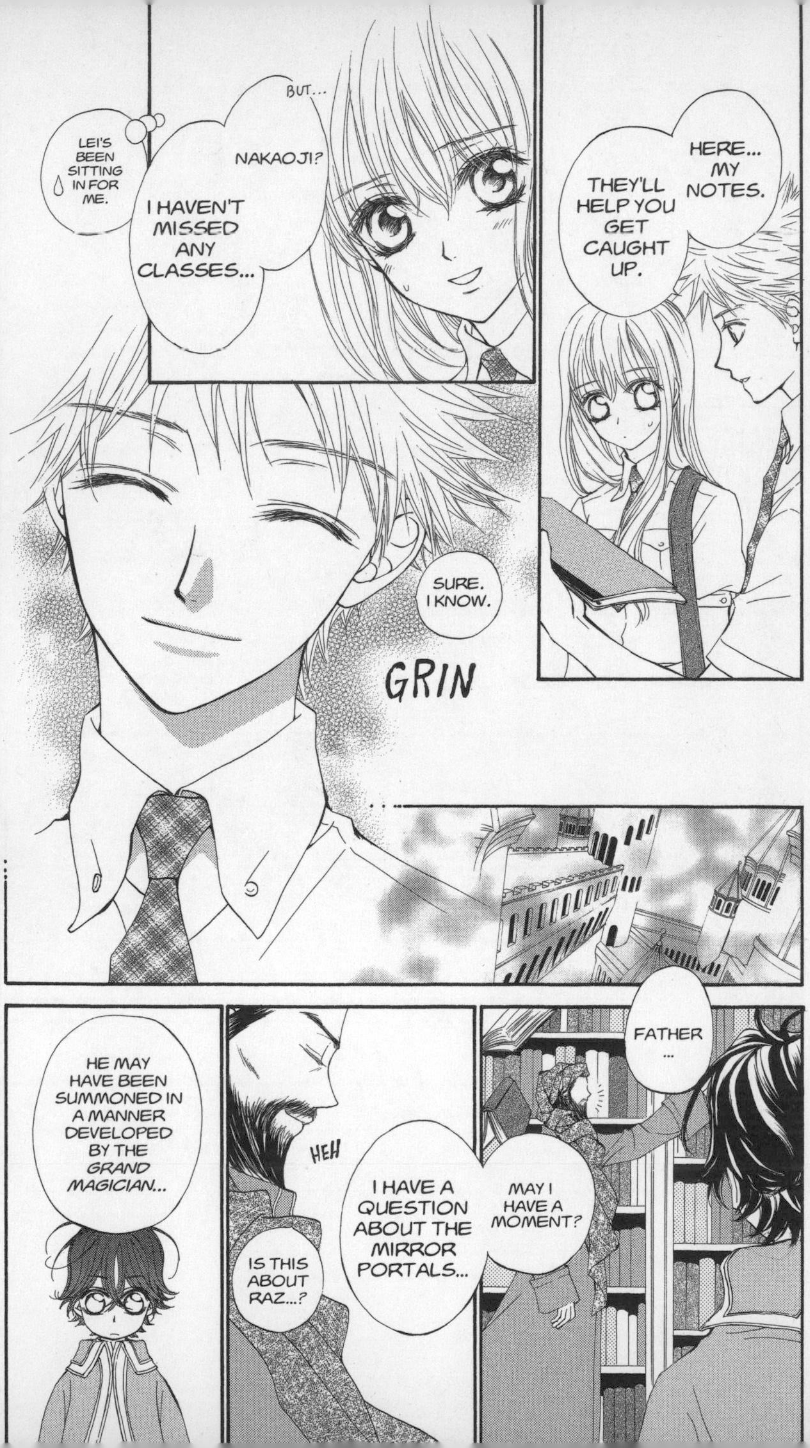
HERE... MY NOTES.
THEY'LL HELP YOU GET CAUGHT UP.
BUT...
NAKAOJI?
I HAVEN'T MISSED ANY CLASSES...
LEI'S BEEN SITTING IN FOR ME.
SURE. I KNOW.
GRIN
FATHER ...
MAY I HAVE A MOMENT?
I HAVE A QUESTION ABOUT THE MIRROR PORTALS...
HEH
IS THIS ABOUT RAZ...?
HE MAY HAVE BEEN SUMMONED IN A MANNER DEVELOPED BY THE *GRAND MAGICIAN*...

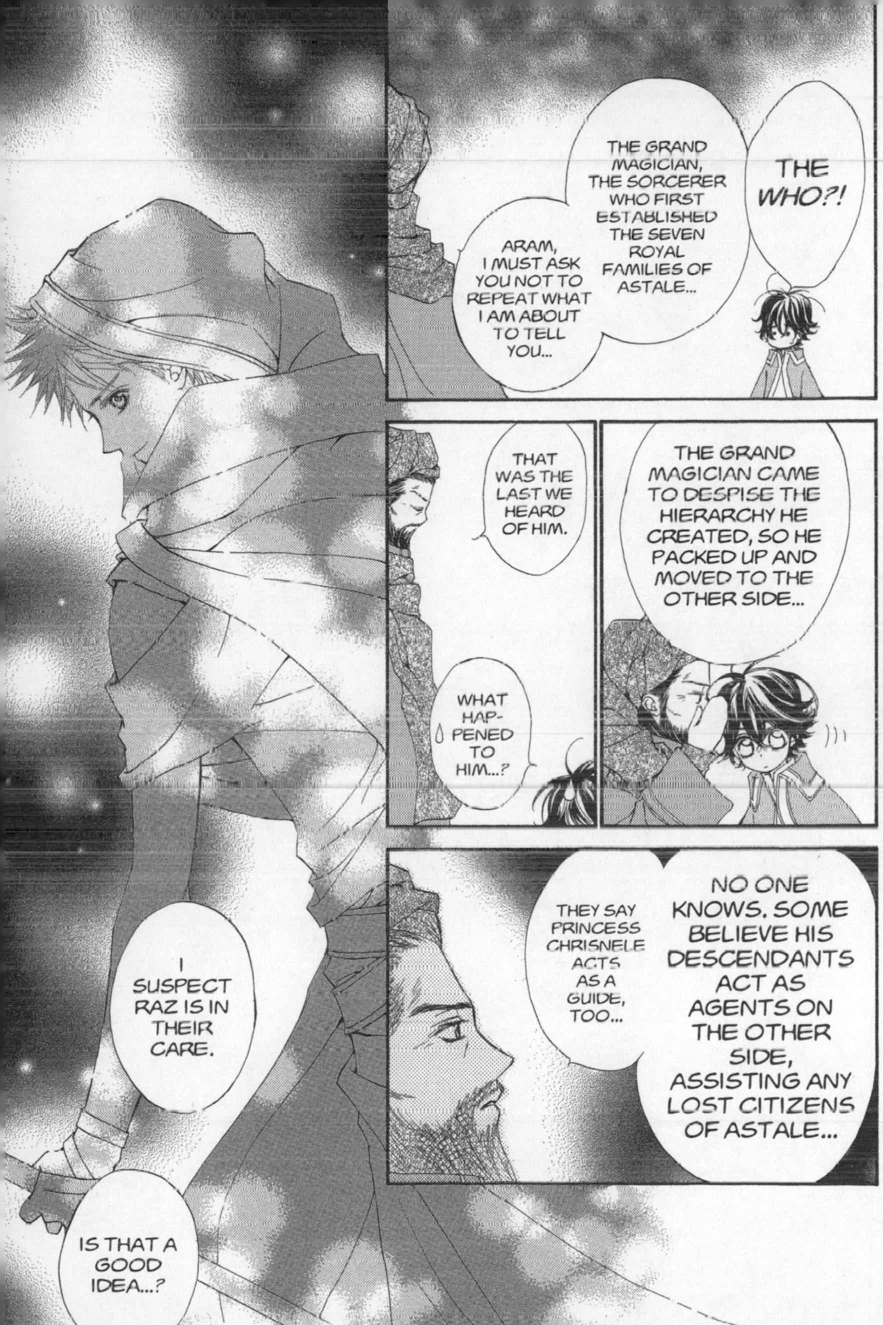
ARAM, I MUST ASK YOU NOT TO REPEAT WHAT I AM ABOUT TO TELL YOU...
THE GRAND MAGICIAN, THE SORCERER WHO FIRST ESTABLISHED THE SEVEN ROYAL FAMILIES OF ASTALE...
THE WHO?!
THE GRAND MAGICIAN CAME TO DESPISE THE HIERARCHY HE CREATED, SO HE PACKED UP AND MOVED TO THE OTHER SIDE...
THAT WAS THE LAST WE HEARD OF HIM.
WHAT HAP-PENED TO HIM...?
NO ONE KNOWS. SOME BELIEVE HIS DESCENDANTS ACT AS AGENTS ON THE OTHER SIDE, ASSISTING ANY LOST CITIZENS OF ASTALE...
THEY SAY PRINCESS CHRISNELE ACTS AS A GUIDE, TOO...
I SUSPECT RAZ IS IN THEIR CARE.
IS THAT A GOOD IDEA...?
MERUPURI~SECRET STORY 1~/END

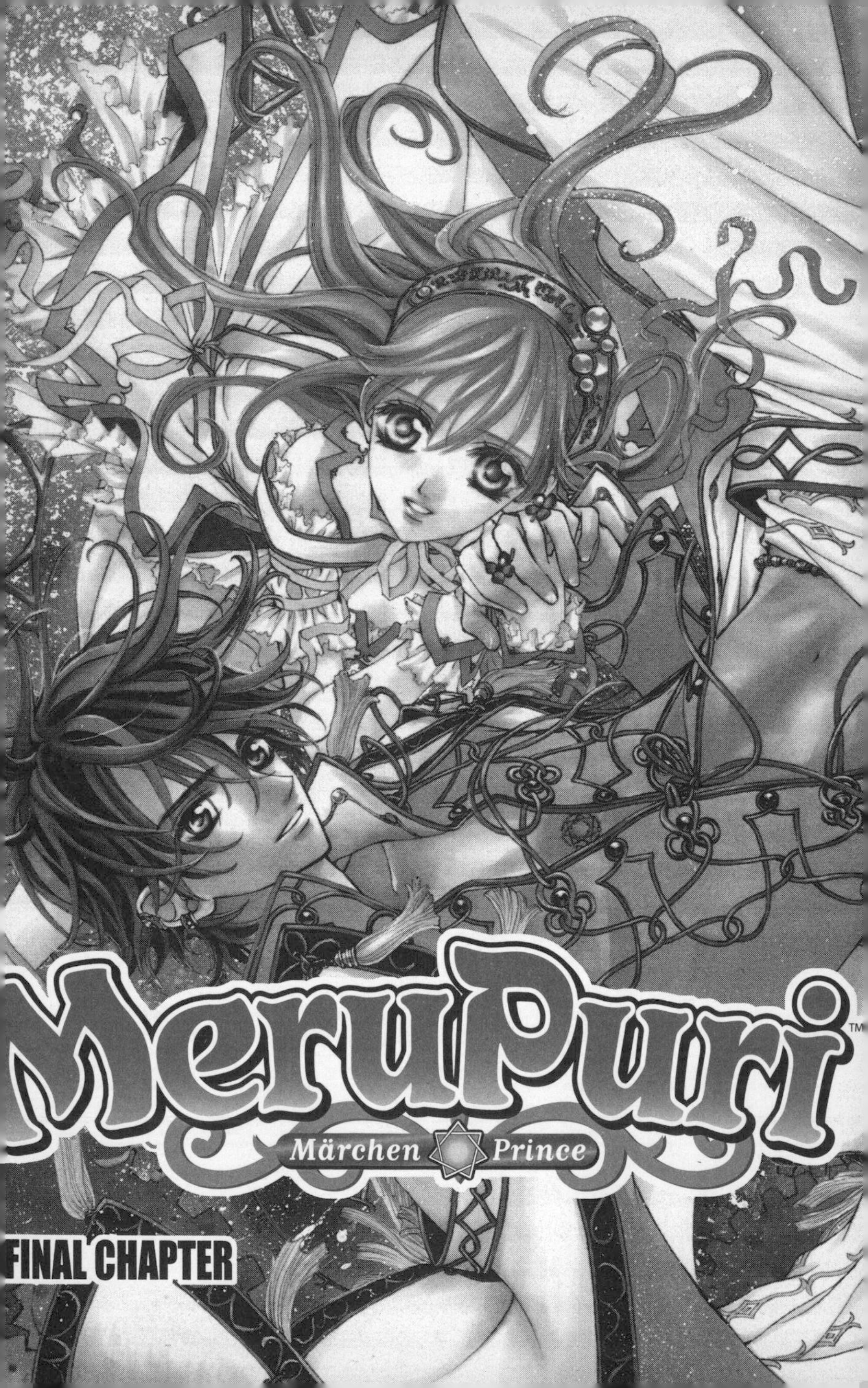
MeruPuri™
Märchen Prince
FINAL CHAPTER

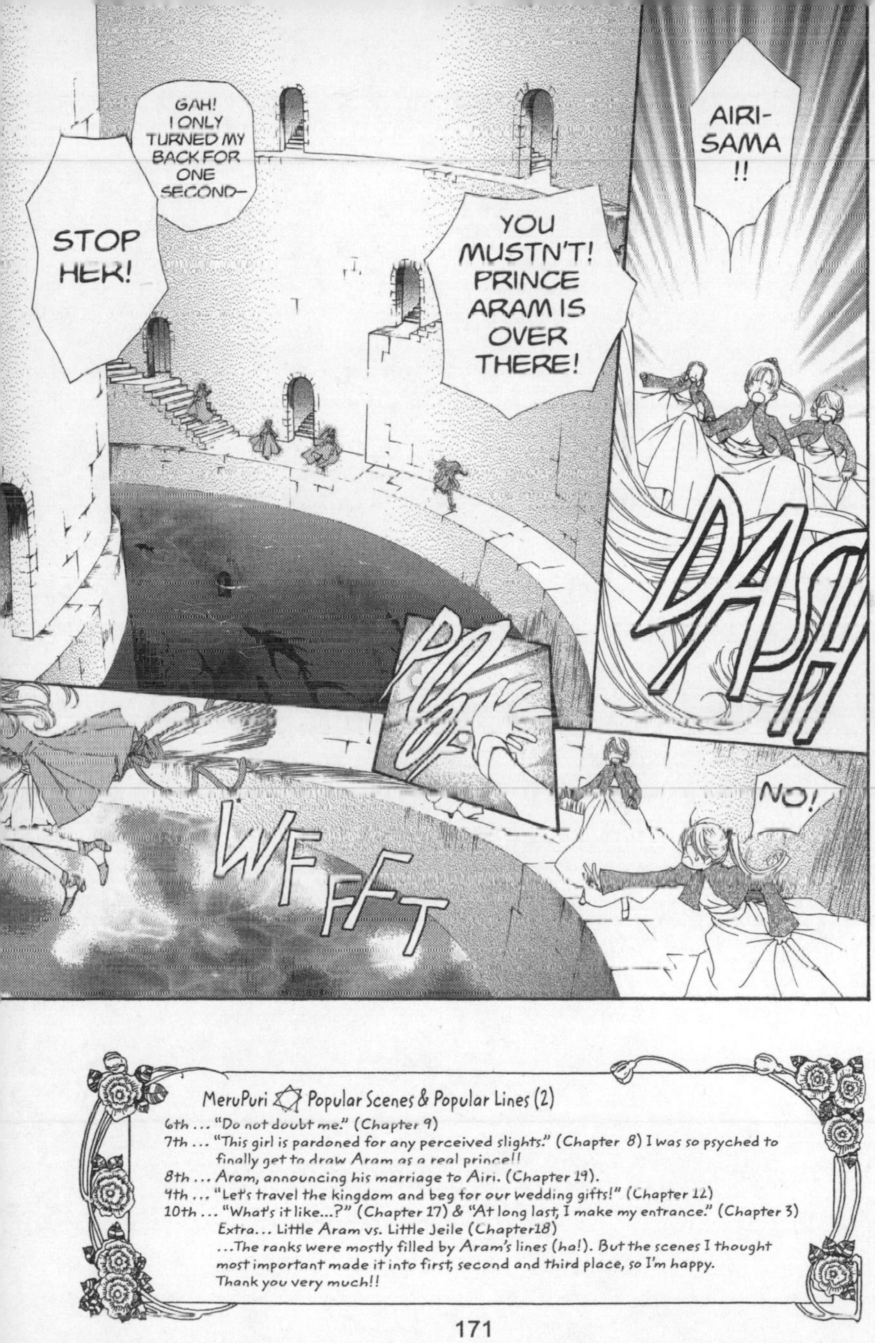
AIRI-SAMA!!
DASH
GAH! I ONLY TURNED MY BACK FOR ONE SECOND–
YOU MUSTN'T! PRINCE ARAM IS OVER THERE!
STOP HER!
NO!
POF
WFFFT

MeruPuri ✡ Popular Scenes & Popular Lines (2)

6th ... "Do not doubt me." (Chapter 9)
7th ... "This girl is pardoned for any perceived slights." (Chapter 8) I was so psyched to finally get to draw Aram as a real prince!!
8th ... Aram, announcing his marriage to Airi. (Chapter 19).
9th ... "Let's travel the kingdom and beg for our wedding gifts!" (Chapter 12)
10th ... "What's it like...?" (Chapter 17) & "At long last, I make my entrance." (Chapter 3)
Extra... Little Aram vs. Little Jeile (Chapter18)
...The ranks were mostly filled by Aram's lines (ha!). But the scenes I thought most important made it into first, second and third place, so I'm happy. Thank you very much!!

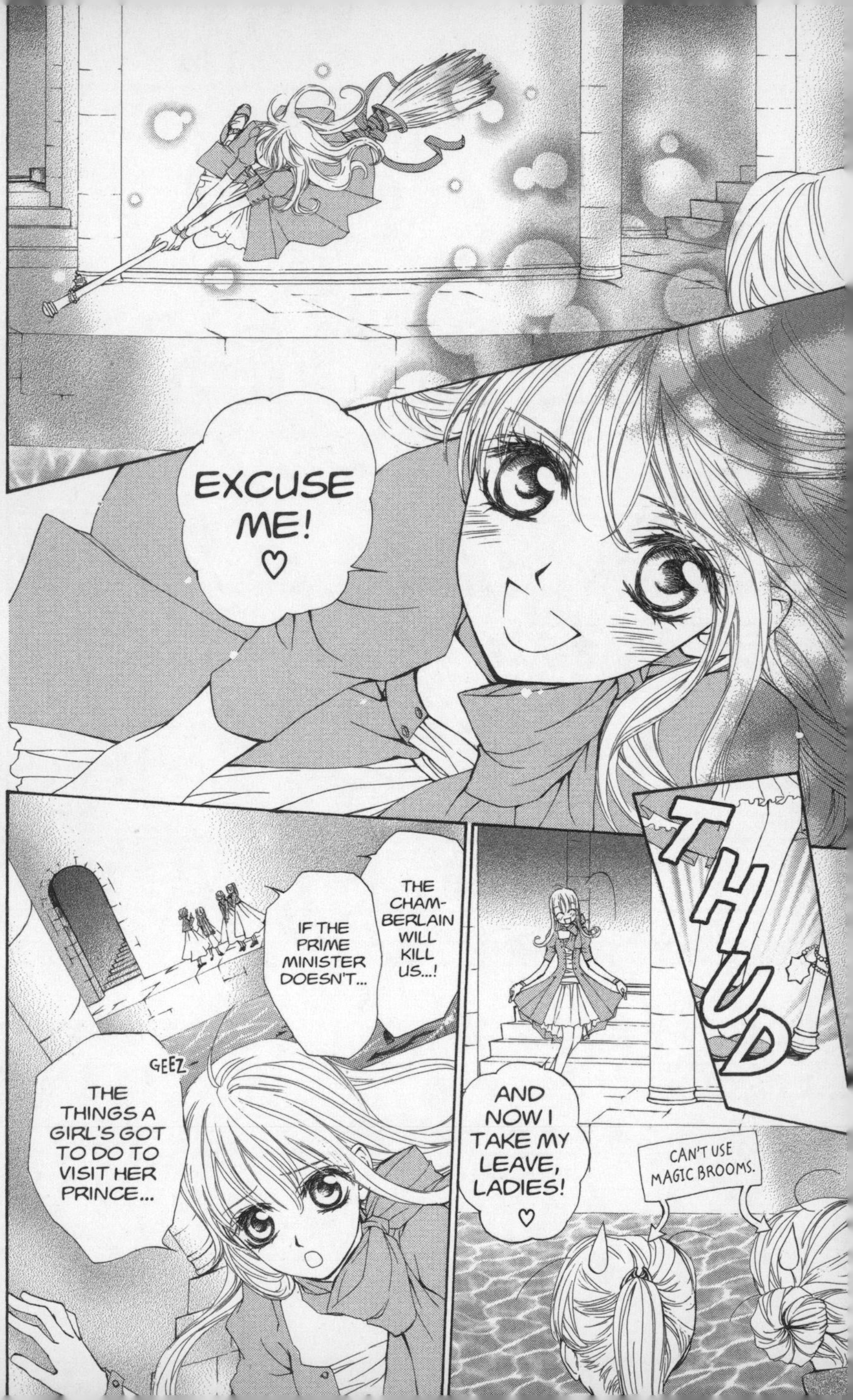
EXCUSE ME! ♡
THUD
AND NOW I TAKE MY LEAVE, LADIES! ♡
CAN'T USE MAGIC BROOMS.
THE CHAM-BERLAIN WILL KILL US...!
IF THE PRIME MINISTER DOESN'T...
GEEZ
THE THINGS A GIRL'S GOT TO DO TO VISIT HER PRINCE...

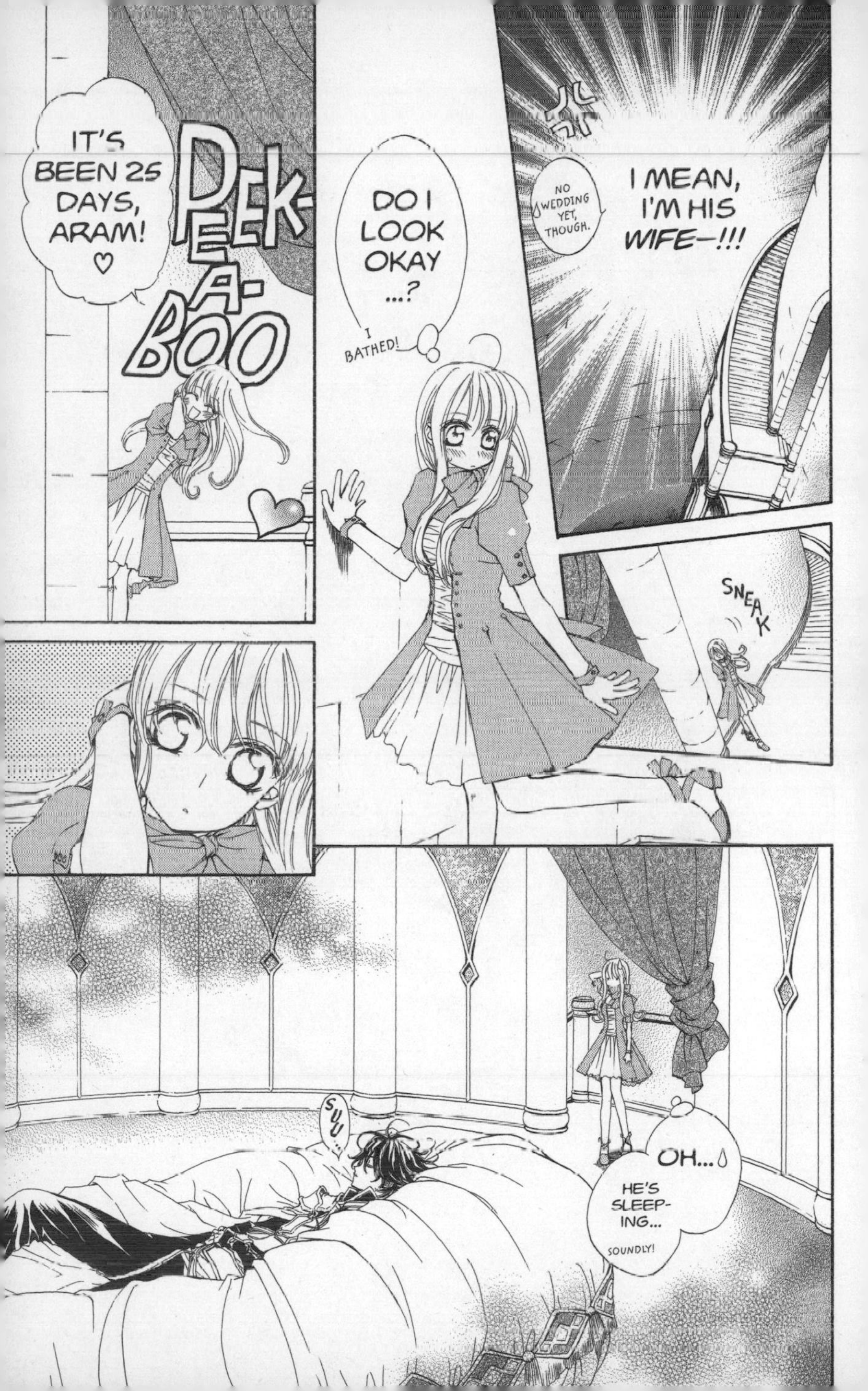
I MEAN, I'M HIS WIFE-!!!
NO WEDDING YET, THOUGH.
SNEAK
DO I LOOK OKAY ...?
I BATHED!
IT'S BEEN 25 DAYS, ARAM! ♡
PEEK-A-BOO
SUU...
OH...
HE'S SLEEPING...
SOUNDLY!

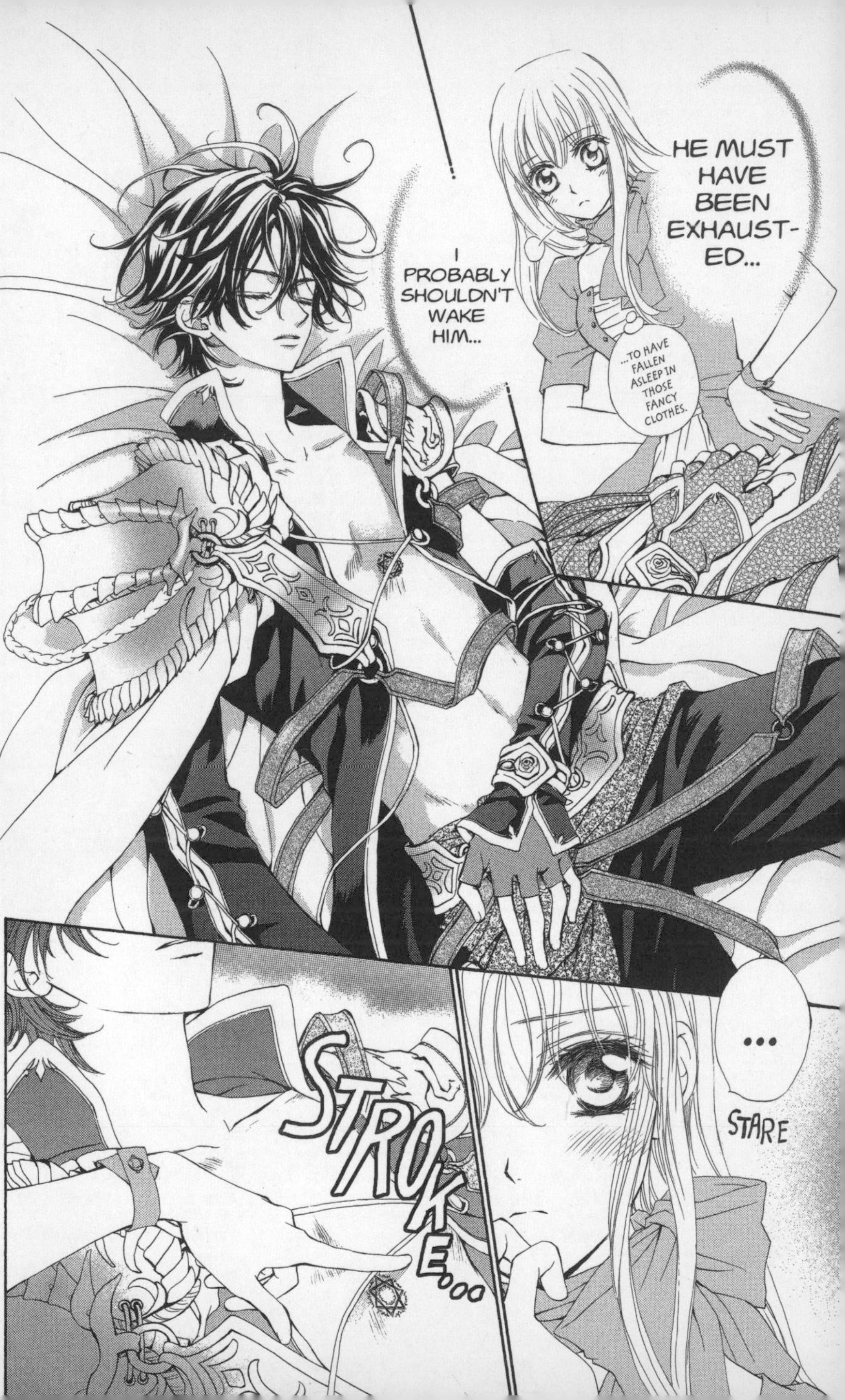
HE MUST HAVE BEEN EXHAUSTED...
...TO HAVE FALLEN ASLEEP IN THOSE FANCY CLOTHES.
I PROBABLY SHOULDN'T WAKE HIM...
...
STARE
STROKE...

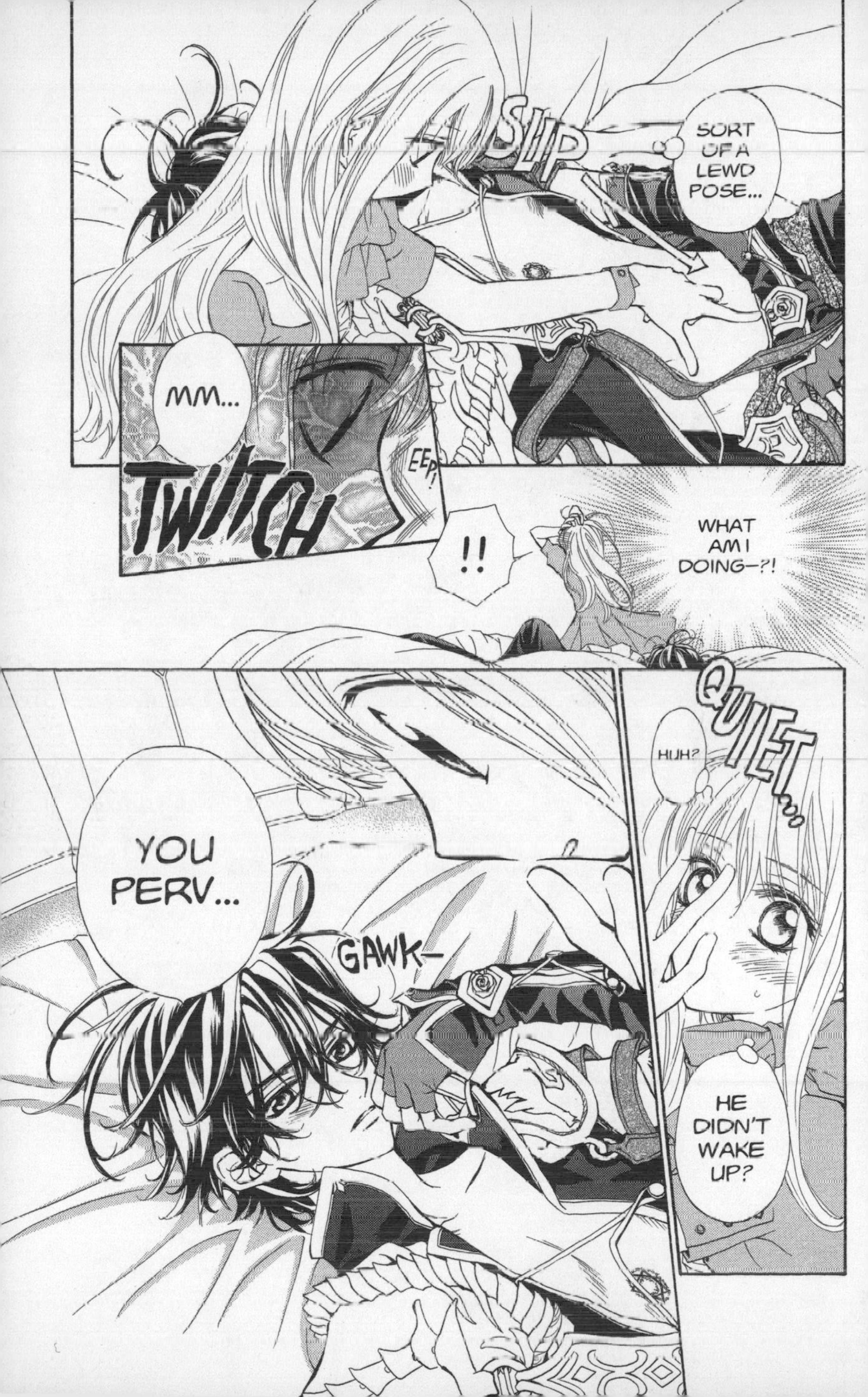
SORT OF A LEWD POSE...
SLIP
EEP!
MM...
TWITCH
WHAT AM I DOING—?!
!!
QUIET...
HUH?
HE DIDN'T WAKE UP?
YOU PERV...
GAWK—

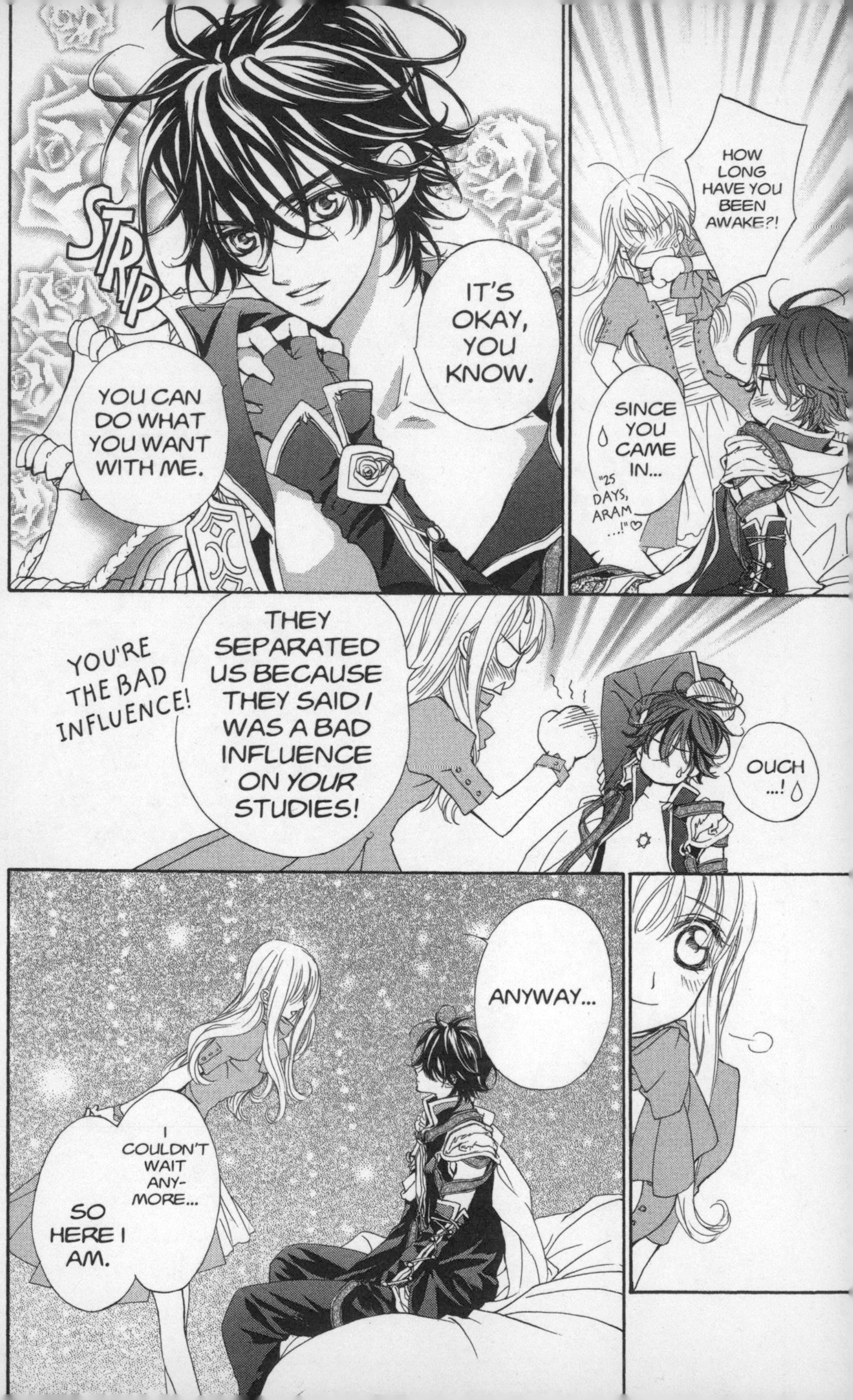
HOW LONG HAVE YOU BEEN AWAKE?!
SINCE YOU CAME IN...
"25 DAYS, ARAM ...!"♡
STRIP
IT'S OKAY, YOU KNOW.
YOU CAN DO WHAT YOU WANT WITH ME.
OUCH ...!
THEY SEPARATED US BECAUSE THEY SAID I WAS A BAD INFLUENCE ON *YOUR* STUDIES!
YOU'RE THE BAD INFLUENCE!
ANYWAY...
I COULDN'T WAIT ANY-MORE...
SO HERE I AM.

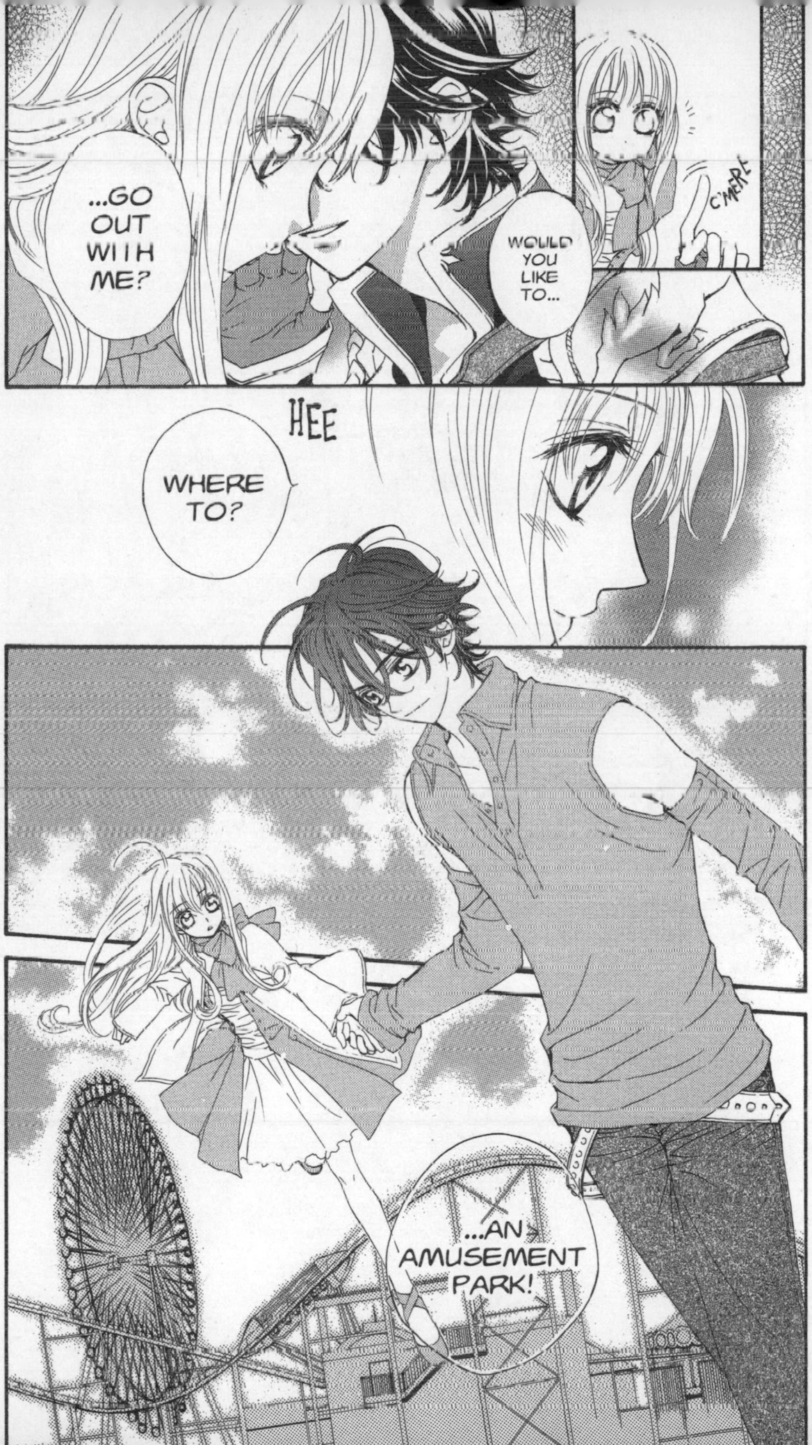
C'MERE
WOULD YOU LIKE TO...
...GO OUT WITH ME?
HEE
WHERE TO?
...AN AMUSEMENT PARK!

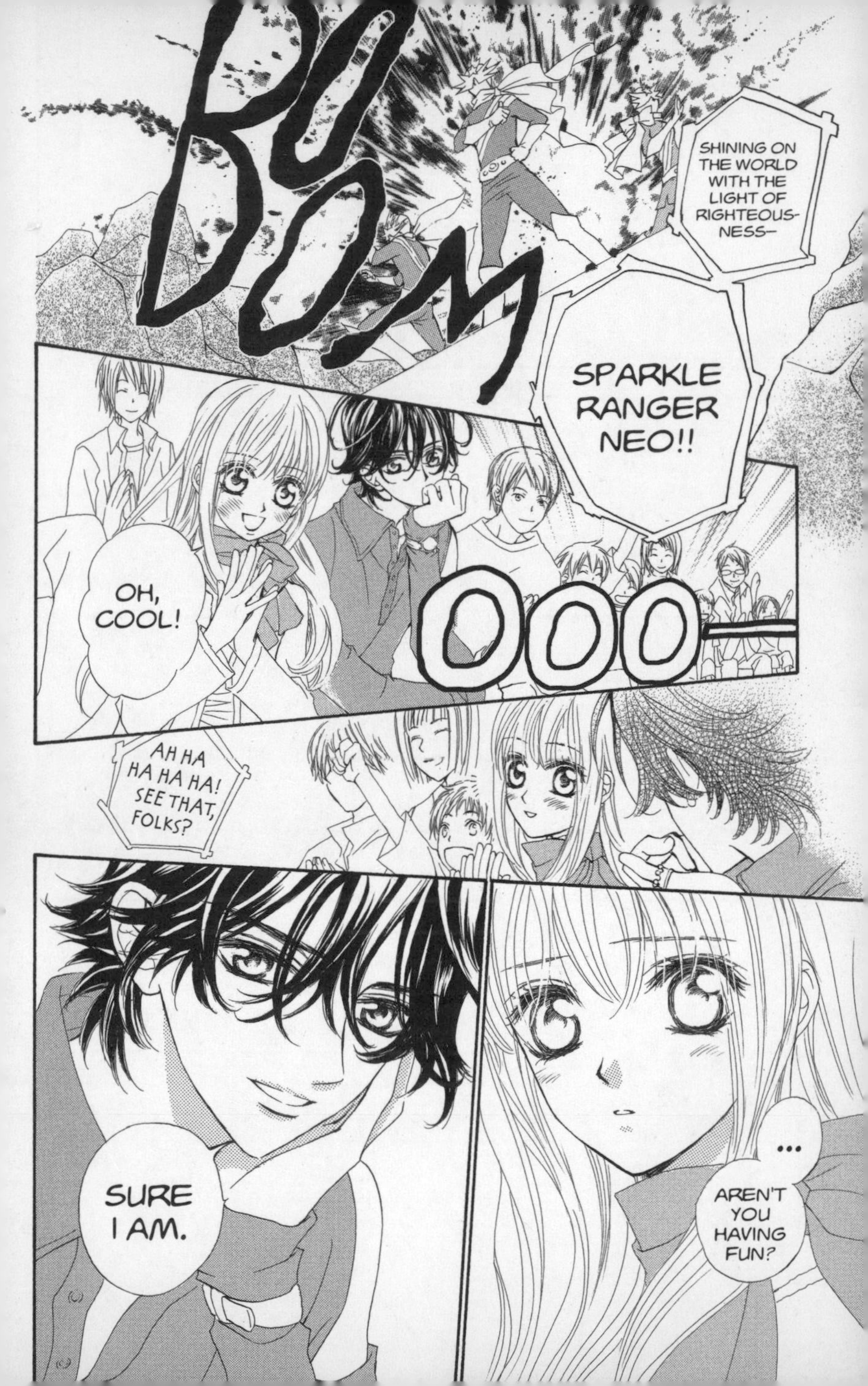
SHINING ON THE WORLD WITH THE LIGHT OF RIGHTEOUS-NESS—
SPARKLE RANGER NEO!!
BU DOM
OOO—
OH, COOL!
AH HA HA HA HA! SEE THAT, FOLKS?
...
AREN'T YOU HAVING FUN?
SURE I AM.

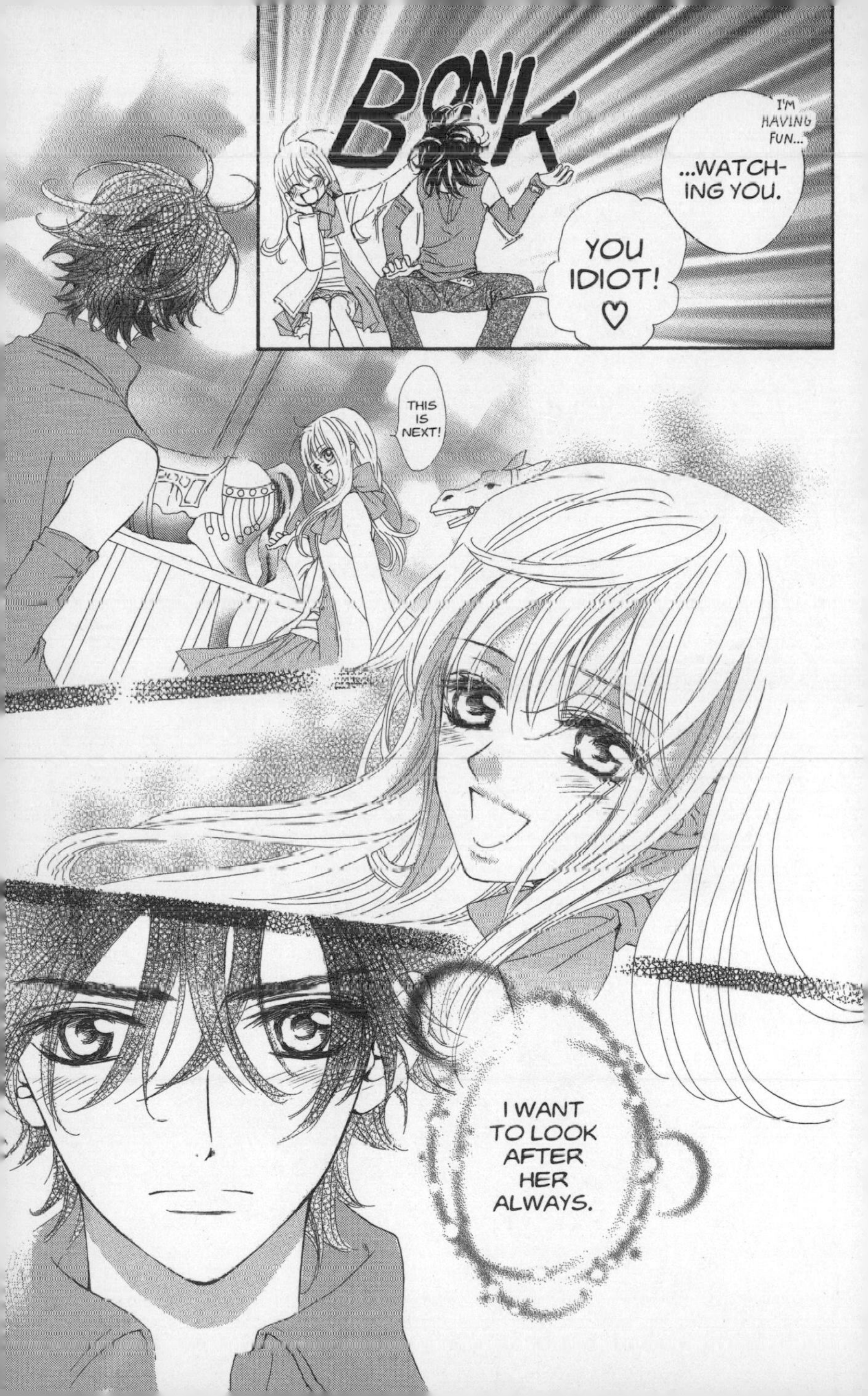
BONK
I'M HAVING FUN...
...WATCHING YOU.
YOU IDIOT! ♡
THIS IS NEXT!
I WANT TO LOOK AFTER HER ALWAYS.

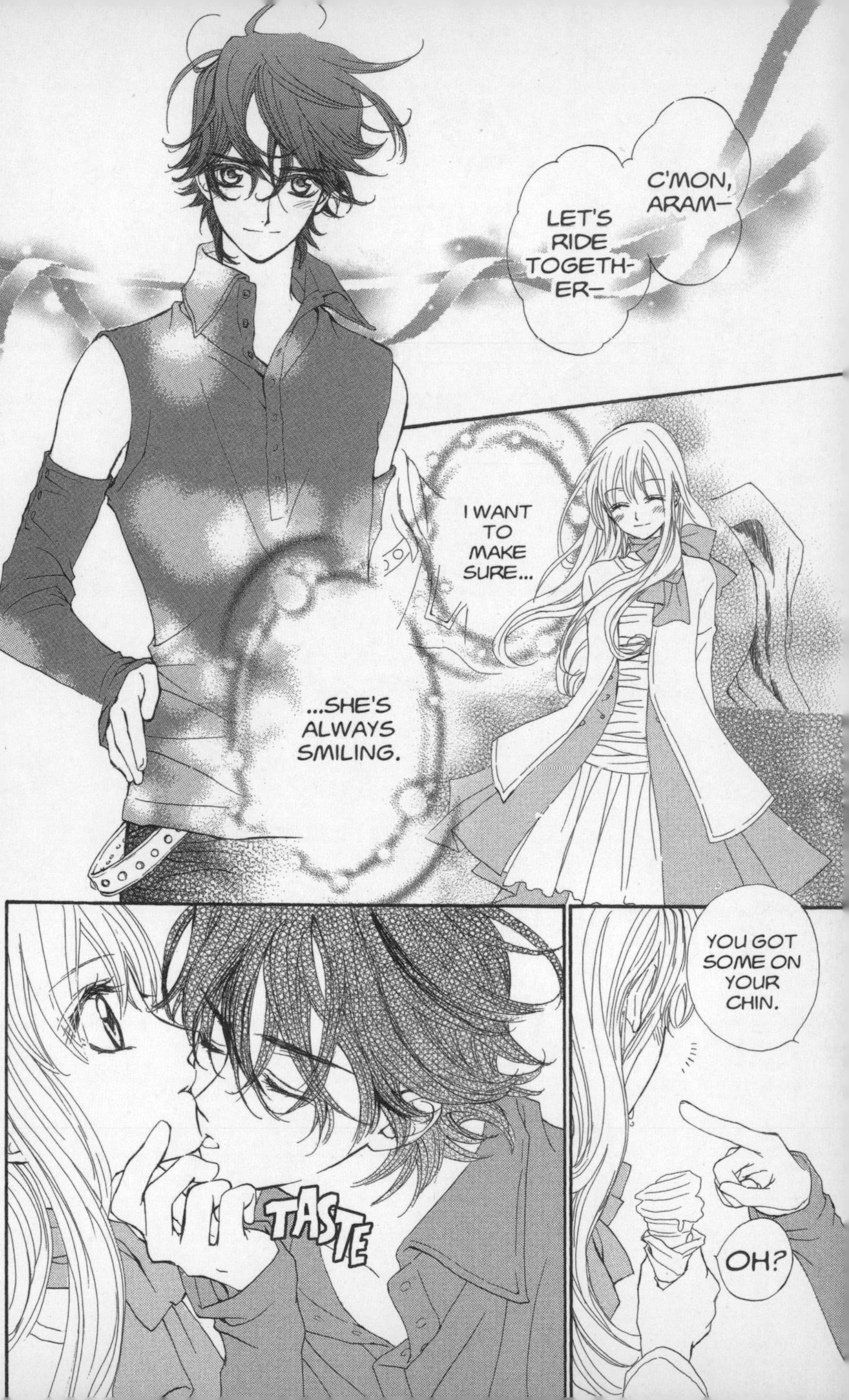
C'MON, ARAM–
LET'S RIDE TOGETH-ER–
I WANT TO MAKE SURE...
...SHE'S ALWAYS SMILING.
YOU GOT SOME ON YOUR CHIN.
OH?
TASTE

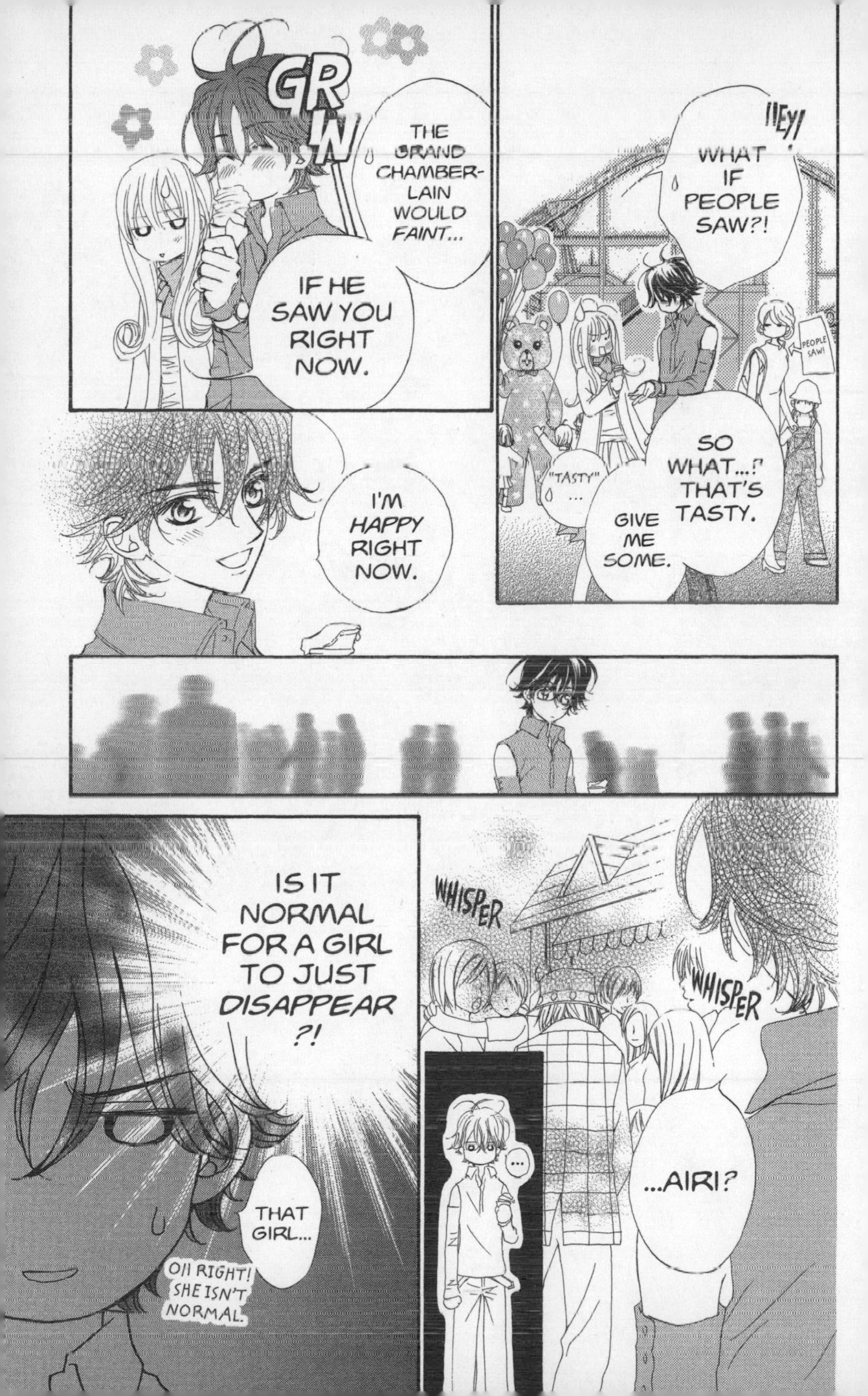
HEY!
WHAT IF PEOPLE SAW?!
PEOPLE SAW!
SO WHAT...!? THAT'S TASTY.
"TASTY" ...
GIVE ME SOME.
GRW
THE GRAND CHAMBER-LAIN WOULD FAINT...
IF HE SAW YOU RIGHT NOW.
I'M *HAPPY* RIGHT NOW.
WHISPER
WHISPER
...AIRI?
...
IS IT NORMAL FOR A GIRL TO JUST *DISAPPEAR*?!
THAT GIRL...
OH RIGHT! SHE ISN'T NORMAL.

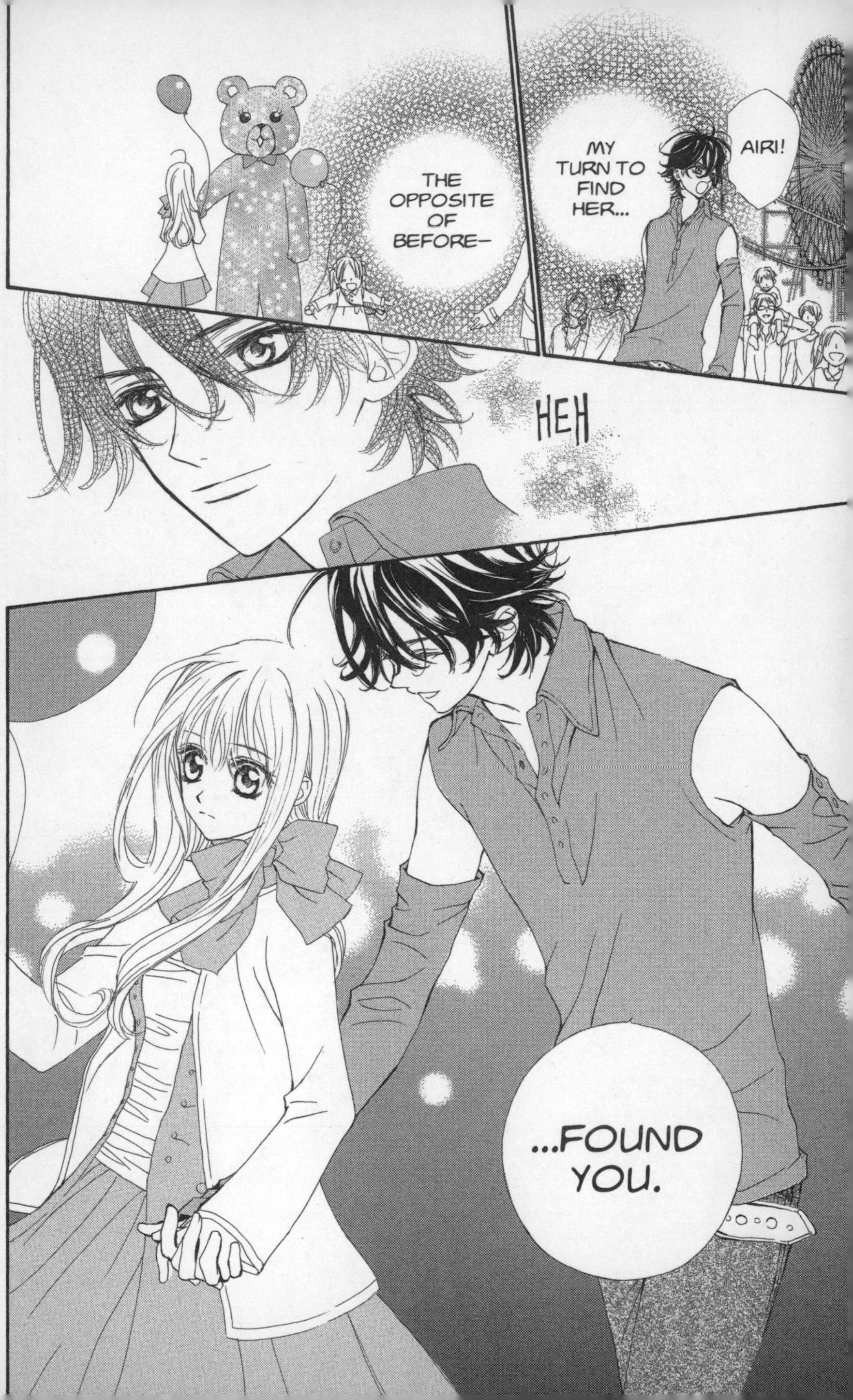
AIRI!
MY TURN TO FIND HER...
THE OPPOSITE OF BEFORE—
HEH...
...FOUND YOU.

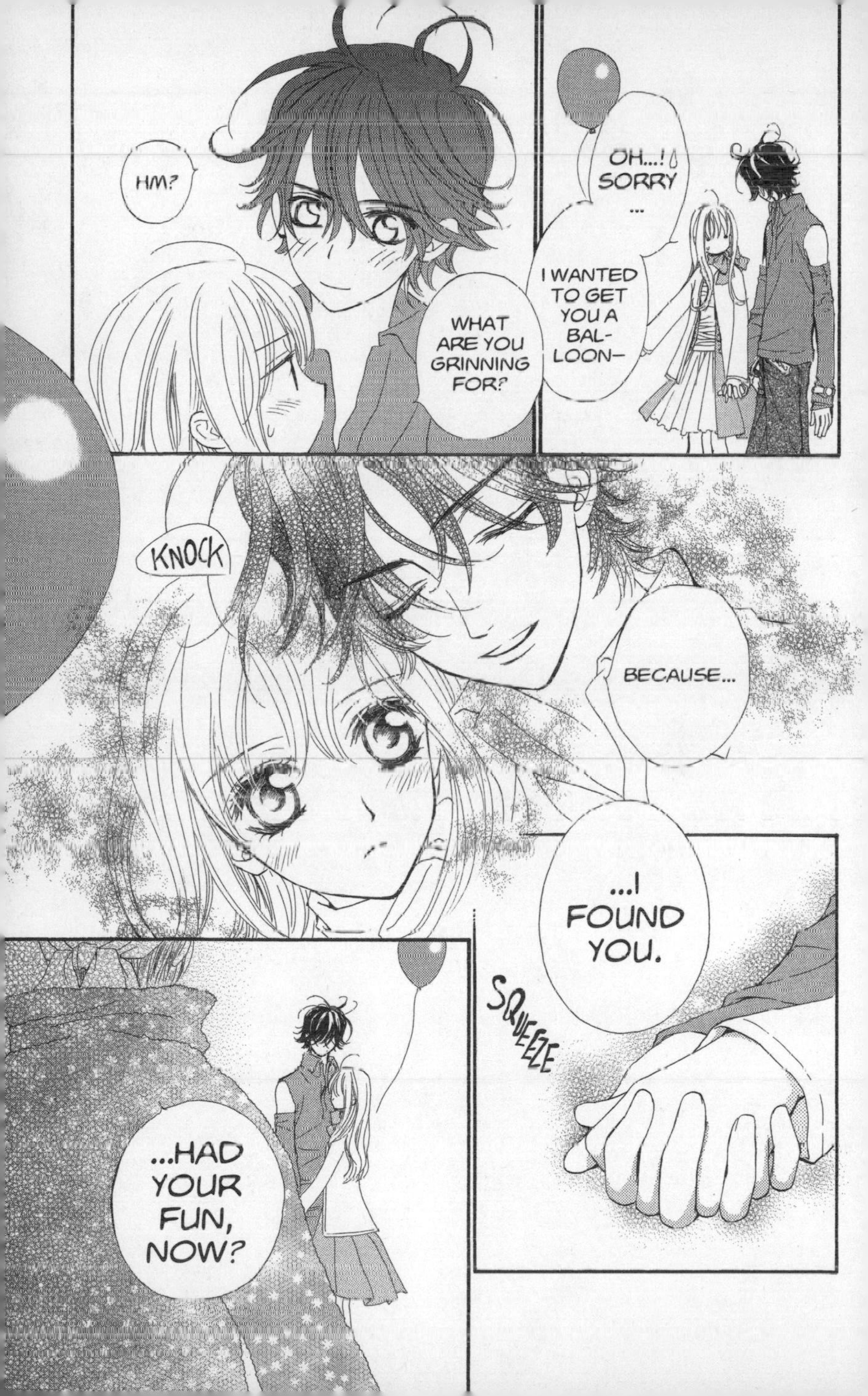
OH...! SORRY ...
I WANTED TO GET YOU A BAL-LOON—
HM?
WHAT ARE YOU GRINNING FOR?
KNOCK
BECAUSE...
...I FOUND YOU.
SQUEEZE
...HAD YOUR FUN, NOW?

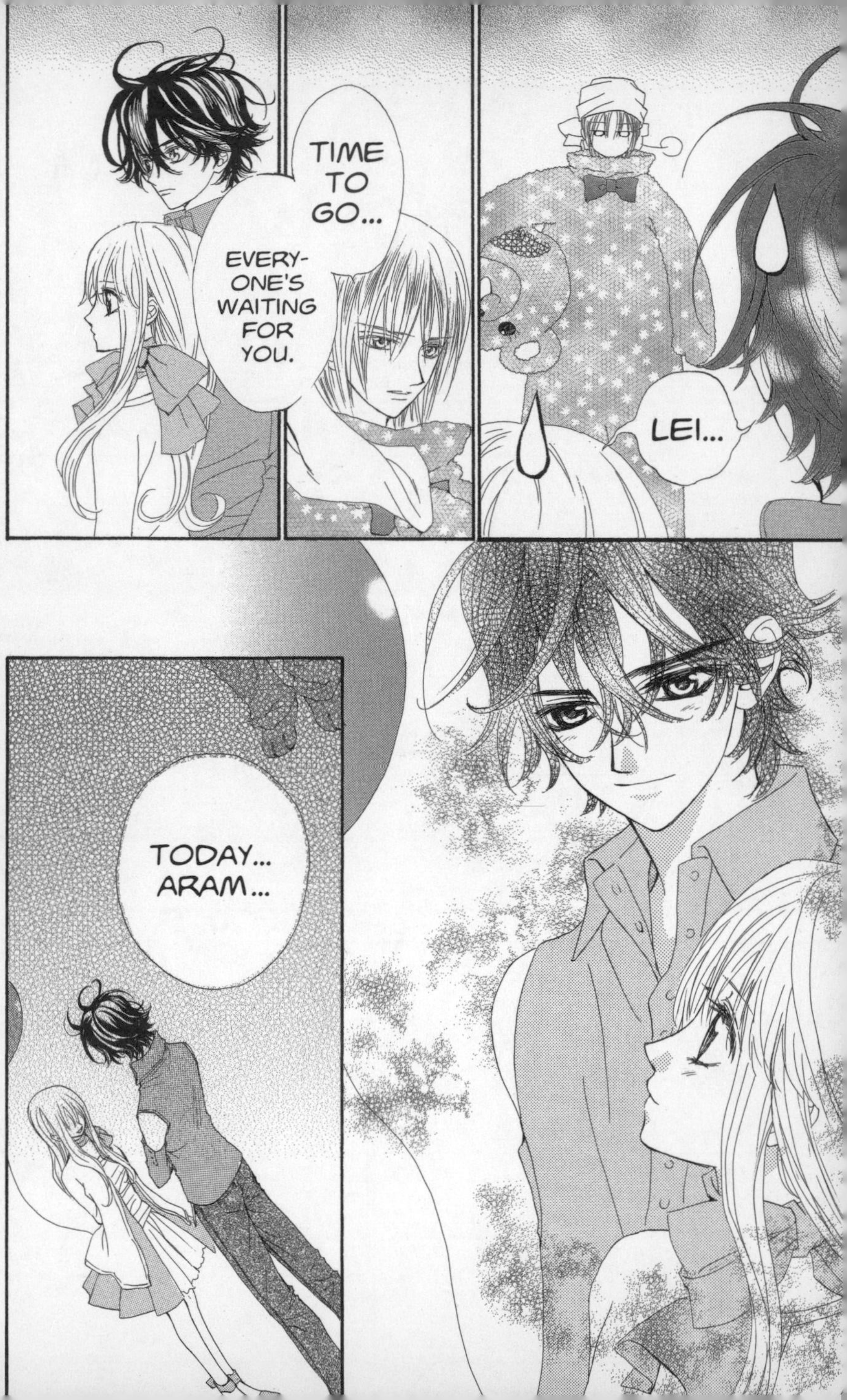
LEI...
TIME TO GO...
EVERYONE'S WAITING FOR YOU.
TODAY... ARAM...

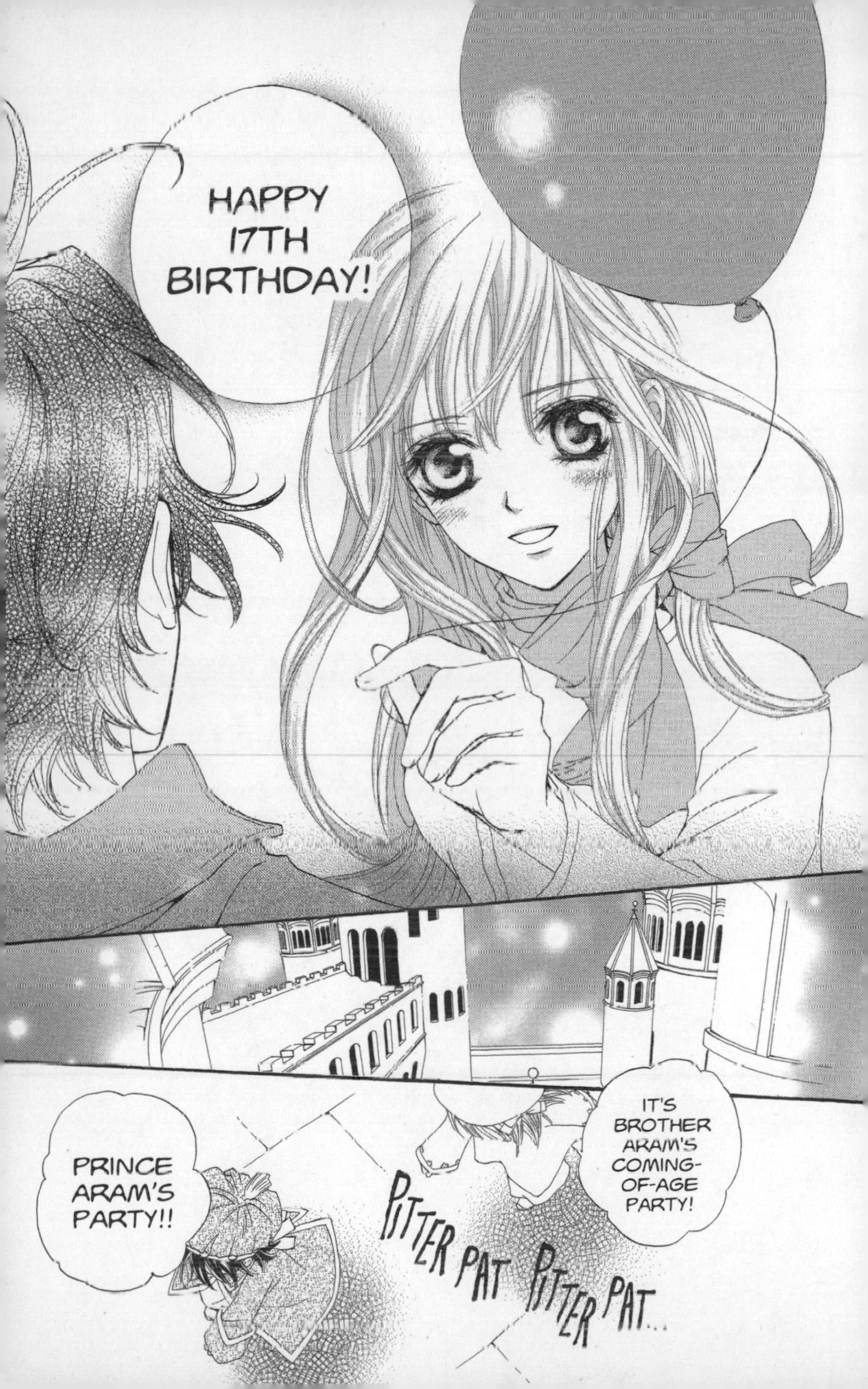
HAPPY 17TH BIRTHDAY!
IT'S BROTHER ARAM'S COMING-OF-AGE PARTY!
PITTER PAT PITTER PAT...
PRINCE ARAM'S PARTY!!

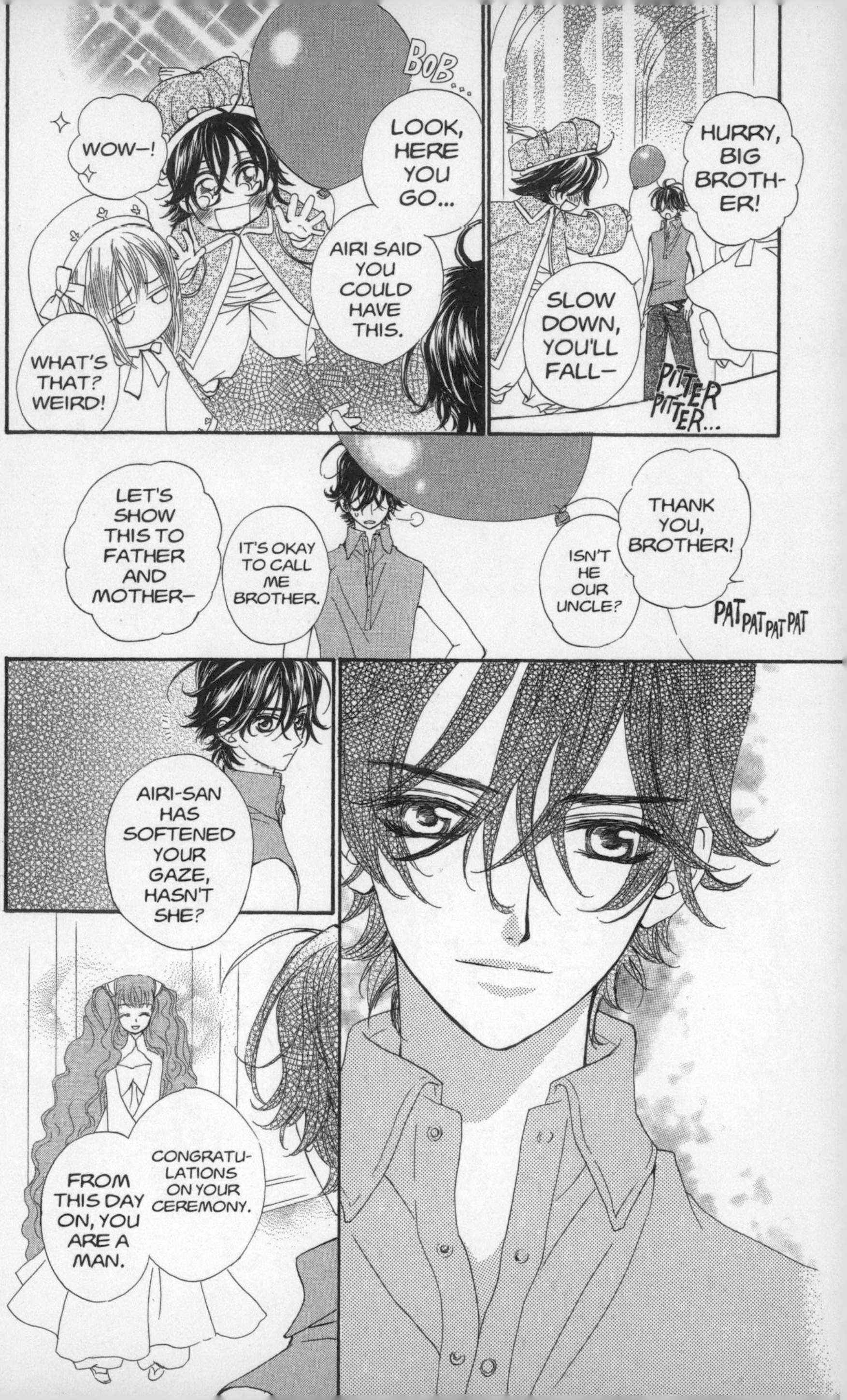
HURRY, BIG BROTH-ER!
SLOW DOWN, YOU'LL FALL—
PITTER PITTER...
BOB...
LOOK, HERE YOU GO...
AIRI SAID YOU COULD HAVE THIS.
WOW—!
WHAT'S THAT? WEIRD!
THANK YOU, BROTHER!
PAT PAT PAT PAT
ISN'T HE OUR UNCLE?
IT'S OKAY TO CALL ME BROTHER.
LET'S SHOW THIS TO FATHER AND MOTHER—
AIRI-SAN HAS SOFTENED YOUR GAZE, HASN'T SHE?
CONGRATU-LATIONS ON YOUR CEREMONY.
FROM THIS DAY ON, YOU ARE A MAN.

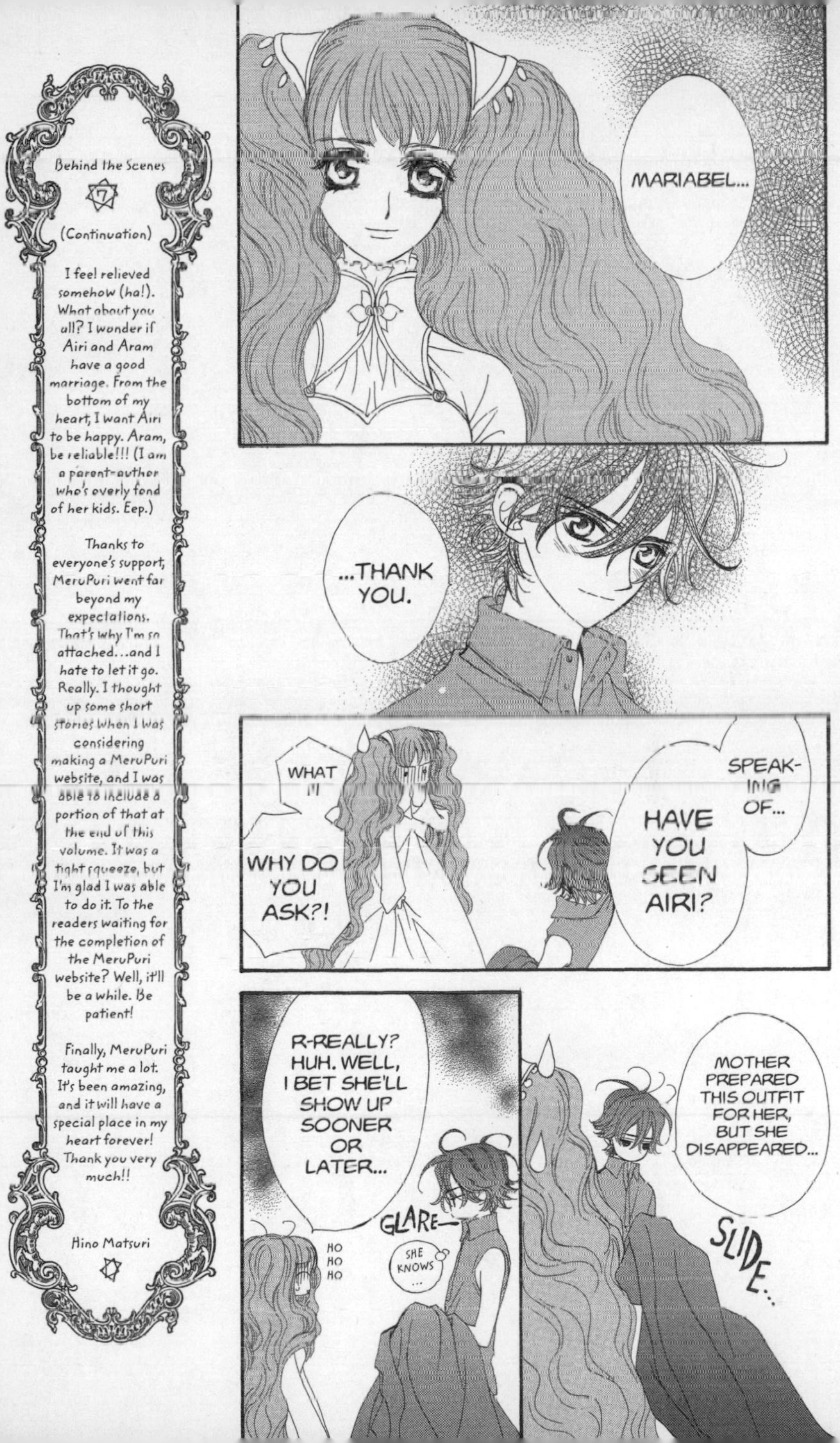
MARIABEL...
...THANK YOU.
SPEAK-ING OF...
HAVE YOU SEEN AIRI?
WHAT!!
WHY DO YOU ASK?!
MOTHER PREPARED THIS OUTFIT FOR HER, BUT SHE DISAPPEARED...
SLIDE...
R-REALLY? HUH. WELL, I BET SHE'LL SHOW UP SOONER OR LATER...
GLARE—
SHE KNOWS...
HO HO HO

Behind the Scenes

7

(Continuation)

I feel relieved somehow (ha!). What about you all? I wonder if Airi and Aram have a good marriage. From the bottom of my heart, I want Airi to be happy. Aram, be reliable!!! (I am a parent-author who's overly fond of her kids. Eep.)

Thanks to everyone's support, MeruPuri went far beyond my expectations. That's why I'm so attached...and I hate to let it go. Really. I thought up some short stories when I was considering making a MeruPuri website, and I was able to include a portion of that at the end of this volume. It was a tight squeeze, but I'm glad I was able to do it. To the readers waiting for the completion of the MeruPuri website? Well, it'll be a while. Be patient!

Finally, MeruPuri taught me a lot. It's been amazing, and it will have a special place in my heart forever! Thank you very much!!

Hino Matsuri

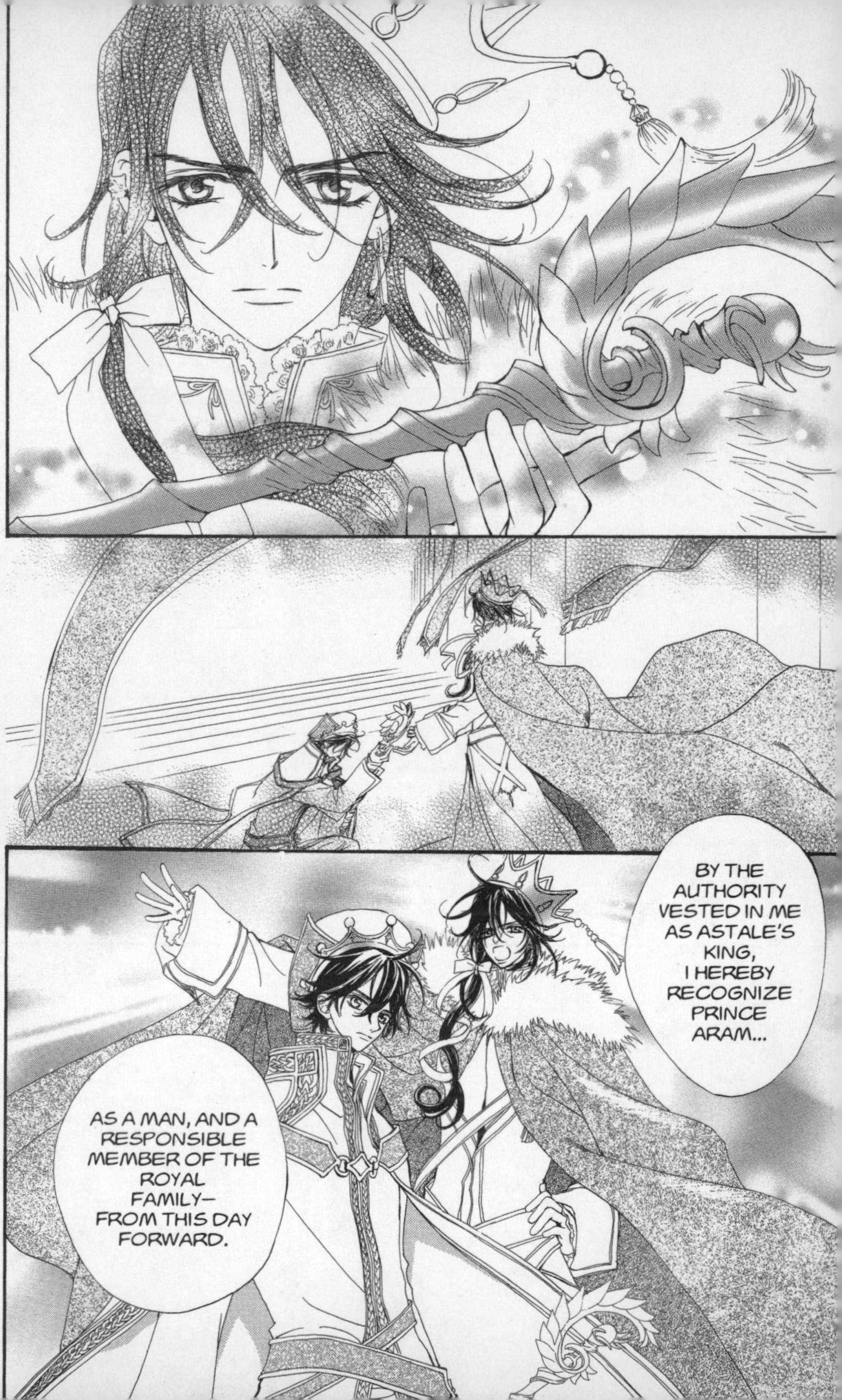
BY THE AUTHORITY VESTED IN ME AS ASTALE'S KING, I HEREBY RECOGNIZE PRINCE ARAM...
AS A MAN, AND A RESPONSIBLE MEMBER OF THE ROYAL FAMILY— FROM THIS DAY FORWARD.

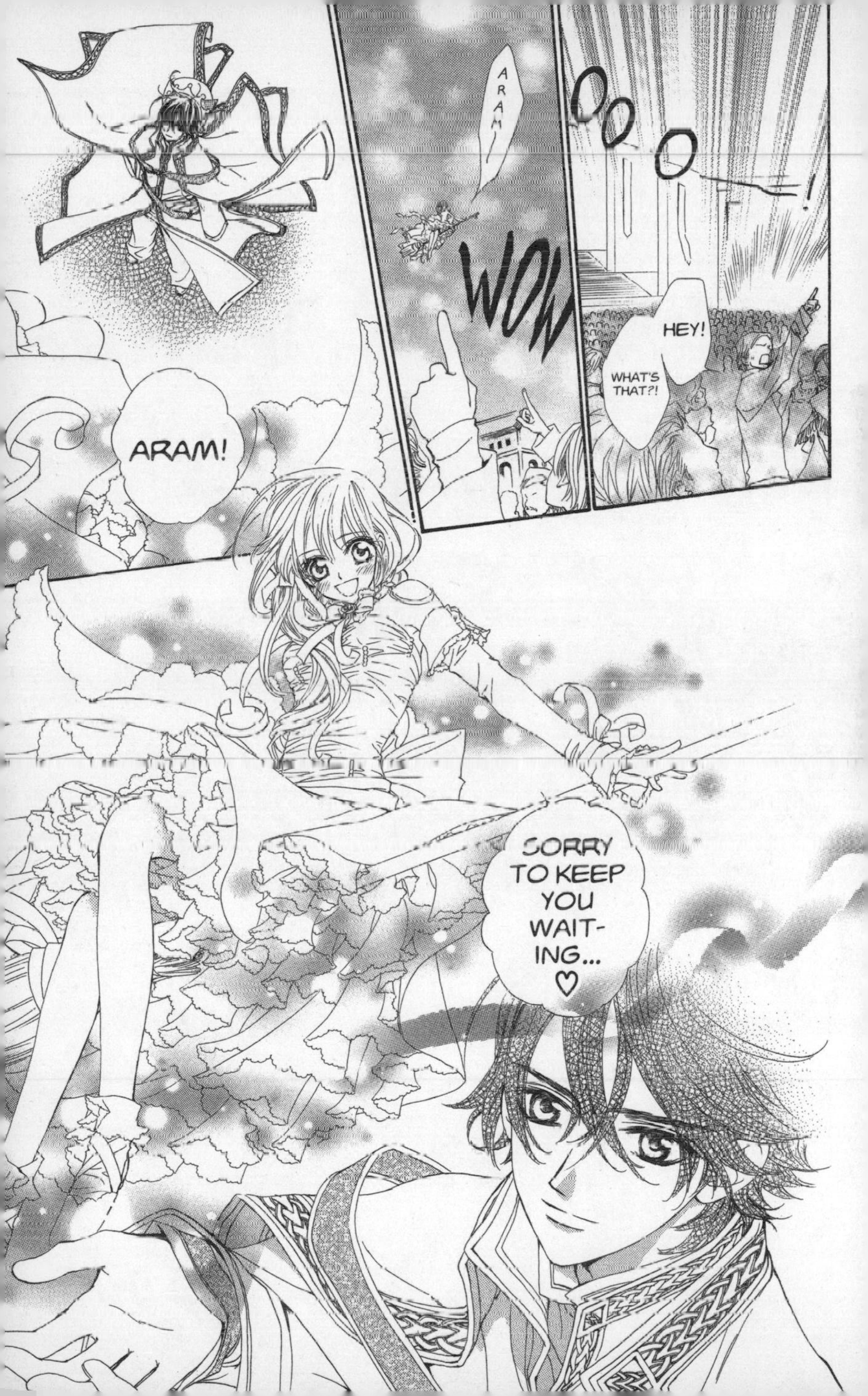
OOOO!
HEY!
WHAT'S THAT?!
ARAM!
WOW
ARAM!
SORRY TO KEEP YOU WAIT-ING... ♡

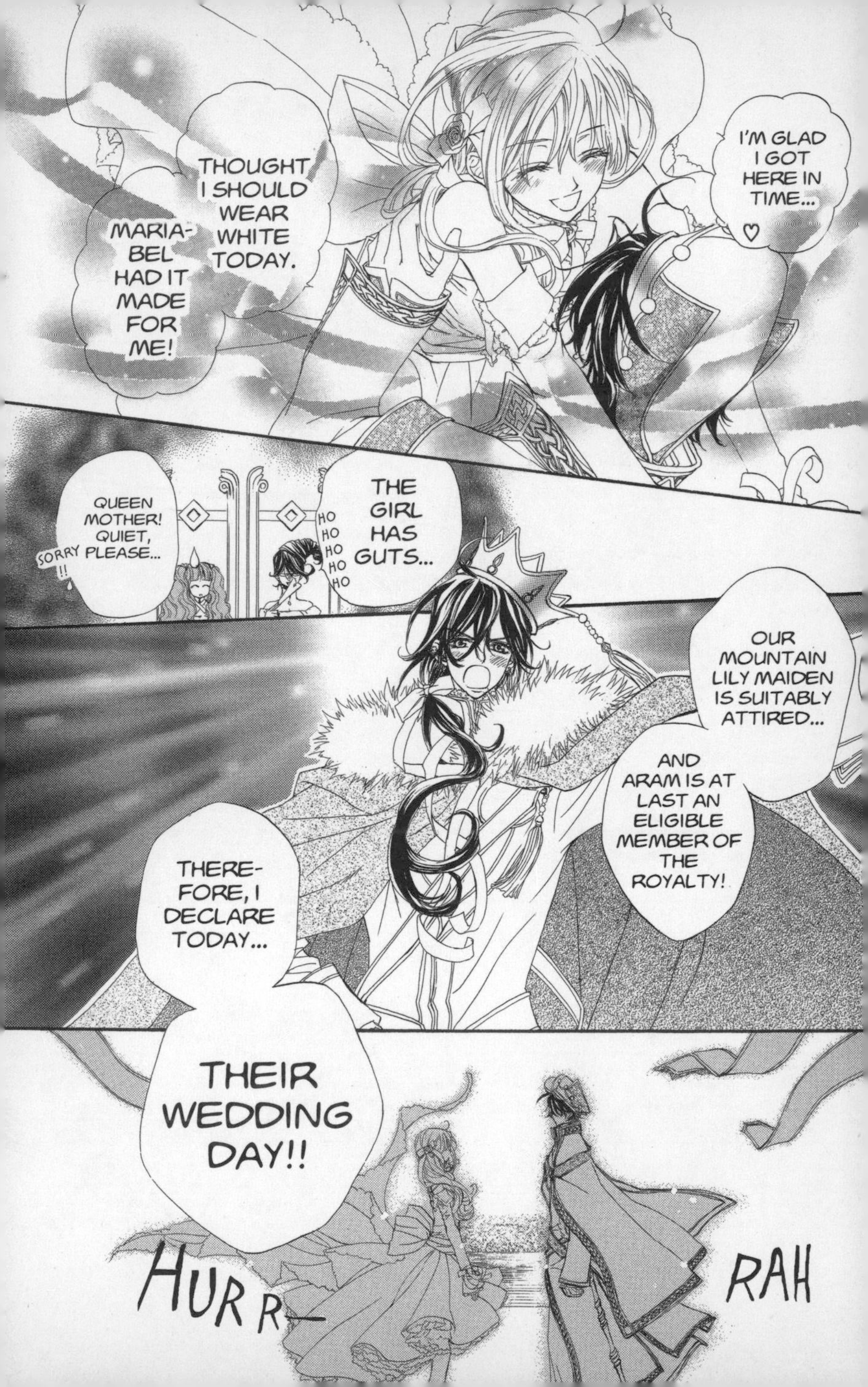
I'M GLAD I GOT HERE IN TIME... ♡
THOUGHT I SHOULD WEAR WHITE TODAY.
MARIA-BEL HAD IT MADE FOR ME!
THE GIRL HAS GUTS...
HO HO HO HO HO
QUEEN MOTHER! QUIET, PLEASE...
SORRY!!
OUR MOUNTAIN LILY MAIDEN IS SUITABLY ATTIRED...
AND ARAM IS AT LAST AN ELIGIBLE MEMBER OF THE ROYALTY!
THEREFORE, I DECLARE TODAY...
THEIR WEDDING DAY!!
HURR—
RAH

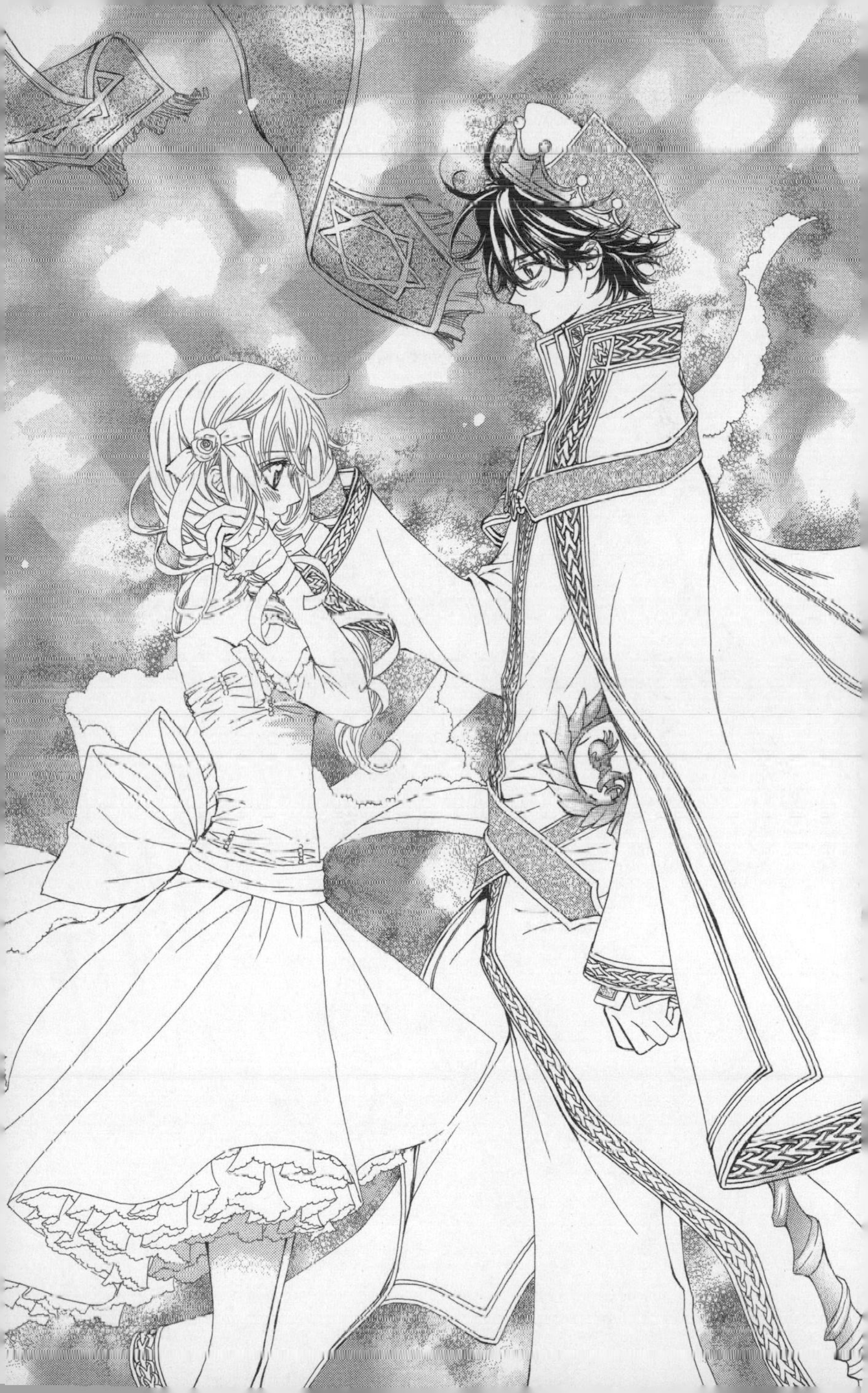

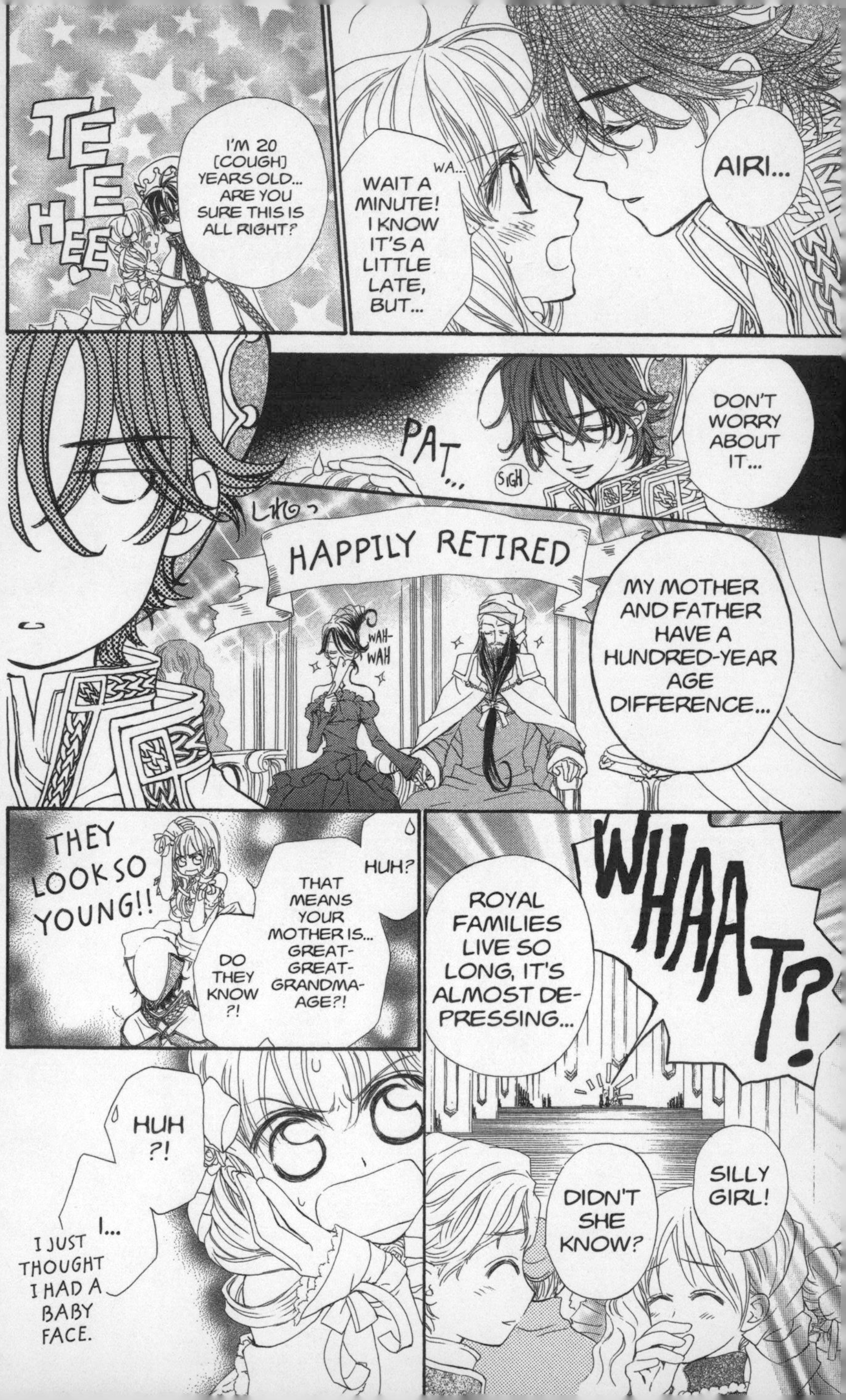
AIRI...
WA...
WAIT A MINUTE! I KNOW IT'S A LITTLE LATE, BUT...
I'M 20 [COUGH] YEARS OLD... ARE YOU SURE THIS IS ALL RIGHT?
TEE HEE
DON'T WORRY ABOUT IT...
PAT...
SIGH
しれっ
HAPPILY RETIRED
MY MOTHER AND FATHER HAVE A HUNDRED-YEAR AGE DIFFERENCE...
WAH-WAH
WHAAT?!
ROYAL FAMILIES LIVE SO LONG, IT'S ALMOST DE-PRESSING...
HUH?
THAT MEANS YOUR MOTHER IS... GREAT-GREAT-GRANDMA-AGE?!
DO THEY KNOW?!
THEY LOOK SO YOUNG!!
SILLY GIRL!
DIDN'T SHE KNOW?
HUH?!
I...
I JUST THOUGHT I HAD A BABY FACE.

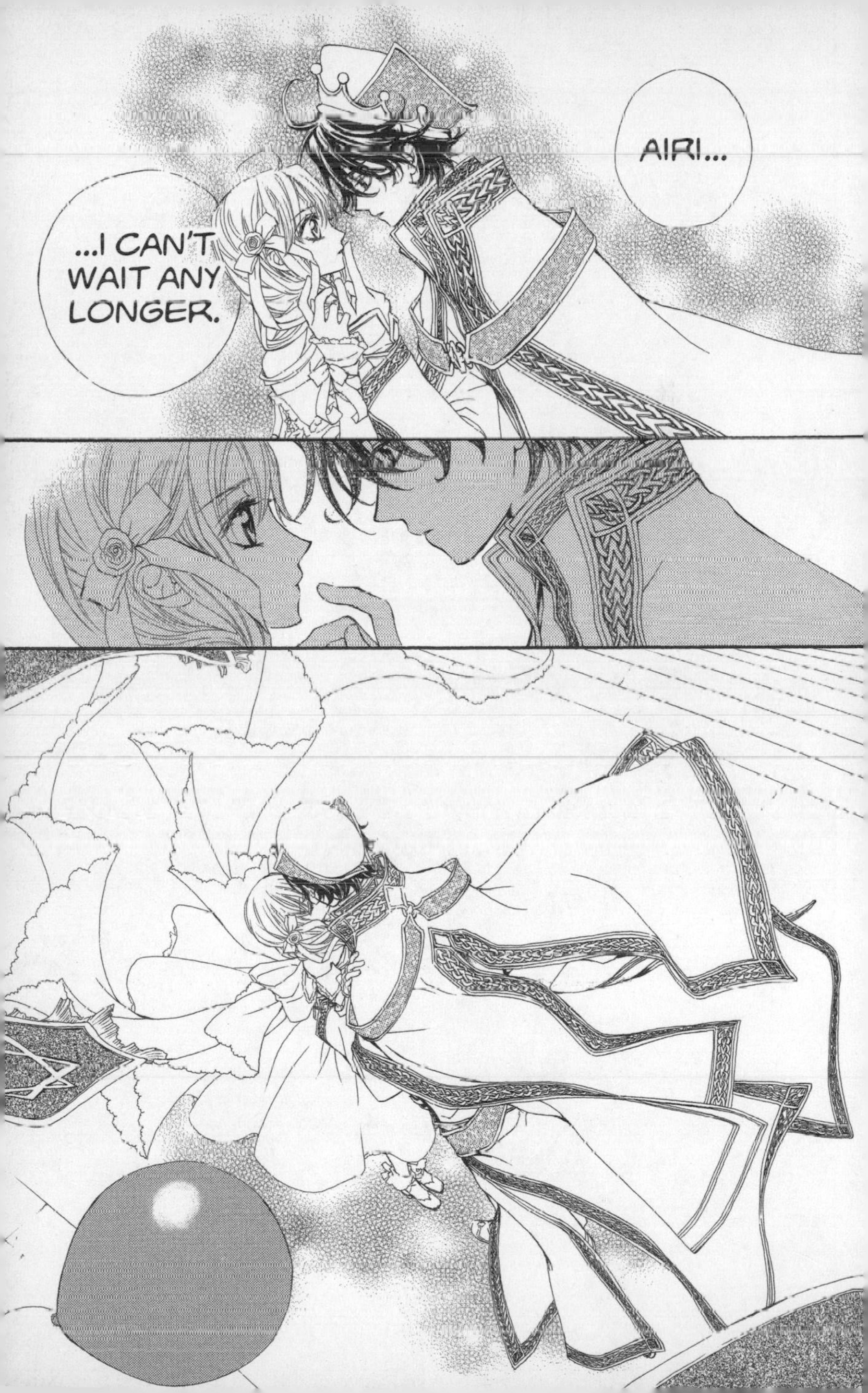
AIRI...
...I CAN'T WAIT ANY LONGER.

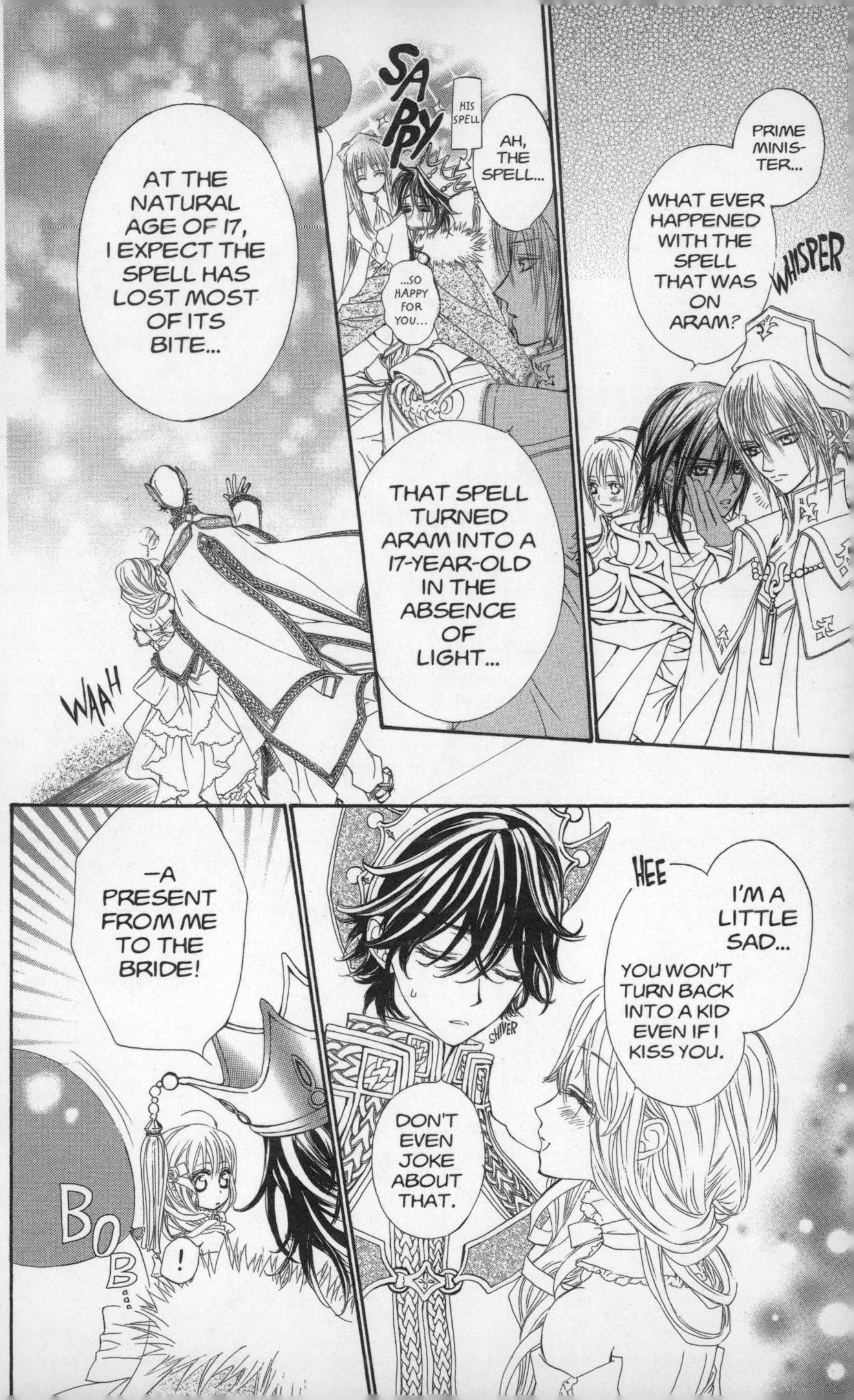
PRIME MINISTER...
WHAT EVER HAPPENED WITH THE SPELL THAT WAS ON ARAM?
WHISPER
AH, THE SPELL...
HIS SPELL
SAPPY
...SO HAPPY FOR YOU...
THAT SPELL TURNED ARAM INTO A 17-YEAR-OLD IN THE ABSENCE OF LIGHT...
AT THE NATURAL AGE OF 17, I EXPECT THE SPELL HAS LOST MOST OF ITS BITE...
WAAH
HEE
I'M A LITTLE SAD...
YOU WON'T TURN BACK INTO A KID EVEN IF I KISS YOU.
SHIVER
DON'T EVEN JOKE ABOUT THAT.
—A PRESENT FROM ME TO THE BRIDE!
BOB...
!

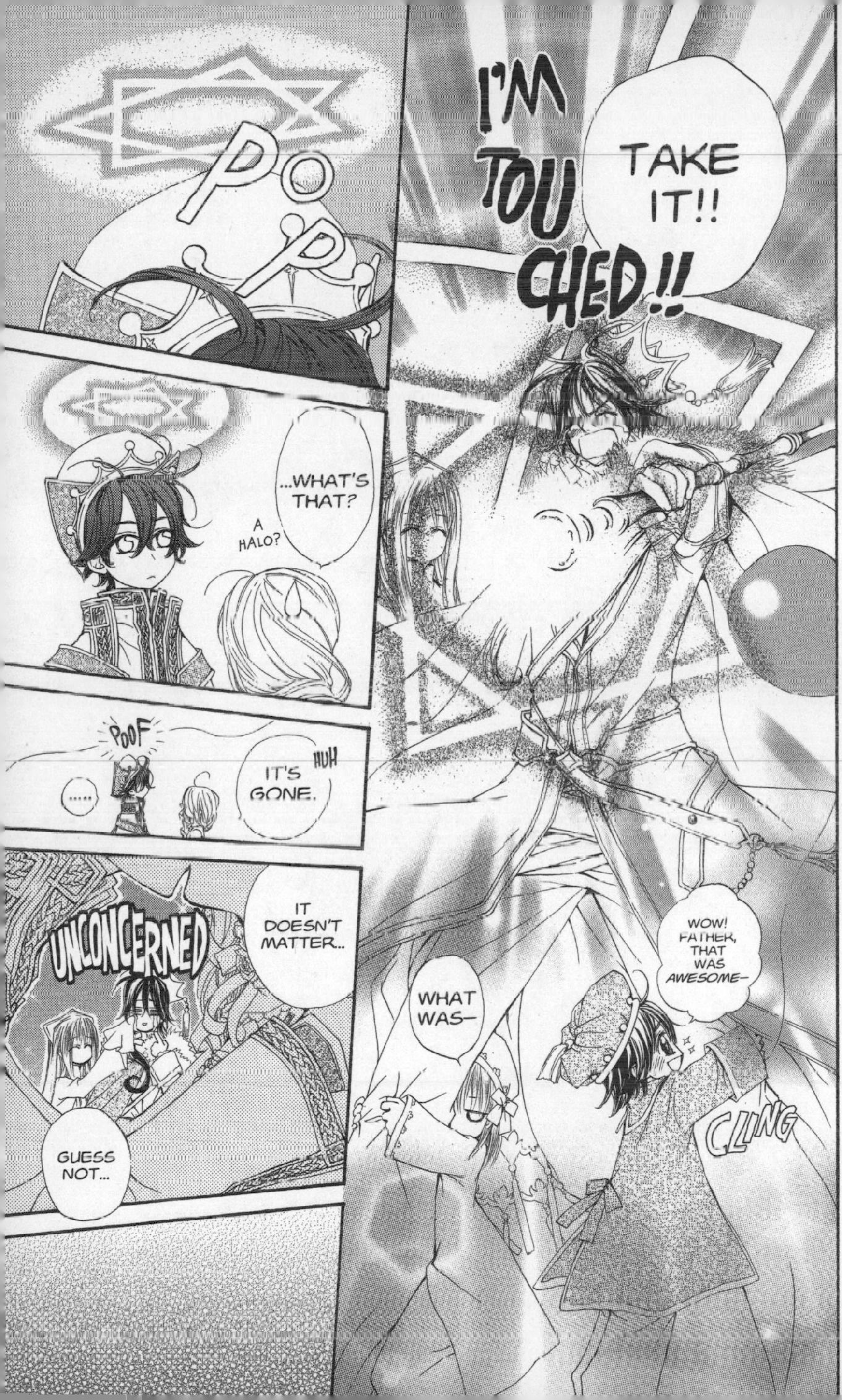
TAKE IT!!
I'M TOUCHED!!
WOW! FATHER, THAT WAS AWESOME—
WHAT WAS—
CLING
POP
...WHAT'S THAT?
A HALO?
HUH
IT'S GONE.
POOF
......
IT DOESN'T MATTER...
UNCONCERNED
GUESS NOT...

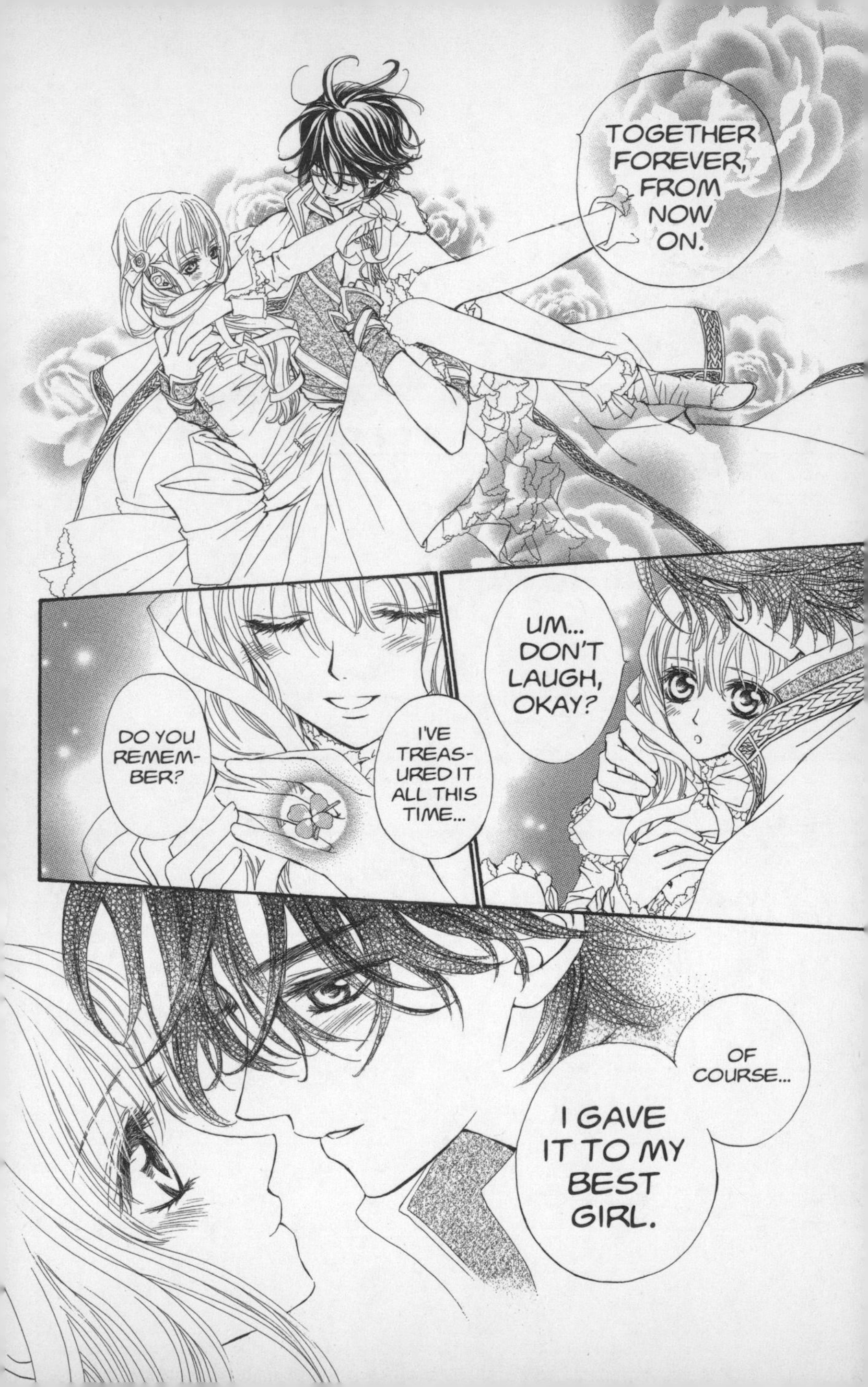
TOGETHER FOREVER, FROM NOW ON.
UM... DON'T LAUGH, OKAY?
I'VE TREASURED IT ALL THIS TIME...
DO YOU REMEMBER?
OF COURSE...
I GAVE IT TO MY BEST GIRL.

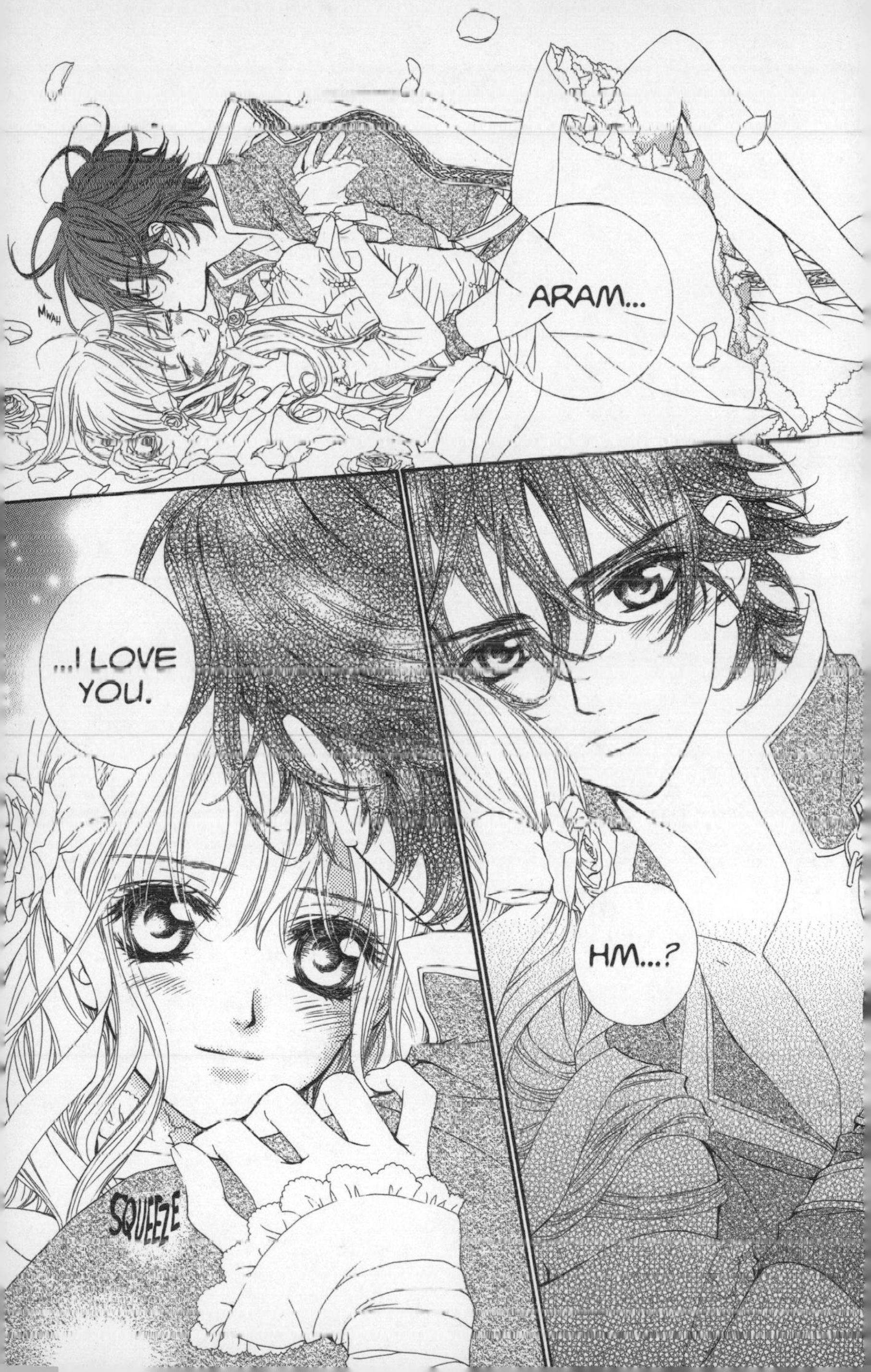
ARAM...
MWAH
HM...?
...I LOVE YOU.
SQUEEZE

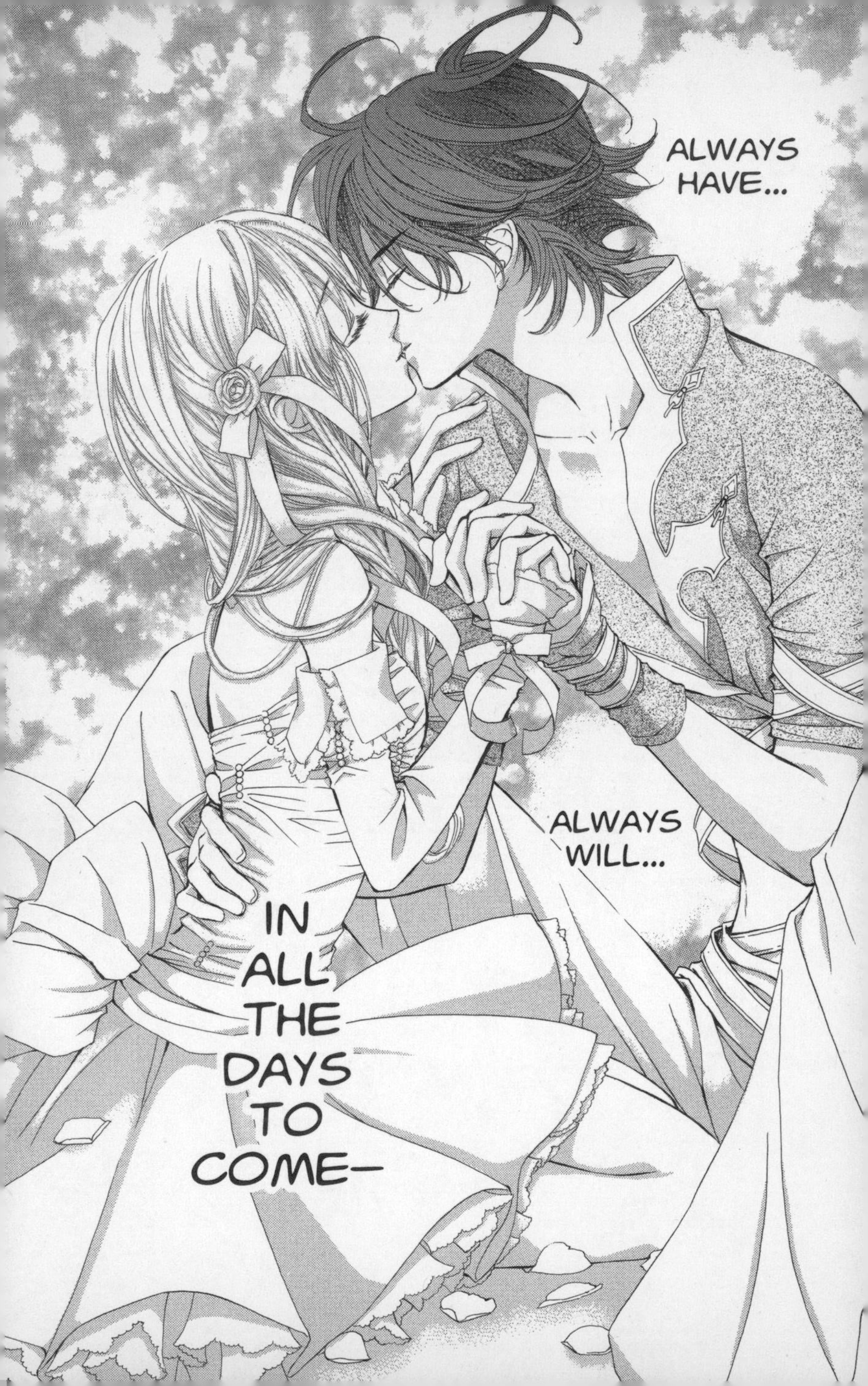
ALWAYS HAVE...
ALWAYS WILL...
IN ALL THE DAYS TO COME—

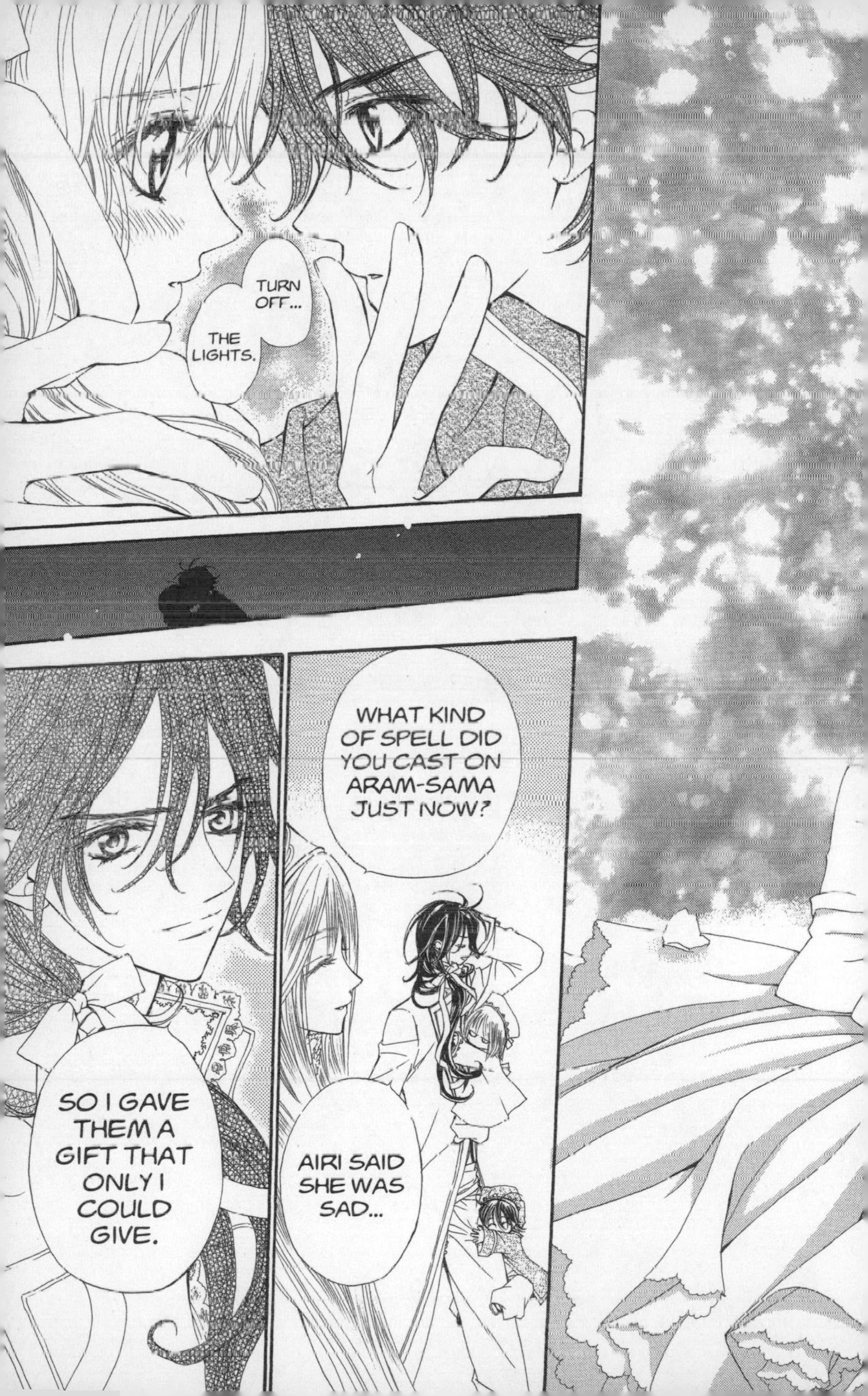
TURN OFF...
THE LIGHTS.
WHAT KIND OF SPELL DID YOU CAST ON ARAM-SAMA JUST NOW?
AIRI SAID SHE WAS SAD...
SO I GAVE THEM A GIFT THAT ONLY I COULD GIVE.

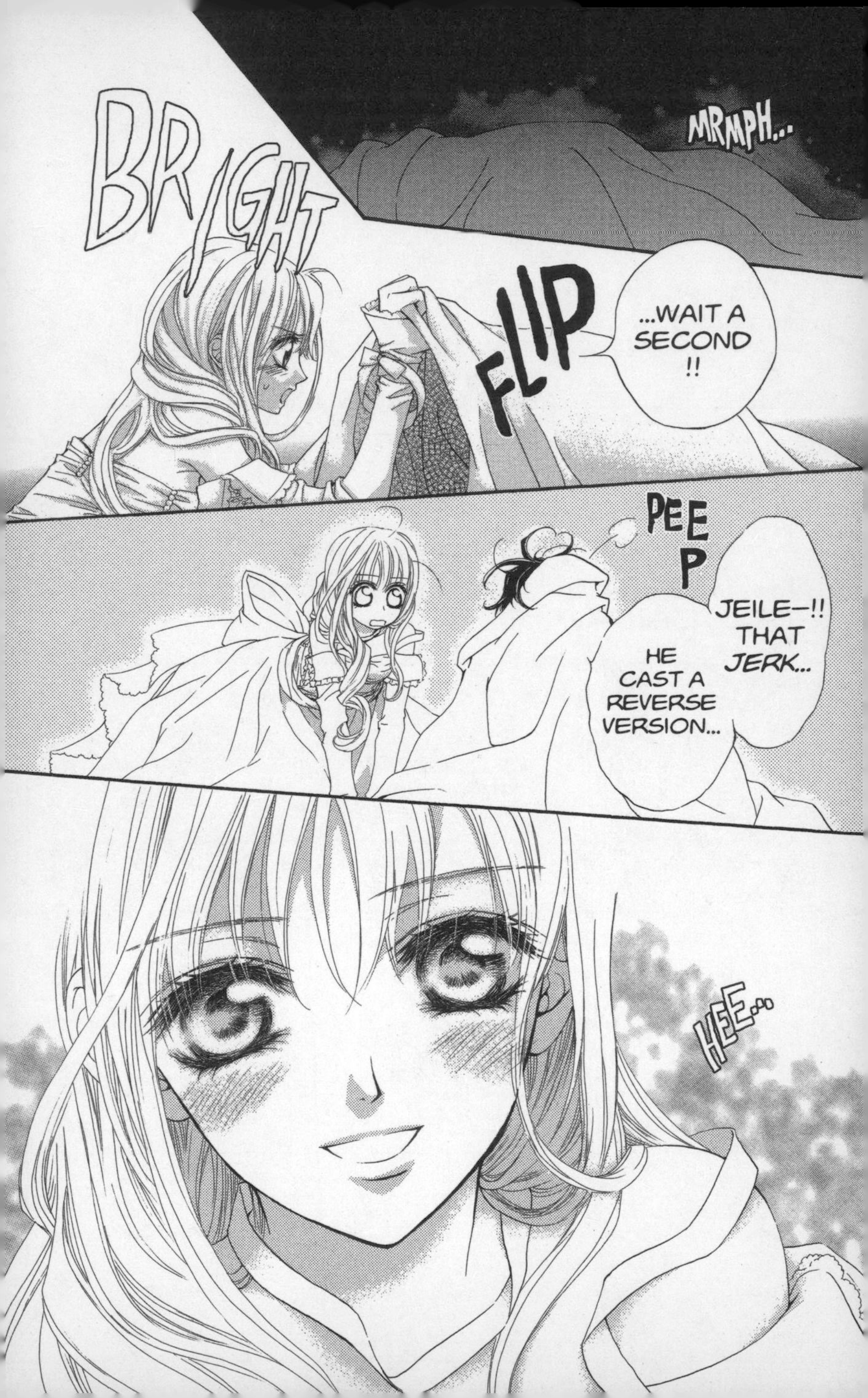
MRMPH...
BRIGHT
...WAIT A SECOND !!
FLIP
PEEP
JEILE—!! THAT JERK...
HE CAST A REVERSE VERSION...
HEE...

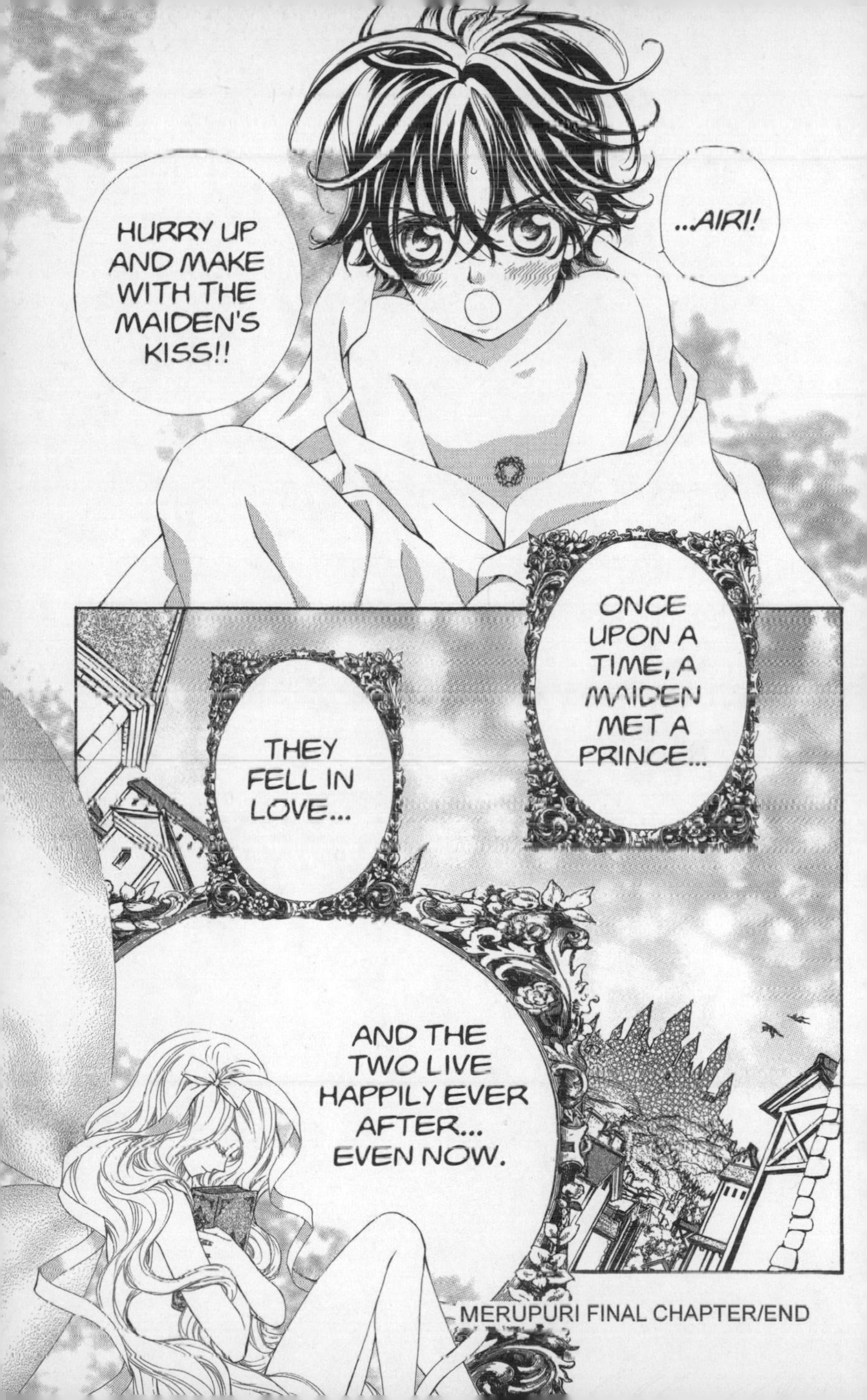
...AIRI!
HURRY UP AND MAKE WITH THE MAIDEN'S KISS!!
ONCE UPON A TIME, A MAIDEN MET A PRINCE...
THEY FELL IN LOVE...
AND THE TWO LIVE HAPPILY EVER AFTER... EVEN NOW.
MERUPURI FINAL CHAPTER/END

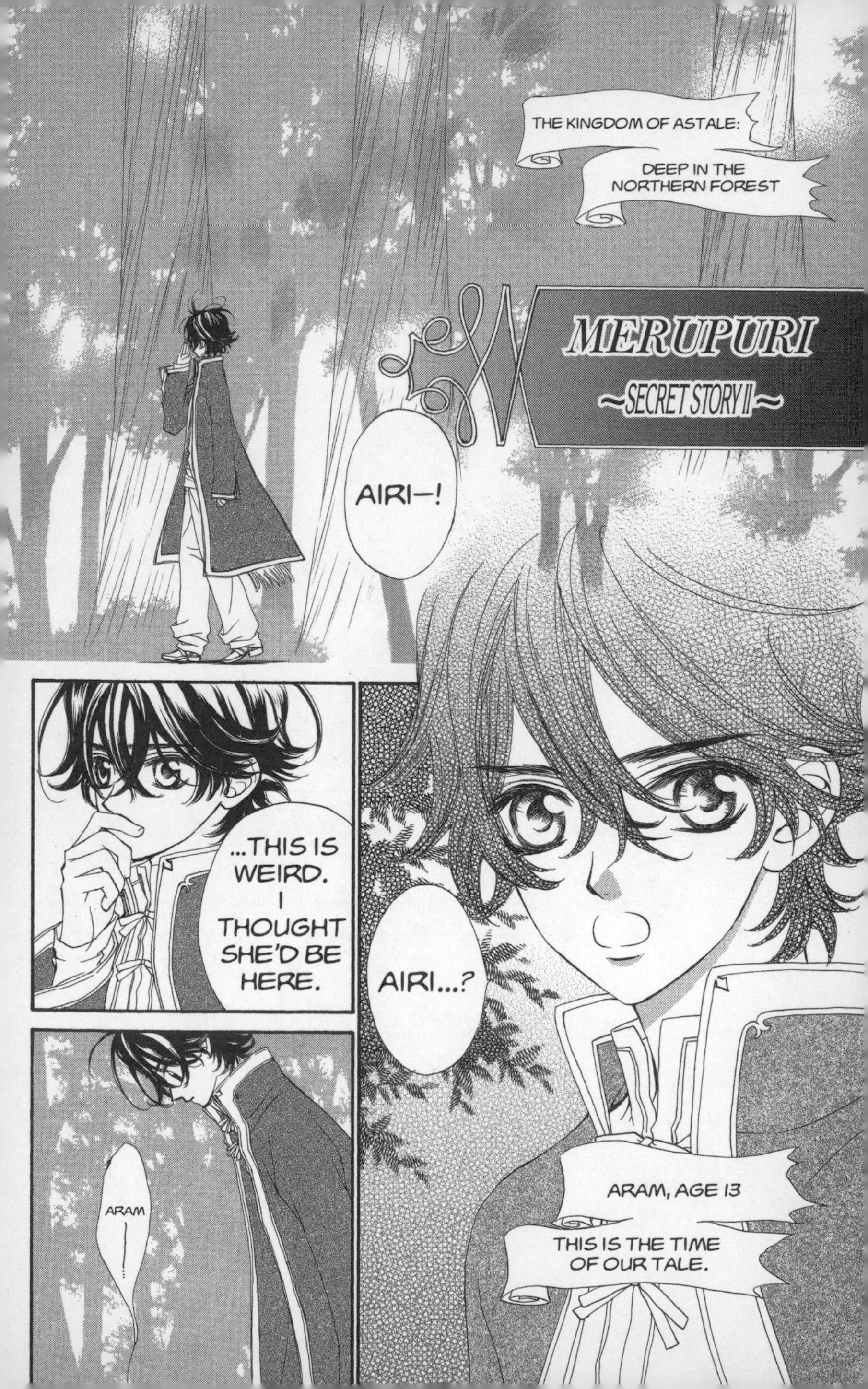
THE KINGDOM OF ASTALE:
DEEP IN THE NORTHERN FOREST
MERUPURI
~SECRET STORY II~
AIRI—!
AIRI...?
ARAM, AGE 13
THIS IS THE TIME OF OUR TALE.
...THIS IS WEIRD. I THOUGHT SHE'D BE HERE.
ARAM
...

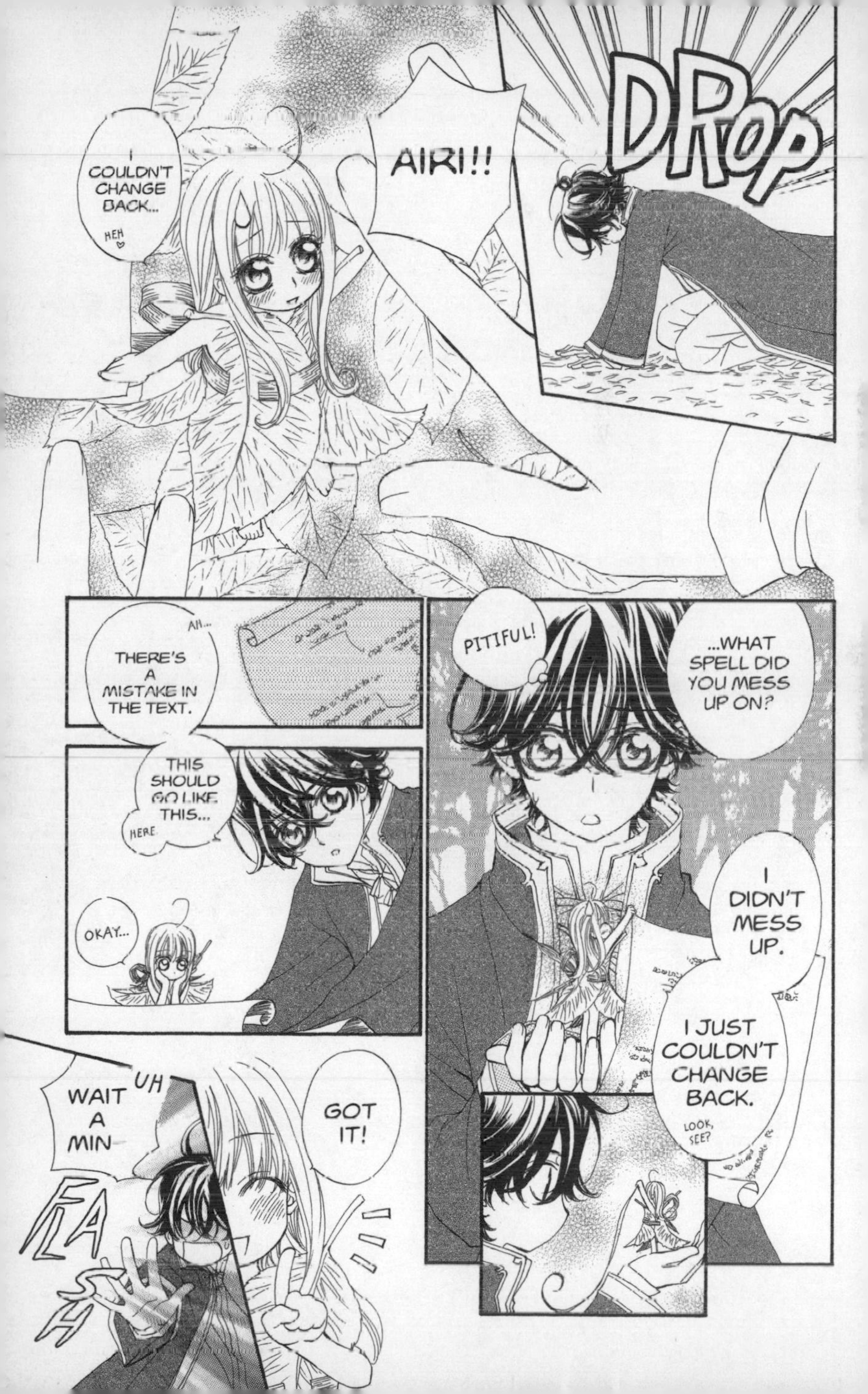
DROP
AIRI!!
I COULDN'T CHANGE BACK...
HEH
...WHAT SPELL DID YOU MESS UP ON?
PITIFUL!
I DIDN'T MESS UP.
I JUST COULDN'T CHANGE BACK.
LOOK, SEE?
AH...
THERE'S A MISTAKE IN THE TEXT.
THIS SHOULD GO LIKE THIS...
HERE
OKAY...
GOT IT!
UH
WAIT A MIN-
FLASH

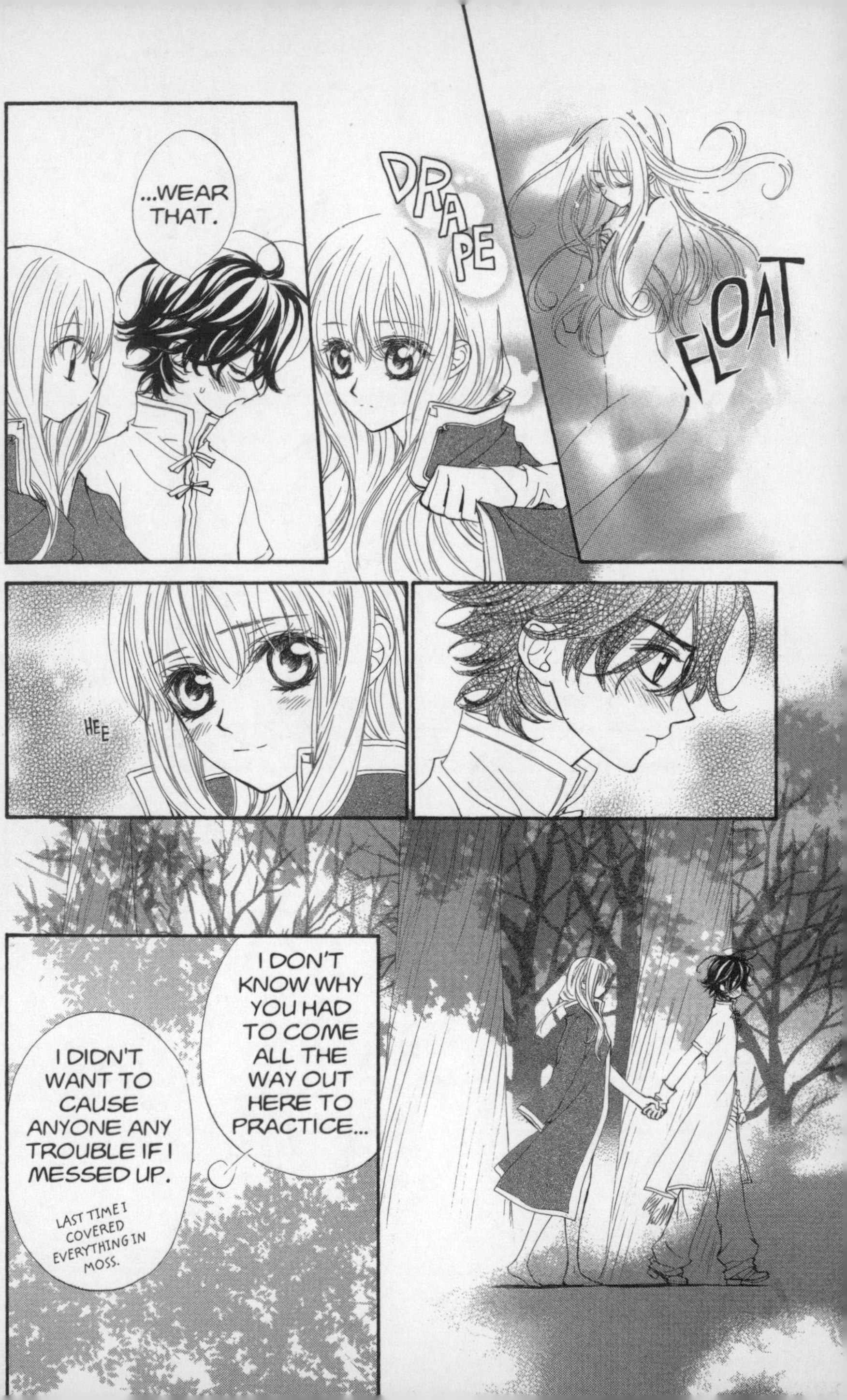
FLOAT
...WEAR THAT.
DRAPE
HEE
I DON'T KNOW WHY YOU HAD TO COME ALL THE WAY OUT HERE TO PRACTICE...
I DIDN'T WANT TO CAUSE ANYONE ANY TROUBLE IF I MESSED UP.
LAST TIME I COVERED EVERYTHING IN MOSS.

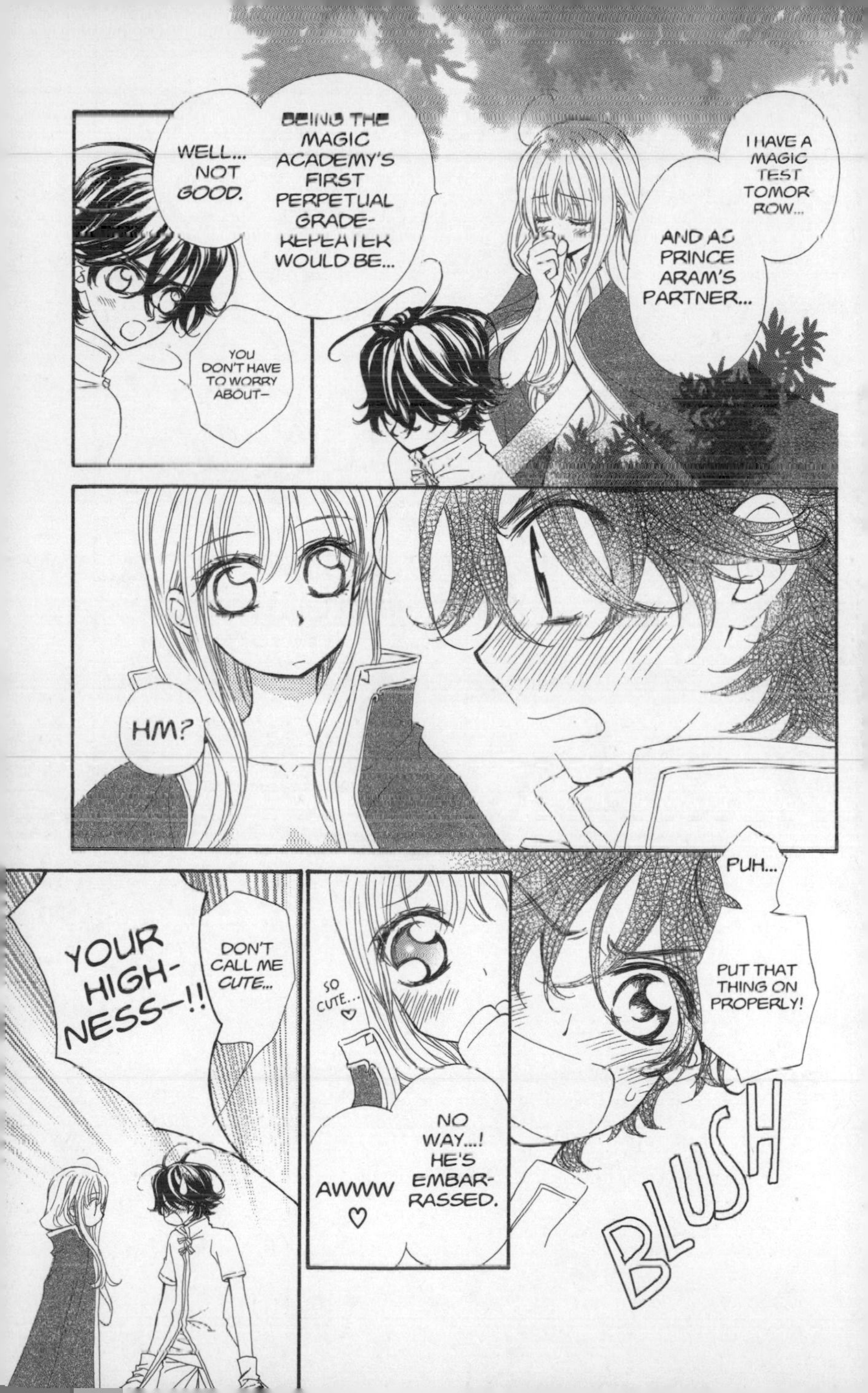

I HAVE A MAGIC TEST TOMORROW...
AND AS PRINCE ARAM'S PARTNER...
BEING THE MAGIC ACADEMY'S FIRST PERPETUAL GRADE-REPEATER WOULD BE...
WELL... NOT GOOD.
YOU DON'T HAVE TO WORRY ABOUT–
HM?
PUH...
PUT THAT THING ON PROPERLY!
BLUSH
SO CUTE... ♡
NO WAY...! HE'S EMBARRASSED.
AWWW ♡
DON'T CALL ME CUTE...
YOUR HIGHNESS–!!

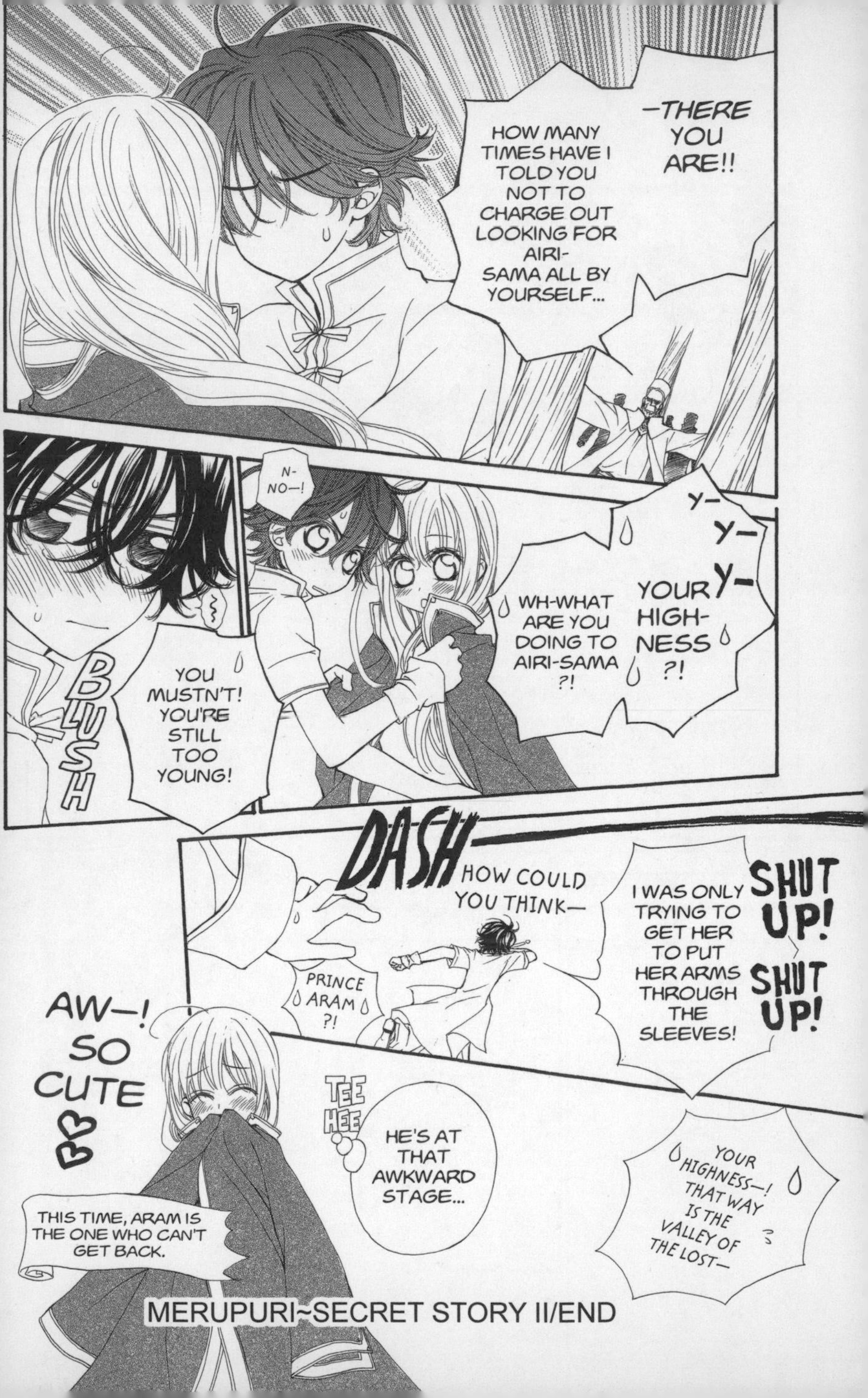

—THERE YOU ARE!!
HOW MANY TIMES HAVE I TOLD YOU NOT TO CHARGE OUT LOOKING FOR AIRI-SAMA ALL BY YOURSELF...
Y— Y— Y— YOUR HIGHNESS ?!
WH-WHAT ARE YOU DOING TO AIRI-SAMA ?!
N- NO—!
YOU MUSTN'T! YOU'RE STILL TOO YOUNG!
BLUSH
SHUT UP! SHUT UP!
I WAS ONLY TRYING TO GET HER TO PUT HER ARMS THROUGH THE SLEEVES!
DASH
HOW COULD YOU THINK—
PRINCE ARAM ?!
YOUR HIGHNESS—! THAT WAY IS THE VALLEY OF THE LOST—
HE'S AT THAT AWKWARD STAGE...
TEE HEE
AW—! SO CUTE
THIS TIME, ARAM IS THE ONE WHO CAN'T GET BACK.
MERUPURI~SECRET STORY II/END

A former bookstore shopkeeper, **Matsuri Hino** burst onto the manga scene with her title *Kono Yume ga Sametara* (When This Dream Is Over), which was published in *LaLa DX* magazine. Hino was a manga artist a mere nine months after she decided to become one.

With the success of her popular series *Toraware no Minouc* (Captive Circumstance), and *MeruPuri*, Hino has established herself as a major player in the world of shojo manga. Her new title, *Vampire Knight*, currently runs in *Monthly LaLa* magazine.

Hino enjoys creative activities and has commented that she would have been either an architect or an apprentice to traditional Japanese craft masters if she did not become a manga artist.

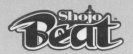

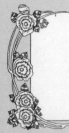

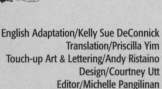

# MERUPURI: MÄRCHEN PRINCE, VOLUME 4
## The Shojo Beat Manga Edition

STORY AND ART BY
**MATSURI HINO**

English Adaptation/Kelly Sue DeConnick
Translation/Priscilla Yim
Touch-up Art & Lettering/Andy Ristaino
Design/Courtney Utt
Editor/Michelle Pangilinan

Editor in Chief, Books/Alvin Lu
Editor in Chief, Magazines/Marc Weidenbaum
VP, Publishing Licensing/Rika Inouye
VP, Sales & Product Marketing/Gonzalo Ferreyra
VP, Creative/Linda Espinosa
Publisher/Hyoe Narita

 A CIP catalogue record for this book is available from the British Library.

Printed in Canada

Published by VIZ Media, LLC
P.O. Box 77010
San Francisco, CA 94107

Shojo Beat Manga Edition
10 9 8 7 6 5 4
First printing, April 2006
Fourth printing, July 2008

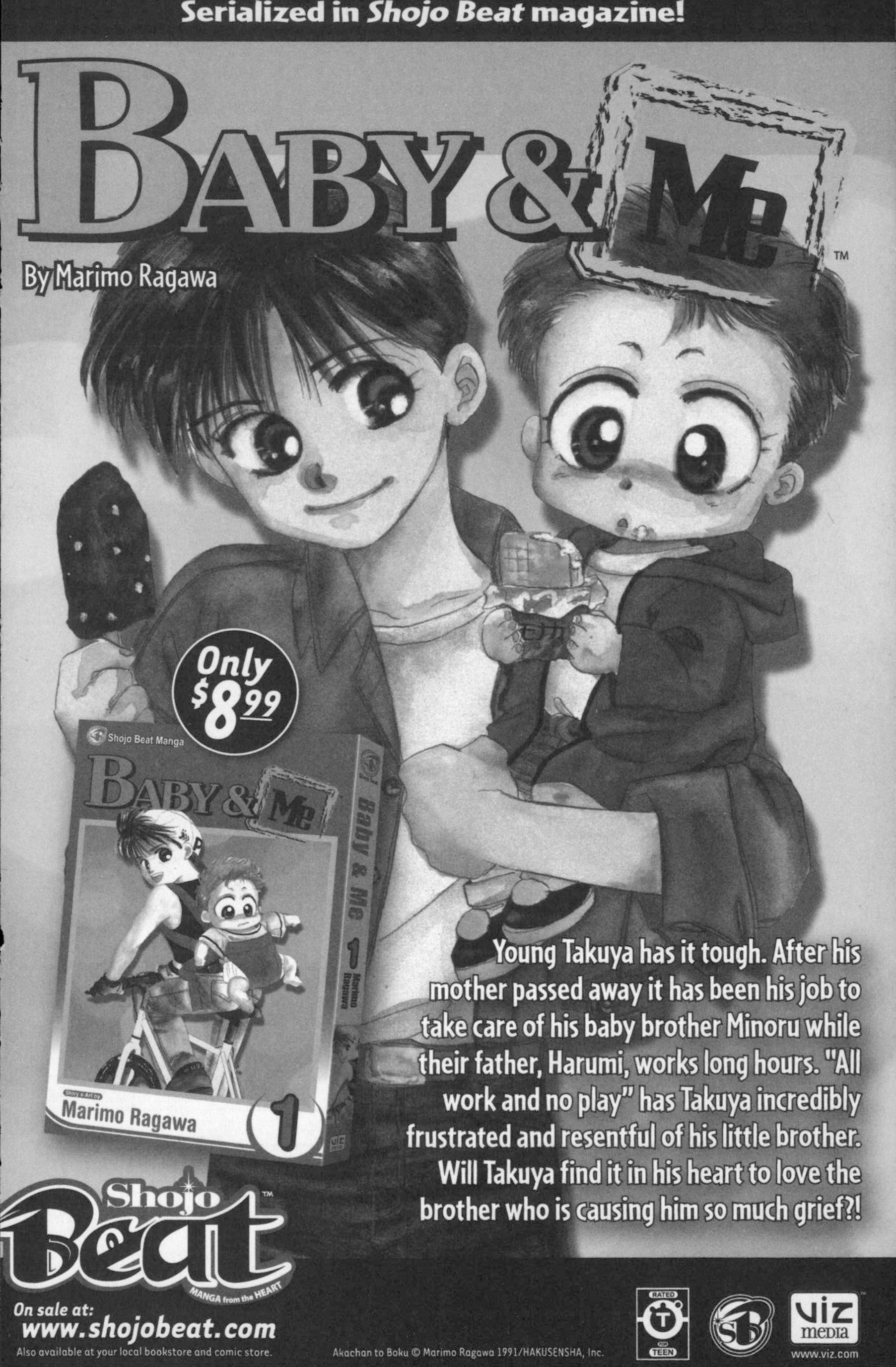
Serialized in Shojo Beat magazine!
BABY & ME™
By Marimo Ragawa
Only $8.99
Shojo Beat Manga
BABY & ME
Baby & Me 1 Marimo Ragawa
Story & Art by Marimo Ragawa 1
Young Takuya has it tough. After his mother passed away it has been his job to take care of his baby brother Minoru while their father, Harumi, works long hours. "All work and no play" has Takuya incredibly frustrated and resentful of his little brother. Will Takuya find it in his heart to love the brother who is causing him so much grief?!
Shojo Beat™ MANGA from the HEART
On sale at:
www.shojobeat.com
Also available at your local bookstore and comic store.
Akachan to Boku © Marimo Ragawa 1991/HAKUSENSHA, Inc.
RATED T FOR TEEN
viz media
www.viz.com

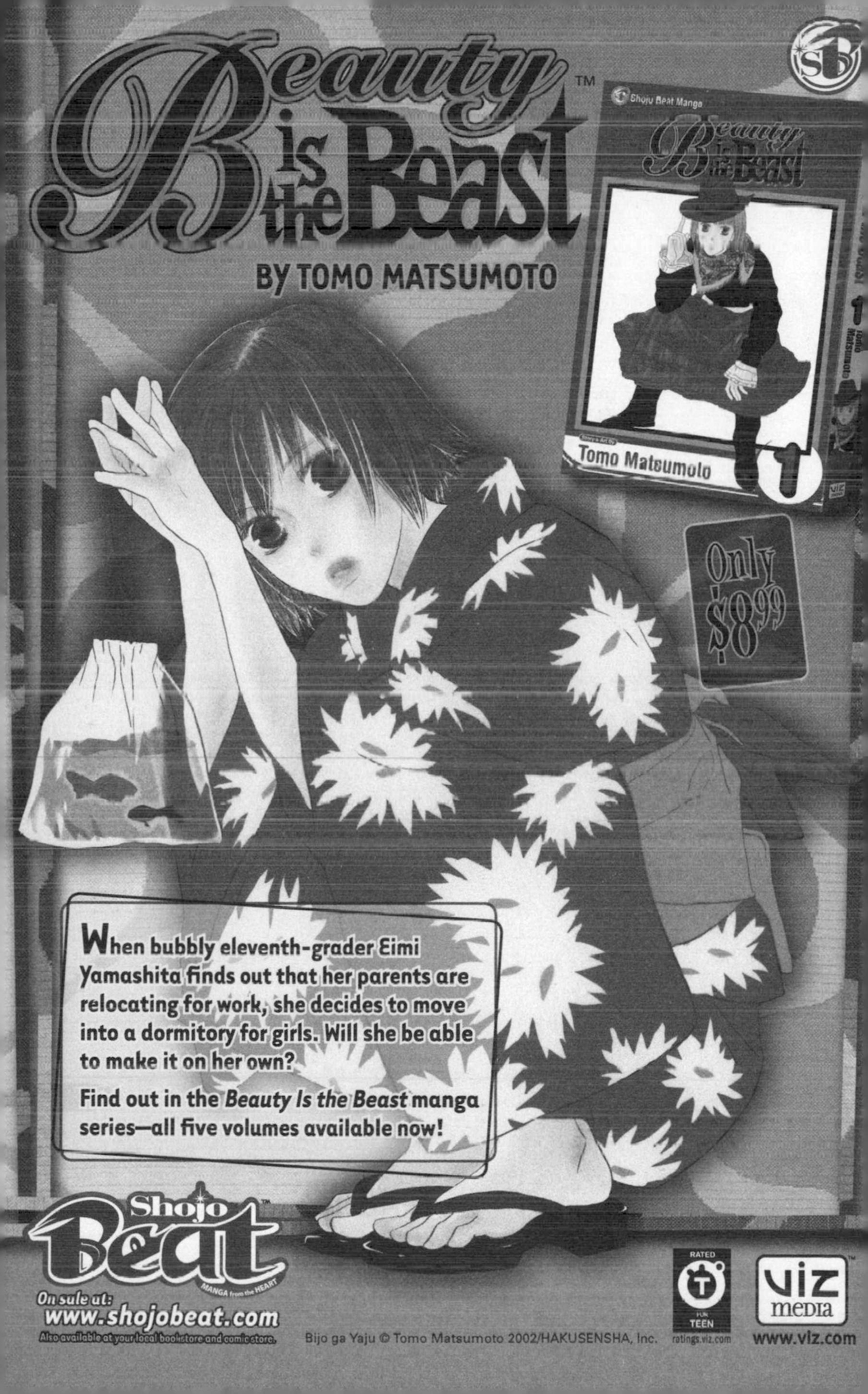
Beauty is the Beast™
BY TOMO MATSUMOTO
Shojo Beat Manga
Beauty is the Beast
Story & Art By
Tomo Matsumoto
1
Only $8.99
When bubbly eleventh-grader Eimi Yamashita finds out that her parents are relocating for work, she decides to move into a dormitory for girls. Will she be able to make it on her own?
Find out in the Beauty Is the Beast manga series—all five volumes available now!
Shojo Beat™
MANGA from the HEART
On sale at:
www.shojobeat.com
Also available at your local bookstore and comic store.
Bijo ga Yaju © Tomo Matsumoto 2002/HAKUSENSHA, Inc.
RATED
T
FOR TEEN
ratings.viz.com
VIZ media
www.viz.com